Responses to Suffering in Classical Rabbinic Literature

RESPONSES TO SUFFERING
IN CLASSICAL RABBINIC
LITERATURE

David Kraemer

New York   Oxford
OXFORD UNIVERSITY PRESS
1995

Oxford University Press

Oxford   New York   Toronto
Delhi   Bombay   Calcutta   Madras   Karachi
Kuala Lumpur   Singapore   Hong Kong   Tokyo
Nairobi   Dar es Salaam   Cape Town
Melbourne   Auckland   Madrid

and associated companies in
Berlin   Ibadan

Copyright © 1995 by David Kraemer

Published by Oxford University Press, Inc.
200 Madison Avenue, New York, New York 10016

Oxford is a registered trademark of Oxford University Press, Inc.

Library of Congress Cataloging-in-Publication Data
Kraemer, David Charles.
Responses to suffering in classical rabbinic literature / David Kraemer.
p. cm.
Includes bibliographical references and index.
ISBN 0-19-508900-6
1. Suffering—Religious aspects—Judaism.   2. Rabbinical
literature—History and criticism.   I. Title.
BM645.S9K7 1995   296.3'11—dc20
93-47291

2 4 6 8 9 7 5 3 1

Printed in the United States of America
on acid-free paper

To my mother,
Phyllis Kraemer,
through whose model
I learned compassion for others

Preface

A number of years ago, when I was a teacher in the Rabbinical School of the Jewish Theological Seminary of America, an abiding friendship developed between a new student, who was considering the rabbinate as a second career, and me. A child had been born to this student and his wife not long before and, during the time he was in my class, it became evident that the child was severely impaired. Empathizing with him, I could not help but ask the questions such pain provokes: Why did God permit this? Why was this innocent child (and his parents) suffering? Where is the justice which God presumably guarantees? In response to my questioning, I undertook to discover what my tradition—the classical rabbinic tradition—had to say about suffering. What I discovered, though often expected, was sometimes quite unexpected, and it became clear to me, as I carried my inquiry forward, that what I had read about rabbinic views on human suffering did not do justice to the variety and complexity of those views. I then decided to conduct a comprehensive study of the relevant materials, and it is the fruits of that study which I offer in the present volume.

This study was a difficult one, one which I "suffered" with, in fits and starts, over a good number of years. As I will detail in the first chapter, there are no earlier studies that treat this subject in a comprehensive manner. Thus, with little on which I could depend, I had to start virtually from the beginning in most matters relevant to this study. The questions which I confronted were many and significant: How should I define my topic? What do I mean by "suffering"? Is it possible to treat this topic independent of a consideration of divine justice and the like? Which methods promise the most fruitful conclusions? And so forth. The answers I arrived at, and the reasons for those answers, are all spelled out in the introductory chapter. But I must emphasize that none of these choices was facile. The multiple early manuscript versions of the book attest to the numerous redirections that were necessary.

Despite the difficulty of this work—a difficulty compounded by the pain of asking such questions and confronting the wrenching human suffering reflected in these materials—this turned out to be a thrilling project, a true labor of love. I began by imagining that my personal doubts would find no company in a literature composed by a group of ancient pietists and discovered instead that I was not alone. There were those expressions which insisted upon acceptance of the perfection of God's justice, to be sure, but there were also voices of challenge, of doubt, and even of anger. Such possibilities were not entertained in all classical rabbinic documents, I discovered. But in certain circumstances and times, the rabbis shared opinions that might surprise even the most seasoned skeptic. There was immense honesty and courage in the voices of these ancient sages. Teachings preserved from earlier rabbinic communities were tested and sometimes challenged, often leading to ends which their original authors could not have intended. But the tradition was a vigorous one, and later rabbis, when they had their doubts, did not hesitate to share them. The orthodoxies of one rabbinic community were not those of another.

As in all scholarly projects, the insights of colleagues contributed significantly to this one as well. Stephen Geller, Claudia Setzer, David Nelson, Burt Vizotsky, Leonard Gordon, and Eliezer Diamond all read sections of the manuscript which pertained to their expertise and each suggested essential improvements. George W. E. Nickelsburg, whom I do not know personally, was kind enough to do the same. His generosity as a scholar and colleague has provided me a model to which I aspire. To him and to the others I offer my deepest gratitude.

The anonymous reader for Oxford University Press demanded significant revisions in an earlier manuscript, a demand for which I am grateful. The reader's insights and critiques were astute, and this is a much better book because of those contributions. To that reader, whoever you may be, I extend my appreciation and respect.

Alvin Sandberg read an earlier version of the manuscript and suggested important improvements of style and formulation. Neither he nor any of the other readers will fully recognize the book as it now appears, but his contributions, like the others', remain significant. Again, I express my gratitude.

The final chapter of this book was written with the support of the Abbell research fund of the Jewish Theological Seminary of America, support for which I am grateful.

Biblical quotations, unless otherwise noted, are taken from the New JPS translation. I am grateful to the Jewish Publication Society for their permission to use this fine translation.

I am fortunate not to have experienced the sort of deep personal suffering which I often discuss in this book. But I have, in recent years, shared such pain with others. It is my prayer that the wisdom of the rabbis will offer some comfort to them, as it has to me.

New York   D. K.
January 1994

Contents

Abbreviations

Arakh.	Arakhin		Naz.	Nazir
A.Z.	Avodah Zarah		Nid.	Niddah
b.	Babylonian Talmud		Qid.	Qiddushin
B.B.	Baba Batra		R.H.	Rosh Hashanah
Ber.	Berakhot		Sanh.	Sanhedrin
Bez.	Beẓah		Shab.	Shabbat
B.M.	Baba Mezia		Sheq.	Sheqalim
B.Q.	Baba Qamma		Shev.	Shevuot
Git.	Gittin		Sot.	Sotah
Hag.	Ḥagigah		Suk.	Sukkah
Hor.	Horayot		Taan.	Taanit
Ket.	Ketubot		Tam.	Tamid
Kil.	Kilaim		Ter.	Terumot
m.	Mishnah		y.	Talmud Yerushalmi
Mak.	Makkot		Yeb.	Yebamot
Meg.	Megillah		Y.K.	Yom haKippurim
Men.	Menaḥot		Zeb.	Zebaḥim
M.Q.	Mo'ed Qatan			

RESPONSES TO SUFFERING IN CLASSICAL RABBINIC LITERATURE

1

Introduction

The more the development [of religion] tends toward the conception of a transcendental unitary god who is universal, the more there arises the problem of how the extraordinary power of such a god may be reconciled with the imperfection of the world that he has created and ruled over.

MAX WEBER, *The Sociology of Religion*

It will be evident without much elaboration that the problem of theodicy appears most sharply in radical and ethical monotheism, that is, within the orbit of Biblical religion. If all rival or minor divinities are radically eliminated, and if not only all power but all ethical values are ascribed to the one God who created all things in this or any other world, then the problem of theodicy becomes a pointed question directed to this very conception. Indeed, more than in any other religious constellation, it may be said that this type of monotheism stands or falls with its capacity to solve the question of theodicy, "How can God permit . . . ?"

PETER L. BERGER, *The Sacred Canopy*

The only thing that gives meaning to human [metaphysical] protest is the idea of a personal god who has created, and is therefore responsible for, everything. . . . Only a personal god can be asked by the rebel for a personal accounting. . . . In this sense it is the God of the Old Testament who is primarily responsible for mobilizing the forces of rebellion.

ALBERT CAMUS, *The Rebel*

Suffering and injustice have forever been part of human experience. Infants die; neighbors rich and poor, good and wicked, are victims of the same disaster; we remain healthy or succumb to illness—all without obvi-

3

ous purpose and often without explanation. But the human animal is distinguished by his or her need for explanations—we want to understand *why* we suffer, why our worlds are disrupted, why we experience loss. This need to ask "why?" is what lies at the root of the problem of suffering.

Suffering is a problem of meaning—of making sense of one's condition. As Clifford Geertz writes, "[T]he problem of suffering is, paradoxically, not how to avoid suffering but how to suffer, how to make of [suffering] . . . something bearable, supportable—something, as we say, sufferable." The variety of experiences we call suffering (such as illness, loss of a loved one, hunger) are to a large degree unavoidable. We would individually like to avoid such suffering, perhaps, but its occurrence is not, of itself, the problem. The problem, again, is that we, as human beings, seek to give meaning and structure to our experience, and suffering is the phenomenon that perhaps most effectively challenges meaning and undermines our sense of order.

The diverse human religious systems stand in significant measure as responses to the problem of suffering.[1] They attempt to explain and often justify suffering, giving it meaning and purpose. The sufferer, consequently, may feel that suffering is not entirely arbitrary or, better, that it serves some divine plan. He or she will thus be protected from the threat of anomie which suffering represents, for potential chaos is cast as part of the divine order.[2]

For reasons we shall consider later, the problem of suffering is probably most acute in "the orbit of Biblical religion."[3] But the degree of difference between biblical and other religions should not be overestimated, for this is, as stated, a common human problem, with solutions that often transcend specific historical and cultural contexts. Among the Greeks, for example, the gods were generally believed to be the source of good, and that alone.[4] The reality of suffering—undeniably "bad" in the common meaning of that term—contradicted the popular sense of divine goodness and so required explanation. Their explanation would cause no surprise for the ancient biblical authors: suffering was a manifestation of divine wrath, provoked by the prior impiety of the sufferer.[5] Impiety could take the form of transgressions against law and tradition in cultic matters, but it also involved murder or other failures to do what was right.[6] The nexus between suffering and impiety was so powerful that suffering could be spoken of as "things that happen to impious men."[7]

Notably, despite this ready explanation of suffering—one which could easily be offered to uphold the justice of the gods—the Greeks did not hold the gods directly responsible for human suffering. Their conviction that the gods could not ordinarily do bad was so powerful that suffering, like other failures or bad experiences, was blamed on fortune or demons (lower-level divine forces).[8] Even in Greek tragedy, which was distinguished from popular religion in important ways with respect to its opinions on these questions, specific gods were not held responsible for suffering; "the gods" in general could be, but one's own cult deity could never directly bring suffering. So while suffering was punishment for impiety, its reality was brought about only by lower divine beings. On both accounts, Greek religion offered a ready solution to the problem of suffering.

In Zoroastrianism, the supreme god Ahura Mazda was believed to be the ultimate judge, ever concerned with justice, the source of all good (Yasht 10, Yasna 30 and 33).[9] Of course, if God is just, then much suffering can readily be understood as punishment for impiety; a god of justice will naturally assure retribution for sinners. But the suffering of righteous individuals is not so readily explained, and common experience demonstrates that the righteous do indeed suffer. Divine justice, therefore, will not suffice to explain all suffering.

Zoroastrianism looked in two different directions to explain evil while affirming justice. First, reward and punishment were assumed to await fulfillment until a future world. Yasna 31 offers a clear formulation of this doctrine:

> O Mazda, thou didst fashion for us in the beginning, by Thy thought, creatures and inner selves and intentions. . . . Thou didst create corporeal life, and acts and words through which he who has free will expresses choices. . . . This I ask, Lord: what punishment shall be for him who promotes power for a wicked man of evil actions? . . . Heavenly glory shall be the future possession of him who comes (to the help of) the just man. A long life of darkness, foul food, the crying of woe—to that existence, O wicked ones, your Inner Self shall lead you by her actions.[10]

Of course, if reward and punishment are completely realized only in some future sphere, then the weight of present experience is lessened and mundane evil, suffering, and injustice become relatively less significant.[11]

The better-known Zoroastrian resolution of the present problems is surely its doctrine of dualism. At the earliest stage, this as yet undeveloped doctrine merely speaks of demons ("demon-created sickness"; Yasht 19),[12] in a fashion virtually identical with Greek paganism. But even in classical texts, this doctrine already finds far more elaborate expression. For example, in Yasna 30, we read of "two primal Spirits . . . the better and the bad." The text continues:

> [T]hose who act well have chosen rightly between the two, not so the evil-doers. And when these two Spirits first came together they created life and not-life, and how at the end Worst Existence shall be for the wicked, but (the House of) Best Purpose for the just man. Of these two Spirits the Wicked One chose achieving the worst things. . . . The Daevas indeed did not choose rightly between these two, for the Deceiver approached them . . . they then rushed to Fury, with whom they afflicted the world and mankind.[13]

There are thus two primal spirits, one of whom is evil. Lesser deities or demons, the Daevas, chose the way of this evil spirit and, in the company of other malevolent forces, bring various afflictions upon mankind. Later Zoroastrian cosmologies, describing the rise of the Evil Spirit, specify that such afflictions include pain and sickness.[14] Whatever the differences between earlier and later traditions, both are clear in assuming the reality and presence of evil forces who, in the course of present history, may act independently of the supreme just god. These demonic forces readily explain, of course, the reality of human suffering.

Turning to biblical religion, we find doctrinal limitations which render a solution to the problem of suffering notably more difficult. In the elite religion represented in the biblical books, demons and other lesser deities were rejected outright. (Popular Israelite and Jewish religion is of course another story. There is widespread evidence that Jews continued to believe in the reality of demons for many centuries.) And, despite persistent evidence of earlier belief in malevolent forces who battled the goodness of YHVH,[15] classical biblical religion described a monotheism which would not countenance the existence of independent evil forces. Thus the solutions of their two greatest neighbors were unavailable to the ancient Israelite and Jewish elite. Yet, at the same time, this religious elite posited a belief in an all-powerful God of history, a God of goodness and justice who cared for the fate of his creatures. Of course, if this is God's nature, then the unavoidable question is, "How can the innocent suffer?" The often incomprehensible suffering that plagues human experience seems to defy so stubbornly what one would expect based upon this biblical conception of God that followers of the biblical tradition would forever be at pains to formulate a coherent response. How incongruous it is, after all, to insist upon a unified God in a shattered world and a just God in a world of injustice.

In light of this biblical conception of God and God's relationship to the world, it is not surprising to find that biblical literature commits significant energies to explaining suffering and injustice. The primary concern of the prophets, a concern which is also central to the Bible's historical books, is explaining the defeat and exile of the biblical kingdoms, north and then south. The Torah, too, devotes significant attention to explaining "falls" of various sorts, and the Torah's coda, the final orations of Deuteronomy, offers as just punishment for disloyalty one of the most horrendous catalogues of suffering ever assembled (Deut. 28:15–68). The Writings, as well, are often directed by this concern, addressing questions of exile (Esther and Daniel), justice (Ecclesiastes), or suffering, pure and simple (Job, many psalms). Having erected a structure which would allow for no unexplained (read: unjust) suffering, virtually all biblical authors found themselves compelled to explain the unexplainable.[16]

Nor was this concern limited to the Bible itself. Jews who lived in the centuries following the Bible carried with them the legacy of this all-powerful, all-knowing, just and caring God. As their history brought pain and bitterness (during the Antiochan persecution, for example, or under the reign of Herod), the answers provided in their sacred scripture often did not suffice. So the religious imagination of these centuries repeatedly returned to the related problems of suffering, evil, and injustice, and a variety of explanations, both eclectic and original, found ample expression. A

Zoroastrian-like dualism was accepted by some Jewish groups, and the notion that suffering increased with the approach of the end of days (apocalypse) became extremely popular. But whatever the preferred solution, the problem remained a central focus. "Why does God permit . . . ?" was a question that Jews could not long ignore.

When we look to the first of the rabbinic writings, the Mishnah, we are confronted with a mysterious silence. The Mishnah, along with its close younger cousin, the Tosefta, has virtually nothing to say about the problems of suffering, evil, and injustice (unless we consider silence to be a statement). Instead, and in contrast with the Bible, the Mishnah and Tosefta are almost exclusively concerned with law, in all of its details (in the entire Bible, only the second half of Exodus through Deuteronomy are primarily devoted to spelling out the law!). Concerning the purity status of common vessels or financial liabilities in case of negligence, the Mishnah speaks at great length; concerning the suffering of the righteous, it says barely a word.

This is all despite the fact that the Mishnah, like much of biblical literature, took shape in the aftermath of immense national tragedies. There is very little reliable evidence for the existence of an organized rabbinic movement before the destruction of the second Jerusalem Temple in the year 70 CE. Only later in that same century do the rabbis appear as a recognizable force on the Judean landscape. There can thus be no question that the destruction and the catastrophic defeat of the Jewish forces in their war with Rome was a significant—perhaps *the* significant—impetus for the development of the rabbinic movement.

At this early stage, however, the rabbis did not yet give their practices and ideologies a definitive form. Such a move would come only in the aftermath of another crisis—the ultimately disastrous rebellion against the Romans under the leadership of Bar Kokhba. This rebellion was a difficult one for the Romans—Dio Cassius records that Hadrian's report to the senate in the course of this war did not employ the customary greeting, "If you and your children are in health, it is well; I and the legions are in health"[17]— and consequently, following their defeat of the rebellious forces, the Romans took severe measures to assure that the Jews would never again rebel. Observance of public Jewish rituals was prohibited on pain of death, Jews were restricted from residing in greater Judea, and the symbol of Jewish pride and faith, Jerusalem, was rebuilt as a pagan city with a pagan shrine at its center. Jews suffered horribly as a result of the war and the decrees that followed, and it would not be easy to rebuild the ruins and heal the wounds. Judea and Judaism within it could never again be the same.

The rabbis emerged from the ashes of this war with the hope that their religious program would help restore the lost equilibrium of the Jewish nation. The degree of popular support for the rabbis and their particular vision of Judaism was surely small at the beginning, but this did not stop them from spelling out that vision in considerable detail. The record of this effort is the Mishnah, completed in the late second or early third century. What does the Mishnah say about the experiences of the prior century or so? How does it explain the seemingly unending suffering of the people, individual and collective?

To repeat, the Mishnah says virtually nothing about these things. Nor does it say much about the more theoretical questions of divine justice or evil. How can this be so? How could the rabbis have ignored problems that had consumed their ancestors for so many centuries, this subsequent to events that made the problems ever more intractable?

It is the task of this book to explore these questions. Is it true, we want to know, that the rabbis, in their earliest programmatic statement, refused to confront problems over which their ancestors had spilled so much blood and ink? If this is indeed true, why is this so? What do the early rabbis do *instead* of addressing these questions and how is their chosen alternative a response to the catastrophic events that led to the development of their form of Judaism? Looking further, do the choices of the earliest rabbis control the choices of their successors? Do the rabbis of the third or fourth centuries begin to address the problems of suffering, divine justice, and evil? How central are these concerns to their deliberations? Does their distinct form of Judaism lead to unique responses to these problems or do they simply return to explanations and responses that already found a voice in the canonical biblical literature? Most important, perhaps, if there is a development in the quantity of attention paid or in the quality of explanations, how can this development be accounted for? Why, if it is so, did earlier rabbis avoid these dilemmas and later rabbis speak to them directly? If we can begin to answer these questions, we will have gained significant insight into the development of the rabbinic religious soul in the formative centuries of this movement. We thus begin with a puzzle, but what we really seek to understand is the experience of a religious civilization during the centuries of its birth and ultimate triumph.

Definitions

Before we commence this study, a number of clarifications are necessary. The reader will soon discover that I have chosen, in the following chapters, to give primary attention to suffering as such and to address questions of national catastrophe or divine justice only as they relate to the problem of suffering. Why this emphasis? To begin with, rabbis did not compose systematic treatises of the familiar philosophical (= Greek) sort on matters such as "theodicy" or "evil." Rabbinic discussions of issues of this kind tend to be coincidental and anecdotal. On rare occasion we do find an extended deliberation, but such instances are the exceptions that prove the rule. In place of such extended theoretical discourses, we find scattered comments and reactions: midrashim (scriptural expositions), recounted stories, sudden words of defense or protest. Thus if we try to force rabbinic traditions into the abstract mold that would be required to discuss "divine justice," we will not be doing justice to the nature of the materials at hand. Instead, we must review the many scattered comments or brief discussions of suffering and the like, seeing if there is a pattern which communicates meaning. Proceeding this way, we will not be asking the rabbis to speak in a mode that is foreign to their nature.

Second, it is my belief that suffering is primary to the other issues just mentioned. All theoretical treatments, be they discussions of evil, theodicy, or "destruction" (as a category), are provoked by the primary experience of suffering. They are attempts to give order and meaning to disordered experience. Discussions that are directed by the more theoretical categories are therefore likely to admit of extreme rationalization or detached intellectualism. Suffering, in contrast, is a personal, even intimate, experience and is far more difficult to distance oneself from completely and consistently. My hope is that by focusing first and primarily on human suffering, as opposed to evil in general, we will meet face-to-face the most difficult and pained responses—those, that is, that are more primary expressions of the human condition. Beginning here, I also hope that we may see more original responses, those that go beyond strictly traditional formulations to explore, in the name of the uniqueness of individual human experience, possibilities not previously considered.

All of this being said, it is obviously impossible to restrict this study to suffering alone, even if we should want to. The sources simply will not permit such a narrow vision. Suffering, in the Bible, the rabbis, and beyond, is often explained as punishment for sin—that is, as a manifestation of divine justice—and where such an explanation seems not to be appropriate it becomes necessary to discuss the sources of evil or otherwise to seek justifications of God's justice in the face of apparent injustice. The primary focus on suffering is heuristic, not doctrinaire. As necessary, examinations of traditions which relate to suffering will extend to encompass the related categories as well.

Of course, for us to focus on the problem of suffering it is necessary to define what we mean by "suffering." The Merriam-Webster Thesaurus (1984) defines suffering as "the state of being in serious trouble or in mental or physical anguish." As synonyms it suggests "distress," "agony," "misery," and "passion," and in its list of related terms it offers "affliction," "trial," tribulation," "anguish," and "grief." What these all bear in common is their sense of the subjective nature of suffering. As suggested earlier in this chapter, suffering is not an objective condition; it is an experience, a feeling of confusion or anguish or grief or anger that results from a particular condition. Practically speaking, then, suffering could be a wide variety of things, from pain to illness to the loss of a loved one to the defeat of one's people in a war to financial loss, and so forth. What is crucial is the evidence that someone is uncomfortable with the situation at hand; what defines the category of suffering is not the nature of the event but the quality of the experience. If someone feels anguish or psychic disruption as a consequence of what has befallen her or him, then we have suffering.

On account of this definition, it will be necessary to extend a rather wide net over rabbinic literature, being sensitive to the possibility of discovering responses to suffering in quite unexpected places. We will begin each exploration with traditions that employ the rabbinic term for suffering, *yissurin* (from YSR = [in intensified form] "to chastise, chasten, try")[18] or the conceptually related *pur°anut* (= "retribution," from PR°, "to pay"). What is crucial, however, is not the use of these terms but evidence of the subjective experience of suffering. As a consequence, the determination of relevant material will be, like the subject matter itself, somewhat subjective, and it will obviously be impossible to review all pertinent traditions. Nevertheless, I am confident that the full range of rabbinic responses is presented here. It is, the reader will find, an impressive and instructive range indeed.

Previous Scholarship and Methodological Considerations

Of course, this is not the first scholarly review of rabbinic opinions which relate to suffering, divine justice, and the like (though it is the first book-length treatment). In what ways does this work differ from what preceded it?

The most noteworthy prior studies of this subject are the essay entitled "The Doctrine of Divine Retribution in Rabbinical Literature" by Solomon Schechter[19] and, far more recently, Ephraim E. Urbach's subchapter, "The Reason for Suffering," with related sections, in his *The Sages: Their Concepts and Beliefs*.[20] Though each makes a valuable contribution—Schechter's essay illustrating the diversity of views that are to be found in rabbinic literature and Urbach's discussion noting important comparisons in contemporary nonrabbinic documents—the works of both are similarly flawed. Their treatments are almost exclusively topical: their choice of texts is determined by the needs of an abstract category and their perception of its logical development. Both assume that attributions of given traditions are accurate, and both disregard completely (for analytical purposes) the different documents in which traditions appear. The latter indifference also leads to a disregard of the contextual formulation of various traditions, thus ignoring completely the opinions of later authors or redactors.

Improving upon these two earlier authors methodologically is Yaakov Elman, whose recent series of studies opens up important new avenues for future study of this subject. Noteworthy are his discussions of differences between Palestinian and Babylonian rabbinic sources that relate to suffering[21] and his inquiry into the unique ideologies of the authors of the Bavli.[22] In the former study, Elman examines rabbinic interpretations of "biblical sources which clearly raise the problem of theodicy."[23] He finds that Palestinian sources are extremely conservative, with later documents rarely going beyond the earliest (tannaitic) rabbinic expressions in these matters. In contrast, he shows that the Babylonian Talmud also allows that suffering may be undeserved, recording explanations that are without precedent in earlier rabbinic sources. In these observations, Elman anticipates important conclusions of this book. In the latter study, Elman claims to be turning his attention to the final compositional hand of the Babylonian Talmud, yet he mostly finds himself drawn to teachings attributed to Rava and his colleagues. In doing so, Elman finds that those ideologies which find a voice for the first time in this Talmud originate mostly with Rava and teachers of his generation. Thus, Elman concludes, the ideological revolution recorded in the Bavli was actually a product of these fourth-century sages.

The methodologies of these authors are no longer accepted by many scholars of rabbinic literature. The major flaw in their method, emphasized so often by Jacob Neusner[24] and finding important expression in an oft-cited article by William Scott Green,[25] is the "gullibility" (Neusner's term) that this methodology represents. The simple question that these earlier authors fail to ask is this: Just because a particular document claims that a certain authority said a certain thing, why should we believe that it is so? Many documents in antiquity attribute opinions or words falsely; ancient historical sensibilities saw nothing wrong with such artificial attributions.[26] Why should we imagine that the rabbis, who did not even claim to write history, were more exacting? Moreover, comparison of parallel traditions in different rabbinic documents or of various citations of the same tradition or story in the same document will quickly reveal how often these citations differ one from the other, either in attribution or in substance. If this is so often true, then how can we give credence to any particular tradition or attribution? As is well known, the Talmuds often admit that there is doubt regarding the correctness of one attribution or another. Are we to assume that there is doubt only when they admit to it, or only when comparison shows such doubt? Or, from the point of view of critical scholarship, is it not more reasonable to doubt the accuracy of attributions unless there is more-or-less convincing external evidence that a tradition should be believed as an exact historical record? Surely the latter is preferable, particularly since rabbinic tradition claims of itself that it was an oral tradition, allegedly transmitting traditions for hundreds of years by a means that scholarship commonly recognizes to be imprecise.[27] All of this is not to say that rabbinic traditions or attributions may never supply historically reliable data—it is possible to demonstrate that, under certain limited conditions, such data are available in the rabbinic record.[28] It is merely to admit that, as a method of inquiry, the assumptions of earlier scholarship are not adequately rigorous and that scholarship conducted according to such assumptions must now be reexamined according to recognized standards.

Let me illustrate the problems with the earlier method with concrete examples. There is a dispute recorded in several classical rabbinic documents regarding the permissibility of examining a beggar (to ascertain his honesty) before giving charity. One view holds that it is permissible to examine before giving clothing but not before giving food, while the other holds that it is permissible to examine before giving food but not before giving clothing. In the Bavli (B.B. 9a), the respective opinions are attributed to

R. Huna and R. Judah (second-generation Babylonian Amoraim), whereas in the Yerushalmi and Leviticus Rabbah (closely related Palestinian rabbinic documents) they are attributed to Rav (first-generation Babylonian) and R. Yoḥanan (first-generation Palestinian). Well, which is it? Are the authors of these opinions first- or second-generation amoraic sages? Are they Babylonians or also Palestinians? The simple fact is that there is no way of answering these questions and thus there is no justification for speaking of the opinions of specific individuals at a particular time and place.

In the specific matter that interests us, two cases addressed by Elman supply illustrative examples.[29] In the first case, Elman identifies two opinions attributed to R. Ammi, one claiming that "there is no suffering without sin, nor death without transgression" (b. Shab. 55a) and the other remarking that "the death of the righteous atones [for others]" (= vicarious atonement, b. M.Q. 28a). On the surface, these two traditions obviously contradict one another, the first assuming that all die for their own sins and the second that the righteous might in effect die for the sins of others. Of course, it is possible to reconcile these opinions with sufficient ingenuity (Elman does just this)—despite the fact that such reconciliation requires a denial of the Talmud's understanding of the Shabbat tradition. But it would be far simpler to admit that the attributions cannot be taken at face value and that these opinions represent the views of different personalities of undefined time and place.

The second example relates to Elman's claim that Rava is particularly at the source of the novel views recorded in the Bavli. Elman makes reference to a teaching at Ber. 5a which shows Rava as the author of an opinion that "allows space for a non–measure for measure principle of Divine justice."[30] But, as Elman notes, the Talmud records an alternative tradition attributing the teaching to R. Ḥisda, and manuscripts preserve a chain of tradition attributing the same teaching ultimately to R. Huna. Furthermore, the Talmud elsewhere attributes the same concept to R. Shimon b. Laqish.[31] Again we are forced to ask, given the multiplicity of traditions regarding the source of this teaching, how can we rely on any one of them? Conclusions erected upon such a foundation rest upon extremely tenuous ground.

But even if the traditions were unanimous in attributing this teaching to Rava, we would still have to question the wisdom of relying upon them to make historical claims. The fact is that Rava's name appears over and over in probably the majority of the Bavli's deliberations. Traditions are attributed to Rava more than to any other sage in this document. For all we know, Rava's name may be a convention of sorts; the question of pre-redactional history is precisely the one we must confront here, and what we have seen suggests that attributions are sufficiently in doubt to avoid building historical scholarship upon them.

These examples could be multiplied many times, but the point has already been made: as a matter of methodological principle, we simply have no warrant for accepting the attributions given in rabbinic documents. We must thus ordinarily read recorded traditions as possibilities articulated at the final level of composition. This conclusion is particularly necessary because, when we are able to compare related traditions in different documents, it quickly becomes evident that "original" traditions are quoted and often molded to serve the purposes of the document as a whole, at its final, redacted level. Several examples of this phenomenon will be found in subsequent chapters, but I will offer one such case to make the scope and consequences of this phenomenon clear.

At Ber. 5b, the Bavli records a narrative which relates the substance of a dialogue between R. Yohanan and his colleagues when they each, in turn, become ill. Asked whether "sufferings are dear to them" each responds "neither they [the sufferings] nor their reward!" There is in this rejection of suffering neither a suggestion of compromise nor a hint that anyone is troubled by the rejection. The implications of this story, in context, are startling and radical, but they are characteristic of positions that the Bavli supports on numerous occasions. In contrast, when a Palestinian document (Song of Songs R. 2, 35) tells this story, it has R. Ḥanina responding to R. Yohanan's statement that his suffering is "more than he can bear" by chastising: "Don't say this but, rather, say—The trustworthy God!" R. Yohanan takes the correction to heart and subsequently responds appropriately to his suffering. Who, then, is the real R. Yohanan, the one who unrepentantly rejects his suffering or the one who allows himself to be corrected for ever having had doubts? Notably, the position attributed to R. Yohanan in the midrashic story fits perfectly the overall view of Palestinian documents which, almost without exception, condemn those who question the justice of suffering. In other words, each narrative serves the purpose of the redactor-author who uses it in his selected context. There is no "original" story here, only a tradition which has been transformed to communicate the message of the later rabbinic author. This case is far from unique. What we have said here pertains not only to these specific instances but to the literature as a whole.

Furthermore, even if we could demonstrate that rabbinic citations are absolutely accurate (which we cannot), we would still have to explain why certain traditions attributed, say, to Hillel, a sage of the early first century, do not appear in any rabbinic document before the sixth century. Presumably such traditions should have been available to the compilers of the Mishnah, for example, in the late second century. Why then were such traditions not quoted at an earlier point? This question is particularly pressing when we are dealing with a tradition which should have been central to the program of the compilers of the earlier document as well as to that of the later documents. If particular traditions or, more often, kinds of traditions were not quoted in earlier documents, it must be because the compilers of those documents did not yet accept or approve of the stated opinions. And what concerns us in a study such as this is not whether some individual at any given time entertained a particular idea, but whether and when that idea came to represent the opinion of a significant religious group (in this case, a group of rabbis). It is thus the author's choice to record an opinion in a canonical document that matters and not the original expression. There-fore, reliable or not, it is our obligation to look to the final documentary record for the history of the ideas we seek. This study must proceed accord-ing to the chronology of the documents at hand and not according to the chronology of sages whose opinions they purportedly record.

A second major problem with the work of earlier scholars is that, because they assume that rabbinic documents actually record the statements of indi-vidual authorities, they tend to read the opinions of the rabbis at the level of the individual, and at that level alone. In other words, because they believe that the particular document in which a citation appears is essen-tially irrelevant, they also deem irrelevant the opinion or opinions of any document at the level of its formulation or redaction.[32] The consequences of this blindness are twofold. First, a major opinion of the rabbinic com-munity, the opinion represented in the final composition of a document, receives almost no hearing in the scholarship of these authors. It is as though we were to read a high court decision by noting only the quoted opinions of lower or earlier courts and ignoring the opinions of the justice who com-piled these other opinions to make the case. Second, these same analyses do not take into account the fact that traditions in rabbinic texts, what-ever their historical reliability in relation to any original version, are selected and arranged by a final author or redactor with a purpose. As I have argued elsewhere, rhetorical analysis, employed for so long in the examination of other literatures, is essential in the interpretation of rabbinic texts as well.[33] Only through sensitivity to the rhetoric of the final composition will the prejudices and predilections of these documents be understood; only with the application of these tools will the impact of the final redactor upon his presumed sources be fully appreciated.

All of this being said, I must emphasize that my siding with Neusner in the scholarly debate regarding the reliability of purported earlier traditions and my agreement with his primary attention to final documents should not be construed as total methodological agreement. In particular, in the matter of the "intertextuality" of rabbinic documents I have a serious dis-agreement with Neusner's conclusions. Neusner has denied what he calls (idiosyncratically) the "intertextuality" of rabbinic documents (he uses the term differently from most literary critics), arguing that the Bavli, for example, speaks in essential isolation from other rabbinic documents (excluding the Mishnah), ignoring their programs and not responding to their ideas.[34] Daniel Boyarin has offered a cogent and fundamentally per-suasive critique of Neusner's position, and there is no need to repeat it here.[35] In my mind, the notion of a self-reflective rabbinic canon is irre-futable, and sensitivity to the echoes, traces, and transformations of earlier vocabularies in later rabbinic documents is essential to the sort of study projected here. Later rabbinic works do refer and respond to earlier tradi-tions and must therefore be read in light of the earlier tradition (as we have it preserved in the documentary record) in order to be fully appreciated. The recognition that later parts of the canon take full meaning only when seen to comment on and transform earlier elements of the canon will contribute immense richness to the analyses of rabbinic documents that follow. While each document is unique, that uniqueness can be appreciated only on the basis of careful and frequent comparison.

The rabbis, of course, did not speak in a vacuum, and they had a considerable and varied tradition on which to build. In order to appreciate the complexity of rabbinic responses, it will be necessary to review this variety and consider the rabbis' substantive relationship to what came before. This is especially true with respect to the tradition of the Hebrew Bible, whose authority the rabbis respected and whose substance they knew intimately. Therefore, Chapter 2 will examine the wide range of responses to suffering that are found in the Hebrew Bible. But reference to the Bible is not enough, for rabbinic religion stands not only on the foundation of biblical religion but also at the end of a long series of postbiblical expressions of Judaism. These expressions, recorded in the earlier Apocrypha and the Dead Sea Scrolls, as well as in the writings of Philo of Alexandria, represent, on the superficial level, directions that the rabbis might have taken but did not. What were these alternative possibilities? Which did the rabbis admit? Which did they reject? Finally, the rabbis were, at the earliest stages at least, but a small proportion of Palestinian, let alone diaspora, Jewry as a whole. Other Jews, non-rabbis, also responded to the tragedy of the destruction of the Temple and later to the Hadrianic persecutions; their responses are found in the writings of the early Christians, in the later Apocryphal books, and in the writings of Josephus. The special nature of rabbinic responses will be fully appreciated only when these alternatives are considered as well. A general review of the relevant material will be found in Chapter 3.

What can we hope to discover in the course of this study? First, and most obviously, we will clarify the history of the development of a set of ideas, that is, those that relate to suffering and the problems of evil and divine justice. We will set out the variety of responses, both traditional and innovative, in their documentary settings, and be able to judge the distance that later rabbinic documents and the communities they represent moved from earlier documents and their communities. In one important area, at least, we will shed light on the development of rabbinic religion.

Second, because we set the rabbinic development against the canonical and traditional background, we will have before us a case study in the reformulation of a religious tradition. We will see how a religion that claims to be traditional reinterprets the canon that stands at its foundation, and how, through reinterpretation or not, it justifies new and even radical formulations to a reading community that presumably remains bound by earlier authoritative traditions. Religions change though they claim to remain the same; here, one kind of history of Judaism will illuminate some of the ways this is done.

Third, we will offer the basis for comparison and critique of recent histories of rabbinic religion which describe the various documentary expressions as responses to particular historical circumstances and events.[36] It is in connection with the present subject that we might expect the influence of history to be most direct and explicit. Thus the contours of the development of this specific set of ideas may reveal much about broader motivations and responses on the part of the rabbinic authors. If what we find regarding suffering corresponds to more general conclusions concerning the religious spirits of these documents, then those conclusions will be strengthened. If our conclusions contradict what has been suggested more generally, then further research and debate will be in order.

Finally, because, as we shall see, the most original and radical responses in rabbinic Judaism to the problem of suffering are found in the Bavli, we will be able, in this study, to add another chapter to the growing literature on the unique intellectual character of that work. To the many other phenomena, both formal and substantive, which first find expression (in rabbinic Judaism) in the Bavli, we will now add the nature of its theological speculation as embodied in the question of suffering, justice, and evil—that is, theodicy. We will witness a document that is both bold and restrained, but rarely submissive—qualities long understood to characterize the Bavli, but never before supported with the kind of detail that this and similar recent studies provide.

2

The Canonical Foundation

The rabbis did not come to the question of human suffering, or to any other question, without prejudice. Their religion was one that, at all of its stages, claimed a profound continuity with the religion of the Hebrew Bible.[1] But this claim was often belied by the reality, and it is clear that rabbinic Judaism differed in significant details from the tradition recorded in the Bible. Consequently, understanding rabbinic Judaism is often a matter of appreciating continuity and difference, that is, the ways in which rabbinic Judaism is continuous with its biblical foundation and those in which it is different.

For the rabbis, even at the earliest stages of their history, the Bible was already a well-defined whole.[2] This is not to say that there were not some final details to be determined; it is quite likely that the precise status of certain books of what came to be known as the Writings (Hebrew: *ketubim*) was still in doubt in early rabbinic Judaism.[3] But the Torah and Prophets had long before been canonized, and so when the rabbis returned to scripture for authoritative opinions they had no significant questions concerning the shape and scope of the canon which bound them. As canon, the Bible was not merely a collection of discrete books; it was one complete book, divinely inspired, some sections more authoritative (the Torah) and some apparently less so (books other than the Torah). Moreover, being divine and therefore eternal, the Bible was not limited by its history—it was *not* read contextually. It spoke now and forever, as a work that weighed in all of its details, and it demanded of the rabbis as of other Jews that they make sense of its immense diversity and richness.[4] This was the Bible upon which the rabbis built.

17

Because we wish to examine canonical precedents for later rabbinic responses to suffering, we will review responses to the same problem in the Bible as the rabbis had it, that is, in the final, canonical Hebrew Bible as preserved in the rabbinic tradition. We will *not* write a history of such responses in biblical times; the rabbis did not read the Bible historically (this was a matter of conscious principle, which the rabbis expressed in the maxim "there is no earlier and later in the Torah"), and thus we gain nothing for present purposes by doing so.[5] Our interest is to outline the authoritative possibilities, those which were unquestionably legitimate in the rabbis' eyes because they were included in the Bible itself. Thus we will proceed in this chapter topically, making reference to major expressions of each type of response. Of course, since this study is an attempt to create a broad typology, a detailed, comprehensive treatment of the biblical materials is not required. Such a study is the subject for another book (actually, for many books).[6] In the present context, we merely seek to understand the biblical opinions as they would reverberate in the consciousness of later rabbinic readers.

The Classical Biblical Position: Retributive Suffering

The mechanism most commonly understood to underlie the vicissitudes of human experience is spelled out from the very beginning of the Torah's narrative drama: suffering, broadly defined, is punishment from God—transgression of the Divine Will finds its direct response in Divine Retribution. Thus the suffering experienced by the descendants of Eve in childbirth, the suffering of Adam and his offspring as they toil in the field, the banishment from the garden, and death itself—all are punishments for ignoring God's command to refrain from consuming the forbidden fruit (Gen. 3). Cain's sentence, dooming him to wander over the face of the earth, is punishment for the murder of his brother (Gen. 4). The flood, destroying all life with the exception of Noah, his family, and small numbers of each animal species, is a retribution for corruption (Gen. 6). The destruction of Sodom and Gomorrah, too, is God's reprisal for the immensity of their sin (Gen. 18).

The same cause-and-effect relationship is evident later in the Torah as well. Miriam is afflicted with leprosy as punishment for maligning her brother Moses (Num. 12). The spies who surveyed the promised land and those who heeded their faithless warning are doomed to perish in the desert as punishment for denying God's word (Num. 13–14). The congregation of Korach, challenging Moses and the God who trusted in him, are destroyed for the same corrupting challenge (Num. 16). Even Moses, for publicly displaying his lack of trust and refusing to follow God's word precisely, is punished by God's refusal to allow him to enter the land (Num. 20). Sickness, wandering, death, and disappointment are all expressions of God's justice, a justice that insists upon obedience to God's will and repays non-obedience with suffering in various degrees.

Exhortative portions of the Torah, particularly those of Deuteronomy, highlight the same lesson. The famous warning of Lev. 26 makes the point precisely: if God's command is not obeyed, all kinds of suffering will result. Included in the list of punishments for transgression are the following:

> I will wreak misery upon you— consumption and fever,[7] which cause the eyes to pine and the body to languish; you shall sow your seed to no purpose, for your enemies shall eat it . . . you shall be routed by your enemies, and your foes shall dominate you. . . . And if, for all that, you do not obey me, I will go on to discipline you sevenfold for your sins. . . . I will make your skies like iron and your earth like copper. . . . Your land shall not yield its produce, nor shall the trees of the land yield their fruit. . . . I will loose wild beasts against you, and they shall bereave you of your children and wipe out your cattle. They shall decimate you, and your roads shall be deserted. (vv. 16–22)

The list continues with punishments of ever-increasing intensity, leading finally to the desolation of the land and the scattering of the people (vv. 31–38). All of this is meant to highlight "their iniquity and the iniquity of their fathers" (v. 40) until "at last shall their obdurate heart humble itself, and they shall atone for their iniquity" (v. 41). Only following such atonement will God finally remember the covenant and restore the suffering people. For present purposes, what is important is that the sin of the people is punished by God and that punishment takes the form of suffering inflicted upon them.

The identical theme is sounded throughout Deuteronomy. In Deut. 4: 25–31, the people are promised exile if they create idols (see also chapter 8, end). In chapter 11 (16–17) the threatened punishment, here for sin in general, is the removal of God's blessing from the land and its produce, and later in the same chapter God promises to curse the people if they do not "obey the commandments of the Lord." In the same vein, many promises of reward for observance convey the clear sense of the consequences of nonobservance; the promise that obedience will lead God to "ward off from you all sickness" (Deut. 7:15), for example, suggests that, conversely, disobedience will lead to all manners of sickness. Almost uniformly, what we have called suffering is explained in the Torah as divine retribution.[8]

But this is not the only explanation offered for suffering even in the Torah. A significant exception to the rule offered above is found in the biblical explanation of the suffering of the Israelites in Egypt. This suffering is, according to the biblical account, a manifestation of this people's covenantal destiny, a destiny promised already by God to Abraham:

> Know well that your offspring shall be strangers in a land not theirs, and they shall be enslaved and oppressed four hundred years; but I will execute judgment on the nation they shall serve, and in the end they shall go free with great wealth. (Gen. 15:13–14)

The slavery and oppression, followed by the redemption therefrom, were essential to the scenario by which this people would be born to God. Their suffering was a fulfillment of divine purpose, therefore, and in no way an expression of judgment. While central to the biblical drama, though—and central as well to the later psyche of this people—the explanation for suffering that was inherent in these events would in the end be mostly irrelevant: later suffering would not be explained in this way. The oppression suffered as a prelude to the exodus was sui generis.

The historical books of the Bible persist in explaining suffering as divine punishment. One of the best examples of this continuing understanding is found in the editorial structuring of the many stories combined in the book of Judges. As the Judge cycle proper begins, immediately following the narration of Joshua's death, the following introduction appears:

> Another generation arose after them, which had not experienced [the deliverance of] the Lord or the deeds that He has wrought for Israel. And the Israelites did what was offensive to the Lord. They worshipped the Baalim and forsook the Lord, the God of their fathers . . . they provoked the Lord. . . . Then the Lord was incensed at Israel, and He handed them over to foes who plundered them. . . . In all their campaigns, the hand of the Lord was against them to their undoing . . . and they were in great distress. Then the Lord raised up chieftains who delivered them from those who plundered them. But they did not heed their chieftains either; they went astray after other gods. . . . They were quick to turn aside. . . . When the Lord raised up chieftains for them, the Lord would be with the chieftain and save them from their enemies. . . . But when the chieftain died, they would again act basely. (Judge. 2:10–19)

The stories as a whole are explained on the basis of the same cycle (see, for example, 3:7, 4:1, 6:1, 8:33). The sin throughout is idolatry, and the punishment is the suffering experienced through defeat.

The narratives of these books commonly suggest the same explanation. For example, the deposition of Saul is explained at 1 Sam. 15 as punishment for his refusal to obey the ban of Amalek. Similarly, it is on account of his sin with Bathsheva that David is threatened with death and other calamities. Only after his expression of remorse is David himself spared, but there is still punishment for his sin, now in the death of his child by Bathsheva (2 Sam. 11–12).

Following the precedent set in Judges, the editorial structure of the royal history is similarly punctuated with formulaic evaluations of each of the kings, suggesting that their fates and the fate of those who follow them are a consequence of their many transgressions (with rare virtuous exceptions appropriately indicated). Thus, we are told, "Omri did what was displeasing to the Lord; he was worse than all who preceded him. He followed all the ways of Jeroboam son of Nebat and the sins which he committed and caused Israel to commit, vexing the Lord, the God of Israel" (1 Kings 16:25–26). In the same fashion, "Ahab son of Omri did what was displeasing to the Lord, more than all who preceded him" (v. 30, same chapter). The promised punishment for Ahab's sins, sounded by Elijah, is his destruction and the destruction of his house. In his case, though, as earlier in that of David, remorse and self-affliction are able to effect a stay in the sentence; the punishment, we are told, would not be executed until the generation of Ahab's son (chapter 22).

Perhaps the most significant repetition of this explanation, a resounding affirmation by virtue of its context, is the justification offered in the biblical texts for the destruction of the Israelite kingdoms, north and south. In the first instance, the defeat is explained in this way:

> This happened because the Israelites sinned against the Lord their God. . . . They worshiped other gods and followed the customs of the nations which the Lord had dispossessed before the Israelites and the customs which the kings of Israel had practiced. . . . They committed wicked acts to vex the Lord. . . . The Lord warned Israel and Judah by every prophet [and] every seer, saying: "Turn back from your wicked ways, and observe my commandments and my laws. . . ." But they did not obey. . . . They rejected all the commandments of the Lord their God. . . . The Lord was incensed at Israel and He banished them from His presence; none was left but the tribe of Judah alone.
>
> Nor did Judah keep the commandments of the Lord their God. . . . So the Lord spurned all the offspring of Israel, and He afflicted them and delivered them into the hands of plunderers, and finally He cast them out from His presence.
>
> So the Israelites were deported from their land to Assyria, as is still the case. (2 Kings 17:7–23)

Simply and unambiguously, the defeat at the hands of Assyria and the destruction of the kingdom is punishment for sin. So, too, would the destruction of what was left of the kingdom in the south be punishment for the sins of Menasseh (chapter 21). The history was one of obedience or transgression and, since the transgression vastly outweighed the obedience, the punishment demanded by divine justice required that this history end in utter desolation.[9]

In general terms, the classical prophets also explain suffering by means of this cause (sin) and effect (punishment = suffering) relationship. This connection may be found in a wide variety of places, too numerous to list here (representative examples may be found at Isa. 3:16–26, 5:24–29; Ezek. 3:17–21, 39:23). Perhaps its most important expression, because of the insistence that each individual is punished for his or her own sins, is the detailed treatise on divine justice in Ezek. 18. Expanding upon Jeremiah's promise that "every one shall die for his own sins" (Jer. 31:30, and compare with the present context also v. 29), Ezekiel spells out at length a calculus of immediate personal responsibility, all with reference to an immediate and not a future reality (see also 33:7–20). Notably, his assertion responds to the complaint of the House of Israel (vv. 25 and 29) that "The way of the Lord is unfair." Ezekiel's retort is that it is the ways of the people that are unfair. By definition, those who are punished through suffering must have transgressed. Only by means of repentance will they be assured of life (v. 32).

Many of the Writings carry forward the same principle. In Psalms, God's justice is widely affirmed. Take, for example, Pss. 34:16–20:

The eyes of the Lord are on the righteous,
His ears attentive to their cry.
The face of the Lord is set against evildoers,
to erase their name from the earth.
They [= the righteous] cry out, and the Lord hears,
and saves them from their troubles. . . .

And so on.[10] Proverbs also repeats this view on numerous occasions. Typical is 3:33: "The curse of the Lord is on the house of the wicked, But He blesses the abode of the righteous."[11] Based upon this assumption, the reasonable conclusion for this author is that the Lord's discipline, intimated to be suffering, will often be manifest and should, as discipline, be wisely and gladly received.[12] In these two statements, the ideology of this book as a whole, at least as it connects with our concern, is succinctly expressed. As the tradition had long taught and traditional Wisdom therefore repeated, failure to fear the Lord—to follow his commandments—was the cause of punishment and the source of suffering.

I have gone on at such length demonstrating the widespread presence of the sin–punishment explanation of suffering in the Bible because of its centrality to biblical ideology as a whole.[13] Though by no means the only explanation (as we shall see below), it is by far the most common explanation and thus the one that is likely to carry the most weight with later Jews. As the rabbis, centuries later, read the Bible and sought explanations for their own suffering, on both the personal and national level, this is the one that would have suggested itself to them most immediately and persistently. Consequently, when we turn, in later chapters, to the various rabbinic explanations, it will be essential to compare the relative prominence given to this explanation with that given to others. A shift in emphasis, even if the same theoretical possibilities are maintained, may be highly significant.

Suffering and Love

A second explanation of suffering, offered especially by Amos, the earliest of the classical prophets, points to the importance of Israel's chosenness and God's unique attention to this people on that account. When we are first introduced to Amos's Lord—a Lord who, before all else, judges the nations—it is made clear that Israel is held to a different, higher standard. Israel's neighbors are punished for acts of extreme violence, Israel (including Judah) herself for having "spurned the Teaching of the Lord" (2:4), for having "sold for silver Those whose cause was just" (2:6). Therefore, if Israel appears to be punished before or more severely than other nations, this seeming injustice can easily be explained: others are not held accountable for the same transgressions as Israel and Judah.

This shift in perspective allows us to understand Israel's afflictions not as cruelty or harsh justice but as a loving, parentlike rebuke. Deuteronomy expresses the notion this way: "As a man chastens his son, so does the Lord, your God, chasten you" (8:5). In consequence of this, suffering is *not* the sign of a relationship (God–Israel) in rupture. On the contrary, God declares that "You alone have I singled out[14] of all the families of the earth—That is why I will call you to account for all your iniquities" (3:2). That God cares to punish through afflictions is a sign of God's love. If God did not care, God would not punish; thus we who are punished must, by that very evidence, be God's select nation.

Proverbs reiterates the same basic idea, but now with relationship to the individual: "For whom the Lord loves, He rebukes, As a father the son whom he favors" (3:12). Again, rebuke from the Lord is an expression of love, much as the parent will discipline the child whom he loves. Suffering, then, may be viewed as an expression of God's love and not as a statement of God's displeasure. Ironically, according to this approach, those who sin and do not suffer are *not* loved by God. After all, God does not even correct them when they have gone astray.

The notion that God's special concern is expressed through suffering is further suggested in the claim that suffering is intended to test, refine, and ultimately improve the sufferer. According to its most likely interpretation, Ps. 11:5 suggests this as an explanation of the suffering of the righteous individual. The verse suggests that "*YHVH zadiq yivḥan*," translated in JPS as "The Lord seeks out the righteous man"— apparently understanding this phrase in apposition to the next, "but loathes the wicked one who loves injustice." Many others, however, have translated "Yahweh [= the Lord] trieth the righteous,"[15] reading the root "BḤN" according to its more common meaning of "trying" or "testing" (see the usage at Ps. 95:9: "when your fathers put Me to the test, *tried* me . . . [emphasis added]). Thus this text may be taken to suggest that suffering is not punishment at all, but a test. If the righteous prevails in this test, of course, he will be improved and ultimately rewarded (see also Psalm 94).

If, already, we are speaking of the righteous individual who suffers, it is appropriate here to consider one of the most striking and certainly the most consequential (by virtue of its adaptation in Christianity) of all biblical explanations of this phenomenon, that is, the vision of the Suffering Servant (Isa. 52:13–53:12). This chapter describes in detail one "servant of the Lord" who will suffer various horrible and disfiguring afflictions, be abhorred and rejected by men, approach death (according to a minimalist interpretation), and be saved only by virtue of having served as atonement for the sins of others. The portions of the prophecy that relate most directly to our concern are these:

> He was despised, shunned by men,
> A man of suffering, familiar with disease . . .
> it was our sickness that he was bearing,
> Our suffering that he endured.
> We accounted him plagued,
> Smitten and afflicted by God;

But he was wounded because of our sins,
Crushed because of our iniquities.
He bore the chastisement that made us whole,
And by his bruises we were healed.
We all went astray like sheep,
Each going his own way;
And the Lord visited upon him
The guilt of all of us.

. . . [H]e was cut off from the land of the living
through the sin of my people, who deserved the punishment.
And his grave was set among the wicked,
And with the rich, in his death—
Though he had done no injustice
And had spoken no falsehood.
But the Lord chose to crush him by disease,
That, if he made himself an offering for guilt,
He might see offspring and have long life,
And that through him the Lord's purpose might prosper. . . .

My righteous servant makes the many righteous,
It is their punishment that he bears. . .
he bore the guilt of the many
And made intercession for sinners. (53:3–12)

A wide variety of interpretations have been suggested to fix the identity of this servant—ranging from particular historical individuals to ideal types to the collective body of the people Israel.[16] For present purposes, the servant's actual identity is immaterial. What is crucial is that he may reasonably be interpreted as symbolizing either the collective body of Israel or an individual, depending upon whether the reader reads[17] in light of the immediate or broader context (the former speaks explicitly of the individual, the latter, on several occasions, identifies the Lord's servant as Israel).[18] Obviously, therefore, this text's unique proposal that the suffering of the righteous might be vicarious atonement for the sins of others may also be applied to either.

Let us look at the details of the prophet's conception. Despite numerous difficulties in this text, it makes absolutely clear that the righteous servant is here understood to suffer not for his own transgressions but for those of others.[19] Those who view him imagine, after the traditional explanation, that *he* is being punished by God, that is, for his own sins (v. 4). But they are blind; he bears the sins of others. Such vicarious retribution has important benefits, though: by virtue of his afflictions others may be healed. On account of his suffering the sins of others will be atoned. He is the sacrifice through whose offering the Lord's purpose will be able to prosper (v. 10).

In this case, clearly, suffering is not punishment for a person's own sins but for the sins of others. What forces the prophet to arrive at such a conclusion? Surely the question which Israel of the exile must every day have confronted: How else can the undeniable suffering of the righteous, side by side with the comfort of the wicked, be understood? To be sure, others, Ezekiel foremost among them, reasserted the older perception of God's execution of justice. But this author no longer agrees with that ancient view. From the perspective of this exilic prophet, both the people as a whole and individual Israelites have suffered far in excess of their measure of guilt. Personal guilt cannot be the point, therefore. Punishment must have been displaced, and there must have been some good reason for such displacement. The prophet's explanation is that displaced suffering effects atonement for those who have indeed sinned. The sacrifice of the righteous will save others from the fate they surely deserve.

Suffering and Future Justice

A very popular biblical solution to the problem of suffering is the projection of justice-realized into some future time (though not a life after death; for this conception, see the next chapter). According to First Isaiah, for example, men of pride and the idols they follow will meet their full destruction only in "a day the Lord of Hosts has ready" (2:12). By the same token, perfect reward also awaits a "day to come" (2:2–4). Isaiah's pronouncements on this matter are not consistent, but at least some measure of God's plan awaits a day to come.

God's response to Habakkuk's complaint (chapter 1) also affirms that justice will be done only in the future. In this prophet's vision, God denies that present appearances are accurate reflections of true reality; "the righteous man is rewarded with life for his fidelity" (2:4) and the wicked will not escape punishment (2:5). If present circumstances are so dismal, when will this all occur? Following the completion of a "set term" and the arrival of "a time that will come." Lest we despair, the assurance is repeated: "Even if it tarries, wait for it still; For it will surely come, without delay" (2:3). There is an end to current suffering, and it is not long off.

The emotion underlying all of this is unmistakable: current experience has become intolerably painful and the promised reward of the righteous and punishment of the wicked simply takes *too long*. According to Yehezkel Kaufmann,[20] Habakkuk's expression anticipates, in a clear and unambiguous way, the response to suffering that would typify later apocalyptic prophecies. There comes an end (*qeẓ*), an end that will not delay. Thus present desperation will quickly be reversed. The future world, in which resolution will be achieved, is due to be realized in short order.

The most dramatic vision of the day-to-come in the classical prophets is also the latest, that of Malachi. Malachi begins by affirming that justice will be done: "those who revere the Lord . . . shall be [the Lord's] treasured possession" (3:16–17). There *will* be a difference between the righteous and the wicked (though, we learn by implication, there might not be now). When will this all be? In "that day," the day of the Lord's judgment. Once again, justice is promised and its fulfillment is projected into a future time.

What distinguishes Malachi's day-to-come from other imaginations of that day, aside from the fact that it will be heralded by Elijah the prophet, is its awesomeness (3:23). That day is described by Malachi as a day of fire (3:2 and 19), a day that will smelt and purify, refine the righteous, and consume the wicked like straw (chapter 3, vv. 3 and 19). It is a day, accordingly, that can barely be endured, but one from which the righteous will emerge triumphant. Furthermore, it is a day when the *individual* will be judged for his sins (3:5). There is no concern for the nations. It is not they who must be judged for their former persecutions of Israel; it is individual Israelites who must give accounting. It is they who will be consumed or healed.

Combining the urgency of Habakkuk and dramatic imagination of Malachi is the latter half of the book of Daniel, the Bible's only full-fledged apocalypse.[21] Werner G. Kummel offers a clear description of this genre. Apocalypse, he writes, is "defined by a distinctive eschatological thought world and by an otherworldly perspective." It "presupposes the penetration of extra-Jewish, i.e., Iranian Hellenistic, concepts into Judaism, especially those of dualism and demonology." Furthermore, its "principal means of expression are parable (allegory) and symbol."[22] Daniel 7–12 offers several excellent examples of this sort of writing, and we take chapter 8 to illustrate the approach of this apocalyptic corpus overall.

The chapter begins with Daniel describing a fantastic vision, one in which an immensely powerful ram is overcome by an even more powerful he-goat. The goat sprouts four horns, one of which "grew as high as the host of heaven" (v. 10). This same horn then "vaunted itself against the very chief of the host; on its account the very offering was suspended, and His holy place was abandoned" (v. 11). Following this, a heavenly being asks how long "the regular offering [will] be forsaken . . . [and] the sanctuary be surrendered" (v. 13). The response is precise: "For 2300 evenings and mornings" (v. 14). Lest there be any confusion, Gabriel then appears to Daniel and tells him that "the vision refers to the time of the end" (v. 17). Then comes the specific interpretation: the ram of the vision is the kings of Media and Persia, the he-goat is the king of Greece (Alexander), and the four horns are the kingdoms that would follow Alexander's demise. The fourth horn, clearly, is Antiochus Epiphanes and the events described are his desecration of the Temple.

The prophecy goes on to detail that the "end of time" will arrive when the persecution has lasted "2300 evenings and mornings," that is, less than seven years. The suffering of those spoken of in the prophecy (unclear to the rabbis, though the original audience, Jews during the Antiochan persecution, would surely have known that it referred to them) is to be short-lived. Moreover, the intensity of their suffering is justified by virtue of the fact that it presages the final redemptive age. The subjective experience of the individual sufferer here is folded into the grand plan of history, and the individual may be comforted with the knowledge that this will all soon come to an end, to be replaced with a world that is far more perfect.

The last and longest of the Daniel visions adds an important element to the solution just reviewed, that is, the explicit promise of resurrection for the righteous (12:2–3). Accepting this view, the justification of chapter 8 is buttressed with the assurance that even those who do not survive until the immanent end-time will nevertheless be delivered from suffering and injustice. The short-term sacrifice that vision seems to require—a sacrifice that, it should be recalled, is hardly short-term for those who lose their lives in the interim—is here eliminated through the expectation that, whatever the individual suffers here and now, this is not necessarily the end of his or her life in any case. Life may resume. Still—and here I anticipate later rabbinic expressions of this same idea—it should be noted that resurrection is expressed in this text as a broad generality: "many of those that sleep in the dust of the earth will awake." It is not clear precisely who these many might be ("the knowledgeable" and "those who lead the many to righteousness" are suggested, but the scope is still unclear), and the assurance that these words hold is not yet related explicitly to the individual. It would be difficult to say whether the individual righteous man or woman could yet submit to threatened suffering with the knowledge that this resurrection can be anticipated with complete confidence.[23]

The Tradition of Complaint

Complaint and accusation as a response to suffering, well-known from the book of Job, are scattered throughout other biblical books as well. The prophecy of Habakkuk, who witnessed with alarm the replacement of the Assyrians with the new Babylonian empire, is one excellent example. Characterized by Yehezkel Kaufmann as a "prophetic Job,"[24] Habakkuk adopts a posture with relationship to God that is a complete reversal of the typical prophetic position: he is the one who initiates dialogue and God the one who responds.[25] This initiative is motivated by an acute sense on Habakkuk's part of the problem of suffering and the injustice that it seems to represent:

> How long, O Lord, shall I cry out
> And You not listen,
> Shall I shout to You, "Violence!"
> And You not save?
> Why do You make me see iniquity
> [Why] do You look upon wrong?—
> Raiding and violence are before me,
> Strife continues and contention goes on.
> That is why decision fails
> And justice never emerges;

> For the villain hedges in the just man—
> Therefore judgment emerges deformed. . . .
> Why do You countenance treachery,
> And stand by idle
> While the one in the wrong devours
> The one in the right? (1:2–4, 13)

Justice does not emerge. God stands by idly. Here we see the problem of divine justice and suffering in its most direct articulation.

Witnessing a later defeat, Jeremiah, like Habakkuk, also brings a claim against God:

> You will win, O Lord, if I make a claim against You,
> Yet I shall present charges against You:
> Why does the way of the wicked prosper?
> Why are the workers of treachery at ease? . . .
> How long must the land languish,
> And the grass of all the countryside dry up?
> Must beasts and birds perish,
> Because of the evil of its inhabitants? (12:1–4)

In substance, the accusation is very much like that of Habakkuk. What distinguishes Jeremiah's approach, and what ties it in a significant way to what we find in Job, is Jeremiah's thought of bringing God to court for present injustice. Here, however, this is all written small. Only in Job does this indictment find full articulation.

Sometimes forgotten for their similarity to these various expressions are the numerous Psalms of Complaint. Of course, the most common response to our problem in the Psalms is to affirm the reality of God's justice. But even such affirmations are not always so simple. The psalmist's confidence is often diluted by the recognition that the problem does exist. When we read, for example, that "Better the little that the righteous man has than the great abundance of the wicked" (37:16), we are unable to ignore the fact that God's abundance is distributed inequitably, often to the benefit of the wicked. Far more explicitly, Psalm 73 devotes most of its length to comments like the following: "I envied the wanton; I saw the wicked at ease. Death has no pangs for them; their body is healthy. They have no part in the travail of men; they are not afflicted like the rest of mankind" (vv. 2–5), or, in contrast, "It was for nothing that I kept my heart pure and washed my hands in innocence, seeing that I have been constantly afflicted, that each morning brings new punishments" (vv. 13–14). Again, we see here the problem at its most acute. It is difficult, in fact, not to be skeptical about the affirmation with which the psalm concludes. This pious affirmation rings a little hollow against the background of this brutal reality. (See also Psalms 92 and 94.)

A more genuine response—at least to modern ears—is the various pleas for amelioration that accompany many similar observations. Thus Psalm

82: "How long will you judge perversely, showing favor to the wicked? Judge the wretched and the orphan, vindicate the lowly and the poor, rescue the wretched and the needy; save them from the hand of the wicked" (vv. 2–3). Or, at length, Psalm 10:

> Why, O Lord, do You stand aloof,
>   heedless in times of trouble?
> The wicked in his arrogance hounds the lowly—
>   may they be caught in the schemes they devise. . . .
> Rise, O Lord!
>   Strike at him, O God!
> Do not forget the lowly. (vv. 1–2, 12)

These and similar expressions[26] typically do not offer explanations of the present dilemma, but the desperation they often reveal may itself be taken as a response. No explanation, then, just prayer—a response that combines both frustration and submission.

The latter of the quoted psalms serves as the first in a series of several psalms that together form a minor treatise on the problem of suffering and evil. The first of these psalms (10) is primarily a recognition of the difficulty and a prayer for its amelioration. The next (11) repeats briefly the complaint (vv. 2–3) and concludes with affirmation. Psalm 12 reiterates the problem and asks again that God respond.

Psalm 13 echoes the same theme, but now with a twist that has important consequences. The complaint here is this: "How long will You hide your face from me?" (v. 2). Notably, the same complaint is repeated in Psalm 88, one of the darkest and most pessimistic of all the psalms; it offers almost no glimmer of hope and highlights only despair. The tone of the latter, in fact, is closest to Habakkuk or Job, with the difference that it despairs even of the possible efficacy of prayer. In any case, the only possibility for explaining the dilemma of the righteous that suggests itself in either of these psalms is this description of God's stance: God has hidden God's face. In willful ignorance of the demands of justice, God has allowed the wicked to flourish and the righteous to suffer. Why would God do so? We are left to speculate. But the suffering *can* be explained by positing (accusing?) that God the judge has withdrawn, choosing not to execute the justice for which God is known.

Finally, Psalm 77 offers the closest parallel in this corpus to Job. The psalm begins by expressing at length the author's sense that he has been rejected by God (vv. 2–11). The response to this, found in the second half of the psalm, is to recall God's wonders by explicit reference to Exodus imagery (a strategy that is not found in Job), but with clear allusions to the creation as well (vv. 18–19). The response emphasizes God's grandeur and wonder, suggesting that, against such works, what is the significance of one individual's disappointment?

Of course, whatever the eloquence of individual complaints in Psalms, the Prophets, or elsewhere, nothing in the Bible approaches the book of

Job for narrative drama and sheer ability to shatter long-held assumptions. The middle dialogue of Job makes reference to virtually all the biblical explanations of suffering reviewed here and calls each, in turn, into question. Its alternative response, already hinted at, is to deny the possibility of explanation. The path by which the book arrives at that conclusion, as well as many of its other details, is important for us to consider in this context. Whatever the rabbis would one day make of this book, its inclusion in the biblical canon made its heterodox notions a permanent part of the authoritative Jewish literature and justified the model that it presents.

The literature on Job is immense, and this is hardly the place to detail the many and various interpretations of this challenging book.[27] A general overview of the book's attitudes, embedded in its broad literary structure (we are interested in the book in its final form, as the rabbis would have known it; source criticism is irrelevant to the present consideration), followed by a review of the variety of explanations that have been offered to make sense of God's response to Job in the final chapters, will be sufficient here.

The book begins by setting the stage for the lengthy dialogue that comprises the bulk of the text. In this introduction, God boasts to his companions in Heaven regarding his servant, Job, "blameless and upright, fearing God and shunning evil" (1:8). The Adversary (= Satan) argues that Job's righteousness is fragile—a luxury of his comfortable condition—and suggests that God test Job's righteousness by causing him to suffer. God obliges by allowing Satan to cause Job to lose his cattle, his children, and finally his own health and comfort. Job's wife encourages him to curse God for his suffering, but he refuses; he does not, as the text says, "sin with his mouth" (at least not yet). At this juncture, three of Job's friends approach him to comfort him and it is here that the drama truly begins.

Job does not, as his wife had urged him, curse God. But he does, in chapter 3, curse the day of his birth. This direction in Job's comments raises an inevitable tension. The reader knows (as Job and his companions do not) that Job's suffering is the product not of sin but of a divine wager. Thus, whatever Job's companions will suggest, the reader can be confident that the correct explanation of Job's suffering cannot be any of the conventional ones. But ancient Israelites would also have known that God is partner in the creation of individual human beings (the Bible relates far and wide that fetal conception is dependent upon God's will) and Job's cursing "his day," therefore, is only one step removed from cursing God. Is such talk proper? Is the continued assertion of his innocence in the following chapters justified? Or is it necessary to remain silent, to submit? Is it possible that Job, who had not earlier sinned, begins to sin at this very moment? This is the question readers must ask as they progress through the following dialogues.

The dialogues (chapters 4–37) pit Job against his colleagues in an often emotional debate over the reason for Job's suffering. The first several exchanges are typical of the dialogue as a whole. Beginning in chapter 4, Eliphaz attempts to put Job at ease through a complicated and not entirely consistent series of arguments.[28] He begins by challenging Job: "Think now, what innocent man ever perished? Where have the upright been destroyed?" (v. 7). If God is just and protects the righteous, then suffering must be punishment for sin. Similarly, but with slightly different nuance, Eliphaz argues that humans are guilty by nature (4:17). Therefore they cannot expect to escape punishment. Alternatively, Eliphaz suggests, suffering might be understood as divine discipline, even when not strictly punishment: "See how happy is the man whom God reproves; Do not reject the discipline of the Almighty" (5:17). Whichever explanation best applies in Job's case, it is clear that acceptance—not rebellion—is the recommended response. Yet Job listens closely to Eliphaz's explanations and continues nonetheless to protest his condition. He maintains that he is in the right (6:29); his suffering is not just punishment for his sin. He will persist, therefore, to complain about his unjust fate (7:11).

Bildad then steps in and indicts Job for his protest. "Will God pervert the right?" he asks, "Will the Almighty pervert justice?" (8:3). No, he insists, "Surely God does not despise the blameless; He gives no support to evildoers" (8:20). Again, the claim is that the system of divine justice is intact. The necessary interpretation of Job's afflictions, therefore, is as it has always been. But Job again denies the truth of this explanation ("He wounds me much for no cause" [9:17]) and escalates his protest by claiming, "It is all one; therefore I say, 'He destroys the blameless and the guilty . . .' The earth is handed over to the wicked one; He covers the eyes of its judges" (9:22–24). The judges are blind and it is God who blinds them. There is no justice to distinguish between the righteous and the wicked. And so the debate goes on.

Job's hopeful "comforters" continue unflinchingly in the same vein. Zophar accuses Job on two levels: first, Job should know that his punishment is even less than his sin (11:6) and besides, God's mystery is too great for Job to understand (v. 7). Eliphaz returns to intimate that Job is truly wicked (15:20). Bildad, too, accuses Job of being wicked (18:5, 21). The several friends later propose that, compared with God, humans, by definition, must be miserable and corrupt, and so deserving of punishment (22:2–5, 25:4–6). And remarkably, even at the end they maintain an insistence that God's justice is intact and that Job, therefore, must be guilty (34:10–12, 36:6–10).[29] But the repetition of this insistence, far from enhancing their argument, undermines the pieties they express and makes the viability of the system they support seem less and less likely; remember: we know all along that Job was, at least before his current protests, completely innocent.[30]

Job continues to insist upon his innocence and to accuse his accusers in kind. They are miserable comforters, he claims (16:2), and their answers are falsehoods (21:34). There is no justice (19:7). It is the wicked, not the righteous, who are in comfort (21:7–9). I am innocent, Job is confident (27:6); there is no truth, as far as he is concerned, in the pieties of old.

Job's insistence upon his innocence comes to a climax in the lengthy statement of chapters 29–31, an extraordinary catalogue of his good deeds. If Job indeed has been the person that he here claims—and the book gives us no reason to believe otherwise—then his suffering is truly insufferable, by himself or by any who know him (including us, the readers). As this catalogue unfolds, the situation in which Job finds himself becomes less and less tolerable, until Job is moved to take the final, extraordinary step—he calls God to court: "O that I had someone to give me a hearing; O that Shaddai would reply to my writ, Or my accuser draw up a true bill!" Now the challenge has been issued. The only question is how God will respond.

God does respond to Job's indictment, and does so powerfully. Basically, God's reply takes the following path. First, the Lord challenges Job's understanding by setting before him the vastness of the Lord's own works of creation, asking what is his possible comprehension in the face of such grandeur (chapters 38–39). Job's immediate response is to retreat to silence (40:4–5). God takes this opportunity, then, to claim that God will, by God's power, overwhelm any who hold themselves aloft in strength or pride. Job's final response is to admit that had not earlier understood:

> Indeed, I spoke without understanding
> Of things beyond me, which I did not know. . . .
> I had heard You with my ears,
> But now I see You with my eyes;
> Therefore I recant and relent,
> Being but dust and ashes. (42:3–6)

How does all of this fit together? How is God's answer any more satisfactory, say, than that of Zophar at 11:7?

Nahum Glatzer reviews the major types of interpretation.[31] Some see the final theophany and response as an affirmation that God's ways are a mystery. If humans cannot comprehend God's creation, that is, why should they imagine that they can understand the precise mechanisms of God's justice? Others see Job's response as a claim that only faith may form a proper and adequate answer. The Lord had, after all, challenged Job's adequacy in thinking that he could thus challenge God; Job's final and more proper response was to submit and to believe. Martin Buber and Yehezkel Kaufmann both understand God's answer to be the theophany itself.[32] God's revelation responds perfectly to Job's demand to confront God. What significance is there to his suffering, after all, in light of God's actual presence?

Stephen Geller follows the main thrust of these several interpretations, but with an important clarification. For Geller, Job is a critique of conventional ancient Near Eastern wisdom, which posited that "the laws of human behavior reflected cosmic order."[33] Job declared instead that "there can be no 'science' of piety." The claim "that the moral order is so directly related to nature as to be a part of it, implicitly binding even God, simply is wrong."[34] When Job triumphed, causing God to reveal himself, that revelation sought to communicate the essential difference between the natural order—which is ultimately inscrutable—and the moral order. The system of divine justice is *not* mechanistic, the author says. God is free from any moral order that we might seek to impose.[35]

For our purposes, it matters little which is the "correct" reading of Job. More crucial is that there are several reasonable readings of the Jobian *deus ex machina*. If so, then any may have been a possibility for the rabbis who held this book to be holy. What is clear is this: the book of Job insists that suffering may be left unexplained. If we hope to offer actual justifications of God's justice, we are bound to fail. We are forced, if we follow the Jobian direction, to be agnostic with respect to the matter of theodicy.

But Job's narrative raised another problem: How are we to respond to apparent injustice? Does piety require absolute acceptance, or is it legitimate to question and challenge? In the end, it is the Lord who answers this question by affirming the position of Job: "I am incensed," the Lord says to Eliphaz, "at you and your two friends, for you have not spoken the truth [or, better, "properly"] about Me as did my servant Job" (42:7, 8). So, whatever the nature of God's substantive answer to Job's plight, we are left with the unambiguous realization that the explanations offered by Job's colleagues were *not* necessary! God does not require that we blindly defend the divine system of justice. The pious individual may legitimately challenge and question, and God approves of doing so. Whether or not later Jews would agree, the canonical status of this view meant that protest would never again *have to be* judged unacceptable.

Suffering in Vain

We turn finally to the last major biblical response to suffering, that of Ecclesiastes (with minor parallels elsewhere; see especially Psalm 49). The most outstanding feature of this book—a feature that responds directly and with brutal honesty to the problem we address—is its unbending recognition and acceptance of what might be called the bitter reality of human experience. A few brief quotes will suffice to exemplify its position:

> For in respect of the fate of man and the fate of beast, they have one and the same fate: as one dies so dies the other, and both have the same lifebreath; man has no superiority over the beast, since both amount to nothing. (3:19)

> In my own brief span of life, I have seen both these things: sometimes a good man perishes in spite of his goodness, and sometimes a wicked one endures in spite of his wickedness. (7:15)

> For the same fate is in store for all: for the righteous, and for the wicked; for the good and pure and for the impure. . . . That is the sad thing about all that goes on under the sun: that the same fate is in store for all. (9:2–3)

And, with the greatest clarity and even intended irony:

> And here is another frustration: the fact that the sentence imposed for evil deeds is not executed swiftly, which is why men are emboldened to do evil— the fact that the sinner may do evil a hundred times and his [punishment]

still be delayed. For although I am aware that "It will be well with those who
revere God since they revere Him, and it will not be well with the scoundrel,
and he will not live long, because he does not revere God"—here is a frustration that occurs in the world: sometimes an upright man is requited according to the conduct of the scoundrel; and sometimes the scoundrel is requited
according to the conduct of the upright. (8:10–14)

So perspicuous is this author's grasp of what surrounds him—and us—that
it is unnecessary even to "update" the manner in which he has described it;
his reality remains absolutely contemporary.

What response does he suggest? At several of the points where the dilemma is expressed, the nature of the necessary response, at least so far as
the author of Ecclesiastes is concerned, is clear. At 3:22, for example: "I
saw that there is nothing better for a man than to enjoy his possessions,
since that is his portion." Since he can be sure of nothing else, a man should
be satisfied with that of which he can be relatively more sure. He should
not, in contrast, hang his fate on the hope of some future recompense: "don't
overdo goodness and don't act the wise man to excess, or you may be dumb-
founded" (7:16). Again, in contrast, what should he do? In the words of
the well-known and oft-misused expression: "For the only good that a man
can have under the sun is to eat and drink and enjoy himself [= eat, drink,
and be merry]. That much can accompany him, in exchange for his wealth,
through the days of life that God has granted him under the sun" (8:15).
There is no promise of justice, in this world or a future world; no sense that
the books will be reconciled. There is here, in fact, no answer to the problems of suffering and injustice at all. In the absence of an answer, says
Ecclesiastes, we can only enjoy what we have. Again, the answers that were
so prominent in the earlier literature seem here to be distant and weak
echoes.

With Ecclesiastes, the range of responses to suffering and the problem
of justice that would find expression in the Hebrew Bible reaches its limit.
And what a range it is! James Sanders categorizes the responses under eight
headings: (1) retributive suffering (= "the orthodox position of the Bible"),
(2) disciplinary suffering, (3) revelational suffering, (4) probational suffering
(= suffering as refining or testing), (5) suffering as illusory or transitory
(= Habakkuk and many psalms), (6) mysterious suffering (only God can
understand = Job), (7) eschatological suffering (= Daniel), and (8) meaningless suffering (= Ecclesiastes).[36] Surely, the precise division could be adjusted,
but this would make little difference, for as important as the precise responses
and explanations is the extraordinary range of biblical possibilities; it is a
range that is, to put it bluntly, astonishing. What is particularly astonishing
is the fact that, in responses that are equally hallowed within the same canon,
we see the same thing and its opposite. So suffering is divine retribution
(many of the documents, including the historical books and Proverbs) or it
is not (Job). Suffering is a meaningful corrective (many of the Prophets and
Proverbs) or it is meaningless (Ecclesiastes). Suffering, as a manifestation
of divine justice, pertains to the individual (Psalms) or only to the nation

within the grand sweep of history (Daniel). Both views are expressed. Neither is declared to be definitive or absolutely authoritative.

For the rabbis who returned to the Bible for authoritative guidance, it was this very range that they would confront. Surely, various responses loomed larger than others, and certain responses typified books (the Torah) that were generally deemed more authoritative. But a far greater variety competed for a hearing, and the rabbis, as they formulated their own responses, could be confident that this full range, at least, could find biblical support. It will be against this variety of authoritative possibilities that the rabbinic choices will be most meaningfully understood.

3

Other Jews, Other Responses

If we were to allow the rabbinic record to direct our inquiry, we would now commence our consideration of rabbinic works proper. As far as the rabbis were concerned, there was no significant Jewish religious creativity between the Bible (which they believed to have been finished in the fifth century BCE) and themselves. But we know reality to have been otherwise, and it would be a significant distortion of the record to ignore the centuries whose spirit is not recorded in the official Jewish (rabbinic) canon. The rabbis do not respond only to the biblical tradition. Living Jewish tradition produced a wide variety of religious expressions in the centuries between the Bible and the rabbis (second century BCE–second century CE), and the rabbis surely were familiar with at least some of these expressions. If they did not choose to follow models which entered Jewish tradition during these centuries, that choice is significant. If they were unconvinced by explanations of suffering which, though without direct biblical precedent, were supported by important groups of Jews in the centuries before the rabbis came upon the scene, then it is essential that we consider what these alternatives might have been. Why were the rabbis not convinced? What in their experience demanded different approaches?

Alternatively, it is possible that the rabbis did indeed incorporate some of these nonbiblical explanations into their own teachings. If the rabbis were in fact merely carrying forth older traditions, then this will affect our understanding of their dealings with the problems of suffering and divine justice. But this evaluation will have to be made with caution: if there is no explicit reference to earlier expressions (as, in fact, there will not be), it will probably be impossible to establish influence. It is possible, of course, that the same general milieu led to similar responses independently. From the perspective of the rabbis, unknowing repetition may be innovation. In cases of this sort, the question of what is uniquely rabbinic will have to be handled with extreme care.

Still, if understanding and appreciation are dependent upon comparison and contrast, we have no choice but to review the evidence of these intervening centuries. Because our goal is to set the stage for rabbinic developments, there is no need to review testimonies that merely repeat views already found in the canonical Bible. These opinions have already been reviewed, and their biblical record is far more important for the rabbis than any subsequent noncanonical repetition. Accordingly, we will direct our attention in this chapter only to opinions that have no strong biblical precedent— those that either recommend notable revisions of biblical views or speak for unprecedented possibilities. As was the case in our consideration of the biblical record, it will be important, as well, for us to consider the degree to which certain views dominate. If Jews in the age before the rabbis seem to have preferred certain explanations of their suffering, we must ask whether the rabbis preferred the same explanations. If they did not, it will be our obligation to try to understand why.

The literature which testifies to the opinions of Jews in the centuries before the rabbis is immense and varied.[1] The documents produced during this period are preserved in a variety of contexts. Some form part of the canon of different Christian churches. Others were discovered in the considerable corpus, much of it previously unknown, commonly known as the "Dead Sea Scrolls." The works of Philo and Josephus, preserved outside the Jewish context, also give us some insight into the variety of opinions that were current in these centuries.

As a whole, these books are closely related to their biblical predecessors. They typically construct their dramas around biblical figures, the genres they employ are mostly based upon models found in the biblical canon, and they are often dependent for their details upon the biblical text.[2] It should come as no surprise, therefore, that many of the ideologies and approaches found in these books are essentially mere repetitions of those found in the Hebrew Bible. This is as much true for responses to suffering as it is for other matters. But there are also original nuances and even new species of response, and it is to these that we turn our attention.

We begin with relatively modest revisions of earlier views. In a context which repeats common biblical explanations of suffering, the Wisdom of Solomon (first century BCE) also adds the view that the sufferer is accepted by God "like the sacrifice of the whole burnt offering (3:6)."[3] This notion may be taken to recall, in part, the approach of Isa. 53 (and to anticipate Paul in his letter to the Romans), but this expression is distinct in several ways. First, its description of the sufferer as sacrifice = burnt offering, in the technical sense, is more explicit and literal than what we find in Isaiah. More important, this context speaks of "the upright" in general, as opposed to some mysterious, righteous servant of the Lord. Thus the possibility that is only dubiously suggested in Isaiah (that the death of any righteous individual will atone) is here stated unmistakably. Finally, there is no indication here, as there was in Isaiah, that the sacrificial atonement is efficacious for others. Here it is the individual's suffering which allows him or her to be accepted as a sacrifice by God. The sacrifice imagined by this author is at the same time more general and more personal than the partial Isaiah precedent.

Later, the Wisdom of Solomon offers another important reinterpretation (now quite explicitly a reinterpretation) of pertinent biblical expressions. At 4:7–9, the author suggests that "an upright man, if he dies before his time, will be at rest,[4] For an honored old age does not depend on length of time and is not measured by the number of one's years, But understanding is gray hair for man, and a blameless life is old age." The Bible had promised length of days to the righteous and, this author asserts, the premature death of such individuals should not be taken as evidence to the contrary. Understood correctly, God's promise of length of days remains in force— nay, is self-fulfilling! Understanding and blameless life are *themselves* the essence of old age and the *zaqen* ("elder") is not the one who has actually lived many years but the one who has acquired wisdom and acted justly. These meritorious pursuits have become, as they would also be in some later rabbinic opinions, their own reward.

Following the preceding expression is an equally significant revision of more traditional notions. The author now proposes that early death is evidence of God's love for the righteous individual because, by means of death, God saves this individual from the company of the wicked. "He was caught up," the author claims, "so that wickedness might not alter his understanding" (4:11). In other words, premature death has here become a saving grace, with death itself the very act of salvation. Understood in this way, premature death is obviously not suffering for the righteous—that notion is a terrible distortion (so this author would claim)! On the contrary, through death this person is saved and death is therefore an act of love.

A notable revision of another biblical justification of suffering appears in 2 Macc. 6:13–16. As also in the Psalms of Solomon (13:6), there is an insistence in 2 Maccabees (by implication but quite obviously) that suffering as correction is different in kind—now radically so—from suffering as punishment. "It is a mark of great benevolence," the author argues,

> not to let the impious alone for a long time but to punish them promptly. For in the case of other nations, the Master is long-suffering and waits before he punishes them until they have reached the full measure of their sins; but in our case he has decided differently, so that he may not take vengeance on us afterward when our sins have reached their height. So he never withdraws his mercy from us, and always though he disciplines us with misfortune, he does not abandon his own people. (6:13–16)

Suffering continues to be punishment, but its apparently inequitable distribution is not to be misunderstood. Jews, like others, sin, and so should also be punished. But Jewish experience shows that Jews suffer far more than other nations! This is evidence, for this author, not of inequity but of divine benevolence, and his accounting is simple. Others who sin will obviously be punished, and because their sins that demand punishment accumulate continually, it is the full accumulation of those sins that will require retribution. Jews, on the other hand, are constantly punished and thus the account of their sins is never permitted to build up. Consequently, the punishment of Jews through suffering will remain relatively minor. Thank God, I suppose the author would say, for small things.

Justice after Death

Typifying documents of this period is the opinion that the scales of divine justice will be properly reconciled only in some future world.[5] This eschatological turn is distinct from biblical precedent in two respects—first, the hope of reconciliation in a future world is far more prevalent than had been the case in biblical literature as a whole, and second, the future world in these texts is not a restored, mundane world but a world after death, either otherworldly or subsequent to resurrection (as was the case, in the Bible, only in Daniel). The former possibility is a significant and radical development, for it posits an essential distinction between body and soul, a distinction without direct biblical precedent.[6]

An excellent example of this development may be found in 1 Enoch 22:9–11,[7] which imagines that

> three[8] places were made in order that they might separate the spirits of the dead. And thus the souls of the righteous have been separated; this is the spring of the water and on it is the light. Likewise a place has been created for sinners when they die and are buried in the earth and judgement has not come upon them during their life. And here their souls will be separated for this great torment, until the great day of judgement and punishment and torment.

Judgment will be fulfilled in a world after death and of death; the souls of those no longer living, this author claims, will be either rewarded or punished on the basis of the accounting of their deeds in life. With less specificity, but with no less confidence, the later chapters of this same book (ordinally, if not clearly chronologically)[9] also hold forth the assurance that the righteous and wicked will in the end be justly repaid (see chapters 96–105). Chapter 104, in particular, anticipates the rabbinic version of this theodicy by suggesting that the angels in heaven write down the names of the righteous so that they may be remembered before "the Great One" and rewarded accordingly.[10] Again, a just reality will be realized only in a future world. Our sense that present experience is unjust, therefore, is based upon incomplete evidence.

The Wisdom of Solomon is equally clear in stating its belief in a place for souls beyond life. The author claims that human beings were originally created for immortality, but on account of Satan's work people were doomed to die (2:23–24). However, though there are no exceptions to the rule of bodily death, "the souls of the upright are in the hand of God" (3:1). It is only the foolish, he goes on, who imagine that the righteous genuinely suffer and die, for, in truth, "they are at peace" (3:3). As we saw argued in this same book above, a corrected perception will remove apparent injustices.

The Book of Jubilees may also imagine a reconciliation in a world after death, now in combination with a final judgment. The assurance of a final judgment is clear: chapter 23 explains Abraham's "premature" (that is, earlier than justice would have required) death by reference to the wickedness of his (= our) time; "all the generations," we are told, "from this time till the day of judgement will grow old quickly" (v. 11).[11] Similarly, the chapter goes on to speak of "those days" (v. 26) and "that time" (v. 30) which will be days of blessing and healing (vv. 29–30), during which the duration of a person's life will again approach a thousand years (v. 27). The reference to future life or resurrection is less clear. Verse 30 speaks of the Lord's servants, who will "be exalted" (= "rise up"),[12] possibly a description of resurrection. The next verse adds, "And their bones shall rest in the earth, and their spirits shall have much joy." If the bones of the righteous are resting in the earth, then presumably the only place where their souls might simultaneously have much joy is in some world other than earth ("Heaven"). Whatever the merit of the former suggestion regarding resurrection, the latter extension certainly seems necessary. At the very least, the anticipation in this chapter of a future final reconciliation is unmistakable.

Second Maccabees also emphasizes that injustices perpetrated in this world will not endure, now explicitly because of the belief that God will resurrect the righteous. Thus, in the well-known story of the martyrdom of the seven brothers (chapter 7),[13] three of the doomed brothers explain their willingness to give their lives by reference to the hope of future life (vv. 9, 11, 14). Of course, the thought of resurrection is not new here. The hope of literal recovery from death may easily be understood to be the meaning of Isa. 26:19,[14] and, as we noted, it is expressed in the latest level of Daniel as a response to the problems raised by the Antiochan persecutions. But there the hope is less precise, more general in scope. Here, for the first time, resurrection has become a kind of personal assurance. The ability to submit to suffering is here enhanced immeasurably with the knowledge that, even if life were now to end, it would not, in fact, be the end. God, the king of the world, will raise the righteous individual to a new life. What does it really matter, then, if a human tyrant or bully takes one's life now?[15]

Come the Apocalypse

The most significant developments in Jewish responses to suffering in the period between the Bible and the rabbis are the introduction of dualistic explanations of mundane evil and, particularly after the defeat of 70 CE, apocalyptic expressions of extraordinary magnitude and urgency.

Even long before the destruction, from the Antiochan persecution, apocalyptic visions already had become popular explanations of the sufferings of the era. For example, one hymn found at Qumran[16] explains Israel's suffering as the travail of childbirth, the birth, that is, of a messiahlike figure who is to accompany a final judgment and salvation. The tone is clearly messianic-apocalyptic, with the explanation of affliction being that the end of historical time approaches.

Apocalyptic expectation also characterizes the sectarian document commonly known as "The War of the Sons of Light and the Sons of Darkness." This scroll urgently anticipates a final battle that will be waged between the forces of light and those of darkness (presumably both here and on high). The triumph, we are told, will be a "time of salvation for the people of God" and, at the same time, "those that have cast [their lot] with Belial shall be doomed to eternal extinction."[17] The fact that detailed prescriptions for the conduct of this war are the substance of this document makes it clear that the war is not imagined to be a distant event.

Another sectarian document from this corpus,[18] the Damascus Covenant, offers a variety of details which relate to the apocalyptic end-time. In this work, the "sons of Zadok" (Ezek. 44:15 = the elect of Israel) are assured "life eternal" in the "last days" that are clearly anticipated (iv, 5; p. 70). Below, the assurance is made more precise. There will be a day, we are told, "on which God will carry out the punishment . . . to which the prophet alluded" (viii, 1–2; p. 76). When will this all occur? "About forty years will elapse from the death of the teacher of the community until all the men who take up arms and relapse in the company of the Man of Falsehood are brought to an end" (viii, 36–38; p. 78). The identities of this "teacher" and the Man of Falsehood are unknown to us—though they may have been known to the Qumran community. In any case, the text makes it clear that the end-time is not far off and, as we should expect, when it comes "salvation shall be revealed for all God-fearing men" (viii, 43; p. 78). Once again travail is but a temporary state. Like those who read Daniel's last visions, so too could individuals who believed this document be confident that restitution and compensation would not be long in coming.

If the hardships experienced by Jews between the Antiochan persecutions and the early decades of the first century generated a perception that the end of time must be approaching, the war with Rome and the destruction of the Temple must have seemed evidence that it had virtually arrived. Indeed, two major apocalypses that can be dated to the decades following the Temple's destruction exhibit just such a sense. The positions of these documents are represented in powerful and moving dramas, and it is worth our considering these deliberations in some detail.

The book known as 4 Ezra (or the Apocalypse of Ezra) is, outside of the first two and last two chapters (which are Christian additions to the original), a clearly Jewish work.[19] The narrative purports to describe a dialogue between Ezra, now in Babylon, and Uriel, the angel of the Lord. The author pictures Ezra as a man deeply troubled by the contrast between the current fate of Israel (purportedly following the destruction of the First Temple) and the comfort and peace of the Babylonians, the conquerors of Israel (3:1–3). He admits that the people have sinned and theoretically, therefore, are properly to be punished, but, as he says, "Do those who live in Babylon do any better? and is it on this account that she has conquered Zion?" (3:28). In fact, Ezra goes on, despite their sins Israel has many merits: "[H]as any other nation known you except Israel? Or what tribes have believed your agreements like that of Jacob? Yet their reward has not appeared, and their labor has not born fruit" (3:32–33).

The angel's initial response is to call Ezra to task for imagining that he understands properly what he sees: "Do you expect to understand the way of the Most High?" (4:2 = 4:11). But Ezra is not convinced; he will not desist. His immediate response is to declare, "It would have been better that we should not be here than to come here and live in ungodliness, and suffer, without understanding why" (4:12). But then he returns to the original indictment, asking "why Israel is given up to the heathen in disgrace; the people whom you loved are given up to the godless tribes" (4:23). Finally, in response, the angel is forced to reveal the truth of what Ezra observes, and here we find this author's explanations of the present sufferings.

The angel's revelation to Ezra is this: "The age is hurrying fast to its end. . . . For the evil . . . is sown, but the harvest of it has not yet come" (4:26–28). So the tragedy of present history portends the end of days. But Ezra is not satisfied; he wants to know, "How long and when shall this [= the end] be?" (4:33). The angel answers, first, in a metaphor; Ezra is made to witness a furnace pass before him, leaving smoke behind, and then a heavy cloud pass before him, leaving behind a few scattered drops. What does this mean? "As the rain is more than the drops, and the fire is more than the smoke, so *the quantity* [*of human history*] *that has passed has far exceeded*, but the drops and the smoke remained" (4:50, emphasis added).[20] Ezra continues to be troubled and he persists in his indictment, but the angel keeps on returning to this answer: "creation is already growing old" (5:55). Even more clearly, in a final vision Ezra is made to see the head of an eagle (= Rome) that has "made itself master of the whole earth, and ruled very oppressively over its inhabitants" (11:32), and a lion then declares to the eagle that the ages of the Most High are completed! "Therefore you will surely disappear, you eagle . . . so that the whole earth may be freed from your violence" (11:44–46). The author makes clear his belief that the present age, under the domination of Rome, is the end of historical time, and the end is so near that "whoever shall have survived all these things . . . shall himself be saved and shall see my salvation" (6:25). Some of those alive today, apparently, will actually experience the final redemption.

This book is distinguished from what came before in its pressing indictment of God's justice on comparative grounds and the unprecedented urgency that is evident in its overall formulation. The author declares that the nation of Israel, sinners and all, should properly be judged in direct comparison with the other nations and that this comparison makes eminently clear that neither we nor they are punished in the measure that true justice would require. It is no longer enough for this author to argue that Israel has sinned and is therefore punished. Just punishment must relate to the quantity and severity of the sin. Certainly, with relation to Rome, it is absurd to claim that Israel is the more wicked party, yet that nation thrives and the nation of Israel suffers. This inequity can be explained only if it is not justice at all that is at the foundation of current circumstances. For this reason, the author, like many before him, is forced to argue that the suffering experienced now is a necessary evil in the course of bringing to fruition the final salvation.

Furthermore, it is no longer adequate—so this author apparently feels—merely to claim that the end is on the way. Ezra is made to press for a specific response: *precisely* how long will it take? And the answer is precise: the end, essentially, is here. The urgency and immediacy of this answer may be understood in two ways. First, the only reasonable explanation, for this author, of the severity of current sufferings is that they are the final, most painful, birth pangs of salvation. Second, because the sufferings are so terrible, the only satisfactory response is to promise that they will be short-lived (again, by comparison, the birthing woman is able to withstand her final pains only because she knows the baby is to be born immediately). The fact that the promise did not come to pass may explain the ultimate failure (within the Jewish community at least) of this book and its approach to win adherents. But the urgency of its message may certainly be understood as an accurate reflection of the response of some Jews—perhaps even most Jews—to the suffering precipitated by the war.

Much the same attitude comes across, perhaps even more dramatically, in 2 Baruch (The Syriac Apocalypse of Baruch).[21] Again in the form of a dialogue, now between Baruch, Jeremiah's scribe, and God, this work is similarly desperate ("Happy is the man who was never born, or the child who died at birth" [10:6]) and the protagonist, Baruch, is similarly indignant at present injustice ("you [Babylon] are prosperous and Zion desolate!" [11:2]). As in 4 Ezra, the first answer is backward-looking (now echoing Amos [see 13:8–9] rather than Job, as was so in 4 Ezra) and, as before, Baruch is not satisfied with traditional answers; he persists in his indictment (see 14:4–7) and alternative responses follow.

The answers, to be sure, hearken back to earlier apocalypses, but the parallel to 4 Ezra is far more intimate.[22] So, we learn, "the time is coming when the days will speed on more swiftly than of old. . . . That is why I have now taken Zion away, so that I may the more speedily punish the world at its appointed time" (20:1–2; see also 83:1). And following, "when Adam sinned and death was decreed . . . then the number of those to be born was fixed . . . my redemption is near and is not far away as it once was" (23:4–7). With somewhat different emphasis, God explains that it is necessary to remove Zion so that the evil world at large may be properly punished—in other words, if you think Israel suffers, wait until you see what is about to come. But the primary emphasis is that the end time is near. However, this is not sufficiently precise for Baruch, and so he, like Ezra, demands a specific accounting (chapter 26). A history of twelve periods is then described, a history that is to reach its culmination in a messianic age and a subsequent resurrection (chapter 30). Lest there be any confusion regarding the passage of these periods, a vision follows whose interpretation makes it clear that a fourth tyrannical kingdom, obviously Rome, will meet its end with the arrival of the Messiah (chapter 39). Hence those who might read this work in the aftermath of the destruction can be sure that they will not have to wait long.

Aside from the obvious ways in which 2 Baruch is similar to 4 Ezra, what stands out in both is their common temporal rhetoric, speaking after a later destruction but setting their narratives in the period following an earlier one. The temporal placement of these books for a post–second-destruction reader is terribly slippery. The narratives claim, of course, to recount events that transpired long before. But the substance of the books does not permit our imagination to remain in that earlier period. The allusions to end time and the speedy passage of history, the promises of messiah and resurrection, the predictions of four kingdoms and their demise—all negate the possibility that we look forward to events that immediately follow the *first* destruction. Any reader will know that none of this accurately describes what occurred subsequent to that destruction (except for the "four kingdoms," of course, though not their demise). So the reader's imagination is directed toward the period following the second destruction, and the promised steps now take on an immediacy in that context. At the same time, the fact that the first destruction did, as it were, come to an end in historical restoration—just as the prophets had promised—assures the same reader that the present promises will also be realized. Clearly, the author of 2 Baruch agrees that present sufferings are unbearable and so he, like the author of 4 Ezra, insists that they must be evidence of an end—a salvation—that is as good as accomplished.[23]

Also shared with 4 Ezra, though here with far greater emphasis, is the view of *who* will merit the imminent redemption. It is "those who have been justified through their obedience to my law . . . who have been saved by their works, Whose hope has been in the law" (56:3, 7) who will "see the marvels in their time." (Note that it is again *in their time*, meaning that some who are now alive will actually witness the final redemption.) This opinion is noteworthy precisely because of the contemporary alternative that it apparently rejects, that is, the view of Paul, who claims "no human being will be justified in his sight by works of the law . . . but on the principle of faith" (Rom. 3:20, 27). For the author of 2 Baruch, the disaster suffered by the people is no evidence that the covenant of law has been rent asunder. On the contrary, it remains true that only obedience to the law has the power to save. The suffering is neither necessarily punishment as such nor rejection; it is fallout from the emergence of the messianic age.

Dualisms

Dualistic explanations for evil are also evidenced in several important documents of this era. The first such expressions are not fully dualistic in their conception of the heavenly powers but instead posit a rebellion on the part of lower divine creatures, the angels, who, contrary to the will of the one supreme God, bring evil into this world.

The most extended exposition of this notion is found in 1 Enoch (especially chapters 6–11). In an expansion of Gen. 5:24–6:5 and beyond, this work describes a rebellion of angels that is supposed to be at the source of the evil at the time of Noah. Teachings promulgated by these angels are said to lead to impiety and corruption (see 8:2), and the flood is brought to eliminate such corruption (chapter 10). Still, in the chapters that follow, it appears that the evil unleashed by the angels is not wiped out completely (see, for example, chapters 15–16).[24] The question is, does the author mean to suggest that these rebellious angels continue to hold sway throughout human history, or is any evil that may still be attributed to them merely vestigial?

Some have understood the intent of the myth to account for the existence of evil until the end-time.[25] But Nickelsburg argues that "1 *Enoch* 6–11 does not depict a world of malevolent angels who continuously direct the course of the nations" and claims that the present narrative should instead be understood as an "*Urzeit–Endzeit* typology"; that is, the current patterns will be recapitulated at the end of time but the conditions that pertain here are not imagined to persist for all of mundane history.[26] John J. Collins similarly argues, on the basis of the larger context, that "the author did not attempt to describe all history" and that the vision of these chapters is not eschatological.[27] Accepting the weight of these arguments, we would conclude that 1 Enoch does not suggest an etiology for all evil for all of history, only an etiology for the evil of the generation of the flood. Whichever the best interpretation, at least some evil is (or has been) the product of forces which the beneficent God does not control.

Various evil spirits are similarly at work in the narrative of Jubilees. As in 1 Enoch, teachings of fallen angels ("the Watchers") are said to be the source of the corruption which necessitated the flood (see 7:21). But Jubilees also makes it clear that the influence of such spirits continues *after* the flood. Thus, though the sons of Noah begin to make war against one another apparently of their own accord, their ongoing corruption is encouraged by various spirits at the direction of Mastema (see chapter 11). Two explanations are offered for this ongoing influence. First, responding to the conflicting demands of Noah and Mastema, God agrees to imprison most evil spirits, but to leave a tenth of their number free "that they might punish before Satan" (10:1–14). Later (15:31–32), the narrator explains that spirits have authority over other nations "to lead them astray" but not over Israel. One way or the other, it is clear that satanic forces continue to exercise power even in the postdeluvian world.

Crucially, the influence of the spirits imagined in Jubilees is not comprehensive. Israel, at least, is (generally) free from their control, and the earlier imprisonment of 90 percent of all such spirits suggests that their intervention in human affairs is seen as occasional, not constant. Some evil may be attributed to their machinations, but other explanations will be necessary to account for the bulk of evil on this earth.

The dualism of Qumran's Code of Discipline (1QS) is far more elaborate and complete than seen before and, in this respect, without direct precedent in biblical or related literature. The system of this document may be summarized as follows.[28] God, in His wisdom, determined the plan of all things before creation. "Nothing can be changed. In His hand lies the government of all things." Part of this plan is the creation in man of two spirits—"the spirits of truth and of perversity"—that will compete "until the final Inquisition." Those who follow the spirit of truth are "under the domination of the Prince of Lights," while those "who practice perversity are under the domination of the Angel of Darkness." This world is the battlefield on which the war between these two forces is fought. All sin is a result of the influence of the Angel of Darkness and "all men's afflictions and all their moments of tribulation are due to this being's malevolent sway." There is assurance, however, that "the God of Israel and the Angel of His truth are always there to help the sons of light." If, despite this support, an individual is seduced by the influence of the Angel of Darkness, then he will suffer a "multitude of afflictions at the hands of all the angels of destruction, everlasting perditions through the angry wrath of an avenging God, eternal horror and perpetual reproach, the disgrace of final annihilation in the Fire . . . ending in extinction without remnant or survival." This is the fate of the individual for the course of present history "until the final age."

But all of this is God's plan only for a set term. Also in God's plan is a final inquisition (= visitation, *pequdah*) when he will destroy absolutely and forever the spirit of perversity. At that time, "God will purge all the acts of man in the crucible of His truth . . . cleansing him by the holy spirit from all the effects of wickedness." The precise time when this end will come is not identified, but the urgency evident in this scenario—as well as the discipline required of the covenanters themselves—makes it clear that it cannot be in the too distant future.

The ideology expressed here is original in the literature that we have examined to this point. It is, to be sure, a piece of apocalyptic eschatology and so finds precedents in Daniel and elsewhere. The influence of malevolent divine beings is also, as we have seen, suggested in Jubilees and 1 Enoch. But the comprehensive nature of the dualism here envisioned has no such precedent and so opens up a new path for justifying suffering and injustice in a specifically Jewish context. In the view of this author, there are, at the origin of all transgression and evil, not merely two tendencies within human beings but two divine forces that ever hold humans under their sway. Ultimately—that is, from the perspective of creation itself—God is responsible for the evil force as well as the good. But, at the level of mundane history, the difficulty of explaining suffering as punishment here and now is eliminated. Individuals sin under the influence of the Angel of Darkness and they must, as a consequence, be justly repaid for their transgression. Moreover, according to the scenario described in this work, the fate of the individual appears to be assigned to the primary influence of one of these forces literally from the very beginning. As described above, the details of justice are maintained, but in fact justice turns out to be barely the point at all. We all participate in a divine (not merely a personal) struggle. Our battle with evil is only a reflection of a far grander battle. As described quite explicitly, the battle will be resolved after "the term for the existence of perversity" has passed, at which point God will destroy the spirit of evil and assure that reward and punishment are meted out in just measure. Again, as is clear from the larger context, the time of the triumph of good and justice is not expected to be far off.

As these several documents illustrate, one of the most popular explanations of present suffering in the literature of this period is that such suffering is a symptom of the approach of the final judgment or battle. Time is short and history thus becomes unstable. The popularity of this view is most likely explained by the widespread suffering and upheaval which typified this age. The threat of extreme Hellenism, the persecutions of Antiochus, the perception that the Hasmoneans usurped the place of those families who should by right occupy the thrones of the kingship and the priesthood, these and other factors made it clear that simpler explanations would no longer suffice. The palpable anticipation of an end-time expressed in these texts makes it clear to us how urgent the need for resolution was for the groups that produced these documents. The fact that this urgent anticipation was unfulfilled should lead us to expect important revisions in generations to follow. This expectation will prepare us to understand more fully the responses of the rabbis in the decades and centuries following the defeat to Rome.

The Hellenistic Jewish View

Two other explanations of suffering—far less dramatic than those just examined—find a place in the literature of the period between the Bible and the rabbis, both without significant precedent in the canonical literature itself. The first is reference to the controlling power of fate—not the apocalyptic and diabolical fate of the Code of Discipline but the more common fate (*tyche*) accepted in the Hellenistic world at large.

A simple reference to the operation of fate in the sufferings of Israel is found in Josephus. In his discussions of the destruction of the Temple, Josephus writes:

> That building, however, God, indeed long since, had sentenced to the flames; but now in the revolution of the years had arrived the fated day, the tenth of the month Lous, the day on which of old it had been burnt by the king of Babylon. . . . Deeply as one must mourn for the most marvelous edifice which

we have ever seen or heard of . . . yet might we draw very great consolation from the thought that there is no escape from Fate. . . . And one may well marvel at the exactness of the cycle of destiny. (*Jewish War* 6.250, 267–68)

Not long after these statements, Josephus adds:

> Reflecting on these things one will find that God cares for men, and by all kinds of premonitory signs shows His people the way of salvation, while they owe their destruction to folly and calamities of their own choosing. Thus the Jews, after the demolition of Antonia, reduced the temple to a square, although they had it recorded in their oracles that the city and the sanctuary would be taken when the temple should become four-square. (*Jewish War* 6.310–11)[29]

Thus, one way or another, the destruction is part of God's design. Either it had been fated to be destroyed at that specific time or it had been decreed that it would be destroyed when the Temple would be made "four-square." In the former scenario, apparently, the people had nothing to do with the destruction; in the latter they were responsible but it was not a direct consequence of their sins. In either case, while the Temple's destruction was properly to be lamented, it could be the source of some comfort as well, for it showed the continuity of divine concern for the world.

In these comments and others, Josephus employs a variety of explanations of Israel's sufferings which often contradict one another. The very fact of these contradictions suggests, I think, that the several explanations he records were widely accepted by the Jewish population of his time. As is evident, Josephus's purpose was not to explain or justify current events by constructing a coherent, logical explanation. Rather, he was addressing a broad audience, and he thus employed the many rhetorical devices that were available to him. In this specific context, it seems likely that he was calling upon various popular explanations of the tragedies of his day in order to win and influence the hearts of his readers. If this estimation is correct, then what we preserve in Josephus is a glimpse of responses that were current among Palestinian Jews in the few decades immediately following the destruction. Fate, as we have seen, was one such popular explanation of their suffering. In this respect, Jews shared significantly in the beliefs of their neighbors.

The final unprecedented response to suffering in this age is what we may only call the Hellenistic Jewish response—actually different responses which are identifiably Hellenistic in their assumptions and means of expression. The major testimonies to these new possibilities are works of the hellenized diaspora, 4 Maccabees and the writings of Philo. Despite the fact that these are products of the diaspora—distant from the stage that would give rise to rabbinic Judaism—they do, nevertheless, reveal how some Jews in the hellenized world, which of course included Palestine, responded to the problem of suffering and God's justice. These alternatives, too, may thus have been available to the rabbis and, for this reason, it is essential that we consider them in this context.

4 Maccabees expands significantly on the stories of the martyrdoms of Eleazar and the seven brothers of 2 Maccabees (chapters 6–7), placing its account in the context of a self-consciously philosophical treatise on the power of reason over emotions. The point of the story for the present author is that if the faith and commitment (= "reason" in the sense with which it is used here) of these endangered Jews could enable them to resist the fear of suffering and death, then reason must clearly be far more powerful than the irrational emotions. While the narrative is heavily influenced by the source in 2 Maccabees, its overall presentation is more profoundly shaped by the purpose for which it is presently used.

For the author of 4 Maccabees, suffering is not, apparently, a problem. For this reason, it seems likely, the centrality of resurrection in the earlier document is no longer evident. If suffering is not a problem, of course, then there is no need to resolve present injustices in some future world. This is not to say that earlier responses to suffering are absent in this text. Eleazar, for example, is made to remark at the moment of his death, "Make my blood an expiation for [Israel], and take my life as a ransom for theirs" (6:29); this notion has obvious precedents elsewhere in the Apocrypha. But the overall tenor of the narrative reveals that the energy driving this author is not the *problem* of suffering, but something else.

In fact, it would be more correct to say that suffering in this text is viewed as an *opportunity*. This is so because the proper endurance of suffering leads to virtue (9:8). Suffering is "a contest . . . for religion's sake" (11:20). It is something to be conquered and, the conquest being good, the contest is to be welcomed.[30] As one of the brothers is made to say explicitly to his oppressor, "A kindly favor . . . have you granted us, you tyrant . . . for by these noble sufferings you enable us to show forth our constancy toward the Law" (11:12).[31] Suffering, to be endured and mastered, is a means to (the demonstration of) virtue. The sufferers are heroes and exempla, evidence of Judaism's stoic ideal. What they experience is proof of their heroism—not a problem at all.

The second author whose writings record opinions of the hellenized diaspora is Philo of Alexandria. His deliberation on the problem of suffering (now stated explicitly as a problem), found in *De providentia*, is less than clear and plagued with contradictions. Some of his explanations, such as the claim that suffering is punishment, are entirely conventional, both in Jewish and Hellenistic contexts. But in his discussion of the suffering of the righteous, at least one of his proposals is unique from the pen of a Jew.

Philo's explanation of the suffering of the righteous lies in the natural cycles that God has established. These cycles—the wind and rain, the seasons after their sorts—are of necessity general in their effects, making no distinction between the wicked and righteous. Those individuals who suffer their effects are, in light of the grandeur of the whole, insignificant, and God's concern is, in any case, for the whole human race (all 2.44, and see also 2.23). Therefore, natural disasters are not "visitations from God . . . for nothing evil at all is caused by God,[32] and these things are generated by changes in the elements" (2.53). If certain individuals who are apparently more righteous experience adversity at the hands of these natural events, Philo goes on to say, "the blame must not be laid on God's ordering of the world, for in the first place it does not follow that if persons are considered good by us they are really such . . . [and] secondly providence or forethought is contented with paying regard to things in the world of most importance . . . not to some chance individual of the insignificant kind" (2.54). Besides, much suffering is the fault of the sufferer for not having taken proper precautions (2.56–58).

In this explanation, at least, Philo understands suffering to be the neutral outcome of natural events. Of course, if this is so, then suffering is no problem, for the notion that God is involved or concerned with the fate of the individual—even the righteous individual, is explicitly denied. People suffer because God has created a world whose forces do not discern. In this vision, the issue is simply not God's justice.

As stated earlier, though these opinions derive from the hellenized Jewish diaspora, there is every reason to believe that they would have been available (in theory if not in this specific formulation) in Palestine as well. After all, Palestine had been in profound contact with Greco-Roman culture and religion for several centuries by the time the rabbis began to formulate their traditions. It is likely, therefore, that the rabbis would have been familiar with such opinions, and their presence or absence in rabbinic literature will thus be significant. It will even be important to consider whether Philo's naturalistic explanation of suffering is paralleled in the rabbis' works for, ironically, it is, in its diminution of the significance of the individual, in crucial respects closer to older biblical conceptions. So, while in one respect—the distancing of God from mundane human affairs—Philo's explanation seems quite opposed to basic rabbinic assumptions, in another respect it is an attractive alternative.

In this chapter and chapter 2 we have seen the variety of responses to suffering that the rabbis might have followed, either by virtue of their canonical status or because of their availability in more contemporary Jewish traditions and beliefs. Will the rabbis continue to refer to these earlier possibilities? Will they prefer certain explanations and ignore others? Will they forge new syntheses, or offer unprecedented responses to human suffering? With the foundation now laid, it is to these questions that we turn in the following chapters.

4

Early Rabbinic Responses: Mishnah and Avot

In the year 70 CE, the Romans destroyed the Temple in Jerusalem, and Jews were left once again without the classical means to atone for their sins, without obvious evidence of God's presence on Earth. Whatever the difficulties of the decades and even centuries leading up to this event, nothing could have been as shattering as this loss. Before, at least, the divinely commanded service, as spelled out in detail in the Torah, could be observed. Now, in a single catastrophic instant, the entire priestly code was rendered irrelevant and, with it, whatever stability and confidence it provided. After so many centuries, Jews once again had to confront in an urgent way the question, Where is God and what is to become of us?

Inevitably, the crisis and confusion of the hour led to various, often contradictory responses. If Josephus is to be taken as a model, some Jews accepted Roman dominance fully, even imagining that the Romans had wished to save the Temple and that it was the Jews, in their stubbornness, who caused its demise. Other Jews, probably relatively few, took the Temple's destruction as evidence of the rupture of the covenant, and turned to a new covenant, tied to the Messiah Jesus, for hope of salvation. More Jews eagerly anticipated the promised end of time, imagining, with the authors of 2 Baruch and 4 Ezra (see Chapter 3), that present sufferings were the birth pangs of the final messianic triumph. The conditions that described Judean reality in the aftermath of the defeat certainly could not—so they must have felt—continue for long.

But most Jews probably looked back to the Bible itself for direction and comfort. After all, the Temple had been destroyed before, and Jews knew, on the basis of biblical models, that repentance would lead to restoration in relatively short order—to be precise, in seventy years or less (see, for example, Jer. 25:11–12). Thus, neither was the destruction an unexplained phenomenon nor was the direction to recovery unknown. Biblical tradition had laid the path many centuries before, and Jews whose lives were directed by biblical truths undoubtedly expected that the Bible's promises would once again be realized.

For this reason, the great messianic rebellion against the Romans, coming only slightly less than seventy years after the destruction of the Temple, will be unexpected to no observer. The time approached for the restoration to begin, and Bar Kokhba fought to make sure it would be realized. For a brief period it looked as though the Jewish forces, with the help of God, would succeed. But then came defeat and persecution, and the biblical expectations that had been significant in fueling the war were now shattered. No biblical pronouncement explained this condition. No apocalyptic visionary could now imagine that the final age would soon arrive.

At this very stage, in the two generations following the Bar Kokhba war, the rabbis first became a significant feature on the religious-political landscape of Palestine. Having begun, in an identifiable way, less than a century before, the rabbinic movement was still extremely small, probably claiming few adherents in the larger Jewish population. Within the movement, loyalties were powerful, cemented by clear master-disciple hierarchies. Disciples owed masters considerable respect, and elaborate rules were developed—at least for official sessions—concerning who could speak before whom, and the like. Still, with the exception of the office of the patriarch (discussed below), rabbinic positions had to be earned, with superior mastery of the tradition being the most important criterion for determining relationships. Thus it was always possible that former disciples could themselves come to be recognized as masters, and there is record of one master being displaced by another. Rabbinic masters were not born, they were (self-) made.

A similar tension characterized the relationship of rabbis and their supporters with nonrabbinic Jews. In the eyes of the rabbis, at least, mastery of the rabbinic Torah was the most important factor in defining a person's status, and rabbis considered a learned *mamzer* superior to an ignorant high-priest (m. Hor. 3:8). Because contact with ignorant Jews could easily lead rabbis into transgression, the rabbis carefully distinguished between themselves and the general population, insisting upon significant separations between sages and their followers, on the one side, and the *ammei ha'arez* (the "people of the land" = common Jews), on the other. Those who supported the rabbis were welcomed; those who did not were condemned without embarrassment. Nevertheless, rabbinic separation was evidently not as extreme as their rhetoric would sometimes suggest, for the rabbis clearly sought to extend their influence over Jewry in general. Their hope was to rabbinize Judaism, and those Jews who, ignorant of the rabbinic way, were once on the outside were encouraged to heed the words of rabbinic teachers and thus find their way in.

These purposes were much advanced, at least *in potentia*, with the acquisition of the patriarchal office by rabbis, particularly R. Judah Hanasi (= the Patriarch). The power of this office, officially recognized by the Roman government, enabled R. Judah and his followers to affect the lives of Palestinian Jews in profound ways. Civil judgments could now be conducted according to the law of the Torah as understood by the rabbis. The market could now be regulated according to rabbinic convention. Though most Jews continued to practice nonrabbinic forms of Judaism, the rabbis were at least in a position to impose their will in matters which related to the official powers of the patriarch.

Mishnah

It was under these circumstances, and with the official sponsorship of R. Judah Hanasi, that the rabbis produced their first statement of law and doctrine, the Mishnah, completed around 200 (R. Judah is viewed in Talmudic tradition as the editor-author of the Mishnah). Given the historical context in which this document was produced, we should expect to find in it significant responses to the events of the day. Yet, carefully as we might look, beyond a few incidental observations that relate to necessary changes in the law, there is little in the Mishnah that relates to history at all, recent or otherwise. The sages behind the Mishnah do not seem to have observed— again, with rare exceptions—that the condition of Jews in Palestine had changed in astonishing ways. (The very name "Palestine," as opposed to Judea, was itself evidence of that change!) Their virtual silence to the changes is one of the Mishnah's most startling features.

But it is not only the silence that startles. Equally surprising is the fact that, despite the destruction of the Temple 130 years before, a major proportion of the Mishnah's laws is devoted to the Temple, its sacrifices, and the maintenance of its purity. This is not only true of the orders *Kodashim* and *Toharot* (Holy Things = sacrifices and the Temple, and "Purities" = laws relating to ritual impurity, which must be avoided by one who wants to enter the Temple precincts) but also of major sections of the Mishnah's Holy Day laws. Thus the major concern of tractate Pesaḥim is the Paschal sacrifice, and the central focus of tractate Yoma is the order of the service in the Temple on Yom Kippur. Tractate Sukkah devotes significant attention to the unique festivities connected with the Festival of Booths in the Temple, and even major sections of a tractate like Shabbat, which seems to be asking the precise definition of labors prohibited on that day, are in fact devoted to the question, "for which labors will a transgressor be liable to bring a sacrifice and for which labors will he be exempt?" Moreover, the Mishnah's description of these many laws is often expressed in the present tense; from the vast majority of the Mishnah's laws, one would have immense difficulty discovering that the Temple service had been halted. On the contrary, most of the Mishnah's explicit rhetoric would lead us to believe that the prior, more perfect world continued without interruption.

Commenting on the Mishnah's broad failure to account for recent history, Neusner writes:

> Nothing in the Mishnah and its description of the Israelite world and way of life makes provision for, or leads us to expect, what the people really were doing in the first half of the period in which the Mishnah took shape. Jews fought two massive wars against Roman armies in the Holy Land. So the Jewish people in the age of the prologue to the Mishnah were making history. Nothing in the Mishnah explains why people should have made wars. *So the framers of the Mishnah were avoiding it.* . . . Their notion of a holy deed does not encompass the battlefield. . . . The principal lines of structure . . . of the Mishnaic system follow the outlines of the village and the cult.[1]

What does this avoidance of history in the Greek sense,[2] this yearning for "ahistorical stasis," represent? Neusner's own answer is this:

> The Mishnah . . . portrays a world fully perfected and so fully at rest. . . . The Mishnah's pretense is that all of these have come to rest. They compose a world in stasis, perfect and complete, made holy because it is complete and perfect.[3]

It is a utopian world, Neusner writes elsewhere,[4] or, in the similar view of a very different contemporary scholar, a world illustrating the ideal, Platonic halakha.[5] Whatever the nuance, one thing is clear: the reaction of the Mishnaic rabbis to the destruction and defeats is to retreat into imagined, eternal perfection. What should be, of course, can be stated once and without compromise, hence the blindness to change. In a world which is ideal in almost all of its details, there is no need to speak of revision and reformulation. For the rabbis of the Mishnah, the problems of the everyday generate no crisis for, in their present conception, the everyday has yielded almost absolutely to the eternal, utopian ideal.

Not unexpectedly, the perfect world of the Mishnah hearkens back to the Bible and particularly to the Torah for many of its directions and underlying conceptions. This is not to say that the Mishnah is dependent absolutely upon those earlier texts (Neusner has discussed in detail the various relationships of Mishnaic law with scripture)[6] but only to recognize the many profound connections. These connections are evident in the emphasis on priestly concerns—much as the priestly corpus comprises the largest portion of the Torah, so do priestly concerns command more attention than others in the Mishnah[7]—as well as in many other details. Surely the Mishnah's ideal world is not the one its authors saw around them every day. Rather, more often than not, their ideal world is the one they saw, through their own interpretive lenses, in the biblical tradition before them.

When we turn to the Mishnah's few traditions which comment on human suffering, we find many of the general trends just outlined resoundingly confirmed. Before looking at the relevant comments, however, it is perhaps most important to note the simple fact that suffering, like history, is a matter of almost no concern to the Mishnah's teachers. As the reader will see shortly, in the Mishnah proper (as opposed to Avot, to be discussed later in this chapter), barely a handful of comments may be taken as reactions, in any obvious way, to the problem of suffering.

In light of our preceding observations, it is not difficult to propose an explanation of this absence. For the rabbis of the late second century, history was suffering and suffering was not sufficiently history (that is to say, it was not sufficiently in the past to put comfortably behind them). Suffering was evidence of the world of the everyday, precisely the world the utopian vision of the Mishnah wished to ignore. To speak of suffering at any length would have required confronting recent events, and that the authors of this work assuredly did not want to do. So they rarely addressed the problems of suffering and divine justice and, as we shall see immediately following, when they did, they did so only to deny that there was a problem at all. In this contention, the Mishnaic texts are almost completely unified.

The Mishnah at Qid. 4:14 records the following tradition:

> R. Shimeon b. Eleazar[8] says: Have you seen in your days an animal or fowl who has a craft? Yet they are sustained without pain. And were they not created except to serve me! But I was created to serve my maker! Doesn't it follow that I should be sustained without pain?! But I did evil and ruined my livelihood. . . .

In this tradition attributed to R. Shimeon b. Eleazar, the Mishnah points out that, by right, human beings should be sustained without pain. This conclusion is available by means of a simple *qal va-homer* (a fortiori deduction). The author reasons that if animals, which were created to serve humans (Gen. 1:28), are sustained without pain, then how much more should it be so that humans, who were created to serve God, should be sustained without pain. Why, then, is this not the case? Because humans have sinned and have therefore been punished. The pain by which they gain their sustenance is this punishment.

The allusion in this Mishnah to the story of Adam and Eve and their expulsion from the Garden of Eden is inescapable: Shimeon recalls that animals were created to serve humans (Gen. 1:26). Humans were created to serve God (implied in the same verse). It is tempting, therefore, to understand his reference to transgression as speaking of the events that precipitated the expulsion from the garden (Gen. 3:17–24). But this is apparently not Shimeon's primary intent (in substance—the rhetorical effect of the ambiguous reference, equating the current "fall" with the fall from the garden, may well be). Rather, Shimeon elaborates that "*I* did evil and *I* ruined *my* livelihood"; the entire expression is in the first-person singular. This emphasis suggests that, had not Shimeon himself sinned, he would have been supported as was fitting, after the manner of the animals (here the superior condition).[9] The Mishnah thus insists that justice is applied directly, not derivatively, to future generations. Suffering (here: pain) is believed to be punishment for sin, on the level of both the individual and the community.

Another Mishnaic text, at Shab. 2:6, supports the same analysis. There the Mishnah explains that "For three sins women die in childbirth: because they are not cautious in [their observance of] niddah [= the requirement for separation during their menstruation (Lev. 15:19–24)], and in hallah [= the separation of the required priestly portion from dough (Num. 15:17–21)], and in the lighting of the [Sabbath] candle." Ignoring the apparent lack of proportion between the sin and the attendant punishment—no justification is offered in the Mishnah for the precise punishment—it remains clear that suffering (here premature and probably painful death) is punishment for sin. The explanation of suffering that was first offered in the earliest canonical documents, and which remained the most prominent of all biblical explanations, is repeated in these texts without apology or apparent modification.

In its more abstract treatments of the question of divine justice and reward and punishment, the Mishnah exhibits the same conservatism evident in its few treatments of suffering. The Mishnah's confidence in a viable system of divine justice, in which reward and punishment are meted out in proper measure, is already evident in the texts reviewed above. Returning to Qiddushin, we find, immediately preceding the portion discussed earlier, the following opinion, attributed to R. Meir:

> R. Meir says: A man should ever teach his son a clean profession and pray to the One who is master of wealth and possessions. For there is no profession in which there is not poverty and wealth; for neither is poverty from the profession nor is wealth from the profession, rather everything is according to his merit.

This tradition suggests unambiguously that reward and punishment are operative in this world. Reward is expressed in material wealth (at least here) and punishment is to be equated with poverty and, as the text that follows this suggests, suffering (of which poverty may be understood as one form). In fact, this text amounts to little more than a reexpression of the Deuteronomic promise.

Also closely tied to scriptural opinions, but slightly more nuanced in its approach, is the Mishnah in the first chapter of Sotah, where we find the well-known principle: "According to the measure that a person measures, with it do we measure him" (= measure-for-measure justice, Mishnah 7). The principle is spelled out in this context because of its association with the trial of the suspected adulteress and the various punishments that await her if there is substance to the suspicion. So, the Mishnah explains:

> *a.* She adorned herself for transgression, [therefore] God (literally, "the place") made her disgusting.
> *b.* She uncovered herself for sin, [therefore] God caused her to be uncovered (see m. Sot. 1:5–6).
> *c.* She began her sin with her thigh and afterward [with] the belly (i.e., that which is within the belly = her womb), [therefore] her thigh will be afflicted first and afterward her belly (following Num. 5:21, but cf. vv. 22 and 27).

Mishnah 8, following this one, demonstrates the application of the same principle to particular biblical figures (Samson and Absalom).

The last Mishnah in the chapter claims that the established pattern also pertains to reward for good deeds. But in each of the illustrations it brings, the precise application of the measure-for-measure principle as applied to divine reward is denied. The clear lesson of the Mishnah is, instead, that the measure of reward is *greater* than the measure of the good deed that it rewards. So, since Miriam waited but one short hour to see what would become of the baby Moses who had been set adrift on the Nile (Exod. 2:4), therefore the Israelites waited for her while she had leprosy for seven days. Similarly, Joseph buried his father Jacob, therefore Moses concerned himself with Joseph's burial. Then, on account of concerning himself with Joseph's burial, Moses had the honor of God's attention to his burial. The pattern demonstrates clearly that reward is actually meted out in greater measure than the deed to which it corresponds.

In evaluating this Mishnah, we must distinguish between its claims regarding divine punishment and those regarding reward. Suffering, our immediate concern, is understood as punishment. In this connection, on the surface, the Mishnah reiterates its confidence in a system of divine justice in which sin is punished by God, and punishment is typically humiliation and suffering. With respect to such punishment, this Mishnah builds on what we saw previously by insisting that each punishment is indeed condign, that is, the system is sound not merely in its general workings but also in the particular.[10] But the other element of this Mishnah—its claims regarding divine reward—shows that the imagined system is not simplistic: greater measures of reward show that God is not only just but also merciful. In contrast, the assertion that God punishes only in a measure corresponding precisely to the sin may be viewed as an insistence on God's mercy. God remains judge and the system of divine justice is intact, but it should not be forgotten that the system is infused, in some measure, with God's mercy as well.

This Mishnah systematizes and gives name to an assumption that has ancient roots. Indeed, the Mishnah's scriptural references show the deep embeddedness of what we might call "poetic justice" in the Bible itself; it is only the precise language employed to describe this principle of justice that appears innovative in comparison.[11] Yet even the language is no innovation, for precise or approximate precedents can be found in a variety of earlier Jewish sources. For example, at Jubilees 4:32 we read: "With the instrument with which one man kills another man, with the same shall he be killed: if he has done a particular injury to another man, the same shall be done to him." The mishnaic statement is merely a generalization of what is suggested with more specific reference here. The Testament of Gad comes even closer: "For by the very same things by which a man transgresses, by them is he punished" (5:11). Finally, the formulation of this principle in the synoptic Gospels is virtually identical to the rabbinic version: "For with the judgment you pronounce you will be judged, and the measure you give will be the measure you get" (Matt. 7:2, also at Mark 4:24 and Luke

6:38). This is clearly a popular principle in Jewish sources, and it requires no particularist ideology to support it.

In fact, it does not even require a Judaic context. Aside from the many pagan myths or Hellenistic histories which could be used to illustrate the ubiquitousness with which poetic justice is claimed, there are even explicit statements which closely approximate the Jewish formulation. Cicero, for example, writes, "the punishment shall fit the offence, so that everyone may be paid in his own coin, violence being punished by death or loss of citizenship, greed by a fine and too great eagerness for the honour of public office by disgrace."[12] He speaks, it is true, in the context of human justice, but it is not difficult to understand how the same principle would be extended by others to divine justice as well.[13]

Mishnah Sotah's measure-for-measure principle, therefore, has a long, multicultural history. It is, by the time of its record in the Mishnah, a profoundly traditional assumption, hinted generally in scripture and assuming its more specific form in subsequent literature. The Mishnah's repetition of this tradition only shows how very traditional it is in its few discussions of these matters. The pattern of the particulars already clearly supports the general observations made earlier: if taken at its word, the Mishnah is highly traditional, highly conservative. The world at large does not require it to be otherwise, for the idealized vision need not account for reality. And the more we search out relevant details, the more these conclusions are reinforced.

Equally confident in their assertion that God judges injustice are the texts in tractates Yoma and Rosh Hashana that speak of the annual period of judgment. In Yoma (8:8–9)[14] we learn only that there is a system that assumes transgression and the consequent need for atonement, accomplished though sacrifice, death, or repentance (or some combination thereof, depending upon the gravity of the sin). Offering greater detail, Mishnah Rosh Hashana (1:2) teaches that "on Rosh Hashana [= 1 Tishrei] all of the world's creatures pass before Him [= God] as in [the review of] a platoon,[15] as it says, 'He who fashions the hearts of them all, who discerns all their doings' (Ps. 33:15)." This is called one of the "four periods in which the world is judged." Though the judgment described here is assuredly not simply on the individual level (a platoon is considered primarily en masse, not as individuals),[16] neither is it exclusively collective (the general will note individuals as they affect the status of the whole). Rather, the operative metaphor evinces a preference for a collective system, with means provided for individual judgments when necessary. In this preference, the Mishnah may be said to reflect a biblical balance in these matters. While the metaphor is thoroughly contemporary, the opinions concerning divine justice are (once again) profoundly grounded in biblical precedents.

The final Mishnah in the first chapter of Qiddushin also assumes a fully viable system of reward and punishment, though here the language creates difficulties in understanding its precise conception of that system. The difficulty is evident at first reading: "Anyone who performs one mitzvah [= commandment, obligation], it is good with him and his days are length-

ened and he inherits the land. But anyone who does not perform one
mitzvah, it is not good with him and his days are not lengthened and he
does not inherit the land." Could the Mishnah possibly intend that the
performance of only one commandment assures someone these rewards,
or that someone who fails to perform even one commandment (or does
this mean "someone who does not perform only one commandment"?) is
denied them? This difficulty caused several Talmudic sages to interpret the
Mishnah as referring to the case of an individual whose sins and merits are
otherwise evenly balanced, in which case this single mitzvah will determine
the appropriate judgment. David Halivni, based upon the Yerushalmi, prefers to interpret the Mishnah as speaking about a single mitzvah that an
individual *always* performs.[17] Whatever the correct interpretation, it is clear
that the Mishnah assumes that there is reward and punishment, thus supporting everything we have seen above.

More striking in this Mishnah is the fact that it promises reward *in this
world*—there is no postponement of justice till the world-to-come. While
this same opinion is evident in the Mishnah in the final chapter of Qiddushin
(discussed earlier), it is not true of other Mishnahs. The first Mishnah in
tractate Pe'a, for example, speaks of those commandments "whose fruits
one eats in this world and whose stock remains for him in the world-to-
come." Similarly, Sanh. 10:1 assures all Israel a place in the world-to-come.
These other traditions show that, like much of the Apocrypha, the Mishnah
too was sometimes forced to look to a future world for a balancing of
accounts.[18] For this reason, Epstein suggests that the present Mishnah is
an ancient one—thus its "anachronistic," literally biblical assurance.[19] However, because this is not the only place where the Mishnah speaks of this-
worldy reward and punishment—and in light of many other prominent
anachronisms in the Mishnah—Epstein's conclusion is unwarranted. It is
more likely that the biblical essence of this Mishnah, and others like it, was
intentional. Understood this way, this Mishnah may be judged, ironically,
as much radical as it is conservative (reactionary redirections are always radical). Despite a powerful tradition to project justice into a future world,
and despite the highly troubling counterevidence in reality, this Mishnah
and others like it return to the Bible for their system of divine justice. Sometimes, the Mishnah believes, this is the purity of the ideal which may still
be asserted.

The extremely limited explicit evidence concerning the Mishnah's opinion of the destruction of the Temple shows still further how unified the
document is in these related matters. Of course, the destruction does not
go entirely unmentioned in the Mishnah. We find here and there, for example, several enactments attributed to R. Yoḥanan b. Zakkai that respond to
the destruction (Suk. 3:13; R.H. 4:1, 3, and 4; Men. 10:5). Other minor
echoes of the event are evident as well (for example, Naz. 5:4). But substantive comments are few.

One important reflection may be found in the last chapter of tractate
Sotah, which describes the gradual diminution of the presence of God in
Israelite history. The text refers to the destruction (the first? the second?

both together?)[20] as one of the pivotal events in an ever bleaker history (see 9:12).[21] What is noteworthy in this Mishnah is its recognition of movement, of change in history. But the movement is pressed into a rigid pattern and most events that, say, the Greeks would consider of historical relevance play no part in that pattern. History serves other, highly limited purposes—so limited, in fact, that this unusual text really changes the broad picture of Mishnaic stasis little, if at all.[22]

More significant, though making its point only by implication, is the requirement in Mishnah Taanit (chapter 4) that the anniversary of the destruction (of the first and the second Temples; see Mishnah 6) be observed by fasting and other restrictions. The restrictions imposed are not mourning customs; for example, in no rabbinic source is there a demand that mourners fast (in fact, on the contrary, they are required to eat). Rather, the ritual restrictions are precisely those imposed on Yom Kippur (see m. Yoma 8:1) and, by analogy, we may say that the present response to the destruction is to seek atonement. Thus the destruction must be viewed as evidence of and punishment for sin (otherwise there would be no need for atonement). This is the only place in the entire Mishnah where an explanation of the destruction is suggested and, not surprisingly, it is fully in accord with the ideology of suffering and punishment expressed elsewhere in the Mishnah.

Compared to the Mishnah as a whole, these few responses to the destruction are insignificant. By and large, the Mishnah simply does not take note of the destruction. Moreover, on only one occasion does the Mishnah even voice hope that the Temple will be rebuilt, and this only in a final coda on a tractate (Tamid).[23] The sense that the Temple even *needs* to be rebuilt is glaringly absent from the Mishnah.

But, of course, one may easily understand the Mishnah's very avoidance of such discussion as an important response to the destruction. The response of the Mishnah to the Temple's destruction is, in effect, denial. As Neusner suggests,[24] the composer(s) of the Mishnah refuse to admit that, in essential terms, anything at all is changed by this catastrophe and the sufferings that accompanied it. From the perspective of "Torah," from the point of view of holiness at its most ideal, there was no catastrophe and there were no sufferings—to speak of. All of that was unimportant. What was important—and ever continues to be—was the utopian, ideal, biblical, and messianic world of the eternal Torah. Since, as Neusner emphasizes, that world finds its home not only in the cult but also in the village, we may participate in that eternal ideal, if only in part, even today. Against such a continuing opportunity, what real importance is there to the sufferings precipitated by war?

It should be apparent that we have merely repeated here, in more specific terms, the generalizations Neusner applied to the Mishnah as a whole. There can be no question that examination of the Mishnah's responses to suffering, divine justice, and the like, convincingly affirms those more general observations and strengthens considerably the thesis that underlies them. The

Mishnah neglects, for the most part, even the now traditional explanations of suffering which found ample expression in the Apocrypha. Indeed, the Mishnah asserts, nothing of genuine significance *has* changed. In matters such as these, the guidance of God's revelation in scripture remains as eternally true as it has always been. And what is that guidance? Sin is punished, God's world is just. If individuals suffer, or if nations experience defeat, they may be sure that God is exacting retribution for failure to heed God's command.

Of course, this could not have been the only response to suffering and catastrophe evident among late-second-century Jews in Palestine. But, it will be recalled, the Mishnah does not speak for Jews, only for the rabbis. How can we explain the success of their refusal to accommodate "new realities," of what some would surely call their blindness to the world around them?

The first answer must be the continued small size and cohesive nature of the rabbinic movement in this early period. On account of these factors, it was possible still for the rabbis to insist upon such traditional explanations and to suppress whatever alternatives may, from time to time, have been entertained. Moreover, in the view of these rabbis, stark contrasts continued to distinguish obedient Jews (= rabbinic Jews) from transgressors (= other Jews), and even more learned rabbis from their followers. The classical dichotomy of right and wrong was embodied in these very groupings. The order of heaven was viewed as residing in the same social order which the rabbis helped to reinforce. Finally, the authority of the rabbis, limited as it was in many areas, was nevertheless still notable; their hold on the patriarchate gave rabbis in the late second century more worldly power than they would have for centuries. The rabbis themselves undoubtedly believed that this mundane authority was somehow an extension of the authority of God, granted them by virtue of their superior mastery of God's Torah. Their own authority was therefore evidence of the continued sway of divine authority over events, big and small, which the rabbis witnessed in their world. Thus, from the rabbis's perspective, nothing in reality genuinely undermined the order of the world as imagined in the Torah. With this limited vision, the rabbis undoubtedly felt that, despite the sufferings which others interpreted as injustice or collapse of the received divine order, the teachings of the ancient tradition in these matters remained valid as before.[25]

Avot

Tractate Avot, commonly considered to be part of the Mishnah, is actually post-Mishnaic in its redaction, as its quotation of traditions attributed to R. Gamliel the son of R. Judah the Patriarch (the redactor of the Mishnah) reveals (see 2:2). For this reason, we have separated our consideration of this tractate from our earlier discussion. Still, it is clear that whoever redacted Avot was closely related to the circles which produced the Mishnah, and it is thus not surprising to find that, in its comments on suffering, this tractate mostly follows the direction suggested in the Mishnah. At the same time, there are a couple of traditions which offer opinions that are distinct in substance or emotion from what we saw earlier, and these merit special consideration in the following pages.

We begin with the commonplace. In a text highly reminiscent of the Shabbat Mishnah quoted earlier, Avot 5:8–9 suggests at length that suffering is punishment for sin:

> Seven types of retribution [= punishment, suffering] come into the world on account of seven types of transgression.
> [If] some [people] tithe [their produce] and some do not tithe, a famine from scarcity comes—[so] some are [consequently] hungry and some are satisfied.
> [If] they [all] decided not to tithe, a famine of [both political] upheaval and of scarcity comes.
> And [if they decided] not to take the hallah [= priestly portion from dough], a famine of [complete] destruction comes.
> Pestilence comes to the world on account of [transgressions punishable by] death that are mentioned in the Torah but which are not given to the [human] court [to enforce] and for [the improper use of] seventh-year fruits [see Exod. 23:11].
> The sword [= war] comes to the world for delay of judgment and distortion of judgment and on account of those who teach Torah not in accordance with the halakha.

And so forth. Obviously, there is here again an assumption that sins are punished by God, and the punishments listed are, without exception, what we would call suffering. In fact, though it is not stated explicitly, it seems clear that all suffering is understood as punishment of one sort or another. Notably, while the sins listed may be either individual (such as those listed later, including vain oaths or desecration of the divine name) or collective, the punishments are all explicitly collective. In this respect, the concern of the text is for corporate Israel and not the individual Jew. This tendency highlights the extreme traditionality of this text for, as in the preexilic biblical books and quite at odds with the preferred focus of later biblical writings, the individual's fate is not considered significant in the final divine accounting.

Avot elsewhere expresses the same ideology in metaphorical language. At 3:16, R. Aqiba is reported as having been accustomed to say

> The store is open and the storekeeper gives credit and the ledger is open and the hand writes and anyone who wishes to borrow may come and borrow, but the collectors go around constantly, every day, and collect from a person both with and without his knowledge [alt.: consent] . . . and the judgment is a judgment of truth and all is fixed for the meal.

God, the storekeeper, is generous in granting "loans" to those in need, but God also has messengers who collect from a person according to his or her "account." Since this collection is described as occurring every day, and because the collecting may be both known and unknown, it seems likely that the commentators are correct when they interpret this reference to "collectors" as speaking of sufferings that individuals experience.[26] Be that as it may, the text here indubitably affirms God's active and ongoing involvement in a system of justice. Hence, whatever the precise nature of the "collection," the agreement of this text with those quoted previously in its assumption that the system of reward and punishment is intact is undeniable.[27] The same basic assumption is found in another Avot tradition (4:11) which suggests that "repentance and good deeds are a shield against retribution [*pur'anut*, ordinarily understood as afflictions]"; if suffering is punishment, then repentance and good deeds will assure that there is no need to punish. Again, the system of divine justice is assumed to be coherent and viable.

The only texts that offer a somewhat different perspective on suffering are those at Avot 1:7 and 4:15. The former text recommends, in the name of Nitai the Arbelite, that one "should not despair as a consequence of reverses" (again *pur'anut*). This brief tradition apparently evinces recognition that suffering is sometimes perceived to be unjust, for otherwise why would there be reason to warn against despair? Despite the subtle admission of the problem, however, this tradition offers no explanation or more elaborate response. Nor, on its own terms, is there a need to do so, for it is clear that it is only the *appearance* of injustice that is deemed problematic. God's system of justice is assumed to be operative. The contrary appearance may be troubling, but it forces no substantive reevaluation.

More explicit, but otherwise not more forthcoming, is the text at 4:15, which allows, in the name of R. Jannai, that (literally) "we have in our hands neither the ease of the wicked nor even the suffering of the righteous." Despite proposed alternative interpretations of this text, it seems likely that it means we cannot understand why the wicked are at peace or why the righteous suffer.[28] If this reading is correct, the text is a concise restatement of the oft-expressed biblical and postbiblical complaint, its present formulation adding nothing substantive to the prior formulations. Furthermore, there is no indication in this tradition that the problem extends beyond our own lack of understanding, and there is no reason to believe that this text does not affirm the full integrity of God's system of justice. Still, this is, along with the previous tradition, a noteworthy statement, for its tone shows clearly that the problem of the suffering of the righteous is at least admitted.

Avot traditions concerning divine justice as such also speak in tones that do not find direct Mishnaic precedent. For example, the emphasis in such traditions on a future world as the arena for judgment (see 2:16, 3:1, and 4:22) is notably more pronounced than in the Mishnah. The Mishnah, as we saw, sometimes prefers a more archaic biblical approach, insisting that justice is realized in this world. Avot, in contrast, looks more consistently to the world to come. In this respect, Avot is closer to the Apocrypha in its

portrayal of the system of divine justice than it is to the Bible. It is traditional but not biblical, related to the Mishnah but distinct from it as well.

Also distinct are several traditions in Avot that seem to be troubled by
the apparent fact that the reward and punishment promised in the Bible
are often not evident in reality. The first hint of such trouble is the text at
2:1, which declares "You do not know the reward of the commandments."
To be sure, the larger tradition assumes a viable system, but the agnostic
posture of the quoted statement reveals that the precise workings of justice
are impossible to perceive. Contrast Mishnah Sotah, in which the measure
of reward and punishment is asserted to adhere to a readily comprehensible rule! This teaching is closest to the Avot tradition examined above
which remarks that "we have in our hands neither the ease of the wicked
nor even the suffering of the righteous." Unlike the Mishnah proper, Avot
is willing to admit that we do not understand. Its vision is not so flawless,
not so perfect that the blemishes do not show through.

Further evidence of the difficulty of reconciling the promise of reward
and punishment with experience is the text at 1:3, which warns against serving the master (= following God's commands) in order to receive reward.
It would not be difficult to read much of the biblical record as offering
precisely such a motivation for obedience, and the caution not to do so
suggests that the biblical promise cannot literally be depended upon. Disappointment confronts one who expects reward for obedience to the divine
command—for this reason alone is it necessary to offer other motivations
for observance. Similarly, a well-known tradition attributed to Ben Azzai
(at 4:2) claims that "the reward of a mitzvah is a[nother] mitzvah and the
payment for a transgression is a[nother] transgression." Why would it be
necessary to deny reward and punishment as biblically conceived and argue
that reward or punishment is no more than the opportunity to perform
another pious deed or transgress another prohibition? Again, it seems likely
that what provokes this sort of approach is the recognition that divine justice
in the classical sense is difficult to assert in view of reality.

What we witness in Avot are slight transformations of the Mishnah's more
literal-minded endorsement of biblical systems, arguments that the system
be supported in the absence of physical reward and in the absence of obvious justice. Obviously, these approaches are also not without biblical precedent, and the Wisdom tradition, in particular, shows clear affinity with
what we see here. The Wisdom of the early rabbis, like biblical Wisdom
before it, begins to admit the evidence of experience with some candor. It
may be that this is a function of the genre itself, but it may also be that the
successors to the Mishnaic rabbis were open to alternatives the Mishnah
didn't admit. Perhaps their greater distance from historical catastrophes
allowed them to be more open to considering the blemishes of recent Jewish experience. Perhaps the growth of the rabbinic movement itself, with
somewhat less distinction between those Jews who were inside and those
outside, forced the dawning of such recognition: the larger group would
be less available to the suppression of different questions or opinions, should

they exist; those who entered from the outside would import some of their own views, and these would be difficult to eliminate completely. Whichever of these explains Avot's teachings, it will be clear that developing rabbinism generally saw fit to go beyond the Mishnah's limited parameters. The first modest evidence of this development is found in the Tosefta, examined in the following chapter.

5

Early Rabbinic Responses: The Tosefta

The next document to emerge from the rabbinic community, in logical and apparently chronological sequence, is the Tosefta, a commentary on and expansion of the Mishnah.[1] The precise dating of this work (as well as of the halakhic midrashim) is notoriously difficult to establish.[2] On the one side, the Tosefta is clearly later than the Mishnah. On the other, many Toseftan traditions are quoted in the Yerushalmi (c. 400) and some are also quoted in the halakhic midrashim. If, therefore, these midrashim are dated to the late third or early fourth century (as I shall argue in the next chapter), then the Tosefta would seem to have taken shape in the mid- to late third century—slightly later, perhaps, than tractate Avot.

In part because of the difficulty of dating the Tosefta, those who have written on this work have seen its development in terms of factors internal to rabbinic Judaism. The reception of the recently promulgated Mishnah, whose authority was apparently respected virtually immediately, is seen to have generated this first commentary and supplement. Undoubtedly, this cause-and-effect relationship is primary to understanding the composition of the Tosefta. However, external factors are never entirely irrelevant to such developments and, particularly when we turn our attention to the subject which concerns us in this book, consideration of the broader context will be absolutely crucial.

The same may be said of the halakhic midrashim, which, again, apparently took shape only slightly later than the Tosefta. Earlier writers have taken at face value the chronological claims inherent in the attributions found in these works, and so have looked to the late first and second centuries for the history relevant to their composition. Neusner, whose basic method I follow here (for reasons spelled out in Chapter 1), accepts a dating of the third or fourth century for these midrashim but neglects that setting for analytical purposes. As also in the case of the Tosefta, Neusner sees the halakhic midrashim as an internal development in rabbinic Judaism, a response to "the crisis precipitated by the Mishnah."[3] But in this case, too, internal factors do not suffice to explain developments in reflections upon human suffering and divine justice. Accordingly, before we examine these late-third-century documents, it is essential to review briefly the history of Jews in Palestine during this period.

The half-century between 235 and 285 was a period of anarchy in the Roman Empire.[4] For a variety of reasons, standing professional armies competed during this period for control of the imperial government, seeking to appoint their own commanders as emperor. Emperors passed quickly in the course of these years, with only the rare one dying a natural death. The ensuing chaos affected the empire, and particularly the provinces, in significant ways.

The aspirations of individual armies and their commanders required financial support. Taxes became onerous, inflation (as a result of the constant minting of devalued coins) ran out of control, trade collapsed, lands were abandoned. Famine was a frequent danger, and birthrates fell alarmingly.[5] Obviously, these were developments which affected not only the government and the armies. The everyday experience of Jews in Palestine (as of citizens of the empire everywhere) deteriorated in ways which were unavoidable and undeniable. The brief recovery that accompanied the age of R. Judah the Patriarch must quickly have seemed a dream. The reality of subjugation to a now anarchic empire presented itself with harsh insistence.[6]

Rabbinic Judaism during this period continued to make inroads in the population as a whole. Rabbinic sources claim that the patriarch, a rabbi, continued to wield considerable power, and though nonrabbinic sources do not, for the most part, support this assessment, it is still likely that the patriarch was officially the most powerful Jew in Palestine at the time.[7] On the back of patriarchal authority, rabbis were able to gain increasing influence. Still, nonrabbinic Jews certainly remained the majority, and rabbinic cohesion continued to be served by reinforcing separations between rabbis and others. The most influential master within the rabbinic movement was R. Yohanan, who made his home at Tiberius. By evidence of later rabbinic documents, his teachings, in the mouths of his numerous disciples, were without rival in their reach and influence. Nevertheless, these teachings have no evident impact on documents coming to completion during this period. It is the names of earlier, tannaitic masters which give authority to these texts.

At first blush, the reality just described has little impact on the Tosefta. As befits a document that takes its cues from the Mishnah, there is little explicit comment in the Tosefta on the problem of suffering. Its few comments on this and related matters show that the position of the Mishnah remains dominant at this stage of rabbinic composition. Still, a few important developments beyond the Mishnaic precedent are already evident, and it is to these that we shall give primary attention.

The Tosefta echoes, at the appropriate locations, the Mishnah's few responses to suffering. For example, in the final chapter of Qiddushin, the Tosefta repeats, essentially unchanged, the Mishnah's tradition claiming that the pain involved in sustaining oneself is punishment for having done wrong. In tractate Shabbat (end chapter 2), to the three things the Mishnah lists as causes for the death of women in childbirth, the Tosefta adds the failure to abide by vows. This echoing is likewise evident in texts which discuss divine justice, each describing various sorts of suffering as punishment for sin.

However, in addition to mere repetition of Mishnaic opinions, we also see in the Tosefta new approaches to the problem of suffering. One such innovation is found in the Tosefta's elaboration of the Mishnah's system for effecting atonement. The Tosefta records, apparently for the first time, a well-known and oft-to-be-repeated tradition, attributed to R. Ishmael, that delineates four levels of sin and four combinations of atoning phenomena that will atone for those sins. Concerning the most severe transgressions, the Tosefta teaches:

> If someone transgressed [sins punishable by] excisions or [by] deaths of the court and repented, [repentance] and the Day of Atonement suspend [judgment] and suffering of the other days of the year effects atonement, as it says, "I will punish their transgression with the rod, [their iniquity with plagues]" (Ps 89:33).
>
> But someone who intentionally desecrated the Name of Heaven and repented, repentance hasn't the power to suspend nor the Day of Atonement to atone. Rather, repentance and the Day of Atonement atone a third, and sufferings atone a third, and the day of death cleanses along with suffering, and regarding this it says, "This iniquity shall never be forgiven you [until you die]" (Isa 22:14)—this teaches that the day of death finally cleanses (Y.K. 4 [5]:8 [p. 252]).[8]

At the most serious levels of transgression, then, suffering is an essential element of the process of atonement. Only if the individual experiences suffering, the rabbis now suggest, will his relationship with God be repaired.

It is essential to note that, while the text of the Tosefta employs a scriptural source to "prove" that suffering has this consequence, the verse of Psalms itself doesn't actually make this suggestion. In its original context, the verse merely repeats the well-known fact that God will punish violators with suffering; what Psalms adds there is the important claim that such punishment is not to be equated with the withdrawal of God's love. The Tosefta, in contrast, suggests that the suffering is, in effect, itself an expression of God's love (this implicitly, not explicitly), for without it God's anger cannot be assuaged.

In earlier contexts, suffering might have had a variety of positive consequences, including correction and self-improvement. But only in the few earlier texts which equate suffering with sacrifice (Wisdom of Solomon,

Hebrews) does the present scheme find genuine precedent. And despite the absence of an explicit statement to this effect, I would argue that the same equation of sacrifice and suffering is being made here. The Mishnah to which this Tosefta responds emphasizes the centrality of sacrifices in effecting atonement.[9] It is clear that, for the Tosefta, suffering has effectively taken the place of sacrifice. In the process, suffering has been removed from its earlier position and given a power that was ascribed to it only rarely before this time.

A shift in sensibility toward suffering in the Tosefta may also be reflected in its definition of the sin of "oppression [= overreaching] by words." The Tosefta remarks:

> Just as there is overreaching in trade, so too is there oppression by words and, moreover, oppression by words is [a] greater [wrong] than oppression with money. . . . If illnesses and sufferings were coming upon him, or [if] he buries his children [who have died prematurely], one should not speak to him as Job's colleagues spoke to him (B.M. 3:25 [p. 79]).

In other words, offering common, pious justifications of a person's suffering (even in a sympathetic, comforting tone)[10] is considered to be oppression. Why is this so? It may be that the Tosefta is uncomfortable with the substance of such justifications. But it also may be that the present author continues to accept their truth and is merely concerned with the emotional pain such "comforting" is likely to cause the sufferer. Which of these alternatives shall we prefer?

The answer to this question may be suggested in another Toseftan text which makes reference to Job. At Sot. 3:6 and following (pp. 160ff.), the Tosefta seeks to demonstrate that "the men of the [generation of] the flood became arrogant only as a result of the good [with which God provided them]." This claim is proved by means of quotations from Job: "Their homes are secure, without fear; They do not feel the rod of God. Their bull breeds and does not fail. . . . They let their infants run loose like sheep. . . . They sing to the music of the timbrel and the lute. . . . They spend their days in happiness" (Job 21:9–13). "That is what caused them," continues the Tosefta, "[to] say to God, 'Leave us alone. . . . What is Shaddai that we should serve him . . . '" (ibid., vv. 14–15). A similar strategy is used at 3:11–12, where the Tosefta makes a similar point regarding the men of Sodom.

The use of Job here has important and ironic consequences. In their original contexts, each of the quoted statements is part of Job's protest, describing the unjust world in which the wicked thrive and escape punishment. The Tosefta claims, in contrast, that the apparently unjust realities described by Job are actually *the cause* of punishment. Rather than being expressions of protest against injustice—as was originally the case—these Jobian outcries are now employed in affirmation of God's justice. Job's intent is erased; the pieties he rejects are reaffirmed. Job is wrong. The system works.

Against this background, we may now perhaps interpret the remark that sufferers should not be comforted after the fashion that Job was comforted. By evidence of its own use of Job's words, we could now say that, in the opinion of the Tosefta, Job's protest (as originally conceived) is wicked. In contrast, we would have to assume, the words of his colleagues are righteous. The problem with the pious justifications of Job's colleagues, therefore, would not be that they were incorrect, but that they did not provide comfort. I state this opinion cautiously, though, because it may not be possible to interpret one Tosefta passage in light of another. It may be that the Tosefta simply does not have a single opinion on such matters.

Even if the problem with Job's friends is the manner in which they try to comfort and not the substance of what they say, it still seems to me significant that such a sensitivity is recorded at all. The Mishnah, when it deigned to explain suffering, had no hesitation offering these ancient "comforting" words. The Tosefta, on the other hand, recognizes that context is crucial. For the Mishnah, it will be recalled, there was rarely a context beyond the world of the ideal Torah. For the Tosefta there is more often a context, as we shall see in greater detail later. This willingness to recognize context—to admit its importance—is a notable development in the rabbinic outlook on the world. It may be the Tosefta's most significant contribution to the evolution of rabbinic responses to suffering.

The Tosefta's discussions of divine justice, though sometimes merely recreating the Mishnah's archaic opinions, also show the rabbinic authors beginning to transcend those opinions and weigh new options.

Tosefta Qid. 1:13–16 (pp. 280–81) is an outgrowth of the exegetical problem we noted in the corresponding Mishnah (Qid. 1:10): Could it be that the performance of only one mitzvah or one transgression will lead to the promised reward or punishment? The Tosefta's solution is a simple one: a person should always imagine that the scales of his relative merits and demerits are balanced and thus a single meritorious act or transgression will tip the scales and lead to complete reward or complete punishment. This is true, the Tosefta adds, not only of individual judgment but also of the judgment of the world as a whole. So when the Mishnah speaks of the controlling power of a single act, it should be taken literally, with the understanding that the imagined foundation for this claim is the case of evenly balanced scales which, on account of a small added weight on either side, will be tipped completely in one direction or the other.

This text's resolution of the Mishnah's problem, providing the conditions according to which the Mishnah can be taken at its precise word, leads us to conclude that judgment is made on the basis of a periodic (or final—this is not clear) comprehensive accounting, and the only relevant question in the act of judgment is the side of the scale on which the majority of acts belong. Such a resolution demands, ironically, that we ignore details in our depiction of divine justice—a single last detail is terribly important, but only because details do not stand on their own. Single acts are (apparently) neither rewarded nor punished; only the combination of them all is.

This allows us to defend divine justice by claiming that no one except God is in a position to do the complete accounting. We are not told the meaning of individual events that might be interpreted as punishment (such as suffering) or reward, but that is not the concern of this Tosefta. It affirms a cumulative divine justice and denies, by implication, discrete acts of small judgment. It is apologetic for the system when viewed over the longer term but unconcerned for everyday injustices.

The latter part of this text turns its attentions to the importance of an individual act in quite a different way. The tradition claims, in the name of R. Shimeon, that the sum total of a person's deeds is unimportant if, in the final hour, he turns in the opposite direction. Thus "if he was absolutely righteous all of his days and rebelled at the end, he caused all [his prior merits] to be lost." By the same token, "if he was absolutely evil all of his days and repented at the end, God receives him." Both positions are supported from Ezek. 33:12, which indeed makes very much the same point (though with the important difference noted below). The Tosefta's claim here is again that the system of justice is operative, but not precisely as envisioned in the prior tradition. Instead, the emphasis now is that God may be merciful until the very end, but also that God will exact retribution even from the belated rebel. In other words, even great quantities of good deeds will not save an individual if, in the end, he turns to evil.

On the one hand, the Tosefta's teaching here is deeply indebted to the system proposed by Ezekiel (and, in somewhat less detail, by Jeremiah). Ezekiel 18:21–24 is particularly straightforward in indicating that a person will be judged according to his latter acts, even if earlier acts are of a very different nature. But there is one essential difference: Ezekiel still speaks of reward (life) or punishment (death) in this world; his prophecy does not await a future world to realize the fruits of justice. The Tosefta, on the other hand, by speaking of a person changing from his accustomed way "all of his days" and assuming a different path at the "end" clearly means to project judgment and justice into a future world, after the fashion of many Apocryphal texts or rabbinic texts outside of the Mishnahs reviewed earlier.

Crucially, by emphasizing and anticipating a final judgment, this Tosefta is at odds with its Mishnaic source in its assumption regarding the venue for justice. The corresponding Mishnah, it will be recalled, was noteworthy for its insistence upon this-worldly justice. The Tosefta, in contrast, also imagines an alternative. It qualifies the present Mishnaic opinion by introducing in this very context a Mishnaic opinion found elsewhere. By doing so, it diminishes the biblical literalism of this Mishnah.

In this connection, it is significant that in its response to the Mishnah's other statement of literal this-worldly reward and punishment (end Qiddushin), the Tosefta also seems to look toward the future world. While the Mishnah claims that neither wealth nor poverty is a product of one's profession, but "all is according to his merit," the Tosefta leaves out this final comment. Might this be evidence of a hesitation to state this principle quite so literally? Furthermore, though the Mishnah in this context says nothing of a future world,[11] the Tosefta goes on to record a tradition, attributed to R. Nehorai, where Torah study is recommended as a constant occupation because "we eat the reward of its [= Torah's] labor in this world and its stock remains in the world-to-come." To be sure, there is some sort of reward (in the language of Mishnah Pe'a, "fruit") in this world, but more promising is the hope of future reward.

Admittedly, it is difficult to argue from silence, and I also understand that the Tosefta does attribute wealth or poverty to God; on what basis other than merit would God distribute these conditions? But this is the only place in context where the Tosefta omits a significant element of the corresponding Mishnah; it otherwise quotes it directly or expands upon it. It is therefore difficult to avoid the conclusion that the omission is intended. Moreover, an inclination toward future judgment, in contrast with the Mishnah, is quite explicit in the Tosefta as it expands upon the Mishnah; hence it seems reasonable to read the omission as significant. It does appear, in fact, that this Tosefta wants to play down the notion of this-worldly justice, preferring instead to anticipate a later judgment.

The other major deliberation on divine justice in the Tosefta is the very lengthy discussion at Sotah chapters 3–4. This text is primarily an expansion of the segment at the end of Mishnah Sotah chapter 1, which exemplifies the principle of measure-for-measure justice (discussed in Chapter 4). Adding many examples to its predecessor, the Tosefta provides powerful reinforcement of the earlier expression. In my reading, two elements of the Tosefta's commentary make significant additions to the earlier treatment.

The first such addition, reviewed already earlier in this chapter, is the Tosefta's rejection of Job's words of protest, making the very injustices he observes into the source of the punishment of the wicked. The second notable expansion is the Tosefta's rendering explicit the Mishnah's less explicit claim that reward exceeds punishment. The statement, at the beginning of Sotah chapter 4 (p. 167), is this: "The measure of good [= reward] is greater than the measure of retribution [by a ratio of] one in five-hundred." This is then supported with scripture:

> With respect to the measure of retribution He [= God] says, "visiting the guilt of the parents upon the children" (Ex 20:5) [but] with respect to the measure of good He says "but showing kindness to the thousandth generation" (ibid. vs. 6); thus the measure of good is greater than the measure of retribution [by a ratio of] one in five-hundred.

This expansion makes the comparison of reward and punishment impossible to miss: God is immensely generous, the Tosefta claims, when it comes to reward. By contrast, the relative insignificance of retribution can be seen as genuinely merciful. If—a person will say to herself—I am assured reward in such extraordinary measure, then I will be willing to tolerate the relatively minor punishment that I must also suffer under this system.

In spirit, there is no question that this Tosefta opposes the tradition in Qiddushin, analyzed previously. This one is concerned with discrete acts—not merely with their sum total—and insists that such acts are rewarded or punished in the present world. The accounting does not, apparently, wait for the end. True, it is possible to reconcile them by claiming that they are complementary, one addressing present justice and one addressing an individual's final justice. The Tosefta at the beginning of Pe'a suggests precisely such a compromise. There are acts, it claims, which are rewarded or punished in this world but which are also included in a final accounting. However, this latter text notwithstanding, it seems that the Qiddushin and Sotah texts are more correctly to be understood as conflicting. These are, after all, primarily hermeneutic expansions of earlier Mishnaic texts, and the expansions are accomplished without concern for each other, only for the earlier texts to which they refer. Therefore, I prefer to leave the Qiddushin and Sotah traditions in basic conflict, recognizing their common claim that the system of justice is operative while noting that they devise different strategies for upholding the ultimate integrity of that system.

In its few reflections on suffering and justice, the Tosefta is little different from the Mishnah on which it comments. The few substantive differences—the explicit recognition of the atoning power of suffering (like sacrifice), the greater preference to anticipate justice in a future world—are in any case thoroughly traditional in Jewish circles by the mid-third century. True, shifts in emphasis can be important, but this is not where the genuine contribution of the Tosefta lies.

The more important difference between the Mishnah and Tosefta is the Tosefta's greater willingness to grant the reality of context, the force of history as it affects the system at large. We saw this already, in a manner that is at least symbolic, in the Tosefta's recognition that common biblical pieties can be "oppressive" if offered as comfort to a sufferer who is yet too much in the midst of suffering. But it is in the Tosefta's comments on the destruction of the Jerusalem Temple that this development is particularly evident.

The Destruction of the Temple and Historical Reality

Like the Mishnah, the Tosefta formulates detailed treatises on matters of the Temple and its sacrifices, giving little indication, in context, that the subject of its attentions no longer exists. However, because the Tosefta takes its cue from the Mishnah, this fact is less significant than it appears. The Mishnah had no model (in postdestruction literature) for its choice of topics; its decision basically to ignore the destruction was thus highly significant, as we discussed. But because the Tosefta followed the Mishnah's lead in this matter, its posture regarding the Temple and sacrifices, as a whole and in their details, may be considered derivative. Its description of an apparently living institution may therefore be downplayed.[12]

I am particularly inclined to downplay its significance because the Tosefta takes relatively more frequent note of the destruction than does the Mishnah, and there is an urgent tone in several of its mentions of that event. The contrast with the Mishnah, for documents that are otherwise similar in these and related matters, is quite striking.

Perhaps the Tosefta's most notable comment relating to the Temple is its asking explicitly why the Temple was destroyed. The discussion, found at the end of tractate Menaḥot, is this:

> R. Joḥanan b. Torta said . . . Why was the first building [= Temple] of Jerusalem destroyed? Because there was in it idol-worship and prohibited sexual relations and the shedding of blood.
>
> But in the latter [Temple] we know that they toiled in Torah and were careful with tithes, [so] why were they exiled?
>
> Because they love money and each one hates his neighbor. . . .
>
> [W]ith respect to the latter building [=Temple], *which will be rebuilt in our lives and in our days*, what is said [in scripture]? "In the days to come, The Mount of the Lord's House shall stand firm above the mountains. . . . And all the nations shall gaze on it with joy . . ." (Is 2:2–3). [emphasis added]

This Tosefta, while not attributing the second, more recent destruction to sin in a restricted sense (if sin = matters specifically prohibited by the Torah), nevertheless makes it clear that wrongdoing is at the root of the catastrophe. Recalling the nature of the wrongdoings described by Amos (chapter 2 and throughout), we may even say that this sort of wrongdoing has a long tradition in prophetic condemnations. Of course, this connection of punishment (the destruction) with wrongdoing is in accord with the prevalent opinion of the Tosefta seen elsewhere, and also with the common opinion of the Mishnah. But the mere fact that the Tosefta addresses the problem of the destruction in this explicit way—unlike the Mishnah before it—is evidence of significant development in the rabbis' willingness to grant the reality and impact of (no longer quite so) recent events.

Also of import, by virtue of its contrast with other expressions, is the part of the tradition which claims that the Temple "will be rebuilt in our lives and in our days" and which, through the quotation from Isaiah, equates the present day (= the time of the speaker) with the age of restoration and redemption. The apparent urgency or profound expectation for restoration exhibited in this statement is remarkable. We have here an author or authors who, despite the passage of two centuries since the destruction and, more crucially, the memory of the failed restoration attempt at the time of Bar Kokhba, are nevertheless willing to express hope that the rebuilding of the Temple is not a distant event. The prophetic promises are understood to refer to this Temple, to this age. And the Temple will be rebuilt during the lives of these very authorities! The contrast between this text and the Mishnah, in both tone and substance, could hardly be more evident. Significantly, the same immediate expectation is repeated in other Tosefta traditions.

For example, the Tosefta at R.H. 2:9 (Erfurt manuscript: 4:3) comments that R. Yohanan b. Zakkai's enactments reacting to the Temple's destruction will be annulled "when the House [= Temple] will be rebuilt [some versions add: speedily in our days]." Even in the unenhanced version, the text exhibits total confidence that the Temple will be rebuilt; it is only a matter of when. At Pisha (Peshaim) 8:4, the Tosefta suggests the law that would apply if permission to rebuild the Temple is given (and, presumably, the rebuilding quickly completed) between the regular Pesah and "Second Pesah" (a month later). Again, the possibility of rebuilding is assumed so confidently that it is necessary to delineate the law relevant in the immediate aftermath of restoration. A similar tone is found in the related comment, at Ter. 10:15, which speaks of the territory of Judah which "will quickly be rebuilt." Most bluntly, Taan. 3:9 (Erfurt: 4:9, p. 430) comments on a time which it calls "*tomorrow*, when the Temple will be rebuilt . . . (emphasis added)." Tomorrow, not in some postponed and unfixable future, the Temple will be rebuilt. The hope of restoration is alive and uncompromised.

Lieberman, in his comments on this latter text, points out that the statement of hope for restoration appears in none of the parallels to this text, despite the fact that the rest of the tradition is repeated, in similar form, in several later documents.[13] As noted, the hope for restoration appears in the Mishnah as the final coda to only one tractate, and the Mishnah is otherwise not characterized by such an expectation. Why the Tosefta expresses such sentiments in these contexts while other rabbinic texts do not we may only surmise. The authors of later documents perhaps were sufficiently sobered by the passing of centuries—and by the failure of the rebuilding effort under the emperor Julian—to recognize that hope for an immediate restoration was foolish. History had proved that such an effort was bound to fail. On the other side, the authorship of the one prior rabbinic work, the Mishnah—though closer even than the Tosefta to the destruction itself— was perhaps constrained by official needs, both internal and external, from voicing such expectations. Furthermore, the more immediate presence of apocalyptic sentiments in the political environment of the Mishnah's compilers may have discouraged them from anticipating too quick a redemption. Whatever the best explanation of the contrast, the Tosefta is unique in its focus on the Temple and its urgently expected restoration. Reference to other echoes of the destruction in the Tosefta reinforces the impression that the event is a special concern in this document.

The most direct response to the destruction in the Tosefta is the much expanded elaboration, in chapter 15 of tractate Sotah, of the consequences of the destruction. After repeating the Mishnah's brief record of the consequences, the Tosefta adds:

R. Shimeon b. Gamliel said: From the day that the Temple was destroyed, it would be proper that we not eat meat and not drink wine [since they were used in the Temple service]. But a court does not decree [restrictions] on the populace that they cannot uphold. He would say: since they [= the Romans] decree upon us that we not learn Torah, we should decree upon Israel that they not marry women [since they do not know marriage and family laws] and, as a consequence, Israel will be ruined and the seed of Abraham will cease. Rather, leave Israel alone [to continue to do as they now do, marrying and having families]; it is better that they should [do these things while transgressing] in error and not [do them] intentionally. (p. 242)[14]

The theme of various responses to and consequences of the destruction continues, until we reach the following conclusion:

Not to mourn at all is impossible, for the decree has already been enacted, but to mourn too much is also impossible. Rather the sages said thus: a man should plaster his home with plaster, and leave a small amount [unplastered] in memory of the Temple. (p. 243)

The comments conclude with a statement encouraging mourning for the destroyed Jerusalem.

Noteworthy in this text is, first, the sheer length of the deliberation on this subject. The theme of the diminution of God's presence in history, in which the present discussion is found, it also greatly expanded in the Tosefta—in comparison to its Mishnaic foundation—and the energy to thus enlarge this treatise may itself be understood as a reaction to the destruction. In this text, there is no suppression of the emotions generated by the destruction. Here and elsewhere,[15] lament is clearly expressed and deemed to be appropriate.

But also important is the recognition in these remarks that, while the urge to mourn excessively might be present, such a reaction would be dangerous. The precise acts of mourning that would be called for, moreover, would be intolerable. So the text advises that mourning be moderated. This does not mean that the cause for mourning, the ruined Temple, should be put out of mind, only that there is a more appropriate response to the destruction than forlorn depression.

Other Tosefta traditions restore the reality of the destruction to the attention of the reader where the Mishnah does not. For example, in the second chapter of tractate Yom Ha-kippurim (5, 6, and 8, pp. 231–34)—against the background of a Mishnah (Yoma) that describes parts of the Temple service of Yom Kippur (without, of course, hinting that the description is archaic)—the Tosefta adds an interpretive narrative in which certain parties are praised for having taken precautions in anticipation of the Temple's destruction. Later (2:13 [3:5], p. 237) we read of a priest who lengthened his prayer in order to pray that the Temple not be destroyed. At Zeb. 13:6, the Tosefta numbers the years that "the latter building" stood, making it impossible to escape the fact that the second Temple is no longer standing. And at Shab. 16:7, the Tosefta adds, gratuitously, that "the fastidiousness of Zechariah b. Aqilas," hinted at earlier in the teaching, led to the Temple's destruction. Whether the Tosefta is referring to the tradition also recorded in the Bavli at Git. 56a or whether the tradition is at this point less devel-

oped matters little. What is important is the fact that the Temple's destruction is emphasized where the Mishnah does not do so, and where, moreover, such emphasis was entirely unnecessary.[16]

There is no escaping the conclusion that the Tosefta is far more impressed
with the Temple's destruction than is the Mishnah. This fact would seem
to suggest, as proposed earlier, that the Tosefta draws a far less static picture of the world than does the Mishnah. The Tosefta admits, in some
degree, the world's imperfection and hopes that things might one day soon
turn again for the better. This understanding is further supported by the
presence of a variety of other references to recent history in the Tosefta as
well. As Neusner remarks, "The presence of Roman troops is acknowl-
edged . . . and what was done 'in the time of danger,' meaning during the
pacification of the country after Bar Kokhba's war, more than seldom is
invoked in law."[17] The reality of recent disasters has consequences. The ideal
imagined in a more restricted way by the Mishnah is not immune to the
events and sufferings which interrupt mundane perfection.

But the Tosefta likewise elaborates on Temple-related concerns at length
without noting the fact that the Temple has been destroyed. And Neusner
is certainly correct in claiming that the Tosefta offers no coherent or extended elaboration of the meaning of history. How are we to interpret this
paradox? Is there history in the Tosefta or is there not? Neusner answers
this question by asking, rhetorically, "how can we speak of a doctrine of
history in a document that knows of only one event, the destruction of the
Temple? . . . The answer, of course, is that under such circumstances, in
the framework of such convictions, there can [be] no history at all."[18]

If we mean by history an elaborate system for correlating events over the
long term, Neusner is certainly correct. But it seems to me that his conclusion is too extreme. First of all, though the Tosefta includes no sequential
history in the Greek sense, it is clear, as we have seen, that historical reality
does have a place in the Tosefta, far more often and in a more significant
way than in the Mishnah. Furthermore, though Neusner sees his conclusion supported by the lack of reference to a personified Messiah in the
Tosefta, he certainly knows that Jewish eschatologies during the period
leading up to the Tosefta in no way demanded a Messiah.[19] The world-to-
come would indeed come, with or without a Messiah, and, as we have seen,
the Tosefta does look toward that future world with greater frequency and
insistence than the Mishnah. Again, in this way the Tosefta recognizes
change, instability, and the hope for improvement. And if the destruction
of the Temple is the only historical event known to the Tosefta (though we
might recognize this claim as hyperbolic), that should not be understood
as a negation of history. On the contrary, the destruction—representing
the actual destruction along with subsequent events and their consequences
(the war of 70 and the Bar Kokhba war were, for purposes of assessing significance, a single war, much as World Wars I and II of this century will
one day certainly be viewed as essentially a single war)—was the most profound source of disruption and suffering that recent Jewish generations

knew. No wonder these events drew rabbinic attention to the exclusion of others. (Yes, these rabbis were not interested in history for its own sake.) What is notable is that the Tosefta is willing to record these events and admit their significance, unlike the Mishnah before it.

Coming between a half-century and a century later than the Mishnah, and in the midst of a decline which brought considerable pain and deprivation, the Tosefta allows for one significant development beyond the powerful Mishnaic precedent: its admission that there is change in history, the world is not perfect, and restoration is something which must be hoped for. The defensive denial of the Mishnah characterizes significant aspects of the Tosefta, but not the whole. Perhaps because of increasing distance from the most catastrophic events in rabbinic history, or perhaps because of the insidious effect of more recent, more modest but unflagging sufferings, the Tosefta's authorship permits itself to be distracted by less-than-ideal realities. True, the events which are the focus of these attentions occurred possibly two centuries before, and more recent suffering is as yet unnoticed. But the Mishnah's pure ideal has been left behind. Would the suffering of the third century make itself felt in rabbinic circles, as the suffering of the first and second century now did in the Tosefta? For an answer to this question, we turn, in the next chapter, to later contemporary expressions, recorded in the halakhic midrashim.

6

Early Rabbinic Responses: The Halakhic Midrashim

The so-called halakhic midrashim, the tannaitic midrashim on the books of Exodus through Deuteronomy, are the next stage in the development of the rabbinic literary corpus. Regrettably, there remains considerable disagreement among scholars in dating these works, with regard both to their substance and (somewhat less so) their final redaction. As in the case of the Tosefta, Albeck here again argues that these are (redactionally) post-Talmudic documents.[1] In what he calls "a good guess," Neusner remarks that they were probably completed around 400 CE—though he does not offer substantive proof for this guess.[2] In my opinion, it is more reasonable to suggest a date of the late third century, for the following reasons. First, these midrashim quote both the Mishnah and, less frequently, the Tosefta, meaning that the earliest possible date of their redaction is the mid-third century. On the other side, they are already quoted in the Yerushalmi, c. 400, making this the latest possible date of their redaction. The remaining question is whether they were completed before the Christianization of the empire and therefore closer to Avot and the Tosefta, or after the triumph of Christianity and thus closer to the Yerushalmi and the early aggadic midrashim. As will be evident to anyone who reads these works, they are, in terms of language, named authorities, and ideologies, far closer to the former than to the latter. Moreover, the qualities which characterize the Yerushalmi and the aggadic midrashim as a consequence of their reaction to the Christian triumph, spelled out in detail by Neusner, are absent from these works. Individual comments may be construed as directed against Christians, but the overall program of these books is not controlled by that concern. In light of these factors, it is likely that these works are earlier, before the Christianization of the empire, and not later. Therefore, the most reasonable surmise concerning their dating seems to be c. 300.

Accordingly, the context for the discussion of these works is approximately the same as the context pertinent for the Tosefta. By the end of the third century, Jews in Palestine had suffered through a half-century or more of chaos and decline. Land had been abandoned, basic necessities became difficult to come by, and the Jewish population of the territory fell. As the experience of postdestruction "exile" became more permanent, the hope for salvation must have been more urgent (psychologically) but more difficult to affirm with confidence. If the rabbis of this period were open to such reflection and discussion, the conditions which might provoke deliberations on suffering were undeniably present.

Perhaps because of his difficulty in dating these books, Neusner, exceptionally, does not read them in the context of their time. He instead thinks that these works bespeak an internal rabbinic development, responding to what he calls "the crisis precipitated by the Mishnah."[3] Noting that the Mishnah had not explicitly laid out its claim of relationship to scripture, but had instead offered its laws mostly in the voice of its own independent authority, Neusner understands the agenda of the midrashim to be filling in the gap, connecting the law of the rabbis with the written law given by God to Moses. These midrashim represent, in his view, a development precipitated by forces internal to the rabbinic movement and not a response to the larger history of the time.

Whatever the merit of Neusner's characterization, and I agree, in large measure, with his understanding of this development, it is still impossible to divorce consideration of these works entirely from the broader historical context. Moreover, the responses to suffering recorded in these pages are more frequent, more detailed, and more profound than what we have seen earlier, and this development is not accounted for by reference to the relation of the Mishnah and the midrashim. Only reference to the malaise of the recent century, and to developments in the rabbinic movement itself, will provide an adequate setting for explaining what we find here.

Before passing to the relevant texts it is also essential that we ask whether these midrashim may be considered together or whether each is distinct, demanding individual examination. In his studies of each work, Neusner has pointed to a variety of differences in their overall approaches.[4] However, in the present matter, I have discovered no significant differences in their responses, and what few differences may suggest themselves are not frequent enough to support conclusions. Moreover, in his comprehensive study of a related subject (responses to the destruction of the second Temple), David Nelson concludes that these midrashim do effectively represent one corpus.[5] Therefore, with respect to the subject at hand, we may approach these various works collectively and speak of their common witness to this stage of the development of rabbinic responses to suffering.

The simple connection between sin and suffering as punishment is commonly repeated in the halakhic midrashim. The Sifra, for example, represents God as saying to Israel: "You have transgressed seven sins; come [now] and accept upon yourselves seven [kinds] of suffering" (*beḥuqotai*, chapter 5, 1). The same assumption is clearly announced in Sifrei Deuteronomy: "[Y]ou, if you are worthy you are rewarded but, if you sin, you are visited with retribution . . ." (Sifrei Deut. 306, p. 333).[6] Death also is conventionally understood as punishment, as in Sifrei Numbers, where R. Shimon b. Eleazar expresses the opinion that Moses and Aaron, like all other mortals, died on account of sin, and continues by claiming that if they had not sinned they would as yet not have died (par. 137, p. 183). In these and other traditions like them, the tradition of the Mishnah, following upon the most common biblical view, is repeated without elaboration or reservation.

Other earlier approaches, less common in the Bible and the Mishnah but no less traditional, are also repeated at this stage. The most typical such response is the idea that the scales of divine justice, apparently improperly tipped in this world, will be restored to their proper position in the world-to-come (see, for example, Sifrei Num. 103, p. 102). A view with shallower roots, repeated in the Mekhilta de'R. Ishmael (henceforth: Mekhilta) (*Yitro, ba-ḥodesh*, par. 7, p. 228) from the Tosefta, is the belief that suffering is essential in effecting atonement for the two most serious categories of sin. As discussed earlier, this formulation had no precise precedent in earlier literature, but the connection with documents that had equated suffering with sacrifice is unmistakable. Understood more broadly, redemptive suffering went back, of course, to second Isaiah. The more literal claim for the redemptive quality of suffering is also found in this literature (for example, Mekhilta *neziqin*, par. 9, p. 280).

At the same time, the halakhic midrashim record lengthy treatises on suffering that, by virtue of their rhetoric in particular, mark new directions in rabbinic responses the problem. The most elaborate treatment of suffering is found in Mekhilta *ba-ḥodesh* (par. 10, pp. 239–41) and is repeated with mostly minor differences in Sifrei Deuteronomy (par. 32, pp. 55–58). Slightly abridged for purposes of conserving space, the text follows.

>   *a.* R. Aqiba says, "With me . . . you shall not make . . ." (Ex. 20:20)— [this teaches] that you should not conduct yourselves with respect to me as others conduct themselves with respect to those [gods] that they fear.
>   *b.* For when good comes upon them, they honor their gods . . . but when suffering comes upon them they curse their gods. . . .
>   *c.* But you, if I bring upon you good, give thanks [and if] I bring upon you suffering, give thanks.
>   *d.* And thus does David say, "I raise the cup of deliverance and invoke the name of the Lord" (Ps. 116:13) [and, at the same time,] "I come upon trouble and sorrow and I invoke the name of the Lord" (ibid., vss. 3–4).[7]
>   *e.* And thus [too] does Job say, "the Lord has given, and the Lord has taken away; blessed be the name of the Lord" (Job 1:21)—[blessing God, therefore, both] for the good measure and for the measure of suffering.
>   *f.* What does his [= Job's] wife say to him? "You still keep your integrity! Blaspheme God and die!" (ibid. 2:9). And so he responds, "You talk as any foolish woman . . ."[8] (ibid. vs. 10). . . .

g. And moreover [it teaches] that *a person should be happier with suffering than with good*, for even if a person experiences good all of his days, he is not forgiven for his sins. And *what causes his sins to be forgiven? Say: suffering.*

h. R. Eleazar b. Jacob says, "Behold, He [= scripture] says, 'Do not reject the discipline of the Lord. . . .' For what reason? 'For whom the Lord loves, He rebukes [as the father the son whom he favors]' (Prov. 3:11–12). You say: come and see, what caused this child to be pleasing to his father? Say: suffering."

i. R. Meir says, "'the Lord your God disciplines you just as a man disciplines his son' (Dt. 8:5). [According to the instruction of this verse] your heart should know: [in Sifrei: you and your heart know] the deeds that you have done and the suffering that I have brought upon you, not according to your deeds have I brought suffering upon you."

Part II

j. R. Yose b. R. Judah says, "precious are sufferings, for the name of the Omnipresent rests upon the one to whom sufferings come . . ."

k. R. Jonathan says, "precious are sufferings, [for] just as the covenant is established by virtue of the land, so too is the covenant established by virtue of suffering . . ."

l. R. Shimeon b. Yoḥai says, "precious are sufferings, for three good gifts did [God] give to Israel, and the nations of the world covet them, and they were not given except by means of sufferings. And what are they? Torah and the Land of Israel and the World-to-Come . . ."

m. You say: what is the way that brings a person to life in the World-to-Come? Say: it is sufferings.

n. R. Neḥemiah says, "precious are sufferings, for *just as sacrifices [cause God to] pardon, so too do sufferings [cause God to] pardon . . .*

o. "And not only so, but *sufferings [cause God to] pardon more than sacrifices. For what reason? Because sacrifices are with [one's] property, but sufferings are with [one's] body. . . .*"

Part III

p. R. Eleazar was once sick, and four elders came in to visit him, [those being] R. Tarfon and R. Joshua and R. Eleazar b. Azariah and R. Aqiba.

q. R. Tarfon responded and said, "Rabbi. You are better for Israel than the solar sphere . . ."

r. R. Joshua responded and said, "Rabbi, you are better for Israel than a drop of rain . . ."

s. R. Eleazar b. Azariah responded and said, "You are better for Israel than a father and a mother . . ."

t. R. Aqiba responded and said, "precious are sufferings."

u. R. Eleazar said to his students, ". . . let me hear the words of my student, Aqiba, who said, precious are sufferings . . ."

To facilitate comment, I have broken this treatise into three segments. The first (a–i) elaborates the theme of praising God for suffering and rejoicing in it, the second (j–o) is united by the common introductory formula, "precious are sufferings," and the last segment (p–u) relates a dramatic narrative that communicates the same message as the middle section of this text. Clearly what we have here is a lengthy apologetic for suffering.

The first segment begins by making the same point as m. Ber. 9:5; that is, a person is required to thank God for the bad that he experiences as well as for the good. Noteworthy in this section is, first, the second proof for this proposition, brought from Job (e–f). In the verses quoted, Job is considered a proper model for pious behavior; he blesses God for the bad that has befallen him and he scolds his wife for suggesting that he do otherwise. As we saw earlier, rabbinic attitudes toward Job are not united in viewing him favorably, so the fact that Job is held up as a model is striking. True, the Job speaking here is the prerebellion Job, but if in the minds of the rabbinic authors the figure of Job were sufficiently blemished by his subsequent rebellious expressions, it would have been difficult to use him as a positive role model in the present context. If Job can be a pious model, perhaps pious people can question God's justice.

The latter part of this first section similarly argues that suffering should be blessed = welcomed, now mostly on the basis of careful quotation from scripture. Important here is the extent to which the apologetic is furthered, for the verses are quoted to increase our desire for suffering while diminishing our sense of its severity. To make these points we are told, first, that suffering causes our sins to be forgiven, but only in the way that punishment restores a child to his parent's good favor. Our suffering is evidence of God's special relationship with us. But the model of a parent punishing a child is important here in another way: since a parent punishes out of love, the punishment a parent metes out is less in degree than would be required by the crime; since God punishes as a parent, God too does not punish according to the full measure of transgression (i). Punishment is not measure-for-measure; it is less than justice would call for. God, in other words, is more merciful than just.

But why conclude that this is the primary sense of the tradition at hand (i)? Why not read "not according to your deeds have I brought suffering upon you" as saying that punishment is in excess of one's sinful deeds? My preference for the former reading is based upon two observations. First, the text suggests that self-reflection will reveal the cause of the punishment. Calling on the individual to be honest with himself, the midrash seems to believe that a true accounting of one's sins will yield the conclusion that the punishment is not uncalled for; on the contrary, it is even less than might be justified. In contrast, it is unlikely that punishment that is greater than the sin could be understood through *self*-reflection. Second, this tradition forms part of a long sequence of apologia for suffering. How would such a purpose be served by saying that suffering is greater than is justified? In light of these observations, surely the first of the suggested readings should be understood as the preferred one.

All this being said, there is little doubt that the noted ambiguity is itself part of the message. Indeed, the comparison to the punishment of a child by a parent opens up another interpretive possibility that has important consequences. Amos, it will be recalled, argued that God more readily punishes Israel , God's beloved people, for lesser sins. On the human plane, as well, it may be appreciated that parental discipline, intended to correct the child, may sometimes be even harsher than the wrongdoing. Considered on either level, it is evident that, just as parental discipline might be less severe than the crime, so too might it be more severe. What distinguishes parental discipline is that it *often does not correspond exactly to the crime.* Correspondence is the way of justice, not of parental love. Thus whichever way parental discipline is imagined, it is correct to say "not according to your deeds have I brought suffering upon you."

In the present context, it is this latter point that is most crucial. This midrash argues explicitly, for the first time in the rabbinic context, that suffering, as discipline (and not as punishment in the penal sense), does *not* correspond exactly with the measure of sin. Contrary to the claim of Mishnah Sotah, this is not a world that is judged according to a measure-for-measure system. If it is not strict justice that we insist upon, then, of course, suffering is far less of a problem. Simply put, if suffering is not punishment, it must be something else. In this simple, brief step, *the necessary relationship of correspondence between sin and suffering has been severed.* Once it has been admitted, as in this text, that the correspondence is not necessary, then it is possible to redefine completely the place of suffering in the system. Crucially, it is also possible, with this redefinition, to confront reality more directly. With this severing accomplished, it is never again necessary to face the reality of suffering and pretend that it is absolutely just. Suffering can now be salvaged, but in a different guise—with a different purpose.

Of course, this is not the first time that this relationship has been severed. Job and Ecclesiastes, in the canonical context, deny the direct and necessary relationship between sin and suffering, and apocalyptic books also claim that present suffering is a matter of fate, and thus not a measured outcome of sin. But the step taken here is significant for two reasons. First, this is the first time in rabbinic literature that the admission of a lack of correspondence is made this explicitly. Elsewhere, to this point, a more archaic biblical perspective has been preferred by the rabbinic authors. Here they begin to recover other, less prominent, biblical alternatives. Second, and crucially, this is *not* an apocalyptic response. Rabbinic literature never admits the apocalyptic possibility, and so the severing of correspondence in the rabbinic context is both more troubling and more radical.

What the different purpose of suffering might be is explored in the second section of this midrash. Here the author argues not merely that suffering is not to be despised, or even, as in the first section, that it leads to a positive outcome, but that suffering carries with it so many profound benefits that it is to be held precious by the sufferer. The first major thrust of the argument (k–m) is that suffering is covenantal. The tradition attributed to Shimeon b. Yoḥai is particularly noteworthy: the three symbols of covenantal fulfillment—the Torah, the Land, and final redemption—are all made conditional upon suffering. Of course if suffering guarantees each of these three things, then suffering genuinely is to be welcomed.

In consideration of the context in which these traditions are expressed, more important is the opinion attributed to R. Nehemiah (n) and its elaboration (o). One of the central problems for emergent rabbinic Judaism and for contemporary Jewish movements was what to do with the Torah's requirement of sacrifices, which, in the absence of the Temple, could apparently no longer be brought. The response of the author of Hebrews (chapters 7 and 9), claiming that Jesus was the perfect, eternal sacrifice, shows the centrality of this dilemma. The present tradition comes remarkably close to that position, but with important differences. In this midrash, sacrifice, while perhaps ideally desirable, is not absolutely essential, because suffering brings God's pardon at least as well as do sacrifices. As it turns out, though, suffering is even more effective than sacrifices, because suffering involves personal, bodily sacrifice, whereas animal sacrifices do not. We who suffer, like Jesus who suffered, replace the sacrifices. Our suffering, like his for Christians, is redemptive. But this similarity is also the most important difference between the two approaches. In the case of Jesus, the suffering of the perfect individual was understood to atone for the sins of the many. In the view of this midrash, in contrast, it is individuals, all imperfect and all sinners, who suffer and thereby effect their own atonement. Our own flesh and blood replace the flesh and blood of the sacrificed animals. Suffering repairs the ruptures that earlier only sacrifices could mend.

The final dramatic narrative gives further proof of the preciousness of suffering, and gives it the support of both scripture (not quoted here) and rabbinic authority. But the point has already been made. And what a point it is indeed. Suffering should be the source of joy! Suffering is dear! Suffering is at the foundation of the covenant! Suffering is redemptive!

As should be clear, it is not, for the most part, the substance of this midrash that is new. Each of its central points can at least find an approximate parallel in earlier Jewish literature. But the attitude expressed and recommended here is nowhere before paralleled. What we see here is a powerful rhetorical attempt to take a painful reality, one in which Jews have suffered horribly as individuals and as a nation, and to transform completely the attitude that a Jew will bring to this reality. If suffering repairs my relationship with God, brings me to Torah, leads me to the land, and assures me life in the world-to-come, then I cannot possibly—or so would seem reasonable—protest this suffering. Relative to the reward, the cost is surely quite minor.

As remarked earlier, the parallel in Sifrei Deuteronomy is virtually identical with the record in the Mekhilta. The most significant difference in the Sifrei version is the bridge to the deliberation on suffering as such. That midrash begins essentially by quoting m. Ber. 9:5, attributing the opinion found in the Mishnah to R. Aqiba. Aqiba comments, in connection with the phrase "[You shall love the Lord your God with all your heart and with all your soul and] with all your might" (*bekhol me'odekha*), that this means you should love God "for each and every measure [*bekhol mida umidda*] with which He measures you, whether with a good measure or with a measure of suffering." The language employed here makes it impossible not to hearken back to the Mishnah in Sotah which, claiming measure-for-measure justice, uses the same terminology. But, as discussed previously, the purpose of the present midrash is to make precisely the opposing argument—that measure-for-measure justice is not the rule. Therefore, the midrash, in its choice of words, assures that the reader will note the contrast. Taking issue with the Mishnah's more simplistic claim, the midrash argues for an understanding of suffering that, while every bit as apologetic for suffering in God's world, nevertheless does not succumb to the simple picture with which the Mishnah suffices.

A brief discussion of death in the Mekhilta (*ba-ḥodesh*, par. 9, p. 237) also shows that the question of divine retribution is more complicated than simple biblical equations might suggest and, like parts of the prior midrash, rends the correspondence between punishment and individual sin. The first comment claims: "If it were possible to remove the Angel of Death, I [God] would remove him, but the decree has already been decreed." That is to say, death is ever-present, by virtue of divine fiat. Having thus been fixed in the world, it is now impossible even for God to remove death. This means, of course, that even if there were to be a perfectly righteous individual she would die because of the universalism of the decree. Accordingly, death is assuredly not simple punishment.

Following this opinion, R. Jose comments: "On this condition did Israel stand at Mount Sinai, on the condition that the Angel of Death have no dominion over them, as it says 'I had taken you for divine beings, sons of the Most High, all of you' (Ps. 82:6); [but] you ruined your deeds, 'therefore you shall die as men do, fall like any prince' (ibid. vs. 7)."[9] As is clear, the connection between sin and death is not broken. The sin of human beings means that they must die. But, once again, the sin of a particular person is not what leads to his individual death. Cause and effect there still is; correspondence there is not.

A similarly complicated comment on death and suffering is recorded later in the Mekhilta (*neziqin*, par. 18, p. 313). The text is this:

> *a.* R. Ishmael and R. Shimeon were once on their way out to be killed [by the Romans, when] R. Shimeon said to R. Ishmael: Rabbi, my heart goes out, for I do not know why I am being killed.
> *b.* R. Ishmael said to R. Shimeon: [Has it never happened] in your days that a person came to you for judgment or for a question and you delayed him until you swallowed [what was in] your pouch or until you fastened your sandal or until you wrapped [yourself in] your shawl? [Remember!] The Torah said "[You shall not ill-treat any widow or orphan.] If you do mistreat . . ." [Ex. 22:21–2] [meaning] either great or minor mistreatment.
> *c.* And for this word, he said to him: You have comforted me, Rabbi.
> *d.* And when R. Shimeon and R. Ishmael were killed, R. Aqiba said to his students: prepare yourselves for suffering. For if good was to come in

our generation, R. Shimeon and R. Ishmael surely would have received it first,

   e. rather, it is revealed and known before the One Who Spoke and the World came into Being that *great suffering is about to come in our generation and* [*God therefore*] *removed them from our midst*

   f. To uphold what is said: "The righteous man perishes, and no one considers; Pious men are taken away, and no one gives thought . . ." and it says "Peace will come, they shall have rest on their couches who walk straightforward."[10] And, at the end, "But as for you, come closer, You sons of a sorceress, you offspring of an adulterer and a harlot!" (Is. 57:1–3).

Here, as in the previous text, suffering and death are claimed to be the consequence of wrongdoing, even of sin proper ("You shall not ill-treat"). But in order to make this argument, even the most insignificant act has to be considered ill-treatment (making someone wait a brief moment while one ties one's sandal), and what is highlighted, again, is not the fact that suffering results from sin but that it is virtually impossible to make a reasonable argument for any direct correspondence between the gravity of the sin and the severity of the punishment (suffering). This midrash goes a significant step beyond even Amos's double standard, demanding of at least the leaders of Israel (the rabbis) a level of righteousness that is nearly impossible to achieve. If that level of righteousness is not achieved, it will be recalled, even the most extreme suffering is justified as punishment. Yet, equally important, this justification is deemed comforting. At least it allows one to avoid the conclusion that God permits suffering for no reason at all.

   The second part of the midrash—the teaching of R. Aqiba to his disciples—confronts the problem of the suffering of the (relatively more) righteous (= Shimeon and Ishmael) with a different set of assumptions. According to this opinion, Shimeon and Ishmael may be seen as a sort of barometer for their generation. If this were to be a generation that would enjoy peace, they would be the first to merit this reward. But, since this is to be a generation of suffering, they must die first to fulfill the prophecy of Isaiah: first the righteous must die and come to their eternal rest, and only then will God call the wicked to account. These righteous individuals are being "removed from our midst" in order to spare them the more severe suffering to come. Their suffering must be considered in relation to the greater burden of suffering that their survivors will bear and, relatively speaking, it is not severe at all. Not since the Wisdom of Solomon has this claim for suffering as an act of grace, of mercy, been made in this manner.

   The majority of texts analyzed to this point have been drawn from the Mekhilta de'R. Ishmael, but the variety of views seen in that midrash is replicated in the others. Sifrei Deuteronomy, for example, parallels the Mekhilta in many of its comments on suffering and death. As in the Mekhilta, the relationship of Sifrei to suffering is extremely apologetic. This is true not only of the lengthy treatise on suffering, which, as noted previously, appears in both documents in almost exactly the same form, but also of other significant responses to the problem of suffering. The relevant comments are united in their observation that, if understood properly, suffering is far less extreme than is commonly imagined and, again if viewed through the proper lens, suffering is by no means unjust.

One such midrash (Sifrei 311, p. 351) makes its argument this way:

> *a.* When Abraham, our father, had not yet come into the world, the Holy One, Blessed be He, judged the world—as if it could be—with a strict [= cruel, severe, merciless] measure.
> *b.* [Thus,] the people of the [generation of the] flood sinned [and God] scattered them like sparks upon the water. The people of the [generation of the] tower [of Babel] sinned [and God] scattered them from one end of the earth to the other. The people of Sodom sinned [and God] flooded them with brimstone and fire.
> *c.* But when Abraham came to the world, he had merit to receive suffering and they [= sufferings] began coming slowly. As it is said, "There was a famine in the land, and Abram went down to Egypt" (Gen. 12:10). And if you should say, Why do sufferings come? Because of the love of Israel: "He fixed the boundaries of peoples / In relation to Israel's numbers" (Dt. 32:8).[11]

The midrash defends the suffering that Jews endure by comparing it with the suffering that others, before Israel, endured. The claim is simply this: the other nations were judged with great harshness, as evidenced by the Torah's record of the punishments of the people of the flood, the tower, and Sodom. But for Abraham and those who followed, harsh judgment was replaced with suffering. This sort of recompense for transgression, the midrash describes, comes gradually—not in a sudden catastrophic incident—and thus is vastly preferable to other forms of punishment. Since all humans sin, they all must be punished. As punishments go, personal suffering is relatively less severe, and so it is reasonable for the midrash to claim that suffering is an expression of God's love for Israel.[12]

Despite the explicit claim of the midrash, it would be a mistake to understand its system in strictly chronological terms. The more important dichotomy is not before Abraham–after Abraham, but Israel–the nations. This must be so because the people of Sodom and Gemorrah were punished *after* Abraham came. It was Abraham, of course, who argued that God should spare those cities. In light of this well-known connection, it must be assumed that the reader of this midrash—and therefore also the writer of this midrash—was aware of the inconsistency that was here created. The unavoidable reading of the present text must, then, be this: before Abraham, no one merited the more humane punishment represented by personal suffering; beginning with Abraham, Abraham and his offspring had such merit.

Very much the same point is made at Sifrei 325 (p. 377). There again the suffering of the nations is compared with the suffering of Israel, and again the suffering of Israel is considered gradual and therefore tolerable. When causing the nations to suffer, God "causes the earth to quake for them," whereas we are merely given over to the domination of the proverbial four kingdoms, where "I am with you to deliver you—declares the Lord" (Jer. 1:8). The argument that the suffering of Israel is gradual, piece-meal, and comparatively less harsh was made earlier in 2 Maccabees (chapter 6). There the narrator, in direct address, prepares the reader for the suffering of the seven brothers, described following, by offering precisely the same justification that we see here. So this strategy, as such, is centuries older than its appearance in this midrash. Still, this is its first appearance in literature that rabbinic Jews will consider authoritative, and it should be accounted as significant for that reason.[13]

The Sifrei also parallels the Mekhilta in its stated view of death. The following deliberation, in the guise of dialogues between Moses and God and then the ministering angels and God, questions first the death of Moses and then the death of Adam. Moses makes his own case (Sifrei 339, p. 388):

> Master of the world! Why do I die? Is it not better that they should say "Moses is good" from sight [= from actually seeing him] than that they should say "Moses is good" based [merely] upon reports? [And] is it not better that they should say "this is Moses who brought us out of Egypt and split the sea for us and brought down the manna for us and performed for us miracles and great deeds" than that they should say "thus and thus was Moses and thus and thus would Moses do?!"

God's response is simple and to the point: "It [= death] is a decree from before me that is equal for all persons." That is, Moses ideally would not have died. Clearly, no claim is being made that Moses died because of his sins. Instead, Moses died as all humans die—this is the divine decree. Therefore, death (at least Moses' death) is not punishment; it is simply the way of the world.

But the latter part of the same midrash, emphasizing the present lesson with regard to Adam, also suggests that death and transgression are related. In these steps, the ministering angels ask God why the first person died. God answers that he died for not having followed God's command (presumably regarding the tree in the garden). The angels then turn their attention to Moses, who, they claim, did perform God's commands. Here God reiterates the earlier response: "It is a decree from before me."

On the one hand, the discussion of Adam suggests that death is clearly tied to transgression. On the other hand, Moses' death is, for this author, evidence that death is not always tied to transgression; it must sometimes be explained as a simple, divine decree. It might be possible to resolve this apparent contradiction by proposing that only Adam's death must have been tied to transgression, but that subsequent deaths are necessary on account of the decree of death precipitated by Adam's sin. I prefer, though, to leave the tension unresolved. It seems more likely that there are arguments in opposition here: one which does not want to abandon the connection between death and sin, the other which admits a reality where death seems inevitable regardless of sin.

In all of the halakhic midrashim we have seen, traditions that relate to suffering are overwhelmingly apologetic; if they do not defend the justice of the system in archaic terms, they instead suggest that suffering is relatively less severe than other possible punishments or claim that suffering has a variety of benefits that should cause the afflicted individual to welcome his suffering. However, the texts examined so far do not entertain the possibility that suffering, whatever its status, does not come from God. One way or another, suffering is assuredly divine in origin.

Yet a careful search yields at least two (so I have found) midrashic texts that unmistakably assume that some suffering, at least, does not originate with God. The first is a well-known text that has commonly been understood to reflect a rabbinic response to the Hadrianic persecutions[14] (Mekhilta *ba-ḥodesh*, par. 6, p. 227). The narrator enumerates the various reasons for which Jews are put to death: "because I circumcised my son . . . because I read Torah . . . because I ate matzah [on Passover]," and so forth. How are these sufferings justified? "These afflictions caused me to be beloved to my Father in heaven." The afflictions, in other words, are not exactly "afflictions of [God's] love"—a justification for suffering that will become prominent in later texts—but they do cause me to be loved by God. Submitting to suffering inflicted by other humans, the sufferer is recognized by God as faithful and God's love for him or her is thereby increased.

There is no hint here that the suffering is in any way punishment for sin. On the contrary, the suffering experienced by the people is avowedly human in origin and obviously unjust. For precisely this reason is God's love for the sufferer increased! Thus, for the first time in the many midrashim we have reviewed, we find allowance for suffering that is not the doing of God. In light of the overall midrashic context, this is a radical allowance.

We must be cautious, however, about reading too much into this tradition. It may well be that the author believes that the wars, destruction, and persecution *began* as punishment for sin and what is here reported is a case of the persecutor—originally performing God's will—going too far. Such an interpretation will merely recall the prophetic view of Babylon (see Isa. 47 and Zech. 1:15). This exposition thus may not be quite as radical as it at first appears. Nevertheless, the admission of human prerogative as a cause for suffering is explicit, and this is a major step, therefore, in severing the necessary connection between suffering and sin.

A second text that similarly unlinks suffering and sin—and allows for a purely human source of suffering—is the midrash at Sifra *beḥuqotai*, chapter 3, 6:

> *a.* "And I broke the bars of your yoke." (Lev. 26:13)
> *b.* They told a parable—to what is the matter similar?
> *c.* To a homeowner who had a plowing cow and lent it to another to plow with it. And that man had ten sons [and] this one came and plowed [with it] and [then] rested and [then] this one came and plowed [with it] and rested, until the cow became exhausted and lay down. [Thereupon] all of the cows came in but this cow did not come in. It was not enough in [the owner's] mind to receive conciliation from that man, rather, he immediately came and broke the yoke and cut the ropes.

d. Similarly, Israel, in this world, one regime comes and enslaves [them] and [then] goes, [then another] regime comes and enslaves [them] and goes. . . . Tomorrow, when the end-time arrives, the Holy One, blessed be He, will not say to the nations, "thus and thus have you done to my children." Rather, He will immediately come and break the yoke and cut the ropes.

Clearly, the persecution of Israel in its various exiles is the work of its hosts, not of God. The parable leaves no room to doubt that this is intended. Probative in this regard is the equation drawn between Israel and the cow. A cow, of course, cannot sin, so the abuse of the cow cannot be seen as punishment. Israel in exile is likewise to be understood as a "dumb cow," abused for no good reason. The borrowers alone are the cause of the suffering, be it of the cow or of Israel.

Again, it may well be that the author imagines that Israel was originally thrust into exile as punishment for its sins, and it may always be wondered why God does not now intervene to end the suffering of the nation (perhaps that very hesitation makes the continuing exile an ongoing punishment from God). Be that as it may, the active persecution of Israel is not claimed to be the act of God. There is limited room, therefore, for understanding suffering as the outcome of human freedom and not, in any direct sense, as punishment from God.

Related Traditions

The exploration of alternatives that is evident in the preceding midrashic–halakhic deliberations on suffering finds little parallel in more theoretical treatments of divine justice or in the few explicit responses to recent national suffering as represented by the destruction of the Temple. In contrast to some texts seen above, where the correspondence between transgression and punishment = suffering is admitted to break down, texts that approach divine justice in the abstract make no such admission. This may be because, as I suggested in my introduction, discussions of personal suffering are less susceptible to detached intellectualization than are discussions of the more theoretical question of justice. Or it may be because, as we shall see, the halakhic midrashim caught upon a single resolution of the problem of divine justice—projection into a future world—that is not available to refutation, and they therefore required no significant alternatives. Whichever of these explanations best accounts for the difference in tone and overall approach between the following texts and those already reviewed, it will be clear in what follows that the difficulties evident in treatments of suffering are not present in this related context.

As has been noted, rabbinic literature in general and the midrashim in particular are often internally inconsistent. There will be no surprise, then, in finding that, despite the obvious denials of measure-for-measure justice found in several of the texts reviewed previously (in particular the lengthy deliberation on suffering in the Mekhilta and Sifrei Deuteronomy), affirmations of measure-for-measure justice are recorded in the very same documents. This affirmation is explicit and common in the Mekhilta (see *vayehi*, intro., pp. 78 and 81, and par. 5, p. 133), where the language of Mishnah Sotah is quoted, in greater or lesser part, almost verbatim. It is also found in another Mekhilta text (*deshira*, par. 2, p. 123), which, though not using the Mishnaic language for "measure-for-measure," does employ the same biblical examples as Mishnah Sotah and quotes the same scriptures in support. These texts obviously occupy the same position as the Mishnah with respect to the question of divine justice, and if there is any difference between these traditions and the Mishnaic model, it is at most a matter of tone: they, like the Tosefta, prefer to emphasize the latter part of the Mishnah's lesson, that God's reward is more generous than God's punishment.[15]

But insistence on this-worldly justice, where the punishment corresponds with the crime, is clearly peripheral in these documents. Far more central is the view that the scales of justice will be balanced only in a world-to-come. This is a widespread notion at the present level of rabbinic expression, and a few examples will illustrate this already well-known approach.

At Mekhilta *deshira* (par. 2, p. 125) God is assumed to be a person's judge immediately after death. Earlier (*vayehi*, par. 5, p. 107) we find one of numerous places in which the Mekhilta declares that God will bring punishment = suffering to the wicked in the world-to-come. The Sifra (*vayiqra*, par. 12, p. 10) emphasizes the reward coming to the righteous in the future world. Despite their different emphases, these texts are obviously in agreement that all will get what is due to them in that future world.[16]

One of the most eloquent statements of this view, stating explicitly that the inequities of this world will be resolved in the world-to-come, is found in the Sifra (*behuqotai*, chapter 2, 5):

> "I will look with favor upon you"[17] (Lev. 26:9)—They told a parable:[18] To what may the thing be compared? To a king who hired many workers and there was one worker who worked for him for many days. The workers came in to collect their wage and that worker came in with them. The king said to that worker: My son, I will look [with favor] upon you. These many who did only a little bit of work, I give them a small wage. But you, I have a significant accounting to figure with you in the future.
>
> So too, Israel was requesting their reward from God in this world, and [at the same time] the nations of the world were requesting their reward. And God said to Israel: My children, I will look [with favor] upon you. These nations of the world did a little bit of work for me and I [therefore] give them a little bit of reward. But you, I will in the future do a significant accounting with you. For this reason it says "I will look with favor upon you."

This midrash may be understood as an apologia for the biblical chapter that serves as its reference. The difficulty with the biblical chapter (Lev. 26), from the perspective of the rabbis composing the present text, is that it promises reward and punishment in this world. Their historical experience obviously belies this promise. The midrash latches on to one of the biblical phrases that may be understood more generally and argues, on its basis, that God's generosity to Israel may be viewed precisely in the fact that God does not—as reality attests—reward Israel in this world. The justification for the absence of present reward, understood now as an intended delay, is that immediate reward comes only to those who have earned reward in small measure; they may be paid quickly and their accounts will thus be settled. But Israel, who has labored long and hard with God, has a significant reward that must be paid, and such great reward cannot be paid quickly or casually. God, therefore, will pay Israel in the future, when the account may be settled properly and in adequate measure. The absence of present reward, in contrast with the apparent reward of the nations, should not, therefore, be interpreted as injustice. The delay is necessitated by the circumstances. Israel, like the faithful laborer, should understand that special reward has to await the opportunity for a full accounting.

Another text on God's justice, agreeing with those just cited that justice is realized only in the world-to-come, asserts with equal vigor that any questioning of God's final justice is utter foolishness. In other words, scripture itself—according to the understanding of the midrash—reveals that reward and punishment await the future judgment, and thus there can be no reasonable questioning of scripture when it asserts "all His ways are just" (Deut. 32:4). The essential elements of the text are these:

a. "His deeds are perfect" (ibid.)—His conduct is perfect with all inhabitants of the world and one may not suspect even the smallest fault in His deeds.

b. "A faithful God"—for He had faith in the world and [thus] created it.

c. "And there is no perversity"[19]—for humans were not created to be evil but to be righteous. . . .

d. "His deeds are perfect" (ibid.)—His conduct is perfect with all inhabitants of the world and *one may not suspect even the smallest fault in His deeds,* for there is no one of them concerning which one may look and say "why did the people of the generation of the flood deserve to be inundated with water, and why did the people of the tower [of Babel] deserve to be scattered from one end of the earth to the other . . . and why did Aaron deserve the priesthood and why did David deserve the monarchy . . . [for] scripture says, "all His ways are just," [meaning] He sits with each and every one in judgment and gives him what he deserves. . . .

e. Another interpretation . . . "His ways are just"—. . . [regarding] the payment of the reward of the righteous and the affliction of the wicked, these have collected nothing of theirs in this world and these have collected nothing of theirs in this world.

f. And from where [do I know] that the righteous have collected nothing of theirs in this world? For it says, "How abundant is the good that *You have in store* for those who fear You" (Ps. 31:20, emphasis added).

g. And from where [do I know] that the wicked have collected nothing of theirs in this world? For it says, "Lo, I have it all put away, Sealed up in My storehouses" (Dt. 32:34).

h. When do these and those collect? "For all His ways are just," tomorrow, when He sits on the throne of judgment, He sits with each and every one and gives him what he deserves.

i. "A faithful God"—just as He pays to a completely righteous person the reward of the commandments that he performed in this world in the

World-to-Come, so too does [God] pay to the completely wicked person the reward of the slight commandment that he performed in this world in this world.

j. And just as [God] collects from the completely wicked person for the sins that he performed in this world in the World-to-Come, so too does [God] collect from the completely righteous person for the slight sin that he performed in this world in this world.

k. "And there is no perversity"—when a person leaves the world all of his deeds come and are detailed before him, and they say to him: "thus and thus did you do on this day and thus and thus did you do on this day. Do you affirm these things?" And he says "yes." They say to him: "sign" . . . and [God] affirms the judgment and says, "I have judged well . . ."

l. Another interpretation: "The Rock!—His deeds are perfect"—When they captured R. Ḥaninah b. Teradion, it was decreed for him that he should be burned with his [Torah] book. They said to him: "It has been decreed for you that you should be burned with your book." He [thereupon] recited this scripture: "The Rock!—His deeds are perfect."

m. They said to his wife: "it has been decreed on your husband that he is to be burned, and upon you to be killed." She recited this scripture: "A faithful God, never false."

n. They said to his daughter: "it has been decreed upon your father to be burned and upon your mother to be killed and upon you to perform labor." She recited this scripture: "wondrous in purpose and mighty indeed, whose eyes observe . . ." (Jer. 32:19).

o. Rabbi said: "*How great are these righteous ones, for in the time of their trouble they summoned three verses for the affirmation of justice . . .*"

p. A philosopher stood before his governor.[20] He said to him: "My master, do not be troubled that you have burnt the Torah, for from the place that it came out it has returned, to its Father's house." He said to him: "To-morrow your fate will be just as [that] of these [described above]." He said to him: "You have given me good news, for tomorrow my portion will be with them for the World-to-Come." [all emphases added]

This beautifully constructed text needs little elaboration. As noted, it again assumes that judgment will take place, finally and perfectly, in the world-to-come (e–k)—even the pagan philosopher is said to be confident of this fact. Moreover, this is considered the clear sense of scripture (f–h). The explanation of apparent present injustices is that the few merits of the wicked and few demerits of the righteous must also, according to the dictates of justice, be properly repaid, and that payment takes place in this world in order that the bulk of reward or punishment—whichever is appropriate— may be duly paid in the world-to-come. To be sure, the deliberation is more elaborate here than elsewhere, and the justification of the claim based upon the reading of scripture also goes a step beyond the like-minded texts cited previously, but in basic substance there is nothing unique in this element of the present text; it is one with the many other halakhic-midrashic texts that displace justice to the future world.

What is new in this text—though not unique to it in the halakhic midrashim—is the obvious apologetic tone that runs throughout. From the very beginning we are warned that God's perfection—God's justice—may *not* be called into question (a, d). The central obligation of human beings, therefore, is to affirm justice, both in this world (l–o) and in the world following death (k). The final narrative (l–o) presses this point most forcefully by praising the great heroism and righteousness of those suffering at the hands of the Roman oppressors who quote these very verses (among others) to affirm the perfect justice of God. Clearly, in light of the experience of R. Ḥaninah b. Teradion and his family, there is no alternative but to assume that such justice will be realized after death.

This insistence that God's justice be affirmed in the face of suffering is our first explicit evidence of what will become (if it is not already) the dominant Palestinian view regarding protest and the questioning of suffering: such responses are impious and are to be condemned. Up to this point, this position has perhaps been implicit. The Mishnah's virtual silence on recent suffering, for example, may be understood as an implicit condemnation of those who would respond otherwise. But, since the issue isn't addressed directly there, there is no need to relate to the question of proper response explicitly. At this stage, however, when the problem of suffering has come under the scrutiny of the rabbinic authors, the question of appropriate responses is likewise subject to discussion. As we shall see, the position evident in this midrash is widely accepted in later Palestinian rabbinic texts, much in contrast with the possibilities that will be admitted in the Bavli. Why this difference develops we will consider at a later stage, though we might already note that the assumptions of the surrounding culture may be influential in this regard. In his *Consolation to His Wife*, Plutarch writes: "For reverent language toward the Deity and serene and uncomplaining attitude toward fortune never fail to yield an excellent return. . . . It ill becomes us to fall into this state by cavilling at our own life for receiving . . . a single stain."[21] If this is the conception of piety of one prominent Greek pagan in the period not too long before the composition of this midrash, then how could the neighboring rabbis demand less?

The defensiveness of this and related midrashim[22] shows an important shift in rabbinic strategy, one which confronts directly the important theological issues generated by the conditions of the time. Obviously there must be those, addressed by the authors of these texts, who are moved by the conditions they witness around them to call God's justice into question; otherwise there would be no need for the extreme defensive tone. Implicitly admitting the problem, these rabbinic authors at the same time insist that they have a solution which is unimpeachable. In contrast, it will be recalled, other texts, both earlier and contemporary, do not even give implicit evidence of the problem. Accordingly, those texts, proposing only pure theory, defend God's justice briefly if at all. But when, as in this midrash, theory is tempered by sensitivity to the human aspects of the problem (here again our attention is drawn to individual human suffering), the claim for justice takes on another form. When the righteous individual and his suffering are in our field of vision, we cannot look aside (so midrashim like this one show) and fail to grapple with the problematic reality.

National Suffering and the Destruction of the Temple

What we just observed in the matter of personal suffering does not extend to related deliberations on national suffering, represented by the destruction of the Temple. The most outstanding feature of the halakhic midrashim, as concerns the question of the Temple's destruction, is that, in those places where the biblical verses detail laws of the Temple and sacrifices, the midrashim interpret those verses with virtually no apparent recognition that the subject of their deliberation is without practical consequence. Like the Mishnah, these midrashim recount the sacrificial laws as details of a seemingly flourishing institution.[23] This being so, it will come as no surprise that these same documents have little to say—at least on an explicit level—about the Temple's destruction, and few traditions give evidence that the destruction was an event worth noting at all.

The Mekhilta has virtually nothing explicit to say about the destruction. At the beginning of *ba-ḥodesh* 1 (p. 203), the text makes reference to the first destruction, but only as a detail in a list and exhibiting no particular concern for the event. Only a text in *shira* 10 (pp. 149–50) hints at any unusual concern for the Temple, here by emphasizing its extreme importance. The destruction of the first Temple, apparently, is spoken of in that context, and perhaps it is the second destruction that provokes the exegetical praise of the institution. However, this connection is not explicit, and the absence of any apparent mourning for the destroyed Temple is as striking as any other feature in this text.

The Sifra—the "Law of the Priests"—obviously has the most to say about the sacrifices and the holy precincts but, like the Mekhilta, it speaks little about the destruction of the first or second Temple. The two explicit mentions of that event (Emor, par. 10, 10, and Emor, chapter 16, 9) are actually brief quotations of the same tradition found at m. Suk. 3:12. These quotations are peripheral in both contexts, and the destruction is clearly not of major concern in either text. As noted, in the vast majority of cases—unlike in these two—the Sifra does not even see a need to update its outdated Temple-related laws.

Sifrei Numbers likewise has little to say about the destruction. Sifrei 64 merely repeats the same insignificant point as Mekhilta *ba-ḥodesh* 1, where the first destruction was understood, by reading subsequent biblical texts, as an event from which the passage of time would be counted. Sifrei 78 also makes reference to the destruction of the first Temple, but only as a historical-exegetical detail.

Only in Sifrei 161 (p. 222) does the *second* destruction finally merit discussion in the halakhic midrash, and here we are also fortunate to learn this author's understanding of the reason for the destruction. The midrash claims that the Temple (which one as yet undesignated) was destroyed because of the shedding of blood. This contention is supported by reference to a story in which two priests, competing for the honor of clearing the altar, raced to the incline of the altar. One, having arrived first, was then stabbed by his jealous brother. Rabbi Zadok thereupon arose and castigated all involved for the fact that this horrible crime could take place in their midst. They, however, were more concerned for the impurity the death would cause than for the death itself, thus compounding their crime by showing their distorted priorities and lack of remorse. This bloodshed and their callous disregard for it are seen to be the crime for which the Temple would thereafter be destroyed.[24] In claiming a specific cause of this nature for the destruction, this midrash is similar to the Tosefta at the end of Menaḥot that connects the destruction to transgression. Significantly, though, the midrash here explains the second destruction on the basis of the same sin (bloodshed) with which the Tosefta (and the Bible; see 2 Kings 21) explains (in part) the first destruction. In this respect the midrash is closer to its biblical source than the Tosefta.

In Sifrei Deuteronomy, finally, there remain few mentions of the Temple's destruction. Two are quite minor: in one (43, p. 102) the destruction is part of the cycle of exile and restoration, in the second (357, p. 425) the destruction is one of many things that Moses is claimed to be shown by God before he dies. The other two references to the destruction,[25] though, are more significant, and each merits independent discussion.

The first text, at Sifrei 61 (p. 127) has R. Gamliel[26] reworking an earlier midrash to say, "You should not do according to their [= the idolators'] deeds, because [if you do] your evil deeds will cause the Temple of your ancestors to be destroyed." Evil deeds are understood to lead to destruction; the destruction is punishment for sin. As in the Sifrei Numbers text above—the only other halakhic midrash that explicitly suggests a reason for the Temple's destruction—the destruction is an act of justice. In this respect, the present traditions are even more classical than the treatments of divine justice reviewed earlier. Those, it will be recalled, mostly delayed punishment to a future world. These two traditions indicate that, at least in connection to the destruction, the claim might still be made that punishment is manifest in this world.[27]

A final Sifrei text (352, p. 410) deals not with the question of why the Temple(s) was (were) destroyed, but with the assurance that it will be restored. Responding to Moses' final blessing of Benjamin, in whose territory the Temple will be built (see p. 409 there), the author interprets the words "he rests between His shoulders" (Deut. 33:12) as referring to a Temple "rebuilt and restored in the future." The midrash then goes on to show, supported by creative readings of scripture, that Abraham, Isaac, and Jacob were each shown visions of the Temple, first built, then destroyed, then restored. The emphasis is on the restoration, with reference to which each thrust of the midrash concludes. Of course, if the bearers of the covenant each saw the restored Temple, then it may safely be assumed that the

Temple will in the future be rebuilt. Such a message is essential, of course, only to an audience whose Temple remains destroyed. This is the only instance in the entire midrash in which this sense of destruction and hope for restoration is so explicit and palpable.

It should be emphasized, again, that my discussion here—as elsewhere—relates only to explicit reference to the Temple's destruction in these documents. Recent work by David Nelson provides the opportunity to illustrate how identification of implicit responses to the destruction might yield evidence of more complicated attitudes to that event.

Nelson's work considers in depth the impact of the destruction upon the halakhic midrashim. In addition to explicit references to the destruction, reviewed above, Nelson reviews a variety of other texts whose postures or attitudes might be construed as responses to the destruction. These include (1) traditions that suggest (implicitly or explicitly) reasons for the destruction (very few in number), (2) discussions of behavioral changes (or the absence thereof) necessitated by the destruction, (3) suggested substitutions for the sacrificial service, (4) what he terms theological responses (discussions of God's relationship to Israel following the destruction, though the destruction is generally not mentioned explicitly in these contexts),[28] and (5) shifts in attitude that might be assumed to stem from the destruction (such as emphasis on the primacy of Moses = the rabbi over Aaron = the priest). Nelson makes an important contribution by offering these texts with detailed analysis, and he shows that the destruction undeniably had its impact.

Our question, however, is not whether the destruction had an impact—that could never really be doubted. The question in this context, rather, is how the destruction is explained and how such explanations relate to explanations of and responses to suffering. In fact, isolating the texts that give evidence of response to the destruction distorts the larger picture, because, as Nelson points out, the texts out of context and read together do not fairly represent the approaches of the documents as a whole. Overall, these responses are not prominent; they are generally difficult to identify in the first place. More prominent is the fact, emphasized in each of Nelson's summaries, that these documents typically give little or no explicit evidence of the destruction—and that is what is crucial in our study. This conclusion supports our own, and the limited evidence may therefore be taken accurately to reflect the tenors of the documents as a whole.

Summary

For the most part, the halakhic midrashim agree with both the Mishnah and the Tosefta that suffering can be justified, and ancient justifications continue to play a significant role. But unlike those other documents, personal suffering disrupts the complacency of the present authors. The difficulty and bitterness break through. They find themselves forced to respond in detail and to marshal their full resources to defend the system. Apologia is the order of the day. Those who respond in a less affirmative manner are condemned.

But this is all true in the halakhic midrashim only where the issue is personal suffering. Where the discussion is divine justice in the abstract, or the suffering of the nation as represented by the destruction of the Temple, these midrashim continue to maintain the position of the Mishnah. As far as the destruction is concerned, there is little to discuss. The Temple is mostly spoken of as a living institution. And though discussions of justice are more extended here than in the Mishnah (where we have but a few relevant comments), they are not different in substance. Again, only in the matter of personal suffering is there evident development here.

Despite their differences, the Tosefta and the halakhic midrashim do share one important feature: they both address one part of the imperfection of their own day where the Mishnah, several generations before, did not. Each in its own way—the Tosefta in confronting the destruction of the Temple and the midrashim in their treatments of personal suffering—grants that the ideal imagined in the Mishnah has yet to be realized. Of course, if there is imperfection, there must be change. If redemption lies in the future, there is something to struggle toward today.

As mentioned earlier, developments internal to these documents as they relate to one another do not explain the present phenomena. Whether as commentary or as scriptural prooftext, these third-century works serve primarily as defenders of the Mishnah, perhaps critiquing its presentation (in the case of the midrashim) but still supporting its substance and extending its authority. The exception to this rule is in the traditions we have examined. If the Mishnah wanted to ignore the destruction, the Tosefta doesn't allow us to turn aside from that reality; if the Mishnah admitted only the ideal, the midrashim are too concerned with suffering and its justification to believe that the world at hand is really ideal. These are important differences in tone and judgment, and exegeses of these documents as a whole do not explain them.

But if we consider these developments against the background of the history of Jews in Palestine in the third century, and the history of rabbinic Judaism in particular, they begin to make sense. First, mere chronological distance from the catastrophes of the first and second century may allow the authors of the Tosefta, and less so those who composed the contemporary midrashim, to begin speaking more directly of those events. Observers of human nature have noted that the first response to personal catastrophe is often denial. Only with the passage of time are those who have experienced loss able to face their losses and begin feeling their pain. Perhaps similar forces are at work here on the communal level. The passage of time itself may have granted these rabbinic authors license to address issues which their teachers were still compelled to avoid.

The newfound midrashic attention to personal suffering may be explained, in part, by reference to the third-century Palestinian setting. We must bear in mind that the third century was marked by a slow, persistent deterioration of conditions. Suffering was not now focused in catastrophic events—as it had been in the prior two centuries—but was spread throughout mundane experience, undeniably and ever more painfully. It seems likely that these deteriorating conditions forced a more direct confrontation with an imperfect, unredeemed reality. Many experiencing the same conditions looked to the mystery religions for salvation. Others, despite the threat of persecutions during this century, turned to Christianity with its promise of salvation. The conditions of the time clearly supported forms of religious expression which focused on mundane suffering and sought means to be liberated from it. Thus if rabbinic Jews in this period redoubled their defense of God's justice while at the same time insisting that suffering would lead to salvation (the midrashim) and that the Temple would soon be rebuilt (the Tosefta), we must be mindful of the fact that this was not an isolated development. It is reasonable to surmise that this was the rabbis' particular expression of a shared religious sensibility.

The rabbinic movement, later in the third century, was experiencing small but still important developments. Lee Levine documents the decline in patriarchal status during this period, as attested in the later rabbinic record.[29] If the rabbinic patriarchate suffered a diminution in power, then the rabbinic movement, which also enjoyed some benefits of the patriarchal prerogative, must similarly have suffered. Even if the movement's popular influence was increasing, as it may well have been, the loss of this stake in official power must have had an impact on the rabbis' status. At the same time, testimony preserved in the Bavli suggests that the power of Palestinian rabbis over the movement as a whole, now with a more significant presence in Babylonia, was in the process of weakening. Babylonian sages were asserting their own right to teach Torah.[30] They no longer necessarily looked for "Torah to come out from Zion." In addition, the flourishing contact between the two rabbinic centers, with messengers constantly relating the teachings of one community in the other, could only have reinforced to the Palestinian rabbis that their movement was increasingly diverse and beyond their immediate influence. To the extent that the Palestinians experienced the Babylonian movement as part of their own, their sense of command of the group and respected status at its center must have diminished accordingly. These shifts in the social and political dimensions of Palestinian rabbinism may also have contributed to the ideological developments traced earlier. Cohesive enough still to insist upon defenses of God's justice, this community was no longer able to suppress the question of suffering and its justifications, even within its own ranks. As structures of inside and outside, center and periphery, became less secure, rabbinic society would no longer support single explanations of its suffering. The classical view remained at the center, to be sure, but other explanations, suppressed in the earlier rabbinic movement, began to find a place by its side.

Whatever the precise factors which contributed to the developments detailed here—and the reasons for even these relatively small changes were undoubtedly multiple and complex—one thing emerges clearly: the attitudes and ideologies of the Mishnah have already yielded to broader possibilities. Though, in fundamental ways, the system proposed by the Mishnah continued serving the needs of rabbinic Jewry in the century following its composition, the insularity of the Mishnah would not serve. Jews, even rabbis, needed to comfort themselves by articulating what they saw and by imagining a time—not too far off—when conditions would improve. It is this need that we see addressed by the rabbis, for the first time, in the Tosefta and the halakhic midrashim.

7

Later Palestinian Documents:
The Yerushalmi

The Talmud of the Land of Israel—the Yerushalmi—is, after the Mishnah, the major halakhic work of the rabbinic community in Palestine in the ancient period. It came to its final shape in the early fifth century, as part of a burst of literary creativity which produced, at approximately the same time, this Talmud, two major aggadic midrashim (Genesis Rabbah and Leviticus Rabbah), and a variety of more minor midrashic compositions. Together, these works comprise the statement of the rabbinic community at a crucial crossroads in Jewish history.

These documents came into being at the tail end of a century of earth-shaking events for Jews. As Neusner enumerates them,[1] these began with the conversion of the Roman emperor Constantine to Christianity in 312, followed by the promise and disappointment of the failed effort to rebuild the Jerusalem Temple under Julian (361), then the reaction against paganism which brought Jews and their holy places before zealous and destructive mobs, and finally the Christianization of the majority of the population of the Roman world.[2] If we add to this the abolition of the office of the Jewish patriarch in Palestine sometime before 429,[3] we will appreciate the gravity of the changes, all with not only practical but also potential theological consequences, which confronted Jews in the early fifth century.

Rome, it will be recalled, was supposed to be the fourth, final kingdom whose downfall would bring the messianic age. Christianity was the bastard, illegitimate claimant to the name Israel. When the emperor of Rome became Christian, these fundamental assumptions held by Jews seemed suddenly and inexplicably wrong. Julian's subsequent reaction, accompanied by the beginning of the restoration, must have seemed a genuine messianic revelation, much as Cyrus and his offer of return had seemed to the second Isaiah centuries before. But the failure of this restoration only made matters worse, and the triumph of Christianity on the popular level, along with the quick deterioration in the safety and status of Jews, must have challenged Jews as fundamentally as the destruction itself. Had the covenant finally failed? Were messianic promises a dangerous illusion?

The precise contours of the rabbinic community whose writings we will examine in this chapter are very difficult to recover. The rabbinic documents produced in this period record traditions attributed to earlier sages; they do not speak explicitly of the period in which they were finally composed. External sources have little to say about Jews in general during this period in Palestine, let alone about the rabbis in particular.[4] Evidence examined by Shaye J. D. Cohen suggests that rabbinic presence and influence remained limited,[5] though, relative to the Jewish community in general (which was now a numerical minority in Palestine, living in the midst of a Christian majority), rabbis must have been a significant factor. In any case, the multiplicity of works produced at this time suggests that the rabbinic community was extremely vibrant, and we know of no outstanding religious competitor on the Palestinian Jewish landscape. Thus it is reasonable to suppose that the rabbis were in a position to influence their neighbors, through careful rhetoric if not on the basis of official recognition. Moreover, the concern for redemption evident in several of their works suggests that they were sensitive to the needs of the larger Jewish population. As far as internal rabbinic structures are concerned, there is no reason to believe that the competitive hierarchy of Torah scholarship had changed.

Neusner reads the rabbinic documents of this period, including the Yerushalmi, as a response to this immense historical and (therefore) theological challenge. In the case of the Yerushalmi, the object of our concern in this chapter, Neusner sees an effort on the part of its authors to construct what he calls "a point-by-point program in defiance of the age: certainty over doubt, authority over disintegration, salvation over chaos, above all, hope and confidence in an age of despair."[6] It is this aspiration, Neusner argues, which explains the Yerushalmi's subservience to the program of the Mishnah, its attempt to clarify that foundation text and decide the law on its basis, its extended argument on behalf of the authority of the rabbi, and its attention to the problem of redemption, which it understands as an outcome of the proper performance of the commandments. Even if some parts of this thesis in the end require modest adjustment (to his credit, Neusner is the only one to have studied the Yerushalmi from the perspective of intellectual-religious history), it will readily be seen how the document is an obvious product of and response to its age.

Reward and Punishment

With respect to the questions of suffering and divine justice, the Yerushalmi conforms fully to its more general character. First, as befits a document that is subservient to the Mishnah, the Yerushalmi—like the Mishnah that charts its direction—has little explicit to say about human suffering (in this way it is also similar to the Tosefta) and it adds almost nothing of substance to earlier approaches to this subject. The most notable development in its relevant traditions is its condemnation of those who respond to suffering with contempt, and this may readily be understood as a gesture on behalf of its search for certainty. In its overall treatment of these questions, the Yerushalmi is far closer to the Tosefta and even the Mishnah than to the halakhic midrashim.

Not unexpectedly, the Yerushalmi's most common assumption is that suffering is punishment for sin. An excellent example of this stance may be found in its commentary on the Mishnah at the end of chapter 1 of Sotah, enunciating the measure-for-measure principle. For the most part, the Yerushalmi (1:7, 17a–b) simply supplements the biblical models already referred to in the Mishnah. These are typical midrashic expansions, many finding precedents in the Tosefta, and there is no evidence of any misgivings either with the Mishnah's principle or with its cases. This position is particularly evident in the baraita quoted at the beginning of the Yerushalmi's commentary, which takes special pains to assure the reader that accounts are carefully and perfectly reconciled.

The text, a Tosefta with an important addition, adduces prooftexts in order to support the Mishnah's measure-for-measure principle as it relates to significant as well as to more minor offenses. With respect to minor offenses the claim, found already in the Tosefta, is that individual acts are combined in the divine accounting and then punished according to their sum. At this point, the baraita (now without precedent) goes on to suggest:

> According to the way of the world, a man stumbles by [doing] a transgression for which [offenders] are liable for death at the hands of Heaven; [subsequently] *his oxen dies, his chicken is lost, his plate is shattered, his finger becomes sore, and [by virtue of these many small afflictions] his account is settled.*
>
> Another matter [or: another opinion]: One joins to another and the account is settled.[7] And how exact is the settlement of the account? [Even] to a single [apparently minor transgression]. [emphasis added]

The relationship among the different parts of this text is difficult to determine. The first part of what is quoted follows the claim that minor offenses are combined, which is supported by a prooftext from Eccles. 7:27, "one by one to find a measure."[8] One would expect, therefore, that the exposition which follows would in some way support what comes before. But the prior text speaks of the combination of smaller offenses; the present tradition—in sharp contrast—speaks of smaller punishments that combine to settle the account of a larger offense. The next part of the baraita, in turn, seems even more difficult to reconcile with what precedes it. If the "one that joins another" here is sins, this point has already been made; if it is punishments, then the point has likewise been made. We are thus confronted with the obvious problem: What does this last tradition add?

It seems that the two traditions quoted above, which are not found, it will be noted, in either the Tosefta or in the Bavli's parallel version of this baraita (Sot. 8b, Sanh. 100a), can most easily be understood by separating them from the substance of what comes before. They are most simply read as differing interpretations of the verse from Ecclesiastes. The first tradition interprets the units being combined for an accounting, described in the verse, as referring to punishments (that is, small punishments are combined to settle accounts of large transgressions), the second opinion interprets the same image as referring to offenses (as the earlier part of the baraita). That this is true of the latter opinion is clear from the final question; it wants to know how exacting the accounting of minor offenses will be. The first tradition, differing with the latter, must, therefore, be referring to punishments.

Whatever the merit of this precise reading, it is in any case clear that the text is arguing for the perfection of the system of divine justice, however that perfection is achieved. Sufferings, large or small, eventually combine to exact payment for a person's measure of sins. Counted one way or another, justice is served; thus there can be no rightful challenge to the claim that God is perfect judge. The Yerushalmi speaks from and for a tradition. As we see here, even its small additions do not generally break new ground.

The Yerushalmi's commitment to this conservative perspective is perhaps most dramatically evident in its deliberations on the great national suffering of earlier generations, represented by the destruction of the Temple and the wars with Rome. As in the Tosefta, note of the destructions of the first and, especially, the second Temple is relatively common in the Yerushalmi. Again, like the Tosefta—and often quoting it—the Yerushalmi doesn't hesitate to add mention of the destruction where the Mishnah neglects such reference (two of many examples may be found at Yoma 41a and Sheq. 48d). But because for the Yerushalmi the tradition is constituted not only by the Mishnah but also by the Tosefta, this tendency demands no particular attention. Following the Tosefta, the Yerushalmi's recollection of these matters may be considered fully traditional.

In only two places does the destruction as such stand at the center of the Yerushalmi's concerns. The first of these deliberations is found at Yoma 1:1 (38c), where attention to the destruction is generated by a tradition that compares the number of high priests who served in the first and second Temples. This discussion leads, by association, to a comparison of the destructions of the two institutions. The relevant comments commence in this way:

> *a.* [T]he first Temple was destroyed only [on account of the fact] that they worshiped idols and engaged in prohibited sexual relations and shed blood.
> *b.* And the same is true with the second [Temple].
> *c.* R. Yoḥanan b. Torta said: . . . We find that the first Temple was destroyed only because they worshiped idols and engaged in prohibited sexual relations and shed blood.

d1. But in the second, we know that they toiled in Torah and were careful in [performing] the commandments and in tithing, and they had [= were characterized by] every good manner,

d2. [so, if they were so good, why was their Temple destroyed?] but they loved money and hated one another for no good reason . . .

This tradition, though recording a difference of opinion, is united in its view that both destructions were punishment for the sins of Israel. The dispute focuses on the precise nature of the sin for which the second Temple was destroyed.

The second opinion (c–d2) is identical with the one recorded in Tosefta Menaḥot (end). It claims that the people who lived during the late second-Temple period were far more meticulous in their observance than those who lived during the existence of the first. It therefore requires another sin—one that was more prophetic, less obvious and conventional—to justify the destruction despite the apparent piety of the population. The traditional justificatory ideology (sin leads to punishment) is maintained but room is made for shifts in experience and perception.

The first opinion is far more startling, particularly since it has no direct precedent in rabbinic literature. It claims, quite simply (b), that the second Temple was destroyed for precisely the same reasons as the first. This opinion may be based upon this authority's different perception of the relevant reality—though, given the contrast between the Bible's explicit record of the sinfulness of the first-Temple community and the available record concerning the second-Temple community, this seems to me unlikely (the opinion of Yoḥanan b. Torta appears to be supported by Josephus, for example). Rather, because this opinion is not recorded earlier and is therefore unlikely to represent a contemporary or near-contemporary evaluation, it is more reasonable to read this opinion as an expression of conservatism on the part of its author; that is, if the Bible or associated tradition explains the first destruction in a certain way, it must be possible to explain the second destruction on the same basis. If both opinions are biblical in their search for sins to pin the blame on, the first opinion is that much more "biblical" in its insistence that, in detail as well as in theory, nothing has really changed.

The text now goes on to argue that the sins uniquely related to the second destruction (d2) are even worse than those associated with the first. This must be so, it is claimed, because the first Temple was rebuilt, whereas the second wasn't. The necessity for this conclusion is eliminated, though, when R. Zeira explains the same reality by positing that those who experienced the first destruction repented, whereas those who experienced the second (including, presumably, the rabbis themselves!) did not. The text continues briefly along this path, struggling with the reality of a Temple that has not, at the time of the speakers, been rebuilt, and it concludes the discussion by remarking: "any generation during which the Temple is not rebuilt, it is accounted to them as though they destroyed it."

This treatment of the continuing unredeemed state of affairs repeats the same extreme conservatism that we noted earlier in this text. If the Temple is not rebuilt, then the generation which continues to experience its destruction must still be sinning in grave enough fashion that the enduring punishment is still justified. The system continues to operate without interruption; if you suffer—on whatever level—you must understand this as punishment. This being so, the only justified response is to identify one's blemish (sin) and to remove it.

The second major treatment of the destruction is found at Taan. 4:5 (68c–69a), accompanying the Mishnah that lists the various catastrophic events that occurred on the seventeenth day of Tamuz and on the ninth day of Ab. Crucially, the latter day witnessed, according to the Mishnah, the destruction of both Temples as well as the capture of Betar at the end of the Bar Kokhba war. By virtue of this connection, the Yerushalmi's discussion reviews the events both individually and in combination. The deliberation is long and detailed, and it would serve no purpose here to review all of the details. Rather, because a single ideology unites the Yerushalmi's justification of all of these catastrophes, we will simply refer to those more limited sections that support and illustrate the Yerushalmi's opinion.

The Yerushalmi's first long discussion concerns the chronology of the events surrounding the destruction of the Temples. A major emphasis of this section is the broad equation of the first and second destructions, an equation which suggests the identity not only of the catastrophes but also of their causes (that is, the nature of the precipitating sins). Such a reading would be in consonance with the same view, unique to the Yerushalmi, seen previously in Yoma. Following the first discussion, there is a detailed and often hyperbolic treatment of the capture of Betar and the consequences of this defeat—with some reference to the Temple's destruction—and from this deliberation, in particular, it becomes clear that the issue, as far as the present author or authors are concerned, is sin and punishment.

This conception of affairs is evident, first, in a story of the siege and capture of Betar. We are told that, during the siege, R. Eleazar ha-Modai prayed, "Master of the world, don't sit in judgment today." According to the narrative, Hadrian finally succeeds in his conquest only when R. Eleazar is killed and his prayer brought to an end; then, of course, God could "sit in judgment." Quite explicitly, then, the whole affair is imagined as an act of God's judgment—if there is judgment and punishment, then there must be sin (where there is smoke there is fire). The catastrophe is punishment from God. Crucially, in the end (according to the narrator), even Hadrian recognizes that this is so.

The same idea is expressed elsewhere in the present text. Below, for example, we learn that Betar was destroyed "because they lit candles after the destruction of the Temple" (R. David Frankel, *qorban ha*c*eda*: "because they were joyful over the destruction of the Temple"). Later, we see opinions which suggest that other defeats were punishment for prostitution or playing ball on the Sabbath or needless disputes or the practice of magic. Overall, there can be no question that the Yerushalmi remains wedded to its initial suggestion—one that, after all, has the most powerful biblical support—that is, God is just and all-powerful, suffering and defeat must therefore be punishment, and the only matter that remains to be clarified in any given instance is the identity of the sin at hand.

The Hint of Alternatives

Here and there in the Yerushalmi's deliberations on suffering we find some important new twists. For example, at Kil. 9:3, 32b = Ket. 12:3, 35a there is a lengthy deliberation on the death of R. Judah the Patriarch and his personal qualities in the face of death. In the midst of this exposition, the Talmud reports that thirteen of the seventeen years that Rabbi resided at Sephorris were spent with toothaches. Why was this so?, the Yerushalmi wants to know. Because "once he was passing and saw a calf on its way to be slaughtered. The calf cried out and said to him: Rabbi, save me! He [Rabbi] said to him [the calf]: for this you were created." In other words, as punishment for his heartless response to the calf, Rabbi suffered tooth-aches for thirteen years. "And how," the Yerushalmi then wants to know, "did he finally return to health? He saw them killing a nest of mice [and] said: leave them alone! It is written 'His mercy is upon all His works' (Ps. 145:9)." So on account of his mercy for these other creatures, Rabbi was rewarded by being delivered from his pain. Suffering is viewed as punishment and reward flows just as surely from good deeds. The ideals of Deut. 11 are repeated here on the individual scale with little revision.

But more interesting in this text is the claim, put in the mouth of R. Jose b. R. Bun, that "during all of those thirteen years no birthing woman died in the Land of Israel or miscarried her fetus."[9] That is, the suffering of this (relatively) righteous man offered protection for others. Again, no explanation is offered for the precise protection that this particular form of suffering provides. But it is clear—in a society where miscarriage and death in childbirth were common and much-feared occurrences—that the form of protection that grew out of Rabbi's suffering was quite extraordinary. The reader could even imagine that, in view of the great benefit of this suffering, Rabbi might gladly have continued to suffer. In any case, this is the most literal expression we have seen to this point of the protective benefits of suffering.[10]

Another story of the suffering of Rabbi suggests a related but distinct understanding of the problem. At Shab. 16:1 (15c) we read of a group of rabbis, including Rabbi (Judah the Prince), who were sitting, studying Lamentations, shortly before the beginning of the fast of the Ninth of Ab. Upon rising to depart to his home,[11] Rabbi injured his finger, in response to which he recited the scripture "many are the torments of the wicked" (Ps. 32:10), suggesting that his injury was punishment for his own sin. Rabbi Ḥiyya refused to accept Rabbi's view of what had transpired, and he responded: "[No!] It is on account of our debt [created by our sins] that this occurred to you, for it is written, 'The breath of our life, the Lord's anointed, was captured in their traps' [meaning, on account of their sins] (Lam. 4:20). . . ."

This narrative refutes directly the conventional view of suffering. Rabbi, in his piety, assumed that his suffering must be punishment for sin, but R. Ḥiyya refused to accept this. His claim, buttressed by scripture, was that Rabbi was suffering for the sin of others. Though this explanation echoes the approach of Isa. 53, and is not distant from the Christian understanding of the sufferings of Jesus (note that, as quoted here, the verse from Lamentations draws a parallel between Rabbi and "the Lord's anointed" = the Messiah), its expression at this stage of the development of the rabbinic canon is notable. Since this appears for the first time in rabbinic texts of this period—nearly the identical tradition is repeated at Lev. R. 15, 4 and the same point, in connection with the suffering of Ezekiel, is also to be found at Lev. R. 28, 6 (p. 662)—it is difficult not to wonder what influence the historical context may have had in motivating such an approach to the problem. Perhaps because of the Christian affection for this paradigm, the rabbis had to naturalize this justification of suffering and claim it as their own. Their reappropriation of this more ancient vision, in light of its recent history in Christianity, is an act of courage and imagination.

Divine Mercy

But these understandings of suffering— even this latter one—are essentially individual voices. They finally find documentary expression here, to be sure, but the reader must look for them. They are not immediately evident in the Yerushalmi's comments on suffering and justice and so should not be given more weight than they actually bear. More crucial, by virtue of its more common appearance, is the Yerushalmi's ready insistence on God's mercy in judgment, an insistence that, while sometimes implicit in earlier texts, is neither as frequent nor as explicit in rabbinic expressions before this.

A brief text at Mak. 2:7 (31d) offers a good example of such traditions. The teaching at hand, attributed to R. Pinḥas, expands upon the characterization in Psalms (25:9) of God as "good and straight." "Why is He good?" the text asks—"because He is straight. And why is He straight? Because he is good." As understood by R. Pinḥas, his goodness is explained in the next part of the same verse: "therefore He shows sinners the way," here taken to mean the way of repentance (*teshuva*). The point, now made explicit, is this: when both wisdom (= Proverbs) and prophecy (= Ezekiel) are asked the punishment of the sinner, the answer is evil or death. But when the Holy One, blessed be He, is asked of the punishment of sinners, God is understood to respond, "Let them repent and they will be forgiven." In the view of this text, God does not seek to punish sinners but prefers to welcome them back and forgive them. If they do not repent, presumably they will indeed be punished, but God prefers to avoid punishment if possible. The justice of God the judge is not in any way restricted here. Still, God's mercy is clearly more important for this author.

The emphasis on God's mercy is also found in a text that is repeated, with only small variations, at Pe'a 1:1 (16b), Qid. 1:9 (61d), and Sanh. 10:1

(27a). The discussion begins with the common view that "if he has mostly merits, he inherits paradise [but] if he has mostly transgressions [to his account] he inherits Gehenna." This tradition generates the obvious question: What if his accounts are evenly balanced? The answer, proven on the basis of various scriptural texts, is that God inclines the balance, wherever possible, toward merit. This, it is said, is what is meant when God is spoken of as being "greatly merciful." The deliberation then proceeds along this same line, concluding with the contention that God, while not otherwise a "forgetter," forgets or covers up the sins of Israel. The thrust of the argument is to avoid an overly exacting picture of judgment and to assure the reader that, where doubt in judgment exists, God will judge mercifully.

The most extraordinary statement of this divine tendency is found at Qid. 1:9 (61d), where we read:

> That which you say [that is, that the scales of relative merits and transgressions are measured precisely, pertains only] to the world-to-come, but in this world, even if 999 angels argue for his liability and [only] one angel argues for his merit, the Holy One, blessed be He, inclines him to the side of merit. . . .
>
> R. Johanan said [that] R. Leazer the son of R. Jose the Galilean says . . . not only the whole angel, but even if 999 aspects of that angel argue for his liability and [only] one aspect argues for his merit, the Holy One, blessed be He, inclines him to the side of merit. . . .
>
> That which you [now] say [refers to] this world, but in the world-to-come, if he has mostly merits, he inherits paradise. . . .

This deliberation, like most others at this stage, clearly assumes that perfect justice will be realized only in the future world. But its picture of this-worldly reality is one in which God is merciful in the extreme—perhaps even too extreme. The problem is that, as imagined here, God is not only merciful enough to grant acquittal to the relatively decent person who has sinned. God is so merciful that, except in the most excessive of cases, even the genuinely wicked individual will prosper in this world. And this text does not even claim that his present good fortune is a way to pay him his insignificant merits now in anticipation of more perfect punishment in the future; this is merely offered as God's way in this world, pure and simple. Is this genuine mercy, or is it a recognition of the bitter reality in which the wicked in fact do not suffer? Justice will be done—so the present author maintains—but the hyperbole of his claim for this-worldly divine mercy allows us to observe that justice has not yet been done. Ironically, the oft-expressed tension between God's justice and God's mercy here winds up undermining our appreciation of both.

Proper Responses to Suffering

The most important feature in all of the Yerushalmi's traditions relating to suffering is its condemnation, found also in the contemporary midrashim, of those who do not accept suffering with graciousness and self-reflection.

The major statement of this position is found in the Yerushalmi's version of the story of R. Aqiba's torture and execution:

a. R. Aqiba was standing to be tortured[12] before Tineus Rufus, the evil one, and the time for recitation of the Shema came.[13]

b. He began to recite the Shema and [thereupon] laughed [in pleasure].

c. He [= Tineus Rufus] said to him: Elder! Either you are a sorcerer[14] or you are being contemptuous of your suffering.

d. He [R. Aqiba] said to him: Drop dead! I am neither a fool nor am I contemptuous of suffering,

e. rather, all my days I have read this verse and I was troubled and said, "When will these three [things] come to my hand [= when will I have the opportunity to uphold these three commands]?"

f. "You shall love the Lord your God with all your heart and with all your soul and with all your might" (Dt. 6:5).

g. I have loved Him with all my heart and I have loved Him with all my substance [= "might"], but with [the commandment requiring] "all my soul" I was not [yet] tested.

h. And now that "with all my soul" has come and the time for reciting the Shema has come, and my will did not revolt, for this reason I recited [Shema] and laughed [= rejoiced].

i. And he had not but completed speaking when his soul departed. (Ber. 9:5, 13b = Sot. 5:7, 20c)

There are several important points that this text makes, not the least of which is the piousness of R. Aqiba in the face of martyrdom. But one of its central concerns—a concern that will become especially clear when this story is compared with the Bavli's version—is to emphasize that R. Aqiba did not rail against his suffering but instead accepted it with joy. This emphasis emerges in particular from Aqiba's response to his persecutor's challenge. Tineus Rufus accuses Aqiba of responding to his suffering with contempt. Not so!, says Aqiba. God forbid that R. Aqiba should not have faced his persecution with appropriate piety! More than anything else, the narrator here wants to make sure that the reader will not imagine this to be a possibility.

The centrality of this concern in the Yerushalmi is highlighted by comparing its version of the story of the afflictions of Naḥum of Gamzu with the better known version of the Bavli. The Yerushalmi (Pe'a, end, 21b) relates that once Naḥum was bringing a gift to the home of his in-laws when he met a certain man who was afflicted with sores. The man asked him for charity, and Naḥum promised that he would give upon his return. When Naḥum returned, he found the man dead. Thereupon, Naḥum prayed that his eyes and hands and legs, which did not have immediate pity on the man, should now become crippled. At this stage, we come upon the most important exchange:

R. Aqiba came up to him. He said to him: Woe to me that I see you like this. He [= Naḥum] said to him: Woe to me that I do not see you like this. He

[R. Aqiba] said to him: Why do you curse me? He said to him: Why [Aqiba] do you have contempt for suffering?

With this comment, the story ends.

It is important to note, first, that suffering (at least that of Naḥum; we know nothing of the source of the suffering of the afflicted man) is here understood as a kind of punishment. But the ordinary cause-and-effect relationship that typically obtains has been complicated here, for Naḥum invited his afflictions; it is difficult to know what would have transpired if he had not done so. In any case, the afflictions correspond symbolically to the nature of Naḥum's sin (his eyes did not see, so he became blind; his hands did not give, so he became crippled; and so on), and their "measure-for-measure" appropriateness supports the conclusion that what we see here is another expression of suffering as punishment. On that level, this story is hardly noteworthy, but for the final exchange between Naḥum and R. Aqiba. Aqiba expresses sorrow that Naḥum suffers these afflictions; Naḥum, in contrast, expresses sorrow that Aqiba does not suffer similar afflictions. Clearly, Naḥum assumes that the suffering has beneficial consequences (atonement for his sin, most likely) and so it is Aqiba who loses by not having a similar experience. But Aqiba apparently doesn't understand this; he interprets Naḥum's comment as a curse! Naḥum corrects him: Why do you seek to repel suffering? Don't you know that suffering has its immediate and unavoidable purpose? Isn't it clear, therefore, that suffering should be accepted graciously and borne willingly? How could you possibly, Aqiba, imagine that suffering is a curse?

The attitude toward suffering that the Yerushalmi recommends in this story is unmistakable. Here, as in the preceding story, it is concerned that the worth of suffering not be impeached. Suffering, it assumes, continues to be an essential manifestation of God's justice, if not mercy; so to question the worth of suffering is to question God.

Contrast this version of the story and the attitude that it recommends with the Bavli's parallel. In the Bavli (Taan. 21a) the story (with minor differences) is told by Naḥum as a response to the question of his students, "Why did this [these afflictions] happen to you?" After he recounts the story as an explanation, the following exchange between Naḥum and his students ensues: "They said to him: Woe to us that we have seen you like this. He said to them: Woe [would be] to me if you did not see me like this!" The exchange reinforces the earlier point: suffering is essential for its power to effect atonement. But also notable, in light of the differences with the Yerushalmi, is the fact that no one is accused of not properly accepting suffering; no one is put in his place for questioning the value or purpose of suffering.

This difference in emphasis is equally evident in the alternative version of this text (found in the Munich and other manuscripts and versions), which has this final exchange:

R. Aqiba [= one of the students] said to him: Woe to me that I have seen you like this. He said to him: Happy you are [= you should be] that you have seen me like this, for if you did not see me like this, you would not have found this [to be so] on my account.

The final statement refers to the fact that, earlier in this narrative as the Bavli records it, Naḥum's suffering has magically protected his students from physical harm. What he is saying to Aqiba is that if not for this suffering, they would not have been thus protected. Again, it is evident here that the narrator has no objection to the questioning of suffering for, while Naḥum does correct Aqiba, he does not criticize him for having assumed the wrong attitude toward suffering. Such concern is the particular province of the Yerushalmi and its sister texts and, as we shall see in more detail in a later chapter, this is a characteristic and crucial difference between the Palestinian and the Babylonian traditions with respect to their views on suffering. The Yerushalmi assumes, with little comment, that suffering performs the function that it always has and thus the questioning of suffering is to be condemned. The Bavli, as already suggested, often models the very approach that its Palestinian counterpart condemns.[15]

The Yerushalmi's comments on suffering and related matters manifest in the particular those characteristics which Neusner observes more generally in the same work. Seeking to overcome the reality of its age, the text strives for certainty and salvation. Its manner is highly traditional—accepting what it has received and affirming the wisdom of old. That wisdom, so dominant in the Yerushalmi's responses to suffering, is offered as evidence of God's continuing love for the Jewish people.

The Yerushalmi's almost exclusive insistence that suffering is punishment for sin represents its commitment to eternal verities. The upheaval of the prior century should not be understood as a challenge to such verities—so their continued and forceful expression in the pages of this document would suggest. On account of these same positions, history, though observed in the Yerushalmi, is deemed insignificant. We continue to suffer because we continue to sin. This simple cause-and-effect formula explains the condition at hand.

The statement of this belief in the specific context of discussions regarding the destruction of the Temple is crucial. It will be recalled that, in the generation prior to the composition of the Yerushalmi, the Temple had almost been rebuilt. Some of the rabbis who worked on creating this document surely witnessed that failed effort and experienced the grave disappointment which followed. By coming back to sin and punishment for explanations, they in part blamed themselves. But they also claimed great strength, for if God's system of justice continued to operate, then they could be sure of final reward. If they were pious and successfully convinced their followers to be likewise observant of God's law, they could have the power to bring about restoration and redemption. In stability, they could find comfort. In responsibility, they could find hope.

They could also find hope in the belief that God is more merciful than just. Whatever the precise balance of the scales of justice, the belief that present sufferings were punishment for sin surely suggested that the sin of the people, even in the Yerushalmi's own generation, was considerable. Could these people ever hope for the scales to tip in another direction? The assertion that divine mercy was more powerful than strict justice allowed that they could. Their own capacity to repent, coupled with God's love of the people, would assure an end to the confused miseries of the early fifth century.

Furthermore—so some few voices suggested—the suffering of the relatively righteous, among whom the rabbis surely counted themselves, could even offer protection to the people. Alternatively, the suffering of these same few individuals could be hoped to diminish the suffering of others. In truth, the experience of the authors of the Yerushalmi told them, suffering would continue. So until repentance could succeed, until divine mercy could conquer strict justice, at least suffering could offer some protection. If the people could not yet be redeemed, then at least suffering would be.

Most crucially, with all of the claims of faith in the eternal verities, and with all of the apologies for the justice and mercy of God's world, it was still necessary to insist that Jews neither question nor challenge the justice of their fate. There was, it is true, a tradition of such pious acceptance in the Greco-Roman world. This tradition surely influenced Jews as it did others. But in the case of Jews, the question of acceptable responses to suffering and apparent injustice was complicated by specific historical factors. The triumph of Christianity—a catastrophic development, in rabbinic eyes—showed what questioning might lead to. The reality of apostate Jews, not spoken of in these texts but surely present during this period, showed as well the dangers of allowing protest to be spoken. So certainty would be maintained in the Yerushalmi, and that certainty had to be, as far as possible, complete. Those who expressed doubts were therefore condemned. Those who might express doubt were warned. The program of protecting Jews from the possible religious consequences of their suffering was complete.

All of this being said, it may have been impossible to insist upon this pious confidence (if only in the internal rabbinic record) if the Palestinian rabbinic community were more scattered or diverse. Our earlier supposition that this community remained relatively small, exerting considerable influence on its own members (the sages and their disciples) and able still to suppress diversity, finds powerful support in the written record we have examined. The program of eternal truths reflects the sense of a relatively isolated community, one which separated itself (or felt separated) in significant ways from its neighbors and knew which side of the separation was good (rabbinic Jewish) and which bad (Christian). The relative certainty offered in the pages of the Yerushalmi is an expression of the ongoing cohesion of the community from which it emerges. The complex range of responses which might have come from a larger, more diverse community under the same conditions thus found only limited expression here.

8

Later Palestinian Documents: The Aggadic Midrashim

As indicated in Chapter 7, the Yerushalmi was not the only rabbinic text to take shape in Palestine in the century following the triumph of Christianity and the failed restoration of the (once and future) glorious Jerusalem temple. Joining the Yerushalmi were the earliest aggadic midrashim—Genesis Rabbah, Leviticus Rabbah, Lamentations Rabbah, and Pesiqta de'R. Kahana.[1] Though they are certainly distinct in their documentary characteristics and programs, these midrashim, along with the Yerushalmi, represent a common approach to the issues at hand. Thus, though a considerable number of traditions discuss suffering in this literature, it is pointless to review them all. Our attention will therefore be applied selectively, seeking to examine representative examples of the full range of opinions (limited as it is) finding expression at this time. Furthermore, because Genesis Rabbah and Leviticus Rabbah are the more ambitious of the four and because they, in any case, record virtually the full range of relevant views evidenced at this level of the developing rabbinic tradition, primary attention will be given in this chapter to these documents.

Neusner's characterization of Genesis Rabbah and Leviticus Rabbah would lead us to expect a conservatively traditional and highly defensive posture in teachings which relate to the matter of suffering. Concerning Genesis Rabbah, Neusner insists that "every word is to be read against the background of the world-historical change that had taken place during the formation of the document,"[2] that same, potentially catastrophic change described at the beginning of the preceding chapter. The entire document, he thus proposes, must be seen as a response to the upheaval and suffering

115

of the age. And what, in Neusner's opinion, is the response of this work? To see in the stories of Genesis the history not only of that earlier age but also of the present age and to understand, therefore, that, though Esau = (Christian) Rome is a sibling of Jacob—a part of Israel—it is the rejected part. As the birthright and blessing went to Jacob, so too must it rest today on Israel = (Rabbinic) Jews. Genesis, in other words, provided the guarantee that the present age seemed to belie.

Leviticus Rabbah, read in the same context, suggests for Neusner a related proposition. For him, "the choice of the book of Leviticus" for sustained topical reflection represented the authors' belief that Leviticus was "that part of the Torah that would present the rules of salvation. . . . If you want to be saved," they argued, "become holy. Since you will be saved through the Torah, study that part of the Torah that tells how to be saved." Earlier, Neusner is more specific concerning what he believes to be this document's unique thesis:

> [T]he sanctification of the cult stands for the salvation of the nation. So the nation now is like the cult then, the ordinary Israelite now like the priest then. The holy way of life lived now, through acts to which merit accrues, corresponds to the holy rites then.[3]

In other words, holy behavior, as translated from Leviticus by the rabbis, would lead to salvation. Though the Temple did not stand, its power was still available to the legitimate Israel.

Even if we agree with David Stern and others that Neusner's claims for the integrity and unity of purpose of these documents are exaggerated,[4] there is no doubt that the themes he identifies commonly occur in these works, and it only stands to reason that their more frequent occurrence at this stage is a response to the events of the prior century and the condition of the time. If, then, we understand the rabbis to deny that the Temple's absence significantly affects our access to atonement and redemption, and if they continue to assert that rabbinic Jews are the legitimate, blessed Israel, we will also not be surprised if suffering is handled defensively and if protest is suppressed. Obviously, the same expectation is created by our earlier review of the Yerushalmi, deriving from the same approximate period. With this in mind, we turn our attention to contemporary midrashic teachings relating to suffering.

Traditional Explanations

These early homiletical midrashim duplicate the Yerushalmi in their powerful traditionality when speaking of suffering and divine justice. Texts that reflect this attitude are many. As expected, suffering is often assumed to be punishment for sin. An excellent illustration of this opinion is the lengthy deliberation on the deaths of the sons of Aaron, Nadab and Abihu (found at Lev. R. 20, 8–12 [pp. 461–72] and at Pesiqta d'R. Kahana [henceforth: Pesiqta] 26, 7–11 [pp. 393–400]). The midrash follows the simple sense of Scripture, where these deaths are indeed punishment for transgression (see Lev. 10:1–3), and the task before the various authorities is merely to identify the precise sin for which they were punished. The only dissenting voice in context is the final tradition, attributed to Ḥiyya b. Abba, who speaks of their death as "the death of the righteous," which, like Yom Kippur, is believed to have atoning powers. This understanding of suffering is also, of course, one with a lengthy pedigree, so even with such variation the midrash remains entirely traditional throughout.

One noteworthy expression of the view that suffering is punishment for sin makes the point in unambiguous and uncompromising terms: "R. Ammi said: There is no death without [prior] sin and no suffering without [prior] iniquity. . . ."[5] (Lev. R. 37, 1). Without detailing the precise relationship between cause and effect, this tradition clearly assumes that both suffering and death are, on some level, punishment. Without sin, therefore, there would be neither suffering nor death. This expression is particularly notable when we anticipate the Bavli's later treatment of the same, because, as we shall see, the Bavli is unable to tolerate so explicit and unmodified a statement of this ancient defense of suffering. In contrast, it is significant that the present author sees fit to record it without comment or modification.

Of course, the notion that suffering is punishment for sin assumes a viable and perfect system of divine justice. The assumption is found far and wide in these documents, and a few brief examples will suffice to illustrate this commonly articulated view. To begin with, sometimes the fact of God's justice is merely stated, without elaboration, as at Gen. R. 14, 1 (p. 126), where the text simply remarks, "[God] created the world with justice." Other texts do elaborate, but with little substantive difference. For example, at Gen. R. 26, 6 (p. 252) the following statements frame the deliberation: "R. Eliezer said: wherever there is no judgment [below] there is judgment [above] . . . [God says] I will no longer suppress my attribute of justice before my attribute of mercy . . . [surely] there is judgment and there is a judge." Likewise, with reference to Sodom and Gomorrah (at 49, 6; p. 504): "I [God] will make known to them that there is an attribute of justice in the world . . . even if I want to keep silent, the judgment of that maiden [against whom violence was done, as reported in the midrash] does not allow me to keep silent." It may be wondered whether the possibility is implied here that other, less grievous wrongs do permit God's attribute of justice to be suppressed but, on the most explicit level, this is but one of many straightforward assertions of that justice.[6]

One affirmation, at Gen. R. 1, 7 (10) (p. 4),[7] reveals some of what is at stake in supporting God's justice. A tradition there, attributed to R. Isaac, remarks that God's creatures "declare all decrees that you [God] decree upon your creatures to be righteous and accept them with faith." This affirmation is thought necessary because "no creature can say that . . . two powers created the world," for, though the word for God is plural in the Torah's creation story (and elsewhere), the verbs that describe the actions of that God are all singular. Thus, whatever one experiences in this world,

whether good or bad, must be the product of that same, single creating
God. Dualism is definitively rejected here (contrast the Code of Discipline,
above, Chapter 3). There is no evil power to account for the presence of
evil. All must be a consequence of the will of the one just God.

The system of divine justice requires, of course, that atonement be made
for transgressions and, as earlier in the rabbinic corpus, suffering here again
is claimed to have the power to effect atonement. We read, for example, in
a text repeated at Gen. R. 65, 9 (p. 717) and 97, 1 (pp. 1241–42):

> *a.* "When Isaac was old [and his eyes were too dim to see]" (Gen.
> 27:1)—R. Judah b. Simon said: Abraham requested [the advent of] old age . . .
>
> *b.* Isaac requested suffering.
>
> *c.* He [= Isaac] said before Him [= God]: Master of [both] worlds! If
> a man dies without [having experienced] suffering, the measure of [strict]
> judgment is stretched out [eternally] before him. But if you cause him to
> suffer, the measure of [strict] judgment is no longer stretched out [eternally]
> before him.
>
> *d.* The Holy One, Blessed be He, said to him: By your life! You have
> requested a good thing! And with you it begins.
>
> *e.* [So] from the beginning of the book until here there is no mention
> of suffering. But as soon as Isaac arose [and made this request] He [= God]
> gave him suffering [as it is said], "When Isaac was old and his eyes were too
> dim."

This text argues forcefully that suffering (in this case, blindness) is good.
It is good, we are told, because it allows one to escape strict justice at the
time of final judgment (following death).

How does suffering accomplish this? The answer to this question may
be the conventional one: that present suffering serves as punishment for
sins already committed. On account of present punishment, future punishment will be unnecessary. However, it is not clear that the midrash is
best understood this way. There is no hint in the midrash itself or in the
biblical text that serves as its basis that sin is the impetus for Isaac's request.
On the contrary, the biblical narrative represents this chapter in isolation
from any larger context; it is introduced with the formulaic "And it came
to pass" (*vayehi*) and it bears no relationship with the chapter that precedes it beyond mere juxtaposition. Thus the force of this tradition is to
suggest that suffering has the power attributed to it (c) independent of its
role in punishment. Suffering itself effects expiation, much as does sacrifice (also not punishment). Surely, since the implied equation of suffering
and sacrifice was made long before in the Tosefta, this idea is well-estab-
lished in the Palestinian rabbinic context. Whatever the better interpretation, the praise of suffering is unambiguous. Furthermore, the elaboration
of the benefits of suffering is immediately supplemented in the text that
follows when we are told that repeated illness (again, suffering) causes a
person to repent—thus also leading to a favorable final judgment. One way
or the other, the benefit of suffering is claimed to far outweigh the pain.

The biblical tradition supplies numerous other responses to suffering that are similarly employed in these midrashim. For example, at Gen. R. 9, 8 (p. 72), the biblical phrase "and behold, it was very good" (Gen. 1:31) is claimed to refer to suffering. How is it, the midrash wants to know, that suffering is "very good"? "Because by means of it creatures attain life in the world-to-come." Why is this so? Because "the way of life is the rebuke that disciplines" (Prov. 6:23). Divine rebuke—that is, suffering—leads a person to life—that is, life in the world-to-come. Suffering is corrective, probably (though not explicitly here) atoning for sin. It therefore has the unique power of assuring the sufferer a place in the future world.

The defense of suffering as reproof, intended to correct and thereby benefit those who suffer, is repeated elsewhere in Genesis Rabbah. At 26, 6 (p. 251), for example, God's frustration with humankind before the flood ("My breath shall not abide in man forever"; Gen. 6:3) is remarked upon in the following way:

> I [= God] said that My spirit should judge them but they did not request it [Freedman translates: "I intended that My spirit should judge [i.e. rule and guide] them, but they refused"[8]], therefore I bend them with suffering [= the flood].

Whatever the precise intent of the first part of this comment, the purpose of suffering is clear: first and foremost, suffering is seen as punishment. But the comments concerning suffering resume. First there is a tradition, in the name of R. Joshua b. Nehemiah, that is apparently corrupted and extremely difficult to clarify. This tradition connects the shortening of a man's days (or the shortening of the days of humans in general) with "bending them with suffering," suggesting, perhaps, that suffering is endemic to the present human condition.[9] More clear is what follows: "R. Aibu said: What caused them to rebel against me? Is it not because I did not bend them with suffering?! This door, what keeps it standing? Its hinges!" The terms used here for bending (with suffering) and hinges employ the same root letters (*s-g-m*). The final association, therefore, is a word play that claims a logical connection on the basis of a linguistic one. The point of this association, as well as the point of the opening comment, is unambiguous: if the generation of the flood had been caused to suffer by God, they would not have rebelled. Suffering, therefore, has a corrective function and works for the improvement of humans. In fact, so it is claimed, suffering is the hinge of the door of humanity—that is, suffering is what allows us to stand. It is the indispensable foundation of human existence. Without suffering, understood in an uncompromisingly positive sense, humanity could not hope to survive.[10]

Another traditional apology for suffering that finds common expression in these documents is the claim that divine justice can be understood only in light of a broad perspective, accounting for a final reconciliation that is to take place in the world-to-come. This is stated, for example, at Lev. R.

29, 2 (p. 672, also at 680), where Jeremiah's statement, "I will chastise you in measure" (Jer. 30:11), is taken to mean: "[I] chastise you with suffering in this world in order to cleanse you of your iniquities for the time to come." Again, present suffering cleans the balances of any sins that might have been accumulated now in order to assure a favorable judgment in the future. As we have said, with such salvation assured, who could complain about present suffering?

Perhaps the most enthusiastic expression of this approach is Gen. R. 33, 1 (pp. 298–99):

> *a.* [It is written:] Your beneficence is like the high mountains; Your justice like the great deep; man and beast You deliver, O Lord." (Ps 36:7)
>
> *b.* R. Ishmael says: The righteous, who received the Torah, which was given from "high mountains," you do them righteousness to the extent of "high mountains."
>
> *c.* But the wicked, who did not accept the Torah, which was given from "high mountains," you are exacting with them even to "the great deep."
>
> *d.* R. Aqiba says: Both these and these is [God] exacting with them to "the great deep" [= to the finest details], [meaning that God] is exacting with the righteous and collects from them for their few evil deeds which they did in this world in order to grant them tranquility and to give them good reward for the world-to-come,
>
> *e.* And [God] grants tranquility to the wicked and gives them reward for the minor mitzvot that they performed in this world in order to exact retribution from them in the world-to-come.

Several additional traditions follow in the same vein. Their point is to emphasize the great future reward coming to the righteous and the similarly immense retribution to be exacted from the wicked in the future.[11]

Suffering and Divine Mercy

Of the many rabbinic notions concerning suffering and divine justice reiterated here from earlier rabbinic expressions, perhaps the most pervasive is the insistence on the ubiquitousness of divine mercy. The reasons for this pervasiveness are, in all probability, both theoretical and historical. The assumed perfection of God's system of justice, outlined above, does not allow for God to judge only according to the principles of strict justice. Indeed, a judge who did so would be cruel and his system highly imperfect. Particularly in the historical context in which these rabbis taught—a context replete with suffering for Jews, where Jews needed more loving divine support and less unfeeling punishment—strict judgment had to be tempered with divine mercy. Accordingly, the claim for such mercy is frequent in these many texts and, for that reason, this theme merits detailed consideration. By virtue of the great number of such traditions, the following discussion merely attempts to represent the range of these claims for divine mercy, but by no means captures the meaning implied in their number.

Divine mercy first found expression in connection with creation itself—
so the midrash (Gen. R. 8, 4; p. 59) claims—when, foreseeing the wicked
who would arise among Adam's offspring, God might well have let the
attribute of justice dominate, judging it better for humans not to be created. The discussion is this:

> R. Berekhiah said: When the Holy One, blessed be He, came to create the
> first human [God] saw righteous and wicked [people] arising from him. [God]
> said: If I create him, the wicked will arise from him. But if I don't create him,
> how will the righteous arise from him? What did the Holy One, blessed be
> He, do? [God] removed the way of the wicked from before [God's] sight
> and joined the attribute of mercy to Himself and created him [= Adam]. . . .

Justice, if applied too strictly, would not have allowed for the creation of
humans. Thus a creation softened by mercy was essential.[12]

Likewise does mercy accompany justice in God's interventions in human
affairs following creation. This point is made in several texts in Leviticus
Rabbah which, along with their affirmations of divine justice, insist on the
simultaneous reality of divine mercy. For example, at 24, 1–2 (pp. 549ff.),
R. Shimeon b. Laqish begins by declaring: "When is the name of the Holy
One, blessed be He, magnified in the world? When He enacts the measure
of justice against the wicked." So divine justice is asserted to be a genuine
reality, a reality supported, the midrash notes, by "many scriptures." But
the text soon proceeds to supplement God's justice with mercy (p. 551):

> R. Huna in the name of R. Aḥa brought [this scripture for comment]: It is
> written, "Of David. A Psalm. I will sing to you of mercy and justice, O Lord,
> I will chant." [Ps 101:1] David said before the Holy One, blessed be He:
> Master of the world! If you do mercy with me, I will sing and if you do jus-
> tice with me, I will sing, whether this or that, "I will chant to the Lord."

God's justice is not an isolated attribute. There might also be, by its side,
divine mercy. But, the final opinion goes on to assert, mercy, even more
than justice, is likely to be at work: "When [God] gave [in this specific
context, to Job], [God] gave with mercy; when [God] took away, [God]
took away with mercy. And not only so, but, when [God] gave, [God]
consulted no creature, but when [God] took away, [God] consulted a
court." God is more likely to be merciful and generous, and more hesitant
to be overly exacting.

This theme—God's preference for mercy over justice—is expressed several times in Leviticus Rabbah, particularly in connection with discussions
of God's judgment on Rosh Hashana. At 29, 6 (5) (p. 674), for example,
though clearly assuming that God acts as judge, the text asserts that, swayed
by the improvement of the deeds of Israel, God will abandon the throne of
judgment and sit instead on the throne of mercy.[13] Similarly, at 29, 9 (8)
(p. 683), the same shift in position—and attitude—is seen to be an outcome of the merit of Abraham and his willingness to offer Isaac on the altar.[14]
Later, at 35, 1 (p. 818), the context changes, but the thrust remains the

same: blessings, rewards for obedience, extend from "*aleph*" to "*tav*" (the first and last letters of the Hebrew alphabet); curses, in contrast, extend from only "*vav*" to "*he*" (two consecutive letters). Reward, in other words, will be extended generously, punishment only begrudgingly.

Pesiqta 23 elaborates upon the theme of divine mercy in an extended exposition on Rosh Hashana as the day of judgment. As this judgment is executed, these traditions collectively emphasize, God is consistently moved to abandon justice in favor of a redemptive mercy. The necessity of this Divine move is explained in a midrash at Pesiqta 16, 4 (pp. 268–69, repeated in similar form at 19, 3, p. 304) describing an expanded dialogue between God and Abraham concerning the judgment of Sodom and Gomorrah. Abraham's claim to God is cogent and persuasive: "If you desire justice, there can be no world; if you desire the world, there can be no [perfect] justice. . . . You desire your world and you desire true justice? If you do not relent a little, the world cannot survive!" As reward for his advocacy, Abraham is "anointed with the oil of gladness over all [his] peers" (Ps. 45:8). God's mercy, overwhelming God's strict justice, is thus essential in God's ongoing judgment of humankind.[15]

The claim for the extent of God's mercy goes still further. As one important midrash (again repeated in both Leviticus Rabbah and Pesiqta d'R. Kahana) suggests, not only is God's judgment conducted with a preference for mercy, but where punishment is necessary, that punishment is also administered with mercy. The text, speaking of God as "the master of mercy" (*ba'al haraḥamim*), offers several scriptural examples to support the claim that "the master of mercy does not first afflict the person [but rather begins punishment with less onerous steps against one's property]." Among the cases collected to illustrate this principle are the sufferings of Job, Maḥlon, and Chilion (Ruth, chapter 1), the plagues that were sent against the Egyptians (note the principle applies to Israel and to the nations alike), and the alleged sequence of the leprous plagues (understood to be brought upon a person as punishment) in Lev. 13–14. The exposition of the latter is worth quoting:

> *a.* In the beginning, He [God] begins with his [the guilty person's] house. If he repents, they [the stones of the house that are thus affected] require "pulling out," [for it says] "and they shall be pulled out" (Lev. 14:40), [but] if he does not repent they require tearing down, [for it says] "the house shall be torn down" (ibid., vs. 45).
>
> *b.* Afterward, He [God] begins with his clothing. If he repents they [the affected parts of the clothing] require tearing, [for it says] "he shall tear it out from the cloth or skin, whether in the warp or in the woof" (Lev. 13:56), [but] if he does not repent, they [the whole garments] require burning [for it says] "it shall be burned" (ibid., vs. 52).
>
> *c.* And afterward, He begins with his body. If he repents, he may leave [temporary isolation], but if he does not repent, "he shall dwell apart outside the camp" (ibid., vs. 46). (Pesiqta 7, 9 [pp. 130–32] and L.R. 17, 4 [pp. 378–82])

This lengthy and obscure series of laws relating to various afflictions or plagues (commonly understood to be leprosy) is now envisioned as a sequence of punishments. The afflicted individual is understood to be guilty and the afflictions themselves are punishments, but only in part. The increasing severity of punishments following one another is claimed to be a goad to repentance. God begins with the least severe hoping that it alone will be sufficient to motivate repentance, thus rendering a full measure of punishment unnecessary. Plainly put, justice might require punishment, but God will punish only with hesitation, and always with the hope that only minor punishment will be necessary to provoke return.

Once the claim has been made that even God's punishment is issued with mercy, certain scriptural tales that describe extreme punishment become difficult to explain. How could God have gone so far as to expel Adam and Eve from the Garden, leaving them forever to toil over the cursed ground? How could God have destroyed nearly all of mankind with a flood? How could God have wiped out the entire cities of Sodom and Gomorrah? Where is the evidence of God's mercy in these catastrophic punishments?

Genesis Rabbah, sensitive to the problem created by the ideology it shares with its sister documents, addresses each of these incidents. Concerning the expulsion from the Garden, the midrash offers what it deems explicit evidence that mercy accompanied strict justice:

> "So the Lord God banished him from the garden of Eden" (Gen. 3:23) . . .
> R. Joshua b. Levi said: When He [God] created him [Adam], He created him
> with the attribute of justice and with the attribute of mercy [see Gen. 2:7],
> and when He expelled him, He expelled him the attribute of justice and with
> the attribute of mercy. (Gen. R. 21, 7; pp. 201–2)

The midrash reads the names of God as they are commonly read in rabbinic literature: "Lord" is equated with God's attribute of mercy and "God" is equated with God's attribute of strict justice. Thus the author merely notes that both appellations are used not only when God creates Adam, but also when God punishes Adam. In the terms that this author assumes, the proof is therefore explicit. God's mercy was a factor even when this seemingly harsh punishment was executed.

The other two incidents are both dealt with in a single midrash (Gen. R. 26, 5; pp. 248–49) and with a single explanation. The severity of each judgment is justified by suggesting that illicit and wanton sexual practices—the offense understood (with scriptural support) to have been committed both by the generation of the flood and by the people of Sodom and Gomorrah—are extreme sins and thus require extreme punishments. There is no place for mercy, the midrash argues, when this is the sin that has been committed. But crucially, it is clear that this sin and its effect on God's mercy are exceptional. On this basis, we may understand why these particular punishments were so severe, but the same explanation also maintains the viability of the claim that God's justice is otherwise tempered by mercy. The assertion of these many midrashim requires a particular perspective, to be sure. To the extent that the argument is effective, God's justice has been valiantly defended.[16]

The Voice of Ambivalence

Unlike the numerous texts examined above, there are also midrashim which, rhetorical analysis will show, do not offer such univocal support of the established responses. A complicated text at Lev. R. 18, 3 (pp. 406–7), for example, addresses the problem of suffering and death in the following way:

> *a.* "The harvest departed [on a day of inheritance[17]]" (Is. 17:11)—[based upon a fanciful reading of the Hebrew root for "departed"] You have brought upon yourselves a harvest of [oppressive] governments, a harvest of suffering, [and] the harvest of the Angel of Death.
>
> *b.* for R. Yoḥanan said . . . at the hour that Israel stood at Mt. Sinai and said, "All that the Lord has spoken we will do and obey" (Ex. 24:7)—at that hour the Holy One, blessed be He, called the Angel of Death and said to him: "Even though I have made you ruler over all my creatures, you have no business with this people . . ."
>
> *c.* This is what is [meant when it is] said: "The tablets were God's work . . . incised upon the tablets." (Ex. 32:16)—read not "incised" (*ḥarut*) but rather "freedom" (*ḥerut*).
>
> *d.* R. Judah and R. Neḥemiah and the rabbis [disputed the interpretation of the verse]; R. Judah said, "freedom from the Angel of Death," and R. Neḥemiah said, "freedom from [oppressive] governments," and the rabbis said, "freedom from suffering."
>
> *e.* "On a day of inheritance"—On the day that I bequeathed to you the Torah
>
> *f.* "And mortal agony" (ibid.)—R. Yoḥanan . . . said: You have brought upon yourselves an affliction. . . .

The midrashic narrative, closely tied to a reading of the verse from Isaiah, describes the course of events that purportedly surrounded the giving of the Torah. At first, as soon as Israel willingly accepted the Torah and its requirements, God responded by freeing them from the domain in which the Angel of Death would be able to exercise his power (b–d, following the interpretation of R. Judah). But subsequently, on that very day (e), they apparently sinned and thereby brought affliction upon themselves (f), including the renewed right of the Angel of Death to act against them (a). This is the "harvest of the Angel of Death" spoken of in the first tradition.

The same narrative could be repeated, as far as this midrash is concerned, replacing "Angel of Death" with "[oppressive] governments" or "suffering" (a and d). In other words, had those at Sinai accepted the Torah and not then sinned, they would forever have been freed from both personal and national suffering. The death and suffering that they do experience are a result of their failure following revelation. In this respect, we remain where we began—sin and suffering as punishment continue to be related.

But more interesting is the hope, imagined to have been realized in that brief period between revelation and sin, that suffering, oppression, and death would in a more perfect world disappear. We might admit that such a hope is natural. But its very expression invites us, the readers, to compare what might have been with what is. And what is, for the authors of this midrash, is a reality consumed by the very harvests (suffering, oppressive governments, the Angel of Death) of which the text speaks. The contrast between the imagined Edenic condition at Sinai and the bitter reality on the outside, set up unavoidably by the authors here, may be taken as a subtle critique of the world of mundane experience.

Also claiming to speak to an earlier biblical reality but subtly addressing more contemporary conditions is the midrash at Lev. R. 23, 9 (pp. 539ff.) which admits that, in limited circumstances, the righteous are punished indiscriminately with the wicked. The text is concerned with the general punishments inflicted upon the generation of the flood and upon the people of Sodom. In it, R. Simlai declares, "Wherever you find whoredom, general, undiscriminating punishment comes to the world and slays both the beautiful[18] and the bad." The midrash then expands upon the gravity of the sin of whoredom. Crucially, while justifying punishment, the midrash explicitly admits that sometimes precise justice is not done. There are certain offenses that allow for a more general punishment, regardless of the merit of individuals. True, no explicit claim is made that this description pertains to the present reality of the rabbis—in context the statement is purely interpretive—but it is not difficult to see how a reader might extend the present explanation to contemporary "punishments" as well.[19]

Leviticus Rabbah 28, 6 (p. 662) also speaks of the suffering of the righteous, revealing through its ironies and silences the ambivalence that such reflection causes. The midrash uses the model of Ezekiel to show that "as long as Israel are in pain, so are the righteous with them in pain." The response in this midrash to the problem of the suffering of the righteous is clear: the righteous share in the suffering of the nation as a whole. If the nation suffers, then so too will the righteous who are a part of it. This is not the same as saying, in archaic biblical fashion, that it is only the nation that we must consider and the fate of the individual dissolves into the common experience. Ezekiel is the prophet who insisted that the individual is judged and punished; it would be perverse to use his model to prove the opposing point. Rather, this suggestion is closer to the opinion, seen earlier, that God goes into exile or suffers with the nation. Here it is the righteous individual who takes that divine role, for what reason we do not know. But as long as this connection is insisted upon—with the necessary recognition that this individual's suffering may not, therefore, be viewed as punishment or correction—we will perhaps be less troubled by any claimed injustice of such suffering. At the same time, we must recognize that this text does not obviously explain how this suffering should be understood (it merely posits the connection); it only indicates ways in which it may *not* be understood. By revealing that conventional explanations of suffering are inadequate and offering silence where an alternative explanation is called for, the midrash suggests critique through ambivalence. The suffering of the righteous does not allow for easy rationalization.

Another text which speaks through silence is Gen. R. 19, 1 (pp. 169–70). There the suggestion is put forth that increased suffering is a consequence of increased knowledge. What provokes this comment is the recognition that the snake in the Garden, called "the shrewdest of all the wild beasts that the Lord God had made" (Gen. 3:1), is also the source of the human suffering. This general position is supported by reference to Ecclesiastes: "For as wisdom grows, vexation grows; To increase learning is to increase heartache" (1:18). The claim is then illustrated with several related observations: animals do not often suffer, humans (who have intelligence) far more often do; scholars, the wisest of Jews, do not require forewarning before they might be convicted of certain crimes, whereas common Jews do (see m. Mak. 1:9); pampered, particular people are more likely to suffer stomach upset than more common folk. This is all summed up in a maxim: "according to the [strength of] the camel is its burden." Simply stated, because humans are able to bear a greater burden, they do. Or, put another way, our capacity to feel and confront suffering is what causes us to experience it more frequently.

This tradition offers an important psychological insight. As we noted in the introductory chapter, the problem of suffering for humans is less its reality than our difficulty understanding it. As is recognized here, it is that very capacity to understand that renders a given experience "suffering" and not merely pain. Thus we suffer—we experience angst—as a direct function of the fact that we are humans. The author here has confronted that ironic reality by making explicit the relation of suffering and understanding.

But this same author has said nothing to justify the pain which is experienced by humans as suffering, and that may be his most radical contribution. It is rare in the Palestinian rabbinic tradition that a text will describe suffering but say nothing to justify it. Why does this midrash not do so? Is suffering so endemic to the human condition, so *natural*, as it were, that it neither needs nor allows for justification? Or is the silence to justification an implicit critique of the condition described? It is fine for us to understand that the stronger "camel" bears the heavier burden. But humans, no matter how strong, are not camels. The insight and analogy allow that there may be understanding, but perhaps no justice. Indeed, by increasing our understanding, the authors have—according to their very principle—increased our (the audience's) suffering, for we now confront the bitter paradox without any apparent justification in sight.

In the two prior cases, I have drawn attention to *what is not said* by the author and suggested that the lack of explanation or justification may be interpreted as evidence of ambivalence, even as an expression of complaint. The claimed import of such rhetorical ambiguities is crucial to the several analyses that follow, so it is necessary here to make explicit the interpretive assumptions which I bring to these texts.

The method employed here is shared by David Stern in a number of his analyses in *Parables in Midrash*.[20] The assumption with which this method begins is that the midrashic expositions actively engage the educated reader ("the audience") in creating and evaluating meanings. Therefore, ambiguities, gaps, imperfect parallels, and the like—all carefully encoded in the text by an authorship which is ever attentive to details—may be understood as part of the intended message. An excellent example of the sort of analysis generated by these assumptions is found in Stern's analysis of Lam. R. 3, 21 (pp. 56–62). The midrash tells of a king who takes a bride and writes her an extravagant marriage settlement (ketubah). After the marriage, the king departs on a journey for many years, whereupon the wife finds herself taunted and encouraged to marry another. But she remains faithful. When the king finally returns, he expresses surprise that she has remained faithful so long. She explains, in response, that it was only on account of the huge ketubah that she was not led astray. By the same token, the midrash continues, at the time of redemption God will express surprise to Israel that she has remained faithful so long. Israel will then reply that it was only on account of the promises of the Torah that she was able to do so.

Concerning this parable and its lessons, Stern articulates the following questions:

> Why must the poor matrona suffer in the king's absence? . . . Why must the king leave his wife in the first place? . . . Does it ever enter the king's mind that, after he departs, the wicked neighbors will test and torment his wife? . . . Is not the king's unexplained absence really an act of unjustified and gratuitous cruelty to his hapless wife?

And so forth.[21]

But these questions are not actually expressed in the text. Is it fair to read them into its message? Stern responds:

> I have posed these questions not to provide answers for them but to show that the doubts they express are indeed raised by the mashal's [parable's] narrative. These doubts point in the direction of a critique of the king's behavior and of the justice of his actions—which is to say, toward a critical interrogation of God and His treatment of Israel. Though never made explicit in the mashal, this critique undercuts the innocent optimism of our initial rhetorical reading of the mashal as praise and consolation. This critique leads, rather, to a second reading which understands the mashal as being closer to complaint than to consolation.[22]

The engaged reader will actively question the narrator along the lines which Stern suggests, as the author must surely have known. These ambiguities, therefore, are part of what the author wants to communicate—part of the message and meaning of the midrash.

Extending our attention to these phenomena to texts which touch directly upon our concern, we may adduce a good number of additional midrashim on suffering and divine justice which exhibit ambivalent or less-than-accepting postures. For example, in a well-known text recorded in Genesis Rabbah (repeated, with minor variations, at 32, 2 [p. 290]; 34, 2 [p. 314]; and 55, 2 [pp. 585–86]), the notion expressed earlier in the maxim "according to the camel is its burden" is used to explain the greater suffering of the righteous:[23]

> *a.* "The Lord trieth the righteous but loathes the wicked one who loves injustice."[24] (Ps. 11:5)—R. Yonatan said: This potter does not check defective vessels, for he could barely strike them once before he would break them. So what does he check? [His] best vessels, for even if he strikes them several times he does not break them.
> *b.* So too, the Holy One, blessed be He, doesn't test the wicked but [only] the righteous, as it says, "The Lord trieth the righteous."
> *c.* R. Yose b. Ḥaninah said: This flax-worker, when he knows that his flax is fine, [he can be certain that] the more he beats it does it improve, and the more that he strikes it does it glisten.
> *d.* [But] when he knows that his flax is poor, [he also knows that] he could barely strike it before it would split.
> *e.* So too, the Holy One, blessed be He, only tests the righteous. . . .
> *f.* R. Eleazar said: [This may be compared] to a house-owner who had two cows, one strong and one weak. Upon which does he place the yoke? [Does he] not [place it] upon the strong [one]?!
> *g.* So too. . . .

This midrash appears in connection with two biblical events: the testing of Noah and the testing of Abraham. These midrashic approaches, with slightly different nuances, justify the testing of the righteous, whereas the wicked, presumably, are at the same time untested.

Before distinguishing the three approaches suggested in this text, let me emphasize that what is here called "testing" is—at least in part—what we have called suffering. This is evident both from the scriptural events to which this midrash refers and from the substance of the midrash itself. The substance of the text most obviously reveals this identity: "testing" is described as striking or beating or the placing of a heavy burden. The question for the midrash is, What nature or quality is necessary to survive these pressures or blows? Its answer is the expected one: the well-constructed vessel, the fine quality material, the strong cow—that is, the righteous individual. The scriptural references also support this analysis, though less obviously. Abraham's test is the demand that he sacrifice his son, a demand that would presumably cause him great emotional anguish (= suffering). Noah is forced to bear witness to the destruction of his generation, to restrict himself to the ark for a lengthy period, and then to emerge into a lonely, unknown world. These experiences, too, must have involved not a little anguish. So, despite the absence of the specific Hebrew term for suffering, this midrash is surely a comment on the problem of the suffering of the righteous.

The general nature of the response to this problem has already been spelled out: the righteous suffer because they are best able to survive the test of suffering. The second statement of this view (c–d) goes further than the others and suggests that such suffering = testing will lead to the improvement of the sufferer, an opinion commonly expressed in earlier literature, beginning with the Hellenistic Apocrypha. The first and third approaches, though, omit such justification. The first merely suggests that the righteous individual is to be compared with the well-wrought pottery vessel (formed perfectly), and the latter prefers the analogy of a strong, healthy cow. In both cases the point is well made—God chooses to test the righteous because they will withstand it. In connection with the first approach (a–b), we might also understand why such testing is necessary; the artisan who suspects that this is a fine vessel needs to test the correctness of his suspicion. Thus is the greater suffering of the righteous justified on logical grounds.

But a closer examination of the analogies reveals several difficulties that may affect our overall understanding of this midrash. In the final analogy, where the owner already knows the strength of the cow—as God, presumably, knows the strength of God's creatures—what need is there for such a burden in the first place? The farmer, surely, needs his yoke to be pulled, but God is not a farmer! Why the need for such a yoke?! Moreover, the first case is an even weaker analogy, because God, unlike the potter, presumably knows the strength of his creatures to begin with (surely the rabbis assumed this to be so!). Why, then, the need to test? The test tells the divine "artisan" nothing that he did not know before, nor does it (according to this analogy) improve the "vessel" in any way. Why such a purposeless test? Why the need for suffering?

This midrash, while it logically defends the greater suffering of the righteous, says almost nothing (outside of the second approach) to explain the necessity of suffering in the first place. The author here speaks through this neglect, allowing his misgivings to show through. If read carefully, the analogies chosen to illustrate the "solution" create more problems than they resolve, for they really emphasize the fact that the most basic question has no obvious answers.

Typically, the questioning side of this midrash is expressed through ambiguity. On the one hand, the greater suffering of the righteous is logically justified. On the other hand, the midrash admits that the system presupposed by such justifications does not yield to comprehensive rationalization. All of the loose ends cannot be tied up. In this respect, this midrash is less confident—less pious—than what we have earlier seen. Again, it allows that, while there may be partial explanations, there are no readily evident justifications.

Also ambivalent and quite complex is the substantial comment on suffering at Gen. R. 92, 1 (pp. 1136–38):

> a. "And God Almighty give you mercy" (Gen. 43:14)—
> b. R. Pinhas in the name of R. Hanin of Sepphoris opened [discussion]:
> c. "Happy is the man whom you discipline, O Lord" (Ps. 94:12), but if he has reservations, "You instruct him in your law" (ibid.).

d. What is written with respect to Abraham? "I will bless you and I will make your name great" (Gen. 12:2). As soon as he went out he was afflicted with famine, *yet he expressed no reservations nor complained of injustice. Similarly you, if suffering comes upon you, do not express reservations or call out in accusation* [*against God*].

e. R. Alexandri said: There is no person without suffering; happy is the person whose [involvement in] Torah [leads to] suffering.[25]

f. R. Joshua b. Levi said: Any suffering that comes upon a person and causes him to cease studying is suffering of reproof. But suffering that comes upon a person and does not cause him to cease studying is suffering of love.

g. Rabbi saw a blind man studying Torah. He said to him: Peace be to you, O free man. He said to him: From where is it known to you that that man [= me] was a slave [that you should now call him "free"]? He said to him: No [I did not mean that]. Rather [I meant] that you would be free in the world-to-come.

h. R. Yudan said: It is written, "[When a man strikes the eye of his slave, male or female, and destroys it, he shall let him go free on account of his eye.] If he knocks out the tooth of his slave, male or female, [he shall let him go free on account of his tooth]" (Ex. 21:[26–]27)—someone upon whom suffering comes, how much the moreso [should he be "free" for the world-to-come].

i. R. Pinḥas in the name of R. Hoshaya said: "Happy is the man whom you discipline, O Yah." "yhvh" is not written here, rather "Yah." Like the one who is being judged before the judge and says "Yah!"[26]

j. So too did Jacob say, "He who will in the future say 'Enough!' to suffering, may He say to my suffering 'Enough!'" as it is said, "And God Almighty give you mercy before the man. . . ." [emphasis added]

The first concern of this text (b–d), already characteristic in the Yerushalmi, is the matter of an appropriate response to suffering. As in the Yerushalmi, the only correct response to personal suffering is acceptance or submission. This is understood to be taught by the model of Abraham, who, immediately after being blessed, begins to suffer hunger (famine). Naturally, by virtue of this juxtaposition, it is difficult to interpret this suffering as a sign of divine displeasure—Abraham's purported acceptance only confirms the unlikelihood of such an interpretation. So Abraham's acceptance is taken to be prescriptive, and the need for an alternative explanation of his suffering leads, by association, to the next segment (e–f), which introduces, for the first time using this precise and explicit language, the notion of "suffering of love."

"Suffering of love" is conceptually not entirely new in rabbinic literature. The association to Prov. 3:12 has already been made in the Mekhilta (*ba=ḥodesh* 10) and its parallel in Sifrei Deuteronomy (par. 32). Nor is the apologetic for suffering new; the same Mekhilta and Sifrei texts, along with others, go on at great length praising the great benefits of suffering. What is new is, first, the language—the fact that such suffering is given a name—and, second, the attempt to say something about the situations in which suffering might or might not be understood as suffering of love. The presence of a name suggests that this notion is already well-developed and widely accepted in rabbinic circles. Given its deep roots, this should come as no surprise. More important, at this stage, is the obvious attempt to give this notion a precise function in the calculus of suffering. Some suffering (that is, the suffering of the relatively righteous) is difficult to explain as punishment. It would be natural to justify such suffering as suffering of (God's) love. But this is acceptable, says R. Joshua, only if the suffering does not lead to an interruption of Torah study. Conceptually, if Torah and its study is the way that God now communicates with humans, suffering that makes study impossible must be God's way of indicating that such communication is undesirable. Obviously, such suffering cannot, on this account, be understood as an expression of God's love—it is the very opposite! This is a justification of suffering that has important applications, therefore, but applications which remain limited. Not all suffering can be so elegantly explained.

The next piece of this text (g–h) serves as a further apology for suffering. The argument, made explicit at h, is that analogy to the law of the Torah itself would require that a person's suffering lead to his "freedom," that is, to his final salvation. The analogy is on one level easy to accept: God is the master and we are the servants. But the law of Exodus describes a master's excessive, perhaps even capricious, affliction of his slave. The analogy implies, therefore, that God's discipline, in the form of suffering, might also be excessive or capricious; on account of that excess, after all, it requires God to grant us "freedom." Quietly but undoubtedly, this analogy declares that there are limits beyond which suffering cannot be justified. It is itself a case, therefore, of what this same midrash above condemned; there are unspoken reservations that indeed must be voiced. If only subtly, the text here begins to work against itself.

The final tradition (i–j), which leads back to the context in Genesis upon which the midrash is purportedly commenting, is difficult to draw out. The version offered here (MS London), rendered more explicit in the Vatican manuscript, again recommends pious acceptance of the judgment expressed in suffering (i). Yet there is again a hint, in the final step, that acceptance is not the only stance that might be supported. Jacob's model apparently allows one to say, "This far, so may it be! But let there be no more suffering!"[27] Clearly, there is a sense that suffering can become excessive. True, following the footsteps of the Yerushalmi, it may be necessary to accept the suffering that has been one's portion to this point, but this does not mean that one must welcome additional suffering.[28] But, then, if one is willing to cry "enough" at anticipated suffering, one must be of the opinion that the benefits of suffering suffered earlier do not outweigh the costs. At best, the acceptance recommended here is only begrudging. Ambivalence, the midrash shows clearly, is the order of the day.

The problems addressed in many of the midrashim above—the appropriate response to suffering, the suffering of the righteous, the possibility of saying "enough"—are also the subject of a midrash in Song of Songs

Rabbah (2, 35). This midrash, like those examined earlier, communicates an essential ambivalence on the issues that concern us. Because of its parallel with a very important Bavli text, it allows us to consider the crucial difference between implied ambivalence and critique, on the one hand, and outright protest, on the other. It also permits us, again, to illustrate the noteworthy difference between the Palestinian tradition, which countenances only the former, and the later Babylonian tradition, which supports also the latter.

The midrash is offered as a comment to Song of Songs 2:16:

a. R. Yoḥanan was afflicted, becoming ill with chills and fever for three and a half years.

b. R. Ḥaninah went up to visit him.

c. He said to him: What is with you?

d. He said to him: It is more that I can bear.

e. He said to him: Don't say this, rather say "the faithful God."

f. When his pain became greater he would say "the faithful God." But when his pain became too great for him, R. Ḥaninah went up to him, recited a word [= an incantation] over him, and he was relieved.

g. After some days, R. Ḥaninah became ill.

h. R. Yoḥanan went up to visit him.

i. He said to him: What is with you?

j. He said to him: How difficult are sufferings!

k. He said to him: But how great is their reward!

l. He said to him: I want neither them nor their reward!

m. He said to him: [Then] why do you not recite that word that you recited over me and [thus] heal yourself]?

n. He said to him: When I was outside, I could act as guarantor for others. But while I am inside, do I not require others to act as guarantors for me?

o. He said to him: "Who feeds among the lilies" (Cant 2:16)—The rod of the Holy One, blessed be He, only comes upon a person whose heart is pliant like a lily.

p. R. Eleazar said: [This may be compared] to a householder who has two cows, one strong and one weak. Which one does he work hard? [Does he] not work the strong one! So, too, the Holy One, blessed be He, does not test the wicked. . . . Whom does He test? The righteous. . . .

q. R. Yose b. R. Ḥaninah said: This flax-worker, when his flax is brittle, he doesn't beat it too much. Why? Because it would burst. . . .

r. R. Yoḥanan said: This potter, when he examines his [clay] furnace, he does not test it with weak jars . . . and with what does he test? With well-made jars. . . . So, too, the Holy One, blessed be He, doesn't test the wicked. So whom does He test? The righteous, as it says, "The Lord will test the righteous." (Ps 11:5)

The explicit message of this midrash is clear. In the first exchange between R. Yoḥanan and R. Ḥaninah (a–f), Ḥaninah condemns Yoḥanan for responding to his suffering by saying "It is more than I can bear," recommending that he instead affirm the faithfulness of God. Yoḥanan does just that. Therefore, when his suffering subsequently increases beyond toleration, R. Ḥaninah considers Yoḥanan fit to be healed. The preferred model has been established: pious acceptance is the proper response to one's suffering.

But when R. Ḥaninah suffers instead (g–n/o), he himself is not able to live up to the ideal behavior that he earlier demanded; he recoils from his own suffering. And when Yoḥanan seeks to justify Ḥaninah's suffering, Ḥaninah rejects his proffered justification; he concludes by saying that he wants neither the suffering nor its promised reward. This is, in the Palestinian context, a remarkably explicit protest against the final worth of suffering, and it is astounding that there is no explicit condemnation of his response in the several comments that follow. We shall return to this point later.

When Ḥaninah expresses to Yoḥanan that he could not heal himself, thus inviting Yoḥanan to step in and heal him, Yoḥanan does no such thing. Instead, he (or the midrash for him) merely quotes the verse from Song of Songs, proposing that those who would not be properly improved by their suffering would not be thus afflicted by God. Again, justification is clearly the primary point of this teaching. Explicit justification continues thereafter, where the claim that suffering is testing—a testing directed by God only at the righteous—is repeated thrice, recreating rationalizations of suffering whose ambivalence we already examined. In the present context, this sequence is distinguished only by the fact that the last analogy is attributed to R. Yoḥanan. The midrash is thus brought to a close by precisely the same master who opened it, and the God who brings such suffering on the righteous is thus justified by the righteous sufferer himself.

On the one hand, the suffering of the (relatively) righteous is defended here. Protest is thus unnecessary, and perhaps even to be condemned. On the other hand, however, the very sage who condemns cavilling at suffering finds himself, when he suffers, doing this very thing. Ideal positions, in other words, must sometimes yield to bitter realities. And, as we have noted, Ḥaninah's protest is not condemned, allowing the possibility, if only by implication, that such a response might sometimes be tolerated. Moreover, the defense of suffering which follows is rife with imperfections which can be motivated only by ambivalence. As we asked earlier, Is God a farmer that he should need us, his cows, to bear the burden of suffering? Does God not know whether we, his vessels, are good or bad, that he should need to test us with blows (suffering)? The ironic protest, the absence of condemnation, and the imperfect analogies all support the conclusion that apology is here joined by ambivalence and complaint. Implicitly but unmistakably, we see in this midrash that suffering is a problem not easily tackled.

When we turn to the Bavli's parallel of these teachings, we see that there are other, more extreme possibilities. The Bavli version, at Ber. 5b, forms the penultimate section of the Bavli's lengthiest consideration of suffering (5a–b; a detailed discussion of this text may be found below in Chapter 10). Without reviewing the Bavli's version here in detail, we may summarize its basic message as follows. There are three nearly identical exchanges, each of which is built on this pattern:

> A. R. Ḥiyya b. Abba became ill. R. Yoḥanan went in to him.
>   1. He said to him: Is suffering dear to you?
>   2. He said to him: Neither it nor its reward.
>   3. He said to him: Give me your hand.
> He gave him his hand and raised him.

R. Yoḥanan is represented in each exchange, a matter of considerable importance in context (see below). The second exchange is supplemented with a discussion of why R. Yoḥanan, who earlier healed R. Ḥiyya b. Abba, cannot subsequently heal himself (like m–n here) and the third begins with a relatively lengthy discussion of why the suffering R. Eleazar is crying; the answer is that R. Yoḥanan's beauty, upon his death, will rot in the ground. This section of the Bavli's exposition then draws to a close with a verbatim repetition of the formula just quoted.

Two points are crucial for understanding the impact of the Bavli's formulation. First, in contrast to the version of Song of Songs Rabbah, in the Bavli the voice of protest is repeated several times and, in immediate context, there is no compromising on that voice. None of the masters involved in this exchange condemns another for his protest (as does R. Ḥaninah here); none offers any sort of justification for suffering. On the contrary, they all agree, in conclusion, that they desire "neither it nor its reward." Second, R. Yoḥanan is not first introduced in this segment. Rather, he forms an integral part of the lengthy earlier deliberation, where it has already been made clear that he suffered the loss of a child and that this experience has caused him considerable pain; in a part of the present exchange not quoted we are brought back to the fact that Yoḥanan suffered this loss. Thus, when we read of Yoḥanan's rebellious response and see his support of the rebellious response of others, we understand that his position is motivated by his own bitter experience. Moreover, both on the personal level and by virtue of the recognized authority of Yoḥanan and his colleagues, we are invited to respond sympathetically to their position and even to identify with it. There can be no serious question that this Bavli text itself legitimates such protest. We are asked to accept the bitterness that personal suffering generates.

The contrast between the Palestinian and Babylonian versions is crucial and, as already noted in Chapter 7, characteristic. The Bavli supports the legitimacy of protest; the Palestinian tradition, on the explicit level, at least, remains apologetic throughout. When the Bavli gives voice to protest, it supplies the motivation that gives such a voice its power; the Palestinian tradition condemns protest or, at most, allows it to be spoken through ambivalence. The bitterness of suffering and the difficulty of explaining it will not be absolutely suppressed in either tradition. But subtle critique and forceful protest are two radically different approaches to the question of how one might legitimately respond to suffering.

The reasons for the difference between the two traditions are impossible to establish with certainty. In later discussions, we will consider the possibility that part of the difference may be a consequence of the divergent sociohistorical settings in which each tradition took shape. But the present expression, in Song of Songs Rabbah, suggests another possible explanation, upon which we speculate only cautiously. One of the specific elements found here but not in the Babylonian parallel is R. Yoḥanan's apology to R. Ḥaninah, "Who feeds among the lilies" (Cant. 2:16)—"The rod of the Holy One, blessed be He, only comes upon a person whose heart is pliant like a lily." In remarking also upon the problem of suffering and divine punishment, Plutarch (admittedly several centuries before the Yerushalmi, and more than a century before the rabbis spoken of in this midrash) writes: "God, we must presume, distinguishes whether the passions of the sick soul to which he administers his justice will in any way yield and make room for repentance" (*De Sera Numinis Vindicta* 551d–e). In other words, according to both Yoḥanan and Plutarch, God's punishment is administered selectively, with an eye to its potential effect upon the sufferer. If the sufferer stands to be improved by the suffering, then God will bring it. If not, God will have to take different steps.

The other, more major difference between the rabbinic traditions is, of course, whether "cavilling" is tolerated. Once again, the parallel in Plutarch is notable. In his *Consolation to His Wife*, he writes, "For reverent language toward the Deity and a serene and uncomplaining attitude toward fortune never fail to yield an excellent return. . . . It ill becomes us to fall into this state by cavilling at our own life for receiving . . . a single stain" (610e–611a). If Plutarch may be taken to represent a common wisdom in the world in which the Western rabbis found themselves (Roman Palestine), then we might suggest that the positions of the Yerushalmi and related midrashim are influenced by the views of their neighbors. Whether or not this is so, it is clear that rabbis in the Roman sphere adopted, for whatever combination of reasons, opinions that are very different from those of their Babylonian colleagues.

Any study of responses to suffering and related themes in this literature would be incomplete without a detailed examination of the longest such deliberation, Gen. R., par. 9 (pp. 67–74). This deliberation offers much of the sort of explicit affirmation seen in earlier texts. But its broad rhetoric is extremely complicated, revealing clear signs of ambivalence or worse, and the text introduces several opinions that stem from obvious discomfort or discontent.

The chapter explores why, when God stepped back to consider creation as a whole, God labeled it "*very* good" (Gen. 1:31). The midrash introduces its discussion by announcing that, from the moment of the completion of creation and forward, it is legitimate to explore the world's mysteries (earlier mysteries should be left completely mysterious). It then points out that the Divine King, unlike human kings, can view all of creation at once, and this capability is what permits God to declare the world "very good." (The interpretation is this: "And God saw *all* that He had made and behold [by virtue of viewing the whole God was able to declare that] it was *very* good.") This suggests, of course, that if humans could do the same (they can't), they would have no problem agreeing with God's evaluation. To drive the point home, the midrash then points out that God's viewing of the world-to-come is what motivated the positive evaluation; obviously this same view is not available to humans! Having emphasized that from the human perspective the search for the world's goodness is doomed to failure, the midrash nevertheless proceeds to explain how those very things which humans experience as bad are still part of the world's goodness.

Included among the various explanations of this evaluation is the claim that the inclusion of death made creation very good (p. 70; here the claim derives from a word play: "*vehinei tov me'od*" is read "*vehinei tov mot*," that is, "and behold, it was very good" is taken to say "and behold, dying is good"), or so too did the creation of the evil inclination (p. 72), suffering (ibid.), hell (ibid.), and divine retribution (p. 73). The argument as a whole is defined earlier: creation was judged "very good" precisely because of those things that humans experience as anything but good. Again, the underlying polemic is clearly directed against a dualistic explanation of the human condition.

Several of the individual deliberations merit consideration. First, how, in the opinion of the midrash, is death thought to be good?

a. R. Ḥama b. Ḥanina and R. Yonatan [both expressed opinions].

b. R. Ḥama b. Ḥanina said: It was appropriate that the first person should not taste the taste of death. So why was he penalized with death? Because the Holy One, blessed be He, saw that Nebuchadnezzar and Hiram, the king of Tyre, would in the future make themselves [as though] gods. For this reason was he [and all of his descendants] penalized with death. . . .

c. R. Yonatan said to him: If so, let [God] decree death for the wicked and not decree death for the righteous!

d. Rather [the real reason for death—even of the righteous—is so] that the wicked not do deceitful repentance, and that [the wicked] not say, "The righteous live [eternally] only because they store up mitzvot and good deeds, so too will we store up mitzvot and good deeds," and thus, their performance [of these deeds] will not be for their own sake [but only for the purpose of receiving reward].

e. R. Yoḥanan and R. Shimeon b. Laqish [both expressed opinions].

f. R. Yoḥanan said: Why was death decreed for the wicked? Because as long as the wicked live they anger the Holy One, blessed be He . . . [but] as soon as they die, they cease angering the Holy One. . . .

g. [So] why was death decreed for the righteous? Because as long as the righteous live they [are forced to] fight with their [evil] inclinations. [But] as soon as they die, they rest. . . .

h. But R. Shimeon b. Laqish said: [the purpose of death is] to give reward to these [= the righteous] in double measure and to exact retribution from these [= the wicked] in double measure.

i. To give reward to the righteous, for they were not deserving of tasting the taste of death and [yet] they accepted upon themselves the taste of death; on account of this "Therefore in their land they shall inherit double" (Isa 61:7).

j. And to exact retribution from the wicked, for the righteous did not deserve tasting the taste of death, and [yet] on account of them [= the wicked] they accepted death upon themselves; on account of this "and shatter them with double destruction" (Jer 17:18).

[Several steps, not relevant to the question of death, intervene here.]

k. . . . R. Samuel b. Isaac said: "Behold, it was very good"—this is [referring to] the Angel of Life. "And behold, it was very good"—this [additional conjunction refers to] the Angel of Death.

l. And is the Angel of Death very good?!

m. Rather [to understand this, this may be compared] to a king who made a meal and invited guests and brought before them a platter filled with all good [things]. He said: Anyone who eats and blesses the king, may he eat and enjoy it. But anyone who eats and does not bless the king, let his head be severed with a sword!

n. So too, anyone who stores up mitzvot and good deeds, behold—here is the Angel of Life. But anyone who does not store up mitzvot and good deeds, behold—here is the Angel of Death. (pp. 70–73)

The midrash is obviously concerned with the justification of death, and is particularly at pains to justify the death of the righteous. Why such a justification is difficult is most clearly evident in the first (a–b) and last (k–n) approaches to the problem: the Angel of Death was created for the wicked (n), for the punishment of those who would brazenly ignore God (b). But the Angel of Life was created for the righteous; given this picture of matters, no good explanation is available to make sense of the death of the righteous (c). Notably, each of these approaches remains committed to the notion that death is punishment. But in the first case, at least, this understanding is admittedly inadequate. Thus these justifications are necessarily joined with several others.

The second justification, in the name of R. Yonatan (d), is the most puzzling. The claim is that the death of the righteous will assure that the wicked not be tempted by the prospect of eternal life to repent and perform mitzvot and good deeds for ulterior motives, that is, to attain eternal life. Instead, the mitzvot should be performed precisely because they are mitzvot (divine commands), out of sheer desire to perform the divine will. Death assures that this will be so, for it eliminates one of the primary selfish motives for obedience. But we cannot ignore the fact that, if death makes it more likely that the wicked will reveal themselves for what they really are, it does nothing for the righteous. Their death is not deserved according to this scheme. Instead, their death is the outcome of a piece of divine social engineering that affects all without discrimination. But how are we to understand this claim? If this midrash intends to justify death by admitting its indiscriminate nature, then this admission is an important and unusual one (in this setting). In any case, this is a highly imperfect apologia. The ambivalence of the apologist here is difficult to miss.

There is one more important problem with the midrash's explanation. The level of pure commitment to the service of God demanded by this argument is extraordinary. Why should it be a problem if the wicked perform good deeds even for ulterior motives? Do the righteous, too, not harbor some hope of reward for their deeds? It is hardly realistic to demand this kind of purity of motives. Moreover, if this level of pure intent is demanded, how could the system finally function? If a wicked person is the one who performs mitzvot and good deeds while hoping to be rewarded for them, then who could be righteous? Though we would not be surprised to see this demand stated as an ideal, it is difficult to believe that it could be universally expected. Moreover, the midrash itself does not seem to sustain this demand. The final explanation that we quoted (m–n) is unconcerned with this distinction. The Angel of Life is waiting for anyone who stores up mitzvot. No reservation is expressed for those who, by those very acts, hope to merit the company of the Angel of Life. Given this contrast, are we meant to take the earlier demand seriously? Again, the difficulties implicit in this apologia are striking, as is the implied admission that the death of the righteous is not easily justified.

The difficulty with constructing an adequate justification for death while simultaneously claiming God's justice is evident from both the explanations examined thus far, neither of which successfully addresses the problem of death and God's justice. The first is rejected by the midrash explicitly (c). The second fails for reasons just suggested: the death of the righteous is claimed to be pragmatic but, by intimation, not necessarily just. The final explanation, referred to briefly, is also problematic. It does not, it is true, admit an explicit willingness to compromise its claim for justice, but it is difficult to ignore the obvious fact—already encountered in several of the earlier approaches but ignored in this final segment—that the righteous do not share the company of the Angel of Life; they die according to the fate of all humanity.

The position of R. Yoḥanan (f–g) is hardly more satisfying. Again, there is no difficulty understanding why the wicked must experience death: "as soon as they die, they cease angering the Holy One." Of course, the righteous do not anger the Holy One, so God should rather prefer their eternal life. What, then, explains their death? The answer: it is a favor to them! The righteous, after all, must constantly, through their lives, struggle with their evil inclinations. Death, alas, permits them to end this struggle. It is this rest, in the opinion of R. Yoḥanan, that justifies their death.

Yet it must be recognized that this is not justice as we have understood it. To be sure, it may be good that the righteous have such rest. But death is a very serious means to achieve it. Moreover, death is ordinarily seen as punishment; this is evident in the various explanations of the death of the wicked. How can it be proper, then, to employ these same means to grant rest to the righteous? Most important, where is the reward of these righteous folk? Is rest all that they merit? Reward is what they were promised, yet Yoḥanan makes no mention of reward.

In the end, of all these explanations of death, only that of R. Shimon b. Laqish is truly satisfactory—and his is one that has, in this and closely related forms, been expressed before. Death is a corridor, as it were, to reward and punishment, and the death of the righteous assures that they—who did not actually deserve death—will be rewarded in double measure. At the same time, the death of the righteous, necessitated by the deserving death of the wicked, also demands that the wicked, who indirectly were responsible for the death of the righteous, be punished in double measure.

Considered not as individual opinions but as a composite text, this midrash has too many flaws, too many loose ends. If we assume that the midrash intends to engage the reader and to elicit his or her response—as I most assuredly do—then we must understand that the questions and inelegances that were apparent to us were part of the message that the midrash wished to communicate. So, as much as assurance, this midrash also communicates hesitation. By intimation, by misstep, and by silence, this midrash voices questions that, even on its own terms, might not be fully resolvable.

A second contemporary midrash requires special attention in this context because of its unique apocalyptic overtones (by virtue of its close exposition of the final verse of Daniel).[29] The discussion, at Pesiqta 17, 5 (pp. 286–87) (and repeated, with minor variations, at Lam. R. 2:3), is as follows:

a. ([In Lam. R.:] "He has withdrawn His right hand in the presence of the foe." [Lam. 2:3])

b. R. Azariah [and] R. Abbahu [said] in the name of Resh Laqish: You find [that] when their sins caused [this punishment] and the enemies entered Jerusalem, they took the mighty of Israel and bound their hands behind them.

c. The Holy One, blessed be He, said: It is written, "I will be with him in distress" (Ps 91:15), [yet now] my children are in pain and I am in comfort?! [Consequently,] as though it were possible, "He withdrew His right hand in the presence of the foe."

d. But, in the end, [God] revealed it to Daniel, as it is said, "But you, go on to the end" (Dan 12:12)

e. [Daniel] said to him: [Am I called] to give judgment and account?!

f. The Holy One, blessed be He, said to him: "you shall rest" (ibid.).

g. He [Daniel] said to Him: An eternal rest?

h. [God] said to him: "and [subsequently] arise." (ibid.)

i. He said to Him: Master of the worlds! With whom [shall I arise]? With the righteous or with the wicked?

j. [God] said to him: "to your destiny" (ibid.), [meaning] with the righteous who are like you.

k. He said to him: When?

l. He [God] said to him: "At the end of days." (ibid.)

m. He said before Him: Master of the worlds! At the end of days [*yamim*] or at the end of the right hand [*yamin*—the Hebrew term for days is written in the later plural form, allowing it to be read also as "right hand"]?

> *n.* [God] said to him: At the end of "the right hand," [meaning] at the end of [the enslavement of] the right hand that is enslaved. [God] said: I have put a limit on [the enslavement of] my right hand. For as long as my children are enslaved, [so too] will my right hand be enslaved. When I have redeemed my children I will redeem my right hand. . . .

The anticipation of the future world—the setting for the final reward of the righteous—pervades this entire text. What makes it notable is its clear sense, along with Daniel, that the arrival of that end-time is already scheduled; those who await it as yet unredeemed will not have to wait forever. Unlike most of rabbinic literature, which suppresses in an extreme way this sort of apocalyptic coloring, here the apocalyptic tenor is less suppressed.[30] The midrash declares (n) that there is a limit to enslavement and that redemption is not only anticipated but scheduled. In this respect, the expectation of redemption is far more palpable than in most rabbinic texts.

But, also like apocalyptic literature, this text assumes a determinate but unknown period during which God's justice, on the national scale, is not yet accomplished. This affinity with the apocalyptic genre is crucial, for it allows an admission that current reality is, indeed, difficult to reconcile with God's justice. The present condition is one of enslavement. Its imperfection is palpable and explicit, and it needs to be resolved. In this manner, the midrash confronts history directly and finds itself forced to respond honestly. We have seen, in earlier chapters, that not all rabbinic documents before this have been willing to confront history so directly, and the Mishnah was willing to deny the import of history virtually outright. By assuming apocalyptic overtones, the present text does the opposite. It makes suffering and injustice an undeniable part of historical time, an imperfect time of change leading (scripture along with the present author guarantees) to redemption. Placing itself in history, this midrash grants the importance of history. In the context we have described, this is a move of great courage.

Lamentations Rabbah

In confronting the problem of history and its unjust imperfection, the midrash examined immediately above is not alone. Because of the theme of its underlying scriptural text (the destruction of the Jerusalem Temple), Lamentations Rabbah addresses recent historical events (the second destruction and the Bar Kokhba defeat) and, by extension, also the problem of suffering and persecution at length. This work thus merits special consideration in this chapter. Fortunately, several recent studies by notable scholars have addressed this midrash in detail, and we may therefore depend upon their research. In reviewing this research, we give special attention only to those few extended texts that relate to our subject and at the same time offer unique approaches to the issue at hand.

A review of the topical program of the midrash makes clear that this document's approach to the problem of suffering is, again on the explicit level, even less varied than the canonical tradition from which it presumably may draw. The analyses of both Jacob Neusner and Shaye J. D. Cohen show that Lamentations Rabbah is of the opinion that suffering is punishment for sin, and that almost exclusively.[31] A quick perusal of this midrash shows the centrality of this theme. Characteristic is the search for individual sins that can be understood to stand at the root of each destruction.[32] Furthermore, there is little room for views which express explicit dissent. In these ways, Lamentations Rabbah stands as another example of the profound conservatism that marks rabbinic documents of this period.

One of many examples of the midrash's position is the lengthy composition in chapter 2 which describes the Bar Kokhba fiasco and the destruction of Betar and environs. No point is served by analyzing the composition as a whole; most of it is a catalogue of the vast destruction that was caused by the war. I simply repeat traditions that, implicitly or explicitly, suggest reasons for the defeat and desolation:[33]

> 1. Three and a half years did Hadrian besiege Betar, and R. Eleazar ha-Modai sat, in sackcloth and ashes, and prayed and said, "Master of the worlds! Don't sit in *judgment* today! Don't sit in *judgment* today!"

The impending disaster is understood as the judgment of God. It may be possible to delay that judgment, but only by virtue of the exceptional merit of R. Eleazar. The basic point remains the same: if the defeat is judgment, it must be punishment for sin.

The centrality of God's place in these events is repeated below, following Bar Kokhba's death, when, seeing the snake wound around the neck of his corpse, Hadrian comments (speaking the truth):

> 2. "If his God had not killed him, who could possibly have taken him?!"

Immediately following, and then in several subsequent traditions, the midrash records various reasons for the disaster:

> 3. Why was [Betar] destroyed? Because they kindled lights on account of [joy over] the destruction of the temple. (A long narrative follows explaining why the residents of Betar took joy in this.)
> 4. Why was [Mt. Shimeon] destroyed? If you say that it was on account of prostitution, was there not one young woman [who was a prostitute] and they expelled her? So why was it destroyed? . . . because they played ball on Shabbat.
> 5. [There were three other cities. And why were they destroyed?] [One] because of internal strife [and one] because of [prohibited] magic [and one] because of prostitution.

All of these explanations pertain to the period following the second destruction. But, lest the reader not recall that sin was also at the root of the first destruction and its attendant events, the midrash makes several such sins explicit: "because they did not observe the sabbatical year . . . and because they tread the winepresses on Shabbat . . . and because they did not engage in the war of Torah." The details may change, but the basic point remains the same.

However, as Cohen suggests,[34] the predominant conventional view is not the only one to find record in Lamentations Rabbah. This midrash differs from other texts of its time and place in at least giving voice to the Jobian complaint and in being willing to consider natural, political causes at the root of the destruction. Moreover, a close reading of texts which do not obviously register complaint or protest shows that the apologetic surface of this midrash is, on more than a few occasions, pocked with a variety of more subtle surrenderings to imperfection.

The ambivalence which accompanies the overall apologetic posture of Lamentations Rabbah is made evident in many of David Stern's analyses. The text we considered earlier in this chapter implicitly accuses God the king of gratuitous and unjustified cruelty toward Israel. This same sort of accusation is carried forward in what Stern calls a "subgenre" of parables in this midrash, labeled by him the "complaint-mashal."[35] In one such text, the author expresses to God: "You! You do not seem to care about Your nation. You leave them among the nations . . ." (quoted at p. 134). In another, the Community of Israel opens its statement to God by declaring "I am accustomed to suffer whatever You bring upon me" and proceeding to complain that God was unfair for having banished Israel (ibid.). Both by implication and in more direct ways, Stern finds that this midrash is often in a position of protesting the injustice of Israel's continued sufferings.

Other Lamentations Rabbah texts remark upon the imperfection of God's justice as it pertains to Israel at far greater length and with remarkable frankness. One outstanding case is the story of the besieging of Jerusalem by Vespasian and the escape from the city of Yoḥanan b. Zakkai (Chapter 1, Buber, pp. 65ff.). This narrative—well-known by virtue of its later record in the Babylonian Talmud—barely addresses the question of why the destruction takes place. To be sure, it makes clear that God's design is in some way at work in the events which transpire; for example, if Vespasian were not about to become king (= emperor), God (according to the testimony of scripture) would not have let Jerusalem fall into his hands.[36] However, when describing the events leading to the destruction as such, the midrash lists a very worldly sequence of events: zealots burn the city's storehouses in order to arouse the people from their passivity; the elimination of supplies leads to famine, and no conciliatory step is able to be taken because the zealots maintain their stubborn insistence on unyielding antagonism to the Roman forces; the destruction ensues. Not only is God not mentioned in the relevant part of the narrative (even by implication), but what is described suggests that mere worldly events are at the source of the destruction. If another, more theological explanation is assumed here, then it is at least striking that "the essence is absent from the book." Certainly the details this text chooses to relate or not relate convey meaning. If an androcentric explanation of the destruction is necessary, then God must have been absent at this crucial time. In other circumstances, we would have no problem describing such absence as criminal negligence.[37]

Another story that describes the destruction, the well-known (again, by virtue of its appearance in the Babylonian Talmud) story of "Kamẓa and Bar Kamẓa," makes the same point with greater clarity and force. The narrative (at Chapter 4, Buber, pp. 142–3) relates that a certain gentleman in Jerusalem made a festive meal and directed his agent to bring his friend Kimẓa (this is the record of his name in Buber's version). Unfortunately, the agent brought the wrong Kimẓa, a fellow who was instead an enemy of the host. Following an ugly exchange, the host refused to allow this Kimẓa to remain, ejecting him forcibly. Since a certain rabbi present at the feast did nothing to prevent this outrage, Kimẓa determined to take revenge. He approached the emperor and claimed that the Jews were rebelling against him. Kimẓa then conspired to make it appear that this was so. As a result, the emperor directed his forces against the Jews and destroyed the Temple. In the end, the failure of the rabbi to condemn the host is identified as the cause of the destruction.

Nowhere here is there mention of God. Nowhere is there explicit mention of sin. The destruction results from hatred, callousness, resignation, and vengefulness. All are human qualities and, while they may be bad, they are not described here as sins—certainly not in the conventional sense. Overall, the events are as prosaic as could be. Unmistakably, the silence here bespeaks a point. The destruction, in the opinion of this narrative, is attributable solely to human causes.

It is tempting to equate this story with the claim made in the Tosefta and elsewhere that Jerusalem was destroyed on account of baseless hatred, where such hatred is clearly understood to be a sin and the destruction a punishment. It seems to me, however, that this would be a mistake. Though this opinion was obviously available in the Palestinian tradition from which this midrash drew, the author of this story chose not to quote it; that choice is significant. Moreover, the complete lack of scriptural or traditional reference here (in contrast the prior text) and its otherwise natural tenor suggest that the author wants to downplay, if not to deny, the element of divine intervention. For these reasons I claim that equation with the earlier tradition ("baseless hatred") would be a mistake. Once again, then, God is absent when Israel suffers its most extreme sufferings. The midrash finds itself in the position of ignoring, and thus implicitly rejecting, the very same conventional explanations it elsewhere supports. Going one step further, we may perhaps even propose that the text's silence to God represents its own claim that God, at the moment of Israel's tragedy, was inexcusably silent.[38]

A final significant text, the last section of proem 24, returns us to the realm of the divine. Its message is entirely other than we have been accustomed to, as careful examination will reveal. But there is some confusion as to the integrity of the text here, and we must thus proceed with caution. The entire narrative is included only in Sephardic manuscripts of the midrash,[39] and Buber judges important sections, and perhaps even the entire present text, as a later borrowing to Lamentations Rabbah.[40] Indeed, the very strangeness of the text, in context, is part of what motivates Buber to make this judgment. It would be a mistake, however, to discount what we will see merely because it is unusual. A more cautious approach requires that we consider this midrash in the context we now find it, while recognizing that its evidence for this stage of the development of Palestinian rabbinism is not as secure as we might like.

The deliberation, attributed to R. Samuel b. Naḥman, describes what occurred in heaven immediately after the destruction of the Temple. The narrative begins with Abraham coming before God and lamenting the destruction, asking what was so horrible with this people (Israel) that they deserved to suffer this humiliation. Seeing that Abraham gets no answer, the ministering angels take up the lament, an act which provokes God to respond. God is finally brought to engage Abraham directly, at which point Abraham addresses the question to God: "Why have you banished your children and given them into the hands of the nations, who have killed them with all kinds of horrible deaths, and have destroyed the Temple, the place where I brought my son Isaac up as a sacrifice before you?" God's answer to Abraham is the expected one: "Your children have sinned and transgressed the entire Torah. . . ." So far, drama, but no surprises.

Then the story takes a significant turn. Challenged by Abraham to bring witnesses to support his claim, God calls upon the Torah and all of the letters of the Hebrew alphabet. As each one comes to render testimony, Abraham dissuades each, in turn, shaming each for even considering testifying against Israel. How could the Torah, for example, testify against Israel, when they had accepted it after all other nations had not? Or how could the *aleph* testify against Israel, who had accepted the commandment that begins with this letter—"I am the Lord, your God . . ."—while others had not? And so forth. The point is clear: whatever the sins of Israel, their merits still put them above all other nations. What justice is there, therefore, in their present condition?

Abraham, Isaac, Jacob, and Moses each then stand before God to remind God of their individual merits. Seeing their extraordinary merits, how could God consider allowing such a fate to befall their descendants? God has no response, so Moses goes ahead, with the guidance of Jeremiah, to find the Babylonian exiles. When they see him, they expect him to redeem them (as he did their ancestors in Egypt). At this point, God is forced to put a stop to matters, so a heavenly voice declares, "*It is a decree from me!*" Moses yields to the inevitable, but promises (on his own word) that the restoration would follow in short order.

Thereupon, Moses returns to the company of the forefathers, who ask what the enemy did to their children. Moses reports in some detail the suffering of the exiles. At this stage, the forefathers begin lamenting what they have heard, laments that amount to no less than accusations. Following, Moses curses the sun for not having darkened when the enemy was approaching the Temple. The sun responds that it would have liked to but was not permitted. The inevitable question is, Not permitted by whom? The answer must be God and the heavenly entourage. God, in other words, cooperates with the enemy. God frustrates the designs of the supporters of Israel.

Moses (not God!) then addresses the captors, asking them not to be overly cruel as they kill and destroy Israel and reminding them that a time will come when "the Master of Heaven will demand an accounting" of them. In context, this is a statement of great irony, for, from all we have seen, it hardly seems as if God is the least bit concerned with what is being done to Israel. In any case, the "Chaldeans" (= Babylonians) ignore Moses' request and proceed with utmost cruelty. This section ends with a mother and father weeping and mourning over their murdered child.

In one version of the midrash, the narrative ends at this point.[41] But another continues by telling of Rachel presenting her case before God, arguing that, as she had overcome her jealousy of her sister Leah and helped Leah deceive Jacob in his bed the night of their wedding, so should God overcome God's jealously of the idols—who are nothing, after all—and have compassion upon Israel. God complies and promises to restore Israel.

Several elements of this narrative deserve special consideration. To begin with, though the conventional explanation of the destruction, offered by God, is where the midrash begins, the conclusion clearly brings us elsewhere. The conventional explanation yields not resignation, but challenge and rebuttal. Asked to prove the claim, God is, in the end, left without any witnesses. We all know the worth of unsupported claims! So the expected answer is unsupported—literally indefensible—and an alternative must be sought.

Before addressing the alternative, we should emphasize the importance of Abraham's rebuttal of God's witnesses. Abraham's argument is, at each stage, that Israel is basically righteous—at least in a relative sense. They have accepted the Torah and have, by and large, observed its precepts. Undoubtedly, they have sinned, but what is their sin compared to that of the nations? Here we return to the indictment typical of the late apocalyptic works (see Chapter 3): What justice is done when Israel suffers for her relatively minor sins while the nations do not suffer for their more severe ones? There is no answer to this question. The indictment of God's justice is clear and forceful.

So what, in the end, is the explanation of the tribulations suffered by Israel? "It is a [divine] decree!" Nothing more than that. This, remarkably, is simply one of Josephus' several explanations (*Wars* 6. 4. 8 [267]), probably reflecting popular opinion. But the rabbis use it here, as far as I know, for the first time. And by relying on this explanation, they admit that there is no other, more reasonable explanation. The destruction was not punishment, not justice, only arbitrary divine will. In this context, no other defense is considered possible.

In one version of the midrash, the narrative ends with the sun describing

God as Israel's enemy (at least effectively so) and with evidence that Moses, Israel's only real hopeful protector here, doesn't have the power to realize his hopes. The last words literally have us crying and hanging our heads with Jewish parents who have witnessed the murder of their own child. The bitter indictment represented in these words is unparalleled. God the villain, unrepentant to the end, is present only in the echo of God's earlier, heartless decree.

The other, extended ending, speaking of God yielding to Rachel's argument, seems to offer God in a more favorable light. At least the narrative ends with the assurance of Israel's restoration. But David Stern argues for a different reading of this section:

> It also implies a devastating critique of God's past deeds. For His wrath, we now learn, has been fueled by jealousy, the envy of idols; and yet, as Rachel reminds God, idols do not even possess "substance." God, in His own words, has been jealous of literally nothing, and Israel has accordingly suffered on account of literally nothing. And when God finally acknowledges His pettiness and puts aside His anger, the sole motive for this change of heart seems to be the shame at being found out to be so petty, not real concern for the Jews' plight.[42]

Even in this version, then, God does not escape scathing indictment. In this single, remarkable text, the anger and bitterness that some Jews must have felt comes through with full force.

Though the subject matter of this midrash concerns the first destruction, it was composed by the rabbis long after the second destruction; there can be no question that the rhetoric directs our attention to the latter time. In this later period, older explanations are unsatisfactory. In this context, Jeremiah, the great accuser of the people, can participate only in silence. So many years after the second destruction, conventional covenantal explanations break down, at least for certain bold authors.

Summary

The most prominent features of the works of this period (reviewed in this chapter and Chapter 7) as they relate to suffering and divine justice are these: (1) The ancient biblical explanation of suffering as punishment for sin in a perfect system of divine justice remains the dominant one on an explicit level. (2) Explicit protest against one's suffering or cavilling at the justice of God is condemned. (3) Nevertheless, ambivalence in these matters is often evident in the formulation of specific texts, and few contemporary compositions even express their complaints or accusations more directly. How are we to understand these features in light of the context in which this literature took shape?

The injustice of the condition in which the Jews found themselves in early fifth-century Palestine was, from the perspective of Jews themselves, undeniable. The "spillover" from the continuing antipagan reaction, the loss of political leadership, subjugation to a proud Christian empire—these were realities that all Palestinian Jews had to confront and explain. But only in the rabbinic teachings examined above do we still preserve a record of contemporary Jewish explanations and reactions.

The rabbis' first reaction to these conditions was to reassert that, properly understood, it was all just. Suffering was still punishment for sin, and those who sinned more would be punished more—in the world-to-come. If fact, so they argued, God was actually merciful, not cruel. And God's mercy would be evident to anyone who could see the whole picture—not yet available to human scrutiny. Of course, if the system of divine justice continued to work as biblically promised and as interpreted by the rabbis, then there was no reason to despair, no reason to conclude that the ancient covenant had been replaced by a new one. If contemporary history remained, in effect, biblical history, then the Bible's promises could still be the source of comfort and hope.

Still, it had to be admitted that contemporary conditions raised serious questions and even doubts. And the triumph of Christianity showed what disastrous ends such questions or doubts might lead to. Asking "Where was God?," "What happened to God's covenantal commitments?," "What is the meaning of my suffering?," and so forth, could lead a person astray. Not surprisingly, then, these rabbis condemned such questions and refused, with the rarest exception, to give them an official hearing. The danger of asking, "This is Torah and this its reward?," recounted in the story of the apostasy of "The Other," demanded that such questioning not be tolerated.

Crucially, the rabbis were apparently in a position not to tolerate the expression of these doubts. As discussed in the preceding chapter, the continued demographic and geographic limitations of the Palestinian rabbis meant that they could, in their official documents, insist upon certain views and suppress others. It seems clear that rabbinic practice was relatively less diverse here than in Babylonia—this condition itself a luxury of the limits just mentioned—and thus the written record did not have to account for a more varied reality. Moreover, by this stage, if the documentary record is to be believed, communications between the Palestinian and Babylonian rabbinic communities had been reduced to a minimum, so the horizon of consciousness of these sages was genuinely limited to their relatively small number. True, it is likely that increasing numbers of Palestinian Jews were now rabbinized, meaning that the powerful cohesion of earlier rabbinic generations may have been compromised by the infusion of larger numbers of outsiders—Jews who, whatever their explicit religious commitments, preserved some of their earlier, nonrabbinic practices. But the written record, at least, speaks to the rabbinic elite, not to the rabbinized population in general (whatever pieces of the popular message it might incorporate). Furthermore, the history of rabbinic political power in Palestine, where the rabbis had once controlled the patriarchal office, would suggest that they had influence even beyond their own numbers in any case. In their own perception, at least, the rabbis could well have believed that their teachings spoke with considerable authority.

At the same time, even in this relatively small community, with all of its built-in defenses, there is no doubt that recent history took its toll, and the multiple texts which reveal ambivalence or worse show how extreme this toll was. Even despite their disavowal of protest and complaint, these rabbinic authors found themselves unable to restrain themselves or their record completely. So, particularly in their more imaginative musings, the ambivalence and complaint sometimes come through clearly. Unlike the Mishnah, they do not censor reality completely; they do not insist upon an ideal and that alone. They argue for a particular understanding of their reality and in doing so reveal how difficult, sometimes, that argument is to make.

But why here, in the aggadic midrashim, do these ambivalent notes sound, whereas in the Yerushalmi, for the most part, they do not? What, beyond the nature of the genres themselves, explains the ambivalence expressed in one but suppressed, mostly successfully, in the other? To begin with, we might suppose that the precise rabbinic circles which produced these various documents were not the same, and that the midrashic circles were more diverse, in sentiment and reality, than the one which composed the Yerushalmi. Indeed, this division of labors has often been assumed; perhaps the record we have examined supports this assumed division. In addition, it has often been argued that midrash is a more popular medium than Talmud (here: the Yerushalmi), and, though I disagree that it is actually a popular communication (see my discussion in the final chapter), it is certainly conceivable that midrash reflects, in elite form, some of the messages which the rabbis sought to communicate more publicly. If the midrashim represent the rabbis in their more subtly persuasive mode, attentive and sensitive to the sentiments of Jews at large, then this too might serve to help explain the ambivalence we have noted. While, in the end, any combination of explanations is at best speculative, the factors here identified cannot be dismissed. At the same time, we should recall that what these documents hold in common is greater than what divides them.

I conclude this chapter with two final midrashim which show unmistakably the toll which history exacted from these rabbinic authors. The first is Lev. R. 19, 5 (pp. 427–29), where Azariah the son of Oded the prophet is made to say (through fanciful interpretation of his words at 2 Chron. 15:3), "In the future, days will come upon Israel in which there will be 'no God of truth,' [meaning] the attribute of justice will not be operating [in the world]." This statement is made at the head of a list of calamities—the end of the high priesthood and the Sanhedrin—that clearly places us within the postdestruction context. So, the authors admit, at the time for which the midrash speaks—its own time—there is no justice. This emotion underlying this admission is reinforced in different terms later, when the midrash speaks of the "hands [of God] that appear weak and the knees [of God] that appear to be failing." Again, in the postdestruction world, God appears to be weak. God allows others to dominate Israel and thus, again, there is no justice.

The midrash calls upon the people to strengthen themselves in the face of such conditions and ultimately holds the people and their sinning responsible for this state of affairs. But, despite this final resort to Deuteronomic reasoning, the earlier admission of apparent injustice and divine weakness is not withdrawn. The truth of earthly experience is admitted to be a terrible one.

The other midrash, Pesiqta supp. 5, 3 (p. 465), goes straight to the problem of the destroyed Temple:

> Israel was waiting and yearning for the time that [God] would return to His House [= the Temple] and take pleasure in His Torah, and even the Holy One, blessed be He, waits and yearns for the time that [God] will return to His House and give pleasure to the congregation of Israel. And when will this be? When He exacts retribution from evil Edom. At that time, Israel says, "Master of the world! He [= Edom] has caused us great pain and has killed our sages and has enslaved us. . . .

The reference, for once, is clearly the second destruction, and that alone. Following that destruction, not only the people but God, too, awaits and yearns for the restoration. When will that restoration occur? "When [God] exacts retribution from Edom." Since Edom, that is, Rome (Byzantium), was the ruling power at the time the midrash was composed, this promise at least assured that there would be no oppressors to succeed the current one. Like apocalyptic texts, this midrash imagines that the present hateful regime is the last before restoration. And perhaps the reader could even hope that the promised restoration would not be far off. But, in the meantime, Rome continues to rule, and Israel waits and yearns for God.

Many of the possible meanings of the present condition of Israel were too bitter to admit. So Israel affirmed God's justice and waited, suffering all the time. Is there any wonder that expressions of this period are apologetic and ambivalent, often at the same time? Given the reality, it is difficult to imagine how it could have been otherwise.

9

The Bavli: Canonical Echoes,
Intimations of Dissent

With the Babylonian Talmud (henceforth: the Bavli) we come to the final and, in the opinion of many, definitive expression of classical rabbinic Judaism. The Bavli is a work of independent spirit, drawing widely on the earlier tradition but allowing no earlier authority to dictate its views. As in so many other matters, the Bavli not only records traditional opinions on suffering and related issues but also expresses opinions that have no rabbinic precedents, opinions that, when viewed against the earlier rabbinic canon, are genuinely radical.

We will consider the range of the Bavli's views in some detail. Because the Bavli typically has so much to say on these subjects—much more than any rabbinic document before it—we will have to be selective, quoting and analyzing either texts which exemplify common responses or those that contribute genuinely new perspectives. In addition, because of the sheer bulk and range of materials in the Bavli, we will devote two chapters and an appendix to analysis. Chapter 9 will give a brief overview of traditional opinions in the Bavli and then begin to examine those texts that give evidence of ambivalence, complaint, or protest. The appendix to this chapter will examine texts which, though mundane in the opinions they express, are important by virtue of their length. Finally, Chapter 10 will examine the most outstanding deliberations on suffering in the Bavli, texts which express new and even radical views. But before commencing our review, it is necessary to comment on the nature of the Bavli and to describe the sort of analysis that it demands.

The Nature of the Bavli

As stated, the Bavli is the longest and most elaborate of all rabbinic documents of Late Antiquity. It purports to be a commentary on the Mishnah but in fact is far more. Although the Bavli does begin by addressing the Mishnah, its theoretical explorations will often take it far beyond the immediate interest of the Mishnah text; in the end, the precise subject it addresses is almost always its own choice. More correctly defined, then, the Bavli is a sophisticated theoretical exploration of matters of law and religion, matters that are often, but not always, suggested by the Mishnah or other earlier rabbinic documents, now part of the canon.[1]

In its deliberations on a Mishnah base-text, the Bavli typically enriches the range of sources available for consideration by quoting other texts, including scripture, sources attributed to Mishnaic authorities but not included in the Mishnah (*baraitot*), and opinions of later Talmudic sages (*amoraim*). With these many sources, the Bavli weaves sophisticated and often lengthy deliberations. These deliberations are often theoretical; the Bavli is not primarily concerned with rendering practical decisions for all matters of Jewish practice. Consequently, the Bavli will often examine two or more contradictory opinions without declaring a preference between them or, with similar intent, it will explore opinions of sages whose authority is for other reasons known to be rejected; such rejection does not negate the value of these opinions for theoretical deliberation.

Because of the richness of the sources quoted in the Bavli, it has been the custom of earlier scholars to give their attention to individual quoted traditions while ignoring the context in which they appear. These traditions have then been understood to represent the opinions of the individual to whom they are attributed, regardless of the chronological gap between the named individual and the ultimate documentary record. The methodological difficulties with this approach are described in Chapter 1. Treating the Bavli as a mere anthology of opinions, these scholars have ignored the deliberative context which gives shape to the whole, thus neglecting the voice of the Bavli itself. The methodological tools necessary to overcome these earlier failings and to get at the Bavli's own, unique, message are those of rhetorical and canonical criticism. By rhetorical criticism, I mean the perspective that considers the text in its final form and reads the signals embedded in the text as they serve, in combination, to convince the reader of this opinion or another. Among the literary features that should attract the reader's attention are the text's structure, repetitions, unexpected turns, contradictions and their resolution, and so forth. It is essential, in this approach, to be aware of how the text plays with the reader's expectations and seeks to sway the reader's interpretations. How do redirections in the progress of the deliberation affect the reader's interpretive responses? If the text first leaves a term or idea ambiguous and then, through a later usage, suggests a particular definition, how does this affect the reader's understanding of the earlier usage? These questions are particularly crucial because the

Bavli leaves frequent gaps that demand the reader's contribution to fill them in. Therefore, a rhetorical reading of the Bavli also requires that alternative "fill-in-the-blanks" always be tried. Where is ambiguity intentionally created? How does such ambiguity affect the sense of the text and the message it does or does not wish to convey?[2]

Canonical criticism, as used here, means the analysis and interpretation of the combination and juxtaposition of ideas in a single document or recognized canon.[3] This approach is particularly important for reading the Bavli because the Bavli will frequently include, in juxtaposition or in more distant contexts, opinions that are contradictory or at least not fully reconcilable. Such contradictions are a product of the nature of the Bavli itself. With respect to matters of doctrine, in particular, the Bavli is far from systematic. Individual approaches need only be fitting for their particular contexts, and the Bavli generally perceives no need to reconcile contradictory expressions[4] (even halakhic matters are sometimes left in opposition, though here there is more clearly a preference for greater consistency). In traditional exegesis these contradictions are often reconciled (it is almost always possible, through ingenious interpretation, to resolve "apparent" contradictions), and in earlier scholarly circles they were attributed to different sources. But such contradictions, typical as they are, cannot so easily be dismissed. Being characteristic of the Bavli's approach, they bespeak something important about its ideologies. Therefore, when speaking of the Bavli's opinion, it is necessary to consider how this and that opinion, though possibly in conflict, work together in the same document.[5] What indecision or challenge do the alternatives suggest?

Furthermore, the Bavli places itself within a canonical tradition. It frequently quotes pieces of that earlier tradition, or, more often, it appropriates and transforms the tradition to serve its own ends. By comparing the Bavli's use of a teaching with the use of that same teaching elsewhere in the canon—through sensitivity to the differences implicit in the specific canonical settings—a whole new set of messages, beyond the apparently literal meaning of the words, will become available. Only by being attentive to the differences and the tensions will the struggles of these authors come to the fore. Only by appreciating the impact of canonical juxtaposition and intracanonical interpretation will the richness of the Bavli's opinions be properly and fully characterized.[6]

Here, as before, the messages we identify may be fully understood only when we account for the sociohistorical context in which the document took shape. Unfortunately, there remains considerable scholarly debate concerning the dating of the Bavli. If we accept that the Bavli's anonymous voice was composed subsequent to the death of the last of the amoraim around 500, and observe, on the other side, that the document was completed before the Arab conquest (there is no hint of these events in the pages of the Bavli), we will at least have narrowed our scope. Furthermore, R. Sherira Gaon reports that "the final years of the Persians were years of persecution and trouble [for the Jews] and they were not able to conduct [study] sessions."[7] There is no good reason to discount this testimony, it being fully in accord with what we know of the last troubled years of the Sasanian Persian empire, and thus it is improbable that the Bavli was composed in these latter years. Indeed, the pages of the Bavli reflect a lengthy period of deliberate composition in a relatively untroubled atmosphere, and it is most likely, therefore, that the project which resulted in the Bavli took place during the latter peaceful years of Khusrau I or, at least, not long thereafter.

What was this period like for the Jews in Babylonia? Beginning in 531, and lasting for forty-eight years, Babylonia was ruled by Khusrau, perhaps the greatest of all Persian kings. Khusrau reordered the administration of the empire, instituted army reforms, and established a new, stable tax system. His armies fought many battles on the frontiers, mostly to their advantage, but the interior was largely empty of a military presence. These were years of security and stability for the residents of the empire. Not surprisingly, Khusrau was very popular with his subjects.[8]

For our purposes, what is most important is that Khusrau was extremely tolerant of minority religions; there is not a single report of a systematic persecution during his years.[9] Indeed, this reality is supported from the Jewish record, for Sherira passes over these years in but a few sentences. Concerning peaceful times, with no persecutions, there is little to say.

But even if the Bavli was composed somewhat earlier, on the heels of scattered persecutions which took place during the fifth century, or somehow later, during the difficulties of the late empire upon which Sherira comments, it would still make little difference. Jews had been living in Babylonia for centuries, sometimes persecuted but mostly at peace. Whatever challenge diaspora as such represented had long before been addressed. Diaspora existence was not a problem for these Jews. Nor, of course, did the domination of Jews by other political powers in Babylonia create any problems of note. Jews had no claim to power in these territories and thus there was no reason to challenge the legitimacy of the power exercised by others. Even scattered persecutions had but little religious consequence. Such events were expected in the diaspora and, as diasporas went, this was rather a benign one. These Jews had no destroyed temple which sat in their midst and whose ongoing ruin they had to explain, no bastard competitor who ruled the roost when hegemony should rightly have been theirs. Simply put, these Jews had no extraordinary spiritual crisis to confront.

The rabbinic community itself continued to be a minority of Babylonian Jewry as a whole.[10] Undoubtedly, ever-increasing numbers of Babylonia's Jews were coming to accept rabbinic ways, and the rabbis exercised influence even beyond the rabbinized population, but they themselves would always remain a small intellectual elite. This meant, on the one hand, that they were distinguished in important ways from Jews around them, particularly by their rituals of Torah study and the deference to scholars which characterized their relations. On the other hand, the rabbis dreamed of rabbinizing all of Jewry, and to do this they maintained regular contact even with nonrabbinized Jews. In some contexts, such as some courts and marketplaces, rabbis exercised official authority over these Jews. But for the most part the rabbis had to depend upon persuasion and good will to gain new adherents.

Ironically, even among their own number, rabbinic power was limited. The rabbis in Babylonia had no recognized center or superior authority. Different teachers had different opinions concerning matters of practice and doctrine, and rabbinic groups in one locale had no choice but to respect the choices and decisions of rabbinic groups elsewhere. Furthermore, though inner-rabbinic hierarchies were strong, they were also fluid, with master status being achieved competitively. There was no equivalent of the patriarchal rabbinic family in the Babylonian rabbinic community.

This state of affairs, historical and social, created conditions that would support greater openness in Babylonian rabbinism. Such openness is evident in the Bavli's ruminations on suffering, as it is in many of its other deliberations. It is to these reflections and responses that we now turn our attention.

The Bavli on Suffering

The Bavli's treatments of suffering are, as suggested, more numerous than those in any other rabbinic document. Even before considering their substance, it is necessary that we appreciate the importance of the relatively greater frequency of such treatments. The Mishnah, we saw, rarely touches upon the question of suffering. It would not have been surprising, therefore, for the Bavli to neglect this topic as well. In fact, as we discovered, "neglect" accurately describes both the Tosefta's and the Yerushalmi's treatments of the matter; as commentaries on the Mishnah, they take their cues from the Mishnah. In contrast, the Bavli makes room for discussions (brief and lengthy) of suffering on many occasions, despite the apparent absence of hooks on which to hang them. The Bavli's willingness to include such discussions shows that, in its opinion, suffering is a topic that reasonably commands attention, demanding rabbinic response. As such, suffering joins the many other questions of religious import that assume their place on the docket of the Bavli's masters.

A good number of the many texts that touch on the question of suffering simply repeat explanations that have already been given ample voice in rabbinic documents preceding the Bavli. This means, of course, that the approach to suffering typified by Deuteronomy, the Pentateuch at large, the historical books, and many of the prophets—according to which suffering is seen as punishment for sin—is repeated often in the Bavli as well.

Perhaps the longest and certainly one of the most forceful Talmudic[11] statements advocating the suffering-is-punishment perspective is the deliberation at Shab. 31b–33b; it discusses which sorts of suffering are punishment for which particular sins. The Talmudic discussion originates with the Mishnah, seen previously in Chapter 5, that describes various sins for which women die in childbirth (Shab. 2:6). The gemara takes its cue from this Mishnaic theme, going on at length (beginning at the bottom of 32a) to enumerate various similar correspondences between sin and suffering as punishment.

The form of the deliberation says much about the message of the text. The first lengthy section repeats many times this formula: "It is taught . . . : On account of the sin of X, Y occurs [where Y = a particular form of suffering seen as punishment for sin X]." Each of these traditions is purportedly a tannaitic tradition, thus claiming highest authority in the rabbinic context. Each is supported by quoting a verse from scripture ("as it says, . . ."), further enhancing the authority of the tradition. Several subordinate discussions create variations in this formalized repetition, but the basic formula is always recovered. Significant among the variations are two traditions which balance their arguments for punishment with corresponding assertions that careful observance of the same obligations will lead to specific rewards.

The pattern is broken, near the bottom of 33a, with an amoraic statement that renders the point far more generally ("R. Oshaya said: Anyone who opens himself up to sins will be afflicted with wounds and bruises, as it says . . ."). This acts as a bridge to a new series of statements (much briefer than the first) that remark, again on tannaitic authority, that "Y [= a certain affliction] is a sign of X [= a certain sin]." That is, not only can one who transgresses a given sin be sure that a particular kind of suffering will follow, but it is also true that if you suffer a certain affliction, you may be sure that you are guilty of a particular sort of sin. These formulas, back-to-back, say it all: the system is so complete that one may begin at either pole and, by means of a simple algebra of sin–punishment, determine what belongs on the other side of the equation.

Crucially, though most claims are supported by reference to scripture (the latter formula—the reverse algebra—includes no such supports), the statements are all expressed as pertaining to the present. This system is eternal. No hint or admission is evident to suggest that anything has changed between "that time" (the times of the Bible) and "this time" (after the destruction, that is, the rabbinic period). This is so despite a small subdiscussion that questions a certain affliction suffered by Samuel the Small, Abbaye, and Rava—an affliction which, in a tradition just quoted, was claimed to be evidence of sin. When Samuel complains of his affliction, fearing that he might be mistaken for a sinner, he is immediately healed. Natural explanations are suggested for the afflictions of the latter two sages. Based upon these latter exceptions to the earlier expressed rule, one might have thought that the Talmud was arguing against the rule as a whole. But this is clearly not so, for the text immediately returns to reassert the general rule and to expand upon it. The matter of the afflictions of these sages commands no further attention. Similar examples are not referred to; the apparent anomalies are easily and quickly explained away and then forgotten. In context, note is merely taken that, when other evidence speaks against the conclusion that this is punishment for sin—such as here, where it is great sages who are suffering—there may be reason to admit an exception. Still, the general rule holds.[12]

Also supporting the claim that divine justice continues to operate, perfectly and in detail, is the lengthy gemara at Sot. 8b–11a. The base-Mishnah (1:7–9), it will be recalled, claims that "According to the measure that a person measures, with it do we measure him" (= measure-for-measure justice). This basic point is supported with several scriptural proofs, showing also that there is measure-for-measure reward as well as measure-for-measure-punishment.

The gemara does not substantively advance the principle expressed in the Mishnah and reiterated in the Tosefta (also quoted in the Talmud text). Crucially, in connection with punishment, the gemara begins by eliminating the possibility that we read the scripture-based substantiation offered in the Mishnah as suggesting that the principle is historically but not currently valid. In the words attributed to R. Joseph: "Even though the measure has been annulled, 'according to the measure' has not been annulled." In other words, though the human court that might administer judgment no longer operates, the principles of justice do. How so?

> One who is liable to be stoned either falls from the roof or a wild animal tramples him. One who is liable to be burned either falls into a fire or a snake bites him. One who is liable to be killed [by the sword] is either captured by the [foreign] government or is attacked by bandits. One who is liable to be strangled either drowns in the river or dies by choking. (8b)

Though historical circumstances might deprive God of the principal means of administering justice in Israel, justice is nevertheless administered. The principle enunciated in the Mishnah applies not only to the biblical figures who are named but to us as well.[13]

A brief story at Shab. 13a–b, while making the same assumption about the reason for suffering, also addresses the problem of apparently contradictory evidence. There we are told of a conscientious student who, besides devoting himself to the study of Torah and rabbinic teachings, served the students of sages. Nevertheless, he died at a young age. His wife then took his *tefillin* (prayer straps) and brought them around to the synagogues and study houses, asking how the principle of observance leading to reward (length of days) could thus have been contradicted. At first, no one had an answer for her. But later they learned that her husband had not been careful to keep himself separate from her in the clean days following her menstrual period before she went to the ritual bath, and the story concludes by noting that this failure to observe the rabbinic stringency was sufficient to warrant his punishment with premature death.

This story admits the apparent injustices that punctuate everyday experience. The relatively righteous do seem to suffer and die before their time without receiving the reward that they should be due. But the admission is expressed only to be rebutted. The story concludes by declaring that the injustice is only apparent. One merely need look deep enough to discover that there is a sin behind every punishment. Suffering may appear unwarranted, but the wise individual should know that this appearance is the consequence of incomplete information. The system does indeed work.

Of course, the Bavli does not stop at this most conventional explanation of suffering. As suggested, traditional views of all sorts also find expression in these pages. A variety of texts record the view that suffering effects atonement for sin (see, for example, Yoma 86a, M.Q. 28a, Sanh. 101a–b, and Sanh. 107a–b). Many others express the common justification of divine justice which argues that the present suffering of the righteous assures great reward in the world-to-come; an extended elaboration of this idea, overruling the base-Mishnah's claim that reward is this-worldly, may be found at Qid. 39b–40b (see the appendix to this chapter for a detailed analysis of that text). Another belief with ancient roots, also finding a place in the Bavli, is the notion that the suffering of a righteous individual will effect atonement for the sins of the many. This is offered, for example, as explanation for the suffering of Ezekiel, at Sanh. 39a.

Sometimes the Bavli recommends, as does earlier rabbinic literature, that those who suffer rejoice in their suffering.[14] This recommendation is articulated simply at Taan. 8a: "Anyone who is happy with the suffering that comes upon him brings salvation to the world, as it says. . . ."[15] Far more elaborate is the text at B.M. 84b–85a, a lengthy, narrative apologetic for suffering that suggests suffering is so beneficial it should be not merely accepted, but even invited. The exemplar of this position in the narrative is R. Eleazar b. R. Shimeon, who, having certain doubts concerning the possible wickedness of some of his actions at an earlier time, invites suffering upon himself, presumably in order to assure atonement. In graphic and gory detail, the text elaborates the various sufferings that R. Eleazar experienced, including "suffering" that extended to his corpse for decades after his death. Crucial to the narrative is the assertion that R. Eleazar was superior to Rabbi (Judah the Patriarch, the esteemed author of the Mishnah) in both Torah learning and deeds; the "deeds" referred to are his voluntary acceptance of suffering, and this is compared to Rabbi's inferior suffering, to be described immediately below (herein and in the Talmudic narrative).

The segment of the text that concentrates on the figure of Rabbi begins with his judgment—in context, deriving from his witness of the suffering of R. Eleazar—that "suffering is precious." Rabbi thus also accepts suffering upon himself for a significant number of years. However, we soon learn, Rabbi's suffering is inferior because it actually came upon him as punishment for a certain wrongdoing.[16] Eleazar's suffering, on the other hand, being completely voluntary, is deemed superior. Nevertheless, the suffering of both has beneficial consequences, for "all of the years of R. Eleazar's suffering no person died prematurely, and all of the years of Rabbi's suffering the world had no need of rain [for produce grew by itself]."

Adumbrated in this narrative is the common notion that suffering is punishment for wrongdoing (in the case of Rabbi) and also the much supported idea that suffering effects atonement (for this reason, it seems clear, R. Eleazar invited his suffering). Similarly finding earlier expression, though with important differences in detail, is the belief that suffering has magical, beneficial qualities, offering protection to the generation as a whole if suffered by a single, more righteous individual. The same claim was made for Rabbi's suffering, it will be recalled, in the Yerushalmi. But there are also notable additions in the current presentation. First, the evaluation of different kinds of suffering with relation to one another, placing suffering that "comes out of love" (as with R. Eleazar, who accepted his voluntarily) at a higher level, is without precedent in the Yerushalmi's version. Here, unlike there, the notion that suffering's benefits are so valuable that suffering might properly be invited upon oneself is made absolutely explicit. In addition— probably provoked, as we said, by the clear benefits of suffering as illustrated by the R. Eleazar story—here Rabbi expresses the opinion that "suffering is dear," a statement also without parallel in the Yerushalmi's version. By doubling the narrative evidence for the immediate benefits of suffering, and by engaging in a one-upsmanship that makes even Rabbi's suffering second-best, the Bavli carves out a resounding apologetic for suffering— one that eliminates any possibility (for the convinced reader) of complaint or even dissatisfaction.[17]

Intimations of Dissent

So, we see, many Bavli texts speak with relative unity of purpose in support of the justice of God's system, where suffering may be understood as punishment, a source of atonement, a protecting gift, or the like. But, as in the aggadic midrashim, explicit justifications of the justice of God's system are some times partially undermined by evident ambivalence. Often subtle, other times not, these texts also form an important component of the Bavli's varied responses to suffering.

Consider, for example, the brief sequence at A.Z. 4a, part of a longer discussion of divine justice. The immediate discussion begins with a repetition of the oft-expressed defense of suffering, but with an important addition:

> "And I rebuked [with suffering], I strengthened their arms, And they consider it evil against Me" (Hosea 7:15)[18]—The Holy One, blessed be He, said: I have said, I will rebuke them with suffering in this world in order to strengthen their arms in the world-to-come, yet "they consider it evil against me."

In the words of the prophet as understood here, God already anticipates that suffering intended to strengthen will be the source of complaint. The point is illustrated with a story that makes reference to a related prophetic pronunciation. In the story, R. Safra is asked by certain opponents to explain the statement of Amos, "You alone have I singled out of all the families of the earth—That is why I will call you to account For all your iniquities" (Amos 3:2). Their question is accompanied by the explicit complaint: "Does one who is angry take it out on whom he loves?!" Safra is silent, leading his opponents to torture him. Following, R. Abbahu offers this explanation for the verse: "To what is it to be compared? To a person who carries claims against two people, one whom he loves and one whom he hates. From the one he loves, he collects little by little; from the one he hates, he collects all at once." In other words, the suffering of Israel, described by Amos, is the slow and patient exacting of a debt by one beloved from another. Those who are hated by God, the other nations, will, in contrast, have their debts collected all at once—a far more painful demand.

This text renders the complaint explicit; How, after all, are we to understand the justification which claims that God causes us to suffer precisely because we are loved? The larger context makes this question particularly poignant. The lengthy deliberation surrounding this, like tractate Avodah Zarah as a whole, concerns the relationship between Israel and the nations. The quality of that relationship in reality is undeniable: the nations (Rome, Persia) dominate; Israel is at best subject and too often suffers. Given such a reality, the problem of Israel's condition and what it seems to say about divine justice is acute. If Israel is God's chosen while the nations neglect even the few commands that are addressed to them (the so-called Seven Commandments of the Children of Noah), how can the present situation be explained? No longer able to deny the bitter truth (as was the Mishnah), the Bavli gives voice to the complaint and, in the person of R. Safra, admits that the problem is so difficult that it will leave some, at least, literally speechless. True, the force of the challenge is not fully granted. By means of a simple analogy—embodying the recognition that the slow exaction of debts is far less painful than their quick exaction—the problem is "solved." Indeed, the solution is by this point an ancient one, expressed long before in various Jewish traditions. Still, the complaint continues to echo, and the ambivalence of the present authorship is palpable. And, as if to assure that we, the readers, will not forget the problem, the protest of Abraham at Sodom and Gemorrah is, in the gemara's next steps, quoted and repeated: it is a profanation to kill the righteous with the wicked. Again an explanation follows, but again answers do not suffice. The system's supports, it is clear, are not immune to attack.

Another treatment of suffering, at B.Q. 60a–b, articulates the complaint somewhat less directly.[19] The deliberation begins with a tradition attributed to R. Shimeon b. Naḥmani in the name of R. Yonatan which says that "retribution [= (here) collective suffering] comes into the world only when there are wicked [people] in the world, and it begins with the righteous." This position is furthered in a subsequent tradition: "R. Joseph taught— . . . When the destroyer has been given permission [to do damage] he does not distinguish between the righteous and the wicked, and, not only so, but he [even] begins with the righteous." The fundamental view, assuming collective punishment, echoes the corporate consciousness that characterizes most of the Bible. Even the next step, declaring that such punishment begins with the righteous, is found first in the Mekhilta (*pisḥa* 11, p. 38). Only the next statement—"[Concerning this claim] R. Joseph cried [and said:] All of this and they [= the righteous] are also put first?!"[20]—is original to the Bavli, but Abbaye's response to R. Joseph's complaint ("It is a favor to them") returns us again to a purportedly ancient view: "Because of evil the righteous was taken away" (Isaiah 57:1). (Rashi: "[It is a favor] so that they will not see the evil that is about to come." Whether or not this is the meaning of the verse, it is still an apology for the premature death of the righteous which has ancient roots.)

The last lengthy section of this deliberation spells out the consequences of the ideology propounded here. Beginning with a tradition also found in the Mekhilta (ibid., though it is here identified as amoraic) and following with numerous texts that are claimed to be tannaitic, the gemara advises that, since the righteousness of an individual does nothing to protect him from suffering that affects the collectivity, he would be wise to avoid dangerous situations completely. This Talmud text carries no promise of the efficacy of an individual's merits in assuring his or her individual protection.

Crucially, the outcome of this discussion is very different from that suggested in the texts reviewed previously. Here there is a breakdown in the relationship between an individual's acts and reward or punishment. But the breakdown is a consequence of a conscious anachronism—in offering a solution, the present authors ignore the concern for the individual that characterizes most of rabbinic ideology and they return, instead, to a corporate conception of justice. They understand that this more ancient conception is not plagued by the same problem as the later rabbinic one. Indeed, it is fair to say that most biblical authors would have supported, without hesitation, the corporate consciousness evident here. But—and this is crucial—rabbinic authors and their readers cannot possibly accept so readily a solution to the problem of suffering which dismisses the independent fate of the individual. By this point, the question of the individual and his or her fate has too long been central to the discussion of divine justice. Moreover, we cannot forget that it is the righteous *individual* who is the focus of this Talmudic discussion, so the anachronism of the answer is highlighted by the fully contemporary quality of the question. The solution begs the reader's indulgence. In the later rabbinic context, such a solution is not without its critical edge.

Up to this stage, the Bavli finds partners in the earlier rabbinic literature. As we saw in earlier chapters, and particularly in the aggadic midrashim, even texts which espouse support of God's perfect justice in their explicit rhetoric find room for subtle and often only implicit complaint in their overall composition. But some texts in the Bavli also allow their misgivings with suffering to emerge with great clarity and even, on occasion, quite explicitly. It is in such deliberations that the Bavli's unique personality becomes most evident.

A modest example is found at Bez. 32b, where a purported baraita remarks, "Three, their lives are not life: one who depends upon his companion's table, one whose wife rules over him, and one whose body is ruled by suffering." These are obviously not good things, for the one who suffers them is better not living. All are conditions that the victim would prefer to eliminate, and thus the attitude expressed here is the very opposite of the accepting posture recommended earlier. An identical attitude is evident in the prayer attributed to Rava at Ber. 17a: "May it be your will, Lord, my God, that I not sin again,[21] and that which I have sinned before you forgive, *but not by means of suffering and horrible illnesses.*"[22] Here, the request is explicit. Suffering is not accepted willingly, whatever its benefits might be. In a voice found only in the Bavli of all classical rabbinic documents, the great Talmudic sage and exemplar is represented as praying, "Please, God, don't make me suffer."

This same emotion is incorporated, in one way or another, in several longer Talmudic treatments. One text that makes ambivalence toward suffering—in this case, death—the centerpiece of its debate is the deliberation at A.Z. 5a:

> *a.* Resh Laqish said: Come and let us express gratitude to our ancestors, for if they had not sinned, we would not have come into the world [Without sin, there would be no death, so what need would there be for children?] . . .
>
> *b.* Is that to say that if they had not sinned they would not have given birth? But is it not written "Be fertile, then, and increase" (Gen 9:7)?
>
> *c.* [This blessing applies only] until Sinai [at which time, receiving the Torah and thereby gaining the means to eliminate sin, death should have ceased and propagation become unnecessary].
>
> *d.* At Sinai it is also written, "Go, say to them, 'Return to your tents,'" (Dt 5:27) [meaning] for [the purpose of] enjoying sexual relations [which presumably lead to children] and is it [also] not written, "that it may go well with them and with their children" (ibid., vs. 26)?
>
> *e.* [These verses are directed only] to those standing on Mt. Sinai [but not to those after who, if they don't sin, will not have children].
>
> *f.* But did Resh Laqish not say: . . . the Holy One, blessed be He, showed to the first person all generations and their interpreters. . . . As soon as He reached R. Aqiba [who lived well after Mt. Sinai—thus the plan from the very beginning was that there would be generations after Sinai]. . . .
>
> *g.* [So] don't say [as in *a*] "we would not have come into the world," rather [say] "it would be as if we did not come into the world [because, if our ancestors did not sin, they would not have died and, in comparison to them—still living—what would we be?]."
>
> *h.* Is that to say that if they had not sinned they would not have died?
>
> *i.* But are the portions of the childless widow and of inheritances [both of which presume death] not written [in the Torah]?
>
> *j.* [They are written only] on condition [that is, if no one died, they would never be applied].
>
> *k.* But are scriptures written only on condition?

l. Yes. . . .

m. They raised an objection: . . . It was impossible [at Sinai] to eliminate the Angel of Death, for *the decree had already been set.* . . . [emphasis
added]

n. He [= Resh Laqish, above at a] said [his opinion] in accordance
with this tanna, who taught—R. Yose says: Israel accepted the Torah only in
order that the Angel of Death have no dominion over them. . . .

Two starkly opposing opinions mark this debate. One, originating with Resh
Laqish at a and then supported at c, e, g, j, l, and n, believes that in the
absence of sin there would have been no death. Death, like all suffering, is
a punishment, so it is only just that, if the people had observed all of the
divine commandments given to them at Sinai, the Angel of Death would
have had no power over them. The second side notes, at b, d, f, and i,
that many scriptures have a plain sense which indicates that death was always
contemplated by God; hence death is ultimately unrelated to transgression.
This opinion is expressed most explicitly at m, where death is described as
a "divine decree," echoing a similar opinion regarding the destruction in
Lamentations Rabbah. If it is a divine decree, of course, then its occurrence
is not a matter of justice as such. If death may be such a decree, and if the
destruction may be a decree, then so too may all suffering be such a decree.
This is a defense—of sorts—of suffering, but only on the basis of absolute
divine authority. No justification of divine justice is proposed in this opinion. It may, in fact, be that its author believes that such justice, as it has
been understood in the Bible and rabbinic literature, does not exist.

The present deliberation is part of a much longer treatment of the relationship between Israel and the nations, divine justice, and suffering, encountered earlier. Never forgetting the urgent problem with which historical
reality confronts Israel, the unit as a whole does not indict God for injustice. But its views are not logically consistent with one another, and one
admits explicitly that death, understood by some to be the most severe of
punishments, may have nothing to do with justice. It is fair to say that the
differences recorded here reflect the different religious imaginations of the
variety of authors who collectively seek to make sense of the problem. The
present text expresses two sides of the debate simultaneously, admitting that,
for some at least, a claim for the existence of rational justice cannot be
defended. The "justice" of death (and, by extension, of lesser suffering) may
be of a more authoritarian sort—God decrees; rational understanding is
therefore beside the point.

A text that reveals its misgivings with suffering in a more one-sided fashion is the brief deliberation at Arakh. 16b–17a, beginning with the question: "What is the limit of suffering?" The proposed answers are these:

1. Anyone who has clothes woven for him which do not fit.
2. Even if one intended that wine be diluted for him with warm water
and it was instead diluted with cold water, or vice versa.

3. Even if one put his clothes on backward (requiring that he remove them and turn them around).

4. Even if one put one's hand into one's pocket to take out three coins and came out with only two.

What is the point of this exercise? the gemara then asks. "For it was taught in the school of R. Ishmael: Anyone for whom forty days passed without suffering has received his [reward for the next] world." As R. Gershom (died c. 1040) explains the question in his commentary: "How small a pain will be considered suffering such that, if this occurs to him within [any] forty days it will be atonement for him and he will not, as a result, receive now his future world?" The answers are the minute, insignificant troubles that are listed above.

It is evident that the list represents a sort of "one-downsmanship." In other words, each proposal goes beyond the previous in the level of insignificance with which it is able to define suffering. Suffering, it is admitted, is "essential" in order to atone for sins; otherwise one will have to, as it were, draw on one's future reserves. But the deliberation goes to ridiculous lengths in identifying "suffering" that is efficacious for purposes of atonement yet minimally onerous for the "sufferer." It is enough to have to turn one's shirt around or return one's hand to one's pocket in order to get the needed number of coins. This will fulfill one's suffering obligation in any given forty-day period.

The obvious question is, Why would the gemara want to reduce the definition of suffering, for these purposes, to such extremes of insignificance? The only reasonable answer, it seems to me, is that the authors of this text, understanding the traditional demand that suffering follow sin in order to effect atonement, wish to pay lip-service to that demand while reducing its actual requirements as much as possible. They do not want to grant the need for genuine suffering, essential as it was in the classical system of justice. They want the requirement to be fulfilled at the absolute minimum level, as anyone who is uncomfortable with the traditional apologies for suffering would. If even these are suffering, then the system of divine justice, as traditionally conceived, is difficult to take seriously.[23]

Still another brief discussion, in the context of a longer deliberation which seeks to show that, despite occasional misleading evidence, idolatry is truly without power, touches on the problem of suffering and healing. The text (A.Z. 55a) returns, more explicitly now, to the position that suffering and justice are distinct and that one cannot (necessarily) be justified by reference to the other. The narrative that makes the point follows:

a. Zunin said to R. Aqiba: My heart and your heart know that there is no substance in idolatry, yet we see people who go [to idolatrous temples] when broken and come [back] restored [how can this be]?

b. He said to him: I will tell you a parable. To what is the thing to be likened? To a trustworthy person in a city with whom all of the people in the city would leave deposits without witnesses. Yet one person came and deposited with him before witnesses. One time, this person forgot and deposited with him without witnesses. His wife said to him, "Come let us deny it." He said to her, "And because this idiot acted improperly, should we lose our source of livelihood?"

   c. So too, when they [presumably God?] send afflictions [= suffering] upon a person, they make [the afflictions] swear that they will not leave until such-and-such a time and by the hand of so-and-so and with such-and-such a remedy. When their time for leaving arrived, he went to an idolatrous temple. They said, "It is proper that we should not leave [because of his sin]" and then they say, "Just because this idiot acts improperly, should we deny our oath?" . . .

In truth, I have great trouble making sense of the parable, beyond the most superficial similarities. ("Should we lose our source of livelihood?"–"should we deny our oath?" Are the trustworthy man and his wife the afflictions? Are the people of the city God? The parallel should not be pressed.) But the nature of the problem (a) and the proposed solution (c) are crystal clear. The problem is everyday experience which contradicts traditional assumptions regarding divine justice. How can this sinner, going to the house of the idol, find himself cured there? Cure should come to those who, following affliction, repent and are therefore atoned! The answer is that there is proper justice ("It is proper" = "*din hu*," "it is just") and there is reality. And reality, as presently imagined, is this: suffering, when it comes upon a person (for reasons that are nowhere mentioned here) is assigned a specific term (it is a decree!); when its term is up, whatever justice might demand, the suffering leaves and the person is healed! Suffering that is an expression of justice is certainly known here. But the common equation, according to which suffering is measured punishment, appropriate to the particular sin, is denied. The truth, as now spelled out, is that it is all quite arbitrary. Expanding upon the immediate narrative, if a righteous person genuinely repents, yet it is not time for his suffering to desist, nothing he has done will matter. Again, to state it quite unambiguously, suffering or healing, as imagined in this text, might be arbitrary and capricious. The justice that is elsewhere imagined does not, according to the present authors, exist.

   It is further essential to note that, despite its attribution to R. Aqiba, this tradition is certainly the opinion of the Bavli. This is evident in the language with which the exchange is introduced—Babylonian Aramaic (with no equivalent Hebrew in manuscript variants)[24]—an unmistakable sign of the hand of the Bavli's final authorship. This conclusion is also supported by the fact that this sequence has no parallel in any earlier rabbinic text. Whatever its actual origin, therefore, only the Bavli finally saw fit to give it voice.

   Undoubtedly, the Bavli's best known discussion of divine justice is the brief sequence at Ber. 7a, which, like the preceding texts, indicates serious misgivings with the conventional view of God's system of justice and the place of suffering in that system. The discussion commences with a question attributed to Moses: "Master of the world! Why is there a righteous person and it is good with him and a righteous person and it is bad with him, a wicked person and it is good with him and a wicked person and it is bad with him?" The first proposed answer, that the difference lies in the parent (is the righteous individual the child of another righteous individual or of a wicked person?) is rejected—the punishment of a child for the sins of a parent, despite biblical expressions to this effect, is simply unacceptable at this level of the tradition. The better answer is one seen also in other texts: it depends on whether the individual is wholly or only partly righteous, wholly or only partly wicked.[25]

The brutal directness with which this text expresses the question is striking. Surely this impression reinforces our broad sense of the Bavli in these matters: it is, indeed, willing to admit the problem, and it does so often. Still, it should be emphasized that there is no compromising of God's justice in what we have quoted so far. "Good" and "bad," comfort or suffering, are here claimed to be expressions of reward or punishment. The brief discussion to this point is every bit as insistent on God's justice as other deliberations seen earlier in this chapter.

The next steps, though, record an alternative:

> And this disputes [the opinion of] R. Meir, for R. Meir said . . . it says, "I will grant the grace that I will grant"—even though he is not worthy; "and show the compassion that I will show," (Ex 33:19)—even though he is not worthy; "He said: you cannot see my face" [meaning, in this context, you cannot understand my ways].

Thus it is admitted, at least according to this opinion, that God's ways may be inscrutable. It may indeed be that God is merciful to those who are not deserving and, presumably, less than merciful to those who are. In this view, God's justice, at least in its present application, may be less than perfect.

This is a difficult admission—and one, we have learned, which characterizes the Bavli. Yet this admission finds far more eloquent expression in several of the texts examined earlier in this chapter, and once it is expressed here, it generates no discussion. It is an alternative that the present author is not interested in pursuing. So, despite the eloquence of the question, this text in no way stands out in the Bavli. It affirms our sense that the challenge may be articulated in these pages and that alternatives are unhesitatingly entertained. Still, the boldest explorations are found elsewhere. The intimations and brief challenges offered in the foregoing texts pale in comparison with the Bavli's boldest and most extended considerations of suffering and divine justice, to be studied in the following chapter.

The Bavli Contrasted with the Palestinian Tradition

In earlier chapters we noted and began to document the fact that, unlike Palestinian rabbinic documents, the Bavli does not condemn those who protest suffering or question God's justice. By way of setting the stage for the Bavli's most radical expressions on suffering (examined in the next chapter), we here return to this point, to illustrate its full extent and to appreciate the Bavli's unique position in this regard.

First, to establish the negative: despite occasional recommendations of "joyful" acceptance of suffering, if one is unable to assume such a stance, the Bavli does not insist. Nor does it condemn those who speak up in protest. This claim which, I have found, applies generally in the Bavli, requires brief reference to a seemingly contradictory tradition at Ber. 62a. The statement reads, as it appears in the printed editions, "the tradition [or, teaching] relating to suffering is silence and prayer." Were this reading to be supported, we would have here modest evidence of agreement with the Yerushalmi's opinion that suffering must be accepted, not protested (see Rashi). But the present text has been emended based upon Rashi's commentary, and all manuscripts have not "tradition" but a term that should probably be taken as "charm (to ward off danger)."[26] Thus the text should read: "A charm *against* suffering is silence and prayer," quite a different sense indeed.[27] In this apparently more original version, the teaching gives advice for avoiding suffering in the first place but says nothing about responses to suffering once it has begun. The difference is crucial because, as indicated, characteristic of the Bavli's overall position is its complete omission of condemnation of those who protest suffering. As we now see, not only is this tradition not an exception but, in fact, it might even be understood to be a manifestation of the Bavli's more contradictory spirit. Why else, after all, advise "charms" against suffering? If suffering is punishment, the only advice necessary should be the avoidance of sin and repentance.

The Bavli's lengthy deliberation on Job (B.B. 15a–16b) also offers important insight into its attitudes toward protest and complaint. The Talmud's evaluation of the rebellious Job, negative but understanding, tells us as much about its sense of the appropriate limits of challenge as any other relevant Talmudic deliberation.

The Bavli's unique reflections on Job (the earliest part of its discussion is shared with prior rabbinic works) begin with its expansion upon the biblical account. The first part of this exposition, beginning near the bottom of 15b, supplies several opinions on Job and his qualities, all praising him. For example, the text emphasizes, in the name of R. Yohanan, that "greater is that which is said [in scripture] about Job than that which is said about Abraham." Scriptures are quoted here to prove the point. Next we learn that Job was not stingy and, then, that Job had what might be called a Midas touch ("anyone who would take a coin from Job would be blessed"). Job himself, the gemara goes on to show, was blessed miraculously, even enjoying a taste of the world-to-come. Crucially, all of the verses expounded here, yielding these various lessons, are drawn from the first chapter of Job. This is a picture of Job before his severest test—and before his rebellion. Everything is still relatively Edenic, and Job may be praised without hesitation. How quickly, however, will things change!

Following an introduction to Satan in the Jobian context, and then a brief digression on the identity and powers of Satan, the gemara returns to expound scripture—now those verses where Job expresses some of his most stinging protests. I quote the central part of the exposition:

a. "For all that, Job did not sin with his lips." (2:10)

b. Rava[28] said: With his lips he did not sin but, in his heart, he sinned.

c. What did he say?[29] "The earth is handed over to the wicked one; He covers the eyes of its judges. If it is not He, then who?"[30] (9:24)

d. Rava said: Job sought to "overturn the bowl" [that is, to upset the balance of the world].

e. Abbaye said to him: Job only spoke concerning Satan [and you have, therefore, misunderstood his intent].

f. This is [also] a tannaitic argument . . . R. Eliezer says: Job sought to overturn the bowl. R. Joshua said to him: Job only spoke against Satan.

g. "You know that I am not guilty, And that there is none to deliver from Your hand." (10:7)

h. Rava said: Job sought to exempt the entire world from judgment. He said before Him, "Master of the world! You created [clean and unclean animals] . . . ; You created the Garden of Eden [and] You created Gehinnom; You created righteous individuals and You created wicked individuals; who has the power to prevent You [from doing as You wish? So, having created the world this way, how can You hold the wicked, whom You Yourself created, responsible for their wickedness]?!

i. And what did his friends respond to him? "You subvert piety And restrain prayer to God" (15:4)—[True,] the Holy One, blessed be He, created the evil inclination, [but] He also created the Torah as a remedy!

j. Rava expounded: What is [the meaning of what is] written, "I received the blessing of the lost; I gladdened the heart of the widow" (29:13)? This teaches that [Job] would rob a field from orphans and improve it and return it to them; "I gladdened the heart of the widow," [teaching] that wherever there was widow whom [others] would not marry, he would go and put his name upon her [Rashi: saying that she was his relative or speaking to her to marry her] and they would come and marry her.

k. "If my anguish were weighed, My calamity laid on the scales," (6:2)

l. Rav said: Dust into the mouth of Job! [He makes himself as though] a colleague of Heaven!

m. "Would there be an arbiter between us / To lay his hand on us both." (9:33)

n. Rav said: Dust into the mouth of Job! Is there a servant who reproves his master?!

o. "I have covenanted with my eyes / Not to gaze on a maiden." (31:1)

p. Rava said: Dust into the mouth of Job! For Job did not [gaze] at another [woman, while] Abraham did not even look at his [woman]. . . .

q. "As a cloud fades away, So whoever goes down to Sheol does not come up." (7:9)

r. Rava said: From here [we learn] that Job denied the resurrection of the dead.

s. "For He crushes me with a storm [or, 'with a hair'—see below]; He wounds me much for no cause." (9:17) *t*. Rabbah said: Job blasphemed with [mention of] a storm and with a storm He [= God] answered him.

u. He blasphemed with a storm, as it is written, "For He crushes me with a storm"—he said before Him: Master of the world! Perhaps the wind of a storm passed before you and caused you to become confused between "Job" [*Iyyov*] and "enemy" [*oyev*]!

v. He answered him with a storm [or, hair], for is written, "Then the Lord replied to Job out of the tempest and said . . ." (38:1)—He said to him: I have created many hairs in a man, and for each and every hair I created a follicle, in order that two hairs not be nourished from the same follicle. For, if two hairs drew nourishment from the same follicle, they would darken the sight of man. [Now] between one follicle and another I did not become confused; between "Job" and "enemy" would I become confused?!

This response of God is followed by others which make precisely the same point.

Generally, this exposition is condemnatory. The condemnation begins with the first comment of Rava (b) and follows in various degrees. So, Job is (properly) accused of seeking to challenge divine judgment (d and h). He is condemned for his hubris (l and n). He is condemned for thinking too highly of himself (p). He is spoken of as being a nonbeliever in basic principles (r) and a blasphemer (t–u). In contrast, Job's colleagues are described as rendering the correct answer to the problem presented by the evil inclination that God created (i) and, needless to say, God's answers to Job's ridiculous assertion (God confused?!) are overwhelmingly convincing. The weight of the evidence would lead us to conclude that the Babylonian authorities whose views are recorded here had little tolerance for the sort of challenge that Job represented.

But this is not the whole picture. To begin with, not all of the evaluations expressed here are negative. Both Abbaye (e) and R. Joshua (f) suggest that Job's challenge is a response to Satan, not an accusation directed at God. Record of Job's ongoing positive qualities is also found (j); in the midst of the longer deliberation on Job's qualities, this can be seen only as an attempt to create a balance. Most important, near the end of this lengthy discussion, we read: "'Job does not speak with knowledge; His words lack understanding.' (34:35) Rava said: From here [we learn] that a man is not held liable for [what he says in] distress." In other words, there were mitigating factors in Job's case. Whatever he might have said, he cannot be held responsible. Like the insanity plea in contemporary jurisprudence, Babylonian Talmudic justice will not convict someone for what he says under duress.

The importance of this conclusion cannot be overemphasized. Generally, we have seen, this text is comfortable with neither Job's protest nor, presumably, similar protests of others. But this discomfort does not yield absolute condemnation. Quite the contrary—a degree of balance is maintained and, crucially, even Job's most extreme statements are, in the end, excused. It is difficult not to anticipate, in this context, the Bavli's own

Jobian expressions, reviewed in the next chapter. It may be that the author of this text would not agree with the opinions expressed in those texts, or even with the way they are stated, but he could excuse such statements. Unlike the Yerushalmi, the Bavli still does not insist upon perfect piety under duress. Piety may be desired, but protest is understood. Such understanding allows, of course, for the plurality of expressions that the Bavli preserves.

Finally, we turn to what is probably the most outstanding example of the Bavli's tolerance of questioning and challenge—its stories of the death of R. Aqiba.

These stories are fully appreciated only when contrasted with the Yerushalmi's far less tolerant alternative. In the Yerushalmi, it will be recalled (for full discussion of this text, see Chapter 7), Aqiba stands in judgment before Tineus Rufus. When the time for reciting the Shema arrives, Aqiba recites and laughs in pleasure. Tineus Rufus, seeing him laugh, says that either Aqiba must be a sorcerer or he must be responding to his suffering with contempt. Aqiba denies both accusations and proceeds to explain his odd behavior. He is unable to finish speaking before he dies.

Now consider the Bavli's first version (Ber. 61b):

a. Our sages taught: Once, the evil government decreed that Israel should not engage themselves in [the study of] Torah.

b. Pappus b. Judah came and found R. Aqiba gathering crowds in public and engaging in [the study of] Torah.

c. He said to him: Aqiba! Are you not afraid of the government?

d. He said to him: I will draw you a parable. . . .

e. They said: It was but a few days before they captured R. Aqiba and imprisoned him. . . .

f. When they took R. Aqiba out to be executed, it was the time for reciting Shema, and they were combing his flesh with iron combs while he accepted upon himself the yoke of the kingdom of heaven [by reciting the Shema].

g. His disciples said to him: *Our master!* [*Are we required to go*] *this far?!* [emphasis added]

h. He said to them: All of my days I was troubled by this verse—"with all of your soul" (Dt 6:5)—[meaning] even if [God] takes your soul. I said, "When will this [obligation] come to my hands, that I may fulfill it? And now that it has come to me, shall I not fulfill it?!

i. He extended [his pronunciation of] "one" (Dt 6:4) until his soul left [him] with [saying] "one."

j. A heavenly voice emerged and said: Happy are you, R. Aqiba, that your soul left with "one."[31]

k. The Ministering Angels said before the Holy One, blessed be He: *Is this the Torah and this its reward?!* "From them that die by your hand, O Lord" (Ps 17:14)[32] [should have been his fate]! [emphasis added]

l. [God] said to them: "Their portion is in life" (ibid.).

m. A heavenly voice emerged and said: Happy are you, R. Aqiba, for you are invited for life in the world-to-come.

Typically, the Bavli's version is longer and more detailed (even without the substantial sections that I have not reproduced). What distinguishes this version, particularly in comparison with the Yerushalmi's version, is the fact that there are four primary perspectives in the narrative rather than two. That is, we have not only R. Aqiba and his persecutor, as in the Yerushalmi, but also always "the other"—including Pappus b. Judah, Aqiba's disciples, and the angels—and God. The perspective of these others is crucial for understanding the force of the story.

Pappus b. Judah questions Aqiba's judgment in ignoring the government's decree (c). The students also question Aqiba for the risks he takes for the sake of Torah, submitting to horrible torture and placing his life on the line (g). The angels question God concerning the justice of what Aqiba suffers (k). In an ascending order, corresponding to the heightened danger to, and suffering of, Aqiba at each stage, these "others" voice precisely the questions that we less pious folk might likewise express. Each question, of course, has an answer, given either by Aqiba or by God, and the answers have important lessons to teach. But so do the questions.

Particularly striking are the questions of the two sets of "disciples," those of Aqiba and of God (the angels). Each group challenges the relationship between Torah and suffering—Aqiba's disciples asking whether it is necessary to submit to severe suffering and even death for the Torah, and the angels asking where the reward for Torah—instead of apparent punishment—is to be found. Crucially, in both instances, the masters (Aqiba and God) respond without condemnation—admitting the force of the challenges and offering contextually reasonable answers. Consider the contrast with the Yerushalmi, where even the Roman persecutor knows that such a challenge is illegitimate! Yet, in the Bavli, the most challenging question—"Is this the Torah and this its reward?"—is voiced by the Ministering Angels themselves!

Lest there be any suspicion that the angels might be misdirected in their challenge, we turn to the related story of Aqiba's death, at Men. 29b, where the challenge is put in the mouth of none other than Moses, who has just witnessed Aqiba's torture. "Is this the Torah and this its reward?" says Moses. Moses!—the greatest of rabbinic heroes. No, there can be no question that, in the opinion of the Bavli, this sort of challenge is absolutely legitimate. It is expressed in its pages, after all, by the wisest of all sources, next to God.

Returning to our contrast with the Yerushalmi, we find that this challenge is also found in its pages. There, at Hag. 2:1 (77b), the text explains the origins of the apostasy of Elisha b. Abuya ("*aḥer*"). One of the explanations suggests that, upon witnessing the tongue of a certain sage being dragged along in the mouth of a dog, Elisha responded by saying, "Is this the Torah and this its reward? [twice] . . . It appears that there is no reward and no revival of the dead!" Thereupon, of course, Elisha became an apostate. Who, then, expresses this question/challenge/doubt in the Yerushalmi? The archetypal apostate himself, Elisha b. Abuya (in the Bavli, this same challenging question is not associated with Elisha)! In the Yerushalmi, such questioning is condemned—not tolerated for a moment. Therefore, it can be only the worst apostate who allows himself to express such a thing. But because, in the Bavli, such doubts and challenging questions are unreservedly legitimate, it is none other than Moses and the Ministering Angels who allow themselves these expressions in its stories. Doubt and question are supported. There is no condemnation whatever of responses to suffering that are less than completely accepting.[33]

The Bavli practices what it preaches. In Chapter 10 we turn to its major expressions of the same challenges and doubts.

APPENDIX

We here consider several major deliberations on divine justice or the destruction of the Temples. The points they make are either utterly traditional or, at least, attested in the earlier rabbinic literature; thus there is no point including extended analysis in the body of this chapter. Nevertheless, the very length of these deliberations makes them significant statements, and I therefore include them here for the reader's consideration.

The Bavli on Divine Justice

Qiddushin 39b–40b (on m. Qid. 1:10) is a lengthy sugya that, as we shall see, little distinguishes the Bavli from rabbinic works that precede it. The Mishnah, again, is this: "Anyone who performs one mitzvah [= commandment, obligation], it is good with him and his days are lengthened and he inherits the land. But anyone who does not perform one mitzvah, it is not good with him and his days are not lengthened and he does not inherit the land." This Mishnah is distinguished by two difficulties. (1) It remarks that a person who performs only one mitzvah merits these many rewards or, conversely, that one who doesn't perform one mitzvah is not thus rewarded; could the performance or nonperformance of only a single mitzvah have this immense power? (2) The Mishnah seems clearly to promise reward in this world, not in some future world. This insistence on this-worldly reward explicitly contradicts other Mishnahs that project reward into the world-to-come. We would expect the gemara to take up these difficulties in its discussions.

In fact, addressing our expectation, the gemara is built on a structure of juxtapositions that highlight a series of contradictions between this Mishnah and other Mishnahs or related tannaitic texts. The first of these approaches quotes the very Mishnah, from the first chapter of Pe'a, that we used to illustrate the Mishnah's belief in a future reward. The gemara is this:

> *a.* [Mishnah] And there is a contradiction: "These are the things that a person eats of their fruits in this world and the fund [= merit, reward] remains for them in the world-to-come. And what are they? Honoring one's father and mother and acts of lovingkindness and[1] bringing peace between a person and his fellow, and Torah study is equivalent to them all."[2] (Pe'a 1:1) [The gemara's problem, as will be clear in the next step, is that this Mishnah says only that "these are the things" that lead to reward, whereas the Mishnah in Qiddushin speaks of the performance of any single mitzvah as leading to reward.]
>
> *b.* R. Judah said: This is what is being said [in the Mishnah in Qiddushin]—"Anyone who performs one mitzvah *above his merits* [meaning that, with this mitzvah, his merits exceed his demerits] it is good with him and he is as one who upholds the entire Torah."
>
> *c.* Consequently, with these [listed in Mishnah Pe'a, should we say that the performance of] only one [will lead to reward]?!

> *d.* R. Shemaya said: [This latter Mishnah means] to say that if it was evenly balanced [= his merits and sins] it [one of these particular mitzvot] will tip the scale [in favor of merits].

Seemingly, the problem that bothers the gemara is that the Mishnah here in Qiddushin speaks of mitzvot in general leading to reward, whereas the Mishnah from Pe'a singles out certain unique mitzvot. The resolution is simple enough: the Mishnah in Qiddushin speaks of one for whom the scales of justice are evenly balanced, thus the performance of one mitzvah will tip the scales in his favor, while the other Mishnah speaks of one concerning whom the scales of justice are evenly balanced at the moment of final accounting; if such a person has, among the meritorious acts, one of these particular acts, then, even though the scales are numerically balanced, they will nevertheless tip in his direction. It is difficult to believe, though, that defining the problem inherent in the present Mishnah required pointing out this alleged contradiction between it and the other Mishnah. In fact, R. Judah's clarifying remark (b) would have made perfect sense—and the problem to which he is responding would have been absolutely clear—even without quoting the second Mishnah. It is necessary to ask, therefore, whether the gemara's citation of the second Mishnah might not, in truth, have another purpose.

The obvious contradiction that leaps out at the reader when these two Mishnahs are juxtaposed is the fact that one speaks of mundane reward while the other postpones final reward to the world-to-come. Why is this obvious contradiction avoided in the gemara's explicit comments and another highlighted instead? Moreover, as will be clear from even a cursory reading of the sugya to follow, anticipation of a future, final reward is central to this text's conception of divine justice but, again, its centrality is softspoken, almost downplayed—as if to say that something so obvious requires no reinforcement. In my opinion, this is the point: the gemara wishes to present the future reconciliation of the accounts of justice as a belief to be taken for granted. But it has an obvious problem with this Mishnah, which does not evidently share that assumption. By focusing its critical lens on a different contradiction, as though ignoring the contradiction concerning belief in future reward, the gemara drives home its point without, however, admitting that it has a problem in this area in the first place.

This same strategy is at the foundation of the gemara's next contradiction and resolution:

> *e.* And "anyone who performs one mitzvah *above his merits* it is good with him"?! But they raised a contradiction: "Anyone whose merits are greater than his sins, it is bad with him and it appears as though he burnt the whole Torah and did not even leave one letter of it, and anyone whose sins are greater than his merits, it is good with him and it appears as though he upheld the entire Torah and didn't omit even a letter of it."
>
> *f.* Abbaye said: Our Mishnah [means that] they make for him a good day and a bad day.[3]

g. Rava said: Who[se opinion] is this? It is R. Jacob, who said that there is no reward for a mitzvah in this world,

h. For it is taught—R. Jacob says: There is no mitzvah written in the Torah whose reward is [written] by its side which is not dependent on the revival of the dead [for the fulfillment of its promised reward]. With regard to honor of one's father and mother it is written, "that you may long endure, and that you may fare well" (Dt 5:16), [and] with regard to the sending off of [the mother from the] nest it is written, "that you may fare well and have a long life" (Dt 22:7); Behold, [what if] his father said to him, "go up to the house and bring me the chicks," and he went up and sent the mother away and took the children, and while returning he fell and died—[so] where is the faring well of this one and where is the long life of this one?! Rather, "that you may fare well" in a world that is all goodness, and "that you have a long life" in a world that is wholly long.

i. And maybe it was never this way!

j. R. Jacob [actually] saw an incident [of this nature]!

k. And maybe [the person who died in this way] was thinking of a sin!

l. The Holy One, blessed be He, does not combine an evil thought with an act.

m. And maybe [this person] was thinking about idol-worship . . . [which is deemed tantamount to an act]!

n. This, too, is what he was saying: If you are of the opinion that there is reward in this world, why didn't his mitzvot [= his merit] protect him so that he would not come to such a thought?

o. But hasn't R. Eleazar said, "those sent out to do a mitzvah are not harmed"?

p. There, it is different [if they are] on their way [but they may be harmed when returning].

q. But didn't R. Eleazar say, "those sent out to do a mitzvah are not harmed either on their way nor when returning"?

r. [In this case] it was a rickety ladder, so the danger was fixed, and wherever the danger is fixed we do not depend upon a miracle,

s. For it is written, "Samuel replied, 'How can I go? If Saul hears of it, he will kill me.'" (I Sam 16:2)

t. R. Joseph said: Had *Aḥer* interpreted this scripture like R. Jacob, his grandson, he would not have sinned.

u. And *Aḥer*, what is it [that he saw which caused him to become an apostate]?

v. There are those who say that he saw a case like this [described above in H] and there are those who say that he saw the tongue of Ḥuzpit, the translator, being dragged by a despicable animal. He said, "The tongue that has brought forth jewels, should it lick the dirt?" [Consequently,] he went out and sinned.

The contradiction that sets up this discussion (e) leads inevitably to the conclusion that resolution of accounts comes in the future world. Only this can be the meaning of the ironic and seemingly cynical text quoted in opposition to the Mishnah. The solution of Rava (g), and possibly even that of Abbaye (f), emphasizes this belief and allows little room for an alternative. The same point is driven home below, in t, where R. Joseph remarks that if Elisha b. Abbuya (*Aḥer*) had understood the necessity of this interpretation of the scriptural promise for reward, he would not have become an apostate. His conclusion obviously being the improper one, then the one who wishes to maintain the proper belief must assume the reality of future justice.

In discussing this sugya, Yaakov Elman makes much of the fact that, unlike the Yerushalmi parallels, this text goes out of its way (in i and following) to insist upon the reality of apparently unjust events—events where worthy people suffer in explicit contradiction to the simple promises of scripture.[4] He also highlights the importance of the conclusion, in r–s, that "fixed harm" must be avoided because when such danger is present no amount of merit will protect the individual. These parts of the deliberation are evidence, he feels, of the Bavli's courageous willingness to face bitter realities and to accept the fact that there are situations which contradict the idealized system of justice promised by scripture.

Surely, the explicit confrontation with these matters in this text is noteworthy, but far less significant, in the end, than Elman believes. Questioning the reality of apparent injustice (i) and emphasizing that such anomalies are a fact of life serve only to disabuse the reader of a naive picture of divine justice that had long ago been replaced by more serviceable alternatives. The admission that "fixed harm," too, may be used to explain the absence of mundane reward of the righteous is only a technical detail in a larger calculus. For nowhere in this text is there a denial of ultimate justice— quite the opposite! The son who falls from the rickety ladder and dies, after honoring his father by fetching the chick and sending away its mother, will still be rewarded, but only in the future world! Yes, the details *are* faced with a brutal honesty, but the view espoused by the text is one that has been assumed for centuries even within the rabbinic community, not to mention earlier Jewish circles. In substance, the Bavli here relies on available views and adds nothing new.

The gemara now goes on to address further difficulties in interpretation, first relating to a contradiction between this Mishnah and another tannaitic text but then, crucially, relating to the Mishnah from Pe'a. It is the Pe'a Mishnah—the one that explicitly focuses on future reward—that now becomes the center of the Talmudic deliberation, making this ideological claim literally central to the sugya as a whole. Furthermore, though, at the end, the deliberation records a text from Tosefta Qiddushin which relates to the present Mishnah, the force of doing so is again to direct our attention to the anticipated final reconciliation of accounts, for in the final opinion of that Tosefta, R. Shimeon b. Yoḥai speaks of individuals who, having been either righteous or wicked their whole lives, have a change of heart in their final moments: What will their judgment (obviously in the future world) be?

Even the text that seemingly commences the discussion of the next Mishnah (40b) persists in emphasizing future judgment, for it speaks of the righteous who get their small punishment in this world in order to enjoy perfect future reward and of the wicked who enjoy their small reward in this world in order to allow perfect punishment in the future world. In fact, it seems to me that that gemara should more properly be understood as the end of the present discussion.[5] Its connection with the next Mishnah is very unclear; in contrast, its relation to the present discussion is direct and obvious. If it is correctly understood as the conclusion of the present sugya, then the Talmud emphasizes, one final time, that reward for the righteous and punishment for the wicked are affairs of the future. The discussion has been framed, beginning and end, by the identical point. The proper response to the troubling evidence of this world is to appreciate that we have only an incomplete picture of God's justice.

This deliberation on divine justice is, it should be evident, entirely traditional. As a matter of sheer theory, this Bavli text is willing to endorse a justification that has endured for many generations. The text is so single-minded in its support of this position, in fact, that it does not even want to admit that the Mishnah upon which it purportedly comments may have a different view.

The Bavli on the Destruction

In the Bavli, there are two major treatments of the destruction of the Temples. The first, at Yoma 9b, repeats the Tosefta from Menḥaot that offers explanations for the destruction of both Temples (see Chapter 5), expanding considerably upon that earlier tradition. Making sense of the Bavli's expansion is a significant challenge because there are several distinct versions of this crucial text, none of which agrees completely with the others in the message that it conveys. The differences evident in the several formulations require that each of the versions be considered independently, without claiming priority for one or the other. We will, by allowing each version to have a voice, see a similar message articulated with various nuances, nuances that do, however, carry important differences of emphasis.

One version is that of the Vilna edition and the Munich manuscript (with slight and insignificant differences):

> *a.* The first Temple, why was it destroyed? Because of three things that were in it: idol worship and prohibited sexual relations and bloodshed. . . [the gemara now expands upon each claim by supplying scriptural support]
> *b.* But the second Temple, where they were engaged in Torah [study] and [the performance of] mitzvot and deeds of lovingkindness, why was it destroyed? Because there was in it baseless hatred.
> *c.* [This is] to teach you that baseless hatred is equivalent to three [grave] transgressions: idol worship and prohibited sexual relations and bloodshed. (all Tosefta Menaḥot 13:22, with differences)
> *d.* They were wicked, but they placed their trust in the Holy One, blessed be He.

e. We have come [with this observation, in d, right back] to the first Temple, for it is written, "Her rulers judge for gifts, Her priests give rulings for a fee, And her prophets divine for pay; Yet they rely upon the Lord, saying, 'The Lord is in our midst; No calamity shall overtake us.'" (Micah 3:11)

f. Therefore, the Holy One, blessed be He, brought upon them three decrees, corresponding to their three transgressions, for it says, "Assuredly, because of you Zion shall be plowed as a field, And Jerusalem shall become heaps of ruins, And the Temple Mount a shrine in the woods." (ibid., 3:12)

g. And in the first Temple was there no baseless hatred? But is it not written, "they shall be cast before the sword together with My people; Oh, strike the thigh [in grief]," (Ezek 21:17) and R. Eleazar said: This refers to people who eat and drink together and [then] stab one another with the swords that are in their tongues?

h. This is referring [only] to the princes of Israel . . . [but not, as in the second Temple, to the whole population].

i. R. Yohanan and R. Eleazar both said: The earlier ones [of the first Temple] whose sin was revealed, the end [of their punishment] was [also] revealed. The later ones [of the second Temple] whose sin was not revealed, the end [of their (= our) punishment] was [also] not revealed.

j. R. Yohanan said: The fingernail of the earlier ones is better than the belly of the latter ones.

k. Resh Laqish said to him: On the contrary! The latter ones are better [for] even though there is enslavement to the [foreign] nations they [are nevertheless able to] engage in [the study of] Torah.

l. He said to him: Let the Temple prove it, for it returned to the earlier ones but it did not return to the latter ones [the second Temple was not rebuilt].

m. They asked R. Eleazar: Are the earlier ones greater or the latter ones?

n. He said to them: Put your eyes on the Temple.

o. There are those who say [that] he said to them: Your witness is the Temple.

The quotation from the Tosefta merely repeats an earlier view, ascribing the destruction to a newly elevated sin and thereby preserving the notion of destruction as punishment. More interesting is the expansion that follows. At d, the gemara observes that "they were wicked," a comment that, in context, refers to those who lived during the late second Temple period. At the same time, we learn that "they placed their trust in the Holy One, blessed be He," but, given the verse quoted in e, it is fair to say that this is speaking of subsequently misplaced trust and is intended as a condemnation (as in Micah). We may take this statement to mean that they erroneously believed that their general observance would assure God's protection; they did not understand that their particular sin, baseless hatred, bore a gravity all its own.

With the next step, e, we are returned to the first Temple. The intent is to equate the sins of the first and second Temples, at least with respect to wickedness and misplaced confidence. However, the punishment that fol-

lows, delineated in f, refers only to the first Temple. Next, the gemara
questions whether the sin of baseless hatred was present in the first Temple
as it was in the second; its response is that this sin was true, during the earlier institution, only of the leaders but not of the people at large. Finally,
the populations of the first and second Temples are explicitly compared and,
in light of the final answers (l–o) and despite the opinion of Resh Laqish
(k), it seems clear that in this gemara the earlier population is preferred to
the latter. The rebuilding of the Temple in the first instance and the absence
of such restoration in the second are taken as clear evidence that things were
better the first time around.

Overall, the concern of this version is more the first destruction than the
second. The only comments that refer exclusively to the second are c–b,
after which we are returned to the first or to comparison between the two.
To be sure, there is, on the one hand, a partial equation between the two
events (c and d–e) but, on the other hand, the final comparison insists
that the equation is incomplete, and the gemara goes out of its way to
emphasize that the sin which characterized the population of the late second Temple had only limited currency in the earlier period. This lack of
complete parity is important, because it explains a crucial difference: the
lack of restoration in the second case is seen as ongoing punishment. This
more severe punishment would make sense only if the sin of the latter were
more severe than that of the former, as the gemara in fact assumes. The
argument is circular, but that very circularity is the most significant point.
Catastrophe is understood as punishment, and the more severe (or persistent) catastrophe must therefore be punishment for the more severe transgression.

A second version, represented by the first printing (the Venice edition)
and others,[6] is nearly identical to the version translated above but with one
crucial difference: it omits the comment, at e, that "we have come [with
this observation right back] to the first Temple." Therefore, what follows
continues to refer to the second Temple, not the first (up to, but not including, g). Thus the prophetic accusation should now be understood to
refer to the latter population, as should the punishments that follow; Micah's
description (at f) will now anticipate the condition of Jerusalem following
the second destruction—and it is a fitting description after all. With this
rhetorical extension of the prophetic vision to the later situation, the comparison that follows is based on a powerful foundation.

The power of this version is in its telescoping of history: the second
destruction is understood in explicitly biblical terms. Not atypically, the
gemara here applies scripture to episodes of later history; the Bible is eternal, and we, therefore, are in a sense living in biblical times. Naturally, if
we read these events biblically, as the gemara insists, then we will see destruction and ongoing desolation as punishment. The sin against which the
punishment is directed is, in this version, not only baseless hatred, but also
the corruption of the leaders (e) and their inappropriate confidence. The
gravity of the wrongs attributed to the latter population is here heightened

considerably. This will also explain, of course—even more than in the first version—why the punishment of this population and its generations continues so long.

A final version, found in the manuscript of Yalqut Shimeoni, in the fragment preserved by Dimitrovsky,[7] and elsewhere,[8] is radically opposed, in its primary emphasis, to the version just reviewed. In this version, the whole discussion of their "wickedness" (d–f) is transposed to a position earlier in the discussion, where it becomes an expansion of the Tosefta's remarks concerning the first Temple. Thus "they were wicked" now refers to the earlier population, as does the remark "they placed their trust in the Holy One, blessed He"—which should now probably be understood as a moderating factor (in the gemara, although this is clearly not its meaning in Micah): true, they did sin, but they also trusted God. According to this order, there is almost no shifting between the discussions of the first destruction and the second—we go back to the first only to ask if there was baseless hatred there too. The overall effect is a far clearer distinction between the two incidents, and the bulk of attention, even more than in the first version reviewed above, is directed at the first Temple. Still, the relative evaluation of the sins that led to each punishment continues to consider the earlier population as less wicked, for they, at least, had trust in God. At the same time, the latter events are less biblical since there is no application of scripture to the second destruction. The only thing that remains biblical about that destruction is the perception that it is punishment for sin. On that point there has been no yielding.

Despite the presence of three different versions, with different emphases and different senses of postbiblical history, there remains absolute unanimity in the belief that both destructions should be understood as God's punishment. Like the Mishnah in Taanit (end), which requires ritual acts of repentance (as on Yom Kippur) in response to the destructions, the gemara here continues to search for guilt. In fact, it need not search very far, for the Tosefta has already supplied the explanation that it seeks and, in substance, the Bavli does not—in this text, in any case—go beyond the much earlier tradition. Moreover, this deliberation is, whatever the precise version, very similar in overall approach to the parallel treatment in the Yerushalmi (Yoma 1:1, 38c)—a telling fact, given the broad conservatism of the Yerushalmi in these matters. The Bavli, like the Yerushalmi before it, here reveals satisfaction with traditional explanations. Its expansion serves only to reinforce what had been expressed before.[9]

The second text that discusses the destruction—now the second destruction exclusively and the several defeats that followed it—is the lengthy, composite narrative at Gitt. 55b–58a. This text is far too long to examine in any detail, but it is possible to capture its overall approach with a more general review. Several elements of this gemara find parallels in the Yerushalmi's second discussion of the destruction, at Taan. 4:5 (68c–69a); the differences communicated in the specific approaches of these two documents will be indicative of characteristic differences in their broad ideologies with regard to the matters we have been studying.

Let us first review the Bavli's deliberation in general outline. The sugya begins with an announcement, attributed to R. Yoḥanan, that "on account of Kamẓa and bar Kamẓa Jerusalem was destroyed, on account of a rooster and a hen Tur Malka was destroyed, on account of the shaft of a litter Beitar was destroyed." Each of these cryptic suggestions is then explained, in turn.

The story of Kamẓa and bar Kamẓa is related first. The basic narrative is similar in many details, and also in overall spirit, to what we saw in Lamentations Rabbah (see Chapter 8). In the Bavli's version, a certain man, a friend of Kamẓa but an enemy of bar Kamẓa, gave a feast and instructed his servant to bring Kamẓa to participate. The servant brought bar Kamẓa instead. The host refused to allow bar Kamẓa to remain, despite the latter's repeated entreaties that he be spared the embarrassment. Being forcibly ejected, bar Kamẓa noted that the rabbis who were present at the feast did not raise their voices to condemn the action of the host, so he decided to take revenge by falsely reporting to the king (= emperor) that "the Jews have rebelled against you." When the king replied in disbelief, bar Kamẓa suggested a test: send a sacrifice to be offered on your behalf at the Temple. Bar Kamẓa caused a blemish in the animal, as a result of which the sacrifice could not be offered. This was taken as evidence of rebellion, so the king sent Nero to take the city. Nero learned that God would take revenge against the one who destroyed the Temple, and he therefore removed himself and sent Vespasian in his place. There follows a detailed description of the siege and final submission of the city.

Because there were ample supplies in the city, the people were able to withstand the siege for a considerable period of time. But the zealots thought this situation intolerable, so they burnt the storehouses, hoping that this would provoke the people to fight. A famine ensued. After establishing that the pacifistic position of the rabbis would have been the correct one, R. Yoḥanan ben Zakkai escaped from the city by means of subterfuge and won Vespasian's support for the founding of a rabbinic school at Yavne. Vespasian, hearing that he had been proclaimed emperor, was replaced by Titus. Titus entered the sanctuary and committed various abominations there; amazement is expressed in the text at God's ability to remain silent in the face of such effrontery. On account of his offense, Titus finally died a horrible death. We are returned, at the end of this immediate account, to the story with which we began: "R. Eleazar said: Come and see how great is the power of shame, for God supported bar Kamẓa and destroyed His house and burnt His sanctuary (or, better, allowed His house to be destroyed and His sanctuary to be burnt?)."

The text now turns to an exposition of the second statement regarding the destruction of Tur Malka. It is told that, in Tur Malka, the custom was that when a bride and groom were brought out, they would lead before them a rooster and hen, "as if to say, be fruitful and multiply like chickens." One day, a Roman division passed and took the rooster and hen from the Jews, whereupon the Jews attacked them. It was then reported to the emperor that "the Jews have rebelled against you" (precisely as above). The emperor then came to attack them but, through a certain turn of events, decided to leave them be. In response, the Jews rejoiced greatly, but the emperor took them to be snubbing their noses at him, so he decided to resume his attack. There follows a lengthy enumeration of the great slaughter and destruction that followed. Several stories that speak of the righteousness of this population are then recounted. "And since they were so righteous, why were they punished?" Abbaye wants to know. "Because they did not mourn over [the destruction of] Jerusalem."

The final approach, explicating the destruction of Beitar (during the Bar Kokhba war) follows the same pattern: the Jews were mistakenly understood to be rebelling, leading the emperor to take actions against them. Most of this exposition is devoted to expanding upon the gravity of the carnage and destruction associated with this war; included among the various illustrations is the Bavli's version of the "woman and her seven sons" story, first told in 2 Maccabees but now associated with the Bar Kokhba war.

The most notable element of this lengthy text, uniting all the explanations of destruction, is the pattern of cause and effect that lies at the heart of each: the Jews are mistakenly understood to be rebelling against the Romans; the emperor responds to this erroneous information by putting down the apparent rebellion. This is a remarkably naturalistic explanation for the subsequent destructions (one which, it will be recalled, was also proposed by the author of 2 Maccabees for the attack by Antiochus upon Jerusalem). In no case does the gemara search for blame in the conventional sense. There is no sin, as such, and therefore no room for punishment.

The same tone is evident in major details of each distinct explanation. The story of Kamza and bar Kamza, leading to the report of revolt, is a story of hatred and resentment—as human as could possibly be. For the most part, God does not even appear in this account; even reference to scripture is slight. Of particular interest is the argument, in the narrative, that the defeat is a consequence of a strategic error: had the zealots taken the advice of the rabbis, instead of forcing a confrontation, there is no reason to believe that the city or Temple would have been destroyed. There are, to be sure, two references to God in immediate connection with the events of the destruction, but those references do little to change the impression just described. First, God is praised for remaining silent in the face of Titus's abominations; the God of the destruction is a God of silence, of self-removal, but not of intervention. Second, God is described, at the end, as supporting bar Kamza by allowing the Temple to be destroyed—I have suggested "allowing" as the better translation because here is the first time in this story that God might even possibly be understood as being directly involved in the destruction. In light of what has preceded, though, I think this understanding would be mistaken, and we would do better to understand God's position as one of passive cooperation. The destruction itself is the mechanical result of human frailties and failures.

Crucially, the only time God is described as being active here is in the miraculous death of Titus, punishing him for his offense in the Temple. But the way the narrative is drawn serves only to emphasize God's withdrawal in the other parts of the narrative. We are told that Titus concluded that God's power is to be found only on the water (he was then traveling by ship back to Rome). He concludes this for two reasons, one explicit and one strongly implied. The explicit reason is the biblical models of Pharaoh and Sisera, both of whom met their end by water (Sisera at the wadi of Qishon; Judg. 4:7). The implied reason is, of course, the fact that God has "obviously" not been able to exert power on land. Otherwise, how could Titus have destroyed God's house and captured the city?! The miraculous death that follows shows that God can exert power, almost spitefully, on land as well. But if God does have the power to influence events on land as well as on water, then how could Titus have succeeded in defeating Jerusalem?! The answer must be as suggested earlier in the gemara: God remained silent and distant. The events of the destruction in which, the narrative formulation makes clear, God played no part must therefore be expressions not of divine laws but of natural political laws.

This is not to say that there is no hint of reference to blame and punishment in this lengthy exposition. Here and there, as in the explanation offered to Abbaye concerning the destruction of Tur Malka, the more conventional justification does appear. But it is by no means the predominant one and, on the contrary, the opposite impression emerges far more forcefully. One may easily read this gemara's explanation of the destruction of Jerusalem and the Temple and ask, "Where is God here? What, if anything, is their sin?" This is particularly evident if we compare the Yerushalmi parallel, where, as we saw, the search for blame is a primary agenda item. Unlike that text, in this discussion there is no reference to the Mishnaic fact that the destructions and the conquest of Beitar occurred on the same date, suggesting that similar divine designs were at the root of them all. Unlike the Yerushalmi version, there is no mention here of the story of R. Eleazar ha-Modai, who asks that God "not sit in judgment today." Nor is there a list of proposed sins that the destructions might be understood as punishment for. This text is perfectly content with offering what we have called naturalistic explanations. For the author or authors who composed this text, the best explanation of the destruction appears simply to be that God stepped back and permitted it. Why this was so, they venture no guess.

The naturalism of this sugya, while different from discussions of the destruction in the Tosefta, the Yerushalmi, or elsewhere in the Bavli, is not entirely new even in the rabbinic context. Virtually the same naturalism characterized, it will be recalled, Lamentations Rabbah's discussion of the same event. Of course, there are some differences in detail, but the ideological assumptions of both are identical. Still, the present assumption is certainly less frequently expressed in the rabbinic canon, and the record of this naturalism in the Bavli does tell us something of its qualities. If the inclusion of such an explanation of the destruction in Lamentations Rabbah —a Palestinian work of far more conventional leanings—was properly the cause of comment, its inclusion in the Bavli causes little surprise. This absence of surprise tells us how far the Bavli has come from its rabbinic predecessors.

10

The Bavli Rebels

I have isolated three Bavli texts that make especially important statements about suffering. The first two represent significant manipulations of earlier traditions in order to express innovative positions. In each case they add their own distinct voices as well, but it is the appropriation of prior voices that makes these deliberations so striking. The third text is almost entirely original, articulating an opinion that, as far as I have been able to discern, is entirely without precedent in all rabbinic tradition. Individually and in combination these texts exemplify the rebellious side of the Bavli.

Shabbat 55a–b

a. R. Ami said: There is no death without sin and no suffering without transgression . . .

b. for it is written, "The person who sins, he alone shall die. A child shall not share the burden of the parent's guilt, nor shall a parent share the burden of a child's guilt; the righteousness of the righteous shall be accounted to him alone, and the wickedness of the wicked shall be accounted to him alone." (Ezek 18:20)

c. There is no suffering without transgression, for it is written, "I will punish their transgression with the rod, their iniquity with plagues." (Ps 89:33)

d. They object [quoting a baraita]: The Ministering Angels said before the Holy One, blessed be He, "Master of the world! For what reason have you punished the first person with death?" He said to them, "I commanded him only one simple commandment, yet he transgressed it!" They said to him, "But didn't Moses and Aaron, who observed the whole Torah, die?" He said to them, "For the same fate is in store for all: for the righteous, and for the wicked . . ." (Eccles 9:2). [This conclusion, claiming that even the completely righteous die, would certainly seem to be a refutation to R. Ami.]

e. [We can defend the opinion of R. Ami by saying that] he expressed [his opinion] like this tanna, who taught: R. Shimeon b. Eleazar says—Even Moses and Aaron died because of their sins, as it says, "Because you did not trust me enough . . ." (Num 20:12)—But had you trusted me, your time for leaving this world would still not have come. [Thus R. Ami's opinion has, for the moment, been defended.]

f. They object [to R. Ami again, quoting another baraita]: Four died because of the urging of the snake [that is, because of the first sin of humankind, and not because of their own sins], and who are they? Benjamin the son of Jacob, Amram the father of Moses, and Jesse the father of David, and Caleb the son of David [all of whom did not sin yet died].

g. And all of them are [known from] tradition, except for Jesse the father of David, concerning whom scripture is explicit. . . .

h. Who is it [that is the author of the unattributed opinion expressed in this baraita, f]?

i. If you say that it is the tanna [who stands behind the baraita that tells] of the Ministering Angels, but there are [also then] Moses and Aaron [whom he says died without having sinned first]!

j. Rather, no, it is R. Shimeon b. Eleazar [who said, in e, that Moses and Aaron also sinned].

k. [If the author of this final baraita is R. Shimeon b. Eleazar, then there is no identified tanna who does not believe that *someone* died without having sinned first. Having thus refuted one part of R. Ami's original claim, the gemara concludes] learn from this [that] *there is death without sin and there is suffering without transgression, and the refutation of R. Ami is a* [*definitive*] *refutation!*[1] [emphasis added]

The tradition that begins this deliberation appears also, we saw, in Lev. R. 37, 1. There it is stated as a simple matter of fact, with no accompanying challenge or question. It is left to the Bavli to collect the evidence that might challenge or even refute this opinion.

For opposition, the Bavli rallies alternative and greater authorities, enlisting, in the process, both contradictory scriptures (Eccles. 9, in d) and baraitot. Most of the steps depend upon quotation of earlier traditions: the first objection (d) is found in Sifrei Deut. 339 and the defense to this objection (e) appears in Sifrei Num. 137. Before we get to the last baraita, the debate is a stalemate (as might be expected when one has access to an earlier tradition that includes such a variety of opinions). But, with a deliberately limiting reading of the last baraita (f and following), the Bavli leads us to a complete refutation of R. Ami's view.

It is worth considering in detail the way in which the Bavli goes about constructing that refutation. The logic is this: there is an unattributed baraita (f) that clearly contradicts R. Ami. Because, in order to contradict one baraita, Ami must find the support of another baraita (in theory, Talmudic sages are not permitted to contradict more authoritative traditions from the period of the Mishnah without the support of another tradition with equivalent authority), the Talmud seeks to identify the author of this problematic baraita. If it is the same as the author of the "Ministering Angels" baraita, then Ami can again simply claim to be aligned with Shimeon b. Eleazar (as at e). But this baraita cannot have the same author as the earlier one; they contradict one another in their list of those who died without first sinning. The Talmud concludes, therefore, that the author must be Shimeon b. Eleazar—the only alternative previously known—and thus R. Ami can find no authoritative support.

The logic of this refutation is labored and ultimately dubious. There is no good reason to assume that there are only two alternatives. Why could this baraita not simply reflect still another opinion (say, that of "the sages," as unattributed traditions are commonly identified in the Bavli) and thus leave Shimeon b. Eleazar to support Ami? From the information with which we are supplied, there is no good reason why this could not be the case. Moreover, why would we understand R. Ami's statement as anything but a general rule intended to express his opinion concerning everyday reality? So what if there are four exceptions? Why could he not grant the exceptions and still insist that the general rule applies? To be sure, the gemara understands his statement as being comprehensive, but this is the gemara's choice. Alternative interpretations could certainly have been suggested to salvage R. Ami's opinion.

This deliberation concludes as it does (though, as shown, this conclusion is hardly necessary) because the author of this text *wants* this to be the conclusion. And he does not quite cover his tracks because he wants it to be apparent that, despite an important and much supported explanation of suffering represented by R. Ami, he insists upon an alternative. Let me spell out why this is so.

Aside from the flawed logic that leads to the text's definitive conclusion, there are two other outstanding elements of its rhetoric that highlight how unnecessary this conclusion is. The first is the broadness of the conclusion. As was noticed even by traditional commentators,[2] it is entirely beyond defense to claim, based upon the evidence at hand, that "there is suffering without transgression." The text on which the refutation is based speaks about death, and death alone. It is entirely conceivable that there could be death without sin—by divine decree—and yet be no suffering without transgression, no suffering that is not somehow punishment. Yet with no direct support the gemara extends its alleged refutation of R. Ami even to his claim for suffering. This gemara insists upon the wrong-headedness of R. Ami. It will not be constrained by the strict limits of its traditional evidence.

The second outstanding feature of the rhetoric of this text is that it arrives at a definitive conclusion at all. The preference of the Bavli is to support amoraic opinions, even several opposing opinions at the same time. It is the hallmark of the Bavli that it finds value in multiple opinions. In light of its overall ideology, definitive refutations are to be recognized as a last resort.[3] In fact, of well over 1,450 instances in the Bavli when an objection from a source of higher authority is introduced, only 118 conclude, as the text does here, by admitting a definitive refutation.[4] This is an astonishingly small number in the context of the Bavli as a whole. And, it must be added, the manner in which some attempted refutations are responded to is extremely forced. Certainly, the logical steps that would be necessary here to support R. Ami are no more strained than many such defenses. For this reason, the forced, almost arbitrary complexion of this conclusion becomes eminently apparent, and it falls to the reader to ask why here, as opposed to most other places, the Talmud is so insistent.

Having recognized the formulative manipulations with which the present author accomplishes his goal, we now turn our consideration to another aspect of this text. I have in mind the fact that, whereas all of the other building blocks of this deliberation are drawn from earlier traditions we can identify independently, the final baraita—upon which the refutation is based—appears nowhere before the Bavli. Of course, this may be pure coincidence; it is possible that the Bavli recorded a tradition that happened not to be recorded elsewhere. However, in light of the fact that all other elements are recorded previously, the absence of an equivalent record for this last baraita is at least suggestive. It is the opinion of some scholars that the Babylonian rabbis did compose their own "baraitot."[5] Is this such a case? Was this "baraita" composed in order to assure that there would be a refutation here? In the end, it really doesn't matter whether this is so. This is, in any case, the first time that the baraita ever merited documentary preservation. This baraita was important to the Bavli, for it supported the conclusion that the Bavli clearly preferred. It allowed for a refutation of R. Ami's conventionally pious opinion.

For purposes of clarity, let me reiterate the position that this gemara so forcefully rejects: it is the opinion that suffering and death are to be understood as punishment for sin, namely, the opinion that originated in the Torah and the Prophets and has been the most commanding explanation of suffering ever since. Yet here, we learn, it is (if understood too literally and too universally) wrong. There is definitive proof, this Bavli text claims, that there are exceptions to this rule. We might add, whether the proof is a contradictory authoritative tradition, as explicitly here, or the evidence of everyday reality, as we might prefer, the conclusion is the same. Remarkably, this author is not even willing, in the end, to consider the possible enduring merit of the traditional position. In his eyes, suffering and justice are two separate discussions.

Finally, it is also necessary to point out that, though this text rejects traditional piety, it offers no alternative explanation. It might be argued that finding such an explanation is not the point of the present discussion; it is concerned with evaluating the opinion represented in R. Ami's statement but has no interest in rationalizing suffering as such. Still, the silence is difficult to dismiss so easily. A text that so definitively rejects the explanation of suffering that has been offered by Jews since the Torah should be sensitive to the void that it leaves. Perhaps the message it finally wishes to communicate is that there are no ready explanations.[6]

Berakhot 5a–b

This text is the longest deliberation (by far) on suffering as such in all classical rabbinic literature. It requires analysis of its many details, but it is far too long to consider at a single, uninterrupted reading. I will thus divide my presentation of the text into the three major sections that I see comprising the text. However, the analyses that follow are cumulative, each building on and responding to the lessons of the prior reading.

Before commencing analysis, it is necessary to say a few words about the nature of the Bavli's intended reader and what that assumption contributes to analysis and, finally, to understanding. This clarification is essential because, as will be evident in what follows, this Bavli text (like many others, but we are interested here in this one) echoes and turns back upon itself, later comments qualifying or contradicting earlier comments on more than a few occasions. The question is, How are we to take these qualifications and contradictions? Are they to be harmonized or allowed to stand in tension? Are we intended to notice contradictions or difficulties at all? Are we to go along with difficult interpretations or claims of meaning, even if they contradict our sense of the meaning of a text? Only by first identifying the assumed reader can we begin to answer these and related questions of interpretation.

To state the matter as briefly as possible, from the nature of this text and so many like it, it appears clear that the Bavli's intended reader is massively literate in biblical and rabbinic tradition, is questioning and critical, and is confident of his own intellectual resources and willing to use them. Assumed competence in biblical and rabbinic tradition is evident from the frequency with which such traditions will be quoted only in part or merely referred to in the Bavli, assuming, though, that the reader will be able to supply the rest of the relevant context and its interpretation. The questioning and critical character of the reader is modeled by the Bavli itself, which invites its reader to engage in the same process. In fact, without such questioning and critical inquiry, the Bavli is frequently impossible to understand. Appreciating the common gaps that characterize the Bavli's expression, we may readily understand that the reader is expected to contribute such critical acumen on his own. Finally, the confidence that the Bavli expects the reader will have in his own intellectual resources is expressed in the fact that the Bavli speaks to its reader as an equal partner in the learning process. This peer—the reader—is engaged directly and is expected to respond and contribute at each stage of the unfolding argument. Thus the passive or submissive reader will have a hard time being part of the process of Talmud. Talmud is an active, demanding, and consequently empowering project.[7]

Given this picture, it seems likely that the reader is intended to approach a text such as this one with critical sensors fully attuned. He will recognize reinterpretations or contradictions. He will be called upon to evaluate such phenomena and to respond. If reasonable reconciliations are available, he will probably be invited to assent to them—but he will not be asked to suspend critical judgment. Thus, where a text works against itself, it will be his responsibility to evaluate the rhetoric of such a move. And, given his assumed confidence, he will be asked to identify with one position or another, but not without challenging himself with the alternative. The text will never be reduced or simplified; he will always be sensitive to its complexities. With this in mind, we now turn to the text at hand.

Transition

    a. And R. Isaac said: Anyone who reads the Shema upon his bed demons separate from him. . . .
    b. R. Shimeon b. Laqish said: Anyone who engages in [the study of] Torah, suffering separates from him, as it says. . . .
    c. R. Yoḥanan said to him, this [idea that you have just expressed] even children in school know it, for it says, "He said, 'If you will heed the Lord your God diligently, doing what is upright in His sight, giving ear to His commandments and keeping all His laws, then I will not bring upon you any of the diseases that I brought upon the Egyptians, for I the Lord am your healer.'" (Ex 15:26)
    d. Rather, anyone for whom it is possible to engage in [the study of] Torah and does not [thus] engage, the Holy One, blessed be He, brings upon him ugly, horrible suffering, as it says. . . .

I describe this exchange as a transition because the text has not yet devoted its attentions exclusively to the question of suffering; what follows does not speak of suffering but of God's generosity in giving the Torah. The primary emphasis here too, therefore, should be understood to be Torah, not suffering. The present opinions wish to emphasize the importance of Torah study; suffering is the threat that looms behind the text's exhortation. It is incidental, not central.[8]

Still, this transition serves the following discussion of suffering in two ways. First, it does build the bridge to the primary discussion of suffering—it is the excuse which allows the text to address this central problem. Second, it emphasizes that there is an opinion—that the study and observance of Torah assures that God will protect the person thus engaged from suffering—that is so obvious that "even the child in the school knows it." As we shall see, when the ensuing deliberation has the opportunity to reflect upon this opinion (from several perspectives but by implication) it turns out that it is not nearly as obvious as is claimed. Thus the introduction of this opinion lulls us into a sense of unwitting confidence. It is this sense that the following deliberation will most challenge.

Part I

A.   Rava, and some say R. Ḥisda, said:[9]

    1. If a man sees suffering coming upon him, he should examine his deeds, as it says, "Let us search and examine our ways, And turn back to the Lord." (Lam 3:40)

    2. If he searched and did not find [his deeds to be the cause of his suffering], he should attribute it to neglect of Torah [study], as it says, "Happy is the man whom you discipline, O Lord, the man You instruct in Your teaching." (Ps 94:12)

    3. And if he attributed it [to the neglect of study] but did not find [his study to be wanting] then it is clear that they are afflictions [= suffering] of [God's] love, as it says, "For whom the Lord loves, He rebukes." (Prov 3:12)

B.   Rava said R. Seḥora said R. Huna said:

    1. Anyone whom the Holy One, blessed be He desires, He afflicts with suffering, for it says, "And the one whom the Lord desires, He crushes with illness." (Isa 53:10)[10]

    2. Is it possible [that this is the case] even if he does not accept them willingly? Scripture says, "if he made himself an offering for guilt" (ibid.)—[meaning] just as an offering is [offered] willingly, so too suffering [must be accepted] willingly.

    3. And if he accepted them [willingly] what is his reward? "He might see offspring and have a long life" (ibid.), and not only so, but his learning will remain with him,[11] as it says, "And that through him the Lord's purpose might prosper." (ibid.)

C.   R. Jacob b. Idi and R. Aḥa b. Ḥanina dispute:

    1. One says: What is suffering of love? Any [suffering] that does not cause the neglect of Torah, for it says, "Happy is the man whom you discipline, O Lord, the man You instruct in Your teaching." (Ps 94:12)

    2. And one says: What is suffering of love? Any [suffering] that does not cause the neglect of prayer, as it says, "Blessed is God who has not turned away my prayer, or His faithful care from me." (Ps 66:20)

    3. R. Aba the son of R. Ḥiyya b. Abba said to them: This is what R. Ḥiyya b. Abba said [that] R. Yoḥanan said—[Both] these and these are suffering of love, as it says, "For whom the Lord loves, He rebukes." (Prov 3:12) Rather, what does scripture [mean when it] says, "the man You instruct in Your teaching?" Don't read "instruct him" [the more literal rendering of this verse] but "[and from your Torah] instruct us," [meaning] this thing You instruct us from your Torah, [that is] *a fortiori* from [the law of the removal by a master of] the tooth or eye [of his slave]; what if [by the removal of] a tooth or an eye, which are but one of a man's limbs, a slave goes out to freedom, suffering, which cleanses the entire body of a person, how much the moreso [should a person "go out to freedom"]!

    3A. And this is [the same as the opinion of] R. Shimeon b. Laqish, for R. Shimeon b. Laqish said: "Covenant" is stated with respect to salt and "covenant" is stated with respect to suffering. "Covenant" is stated with respect to salt, as it is written, "you shall not omit . . . the salt of your covenant," (Lev 2:13) and "covenant" is stated with respect to suffering, as it is written [following the long recitation of afflictions that Israel will suffer if she does not obey God's will], "These are the terms of the covenant" (Deut 28:69)—just as with "covenant" spoken of with respect to salt, the salt sweetens the meat,[12] so too with "covenant" spoken of with respect to suffering, the suffering cleanses all of a person's transgressions.

First, it is necessary to clarify the system by which the translation of the text is presented here. It will immediately be evident that I am following a different system than that followed elsewhere. Ordinarily, my divisions of the text are intended to recreate the smallest units of expression, thereby facilitating reference. But here, my intent is to delineate the substantive structure of the text, showing where the expression of a single coherent idea leads to the expression of another, distinct coherent idea. Where such expressions subdivide into substantive (not formal) units, I indicate such divisions as well. For example, at A, the statement of Rava (or R. Hisda) divides into three distinct ideas: (1) the first response to suffering, (2) the first fallback position (What if sin, in the normal sense, is not at the root of a person's suffering?), and (3) the final, safety position (if 2 doesn't work, there is still an explanation available). Though each of these statements relates to the previous one, each could nevertheless be formulated independently with little adjustment and still express a perfectly coherent idea ("If a person suffers, yet neither sins nor neglects Torah study, it must be suffering of love."). In contrast, in C, though there are three expressions relating to suffering of love (What is and what isn't?), the final opinion (3) is built on a series of individual steps and is then supported (or correlated) with a related opinion, itself built on a series of steps (3A). The point, throughout, is a single one: suffering—apparently (at this point, but see later) potentially any suffering—is an expression of God's love because it cleanses one of one's sins and thereby leads to "freedom." To be sure, this idea takes many formal steps to express. But there is a single, basic idea here nonetheless.[13]

Now to the substance of this first part of the deliberation. The overall concern of part I is what is called "sufferings of [God's] love," a concept with an ancient history whose present appellation waited, nevertheless, to Genesis Rabbah. The idea contained in this term is a simple one: as a parent will reprove a child with love, so too will God reprove individuals (see Deut. 8:5, quoted below in this text). Suffering has undeniable positive consequences; it should therefore be understood as a good gift from God. The present deliberation seeks to define precisely when suffering can be understood as an expression of God's love. In A we learn that the more conventional explanation of suffering should be preferred; we should first consider sin as the possible source of suffering. At this point, suffering of love is seen as a kind of last resort. But in the following steps, suffering of love becomes the exclusive concern of the authorities. In B it is immediately recognized that some might have trouble accepting the notion that suffering is an expression of divine love. Therefore, the text explains that suffering will be suffering of love only if that suffering is accepted out of love. If it is, then the suffering will lead to great reward. In C we learn that, in the opinion of some, certain suffering—that suffering which leads to a breakdown of communications with God—cannot be suffering of love; if God loved us, why would God remove the possibility of communication? But the final opinion in this section remarks that even such suffering is not to be excluded from the category of suffering of love. Suffering in general is considered, on two accounts (the logical relation to the minor suffering of a slave and the relation of suffering to "covenant"), potentially a manifestation of divine love.

Outstanding in the formulation of this deliberation is the clear and consistent formal structuring. The tripartite expression of ideas, typical of many Talmudic texts, predominates. This structuring gives the deliberation a very distinctive voice and, as we shall see, demands that diversions from this formal structure be given particular notice. At present, the balance and order of the text create a confident context for the articulation of mostly traditional ideas—those already widely expressed in scripture and earlier rabbinic literature. Supporting the impression of traditionality is the regular reference to scriptural prooftexts. In fact, each of the lessons supported by scripture is relatively straightforward; one is left with the impression that these opinions do, for the most part, indeed reside in scripture. Thus the voice of biblical tradition looms large. If one were to go no further, this would represent a thoroughly traditional expression.

Yet this air of confident traditionality is not entirely without qualifications. The first such qualification is the admission, in B, that suffering of love is conditional. Suffering will be suffering of love only if it is accepted out of love, that is, willingly. If there is hesitation or misgiving on the part of the sufferer, then it is not suffering of love. Implicit in this statement, of course, is the recognition that such acceptance might not be easy; as we shall see later in the text, even the most pious individuals might not accept suffering. The second reservation is found in the dispute, in C, with regard to the possible disqualification of certain kinds of suffering from the said category. The reasons for suggested disqualification are well understood: If you can't speak to God (prayer) or God won't speak to you (through study of Torah), then how can this be suffering of love? Stated in other terms, this disqualification applies to extreme suffering. By insisting on these exceptions, these opinions open up the possibility that certain extreme forms of suffering might go searching for, but not find, a ready explanation. For this reason, we are relieved when the final opinions reject these exceptions. Still, as we shall soon discover, this rejection is a setup. Even R. Yoḥanan, to whom this opinion is attributed, insists that certain suffering cannot be suffering of love. In retrospect, this easy acceptance will appear ironic indeed.

The next major section of this deliberation begins by quoting a teaching known already from the halakhic midrashim.

Part II

A. It is taught: R. Shimeon b. Yoḥai says: Three good gifts did the Holy One, blessed be He, give to Israel, and all were given only by means of suffering. And what are they?
   1. Torah,
   2. and the Land of Israel,
   3. and the world-to-come.
A1. From where [do we learn] Torah? As it says, "Happy is the man whom you discipline, O Lord, the man You instruct in Your teaching." (Ps 94:12)
A2. The Land of Israel? For it says, "the Lord your God disciplines you just as a man disciplines his son," and it is written after it, "For the Lord your God is bringing you into a good land." (Dt 8:5, 8:7)
A3. The world-to-come? For it is written, "For the commandment is a lamp, The teaching is a light, And the way to [future] life is the rebuke that disciplines." (Prov 6:23)
B. 1. A Tanna taught before R. Yoḥanan: Anyone who engages in (1) Torah or (2) deeds of lovingkindness or (3) buries his children, all of his sins are forgiven him.
   2. R. Yoḥanan said to him: It is fine with Torah and deeds of lovingkindness, for it is written, "Iniquity is expiated by loyalty [= kind deeds] and faithfulness [= truth]" (Prov 16:6)—"loyalty," this is acts of lovingkindness, for it says, "He who strives to do good and kind deeds / Attains life, success, and honor" (Prov 21:21); "faithfulness," this is Torah, for it says, "Buy truth and never sell it." (Prov 23:23). But burying one's children, where is this from?
   3. That elder taught in the name of R. Shimeon b. Yoḥai: It is derived by a scriptural equation of "iniquity" and "iniquity;" it is written here "Iniquity is expiated by loyalty and faithfulness" and it is written there "but visit the iniquity of the fathers upon their children." (Jer 32:18)
C. R. Yoḥanan said: Sores and "children" are not suffering of love.
   1. And are sores not? But is it not taught: Anyone who has any one of these four appearances of skin-ailment, they are none other than an altar of atonement.
      a. They might be an altar of atonement, but they are not suffering of love;
      b. And if you wish I will say: this [the teaching in C.1] relates to us [in Babylonia, for skin ailments do not disqualify us from anything] and this [R. Yoḥanan's statement] relates to them [for, in the Land of Israel, skin ailments cause certain disqualifications due to impurity];
      c. And if you wish I will say: this [the teaching in C.1] is [speaking of a case where the skin affliction is] private [= in a covered location on the body] and this [R. Yoḥanan's statement] is [speaking of a case where the skin affliction] is public.
   2. And are "children" not?
      a. How is this to be imagined? If you say that [we are talking about a case where] he had them and they died, did not R. Yoḥanan say "this is the bone of my tenth son!"[14]
      b. Rather, this [R. Yoḥanan's statement above at C] is where he did

not have them at all and this [his statement here at C.2.a, assumed to support the notion of suffering of love] is where he had them and they died.

I designate this section of text as a single major unit by virtue of the connection of each step with the one preceding it, though the last step (C) is less immediately related to the first (A, that is, beyond the overall theme of suffering of love). So A is related to B by the designation of tannaitic authority, by its inclusion of Torah, by its tripartite structure, and by its attribution of the final answer to R. Shimeon b. Yoḥai (at B.3), the alleged author of the opinion in A. B is related to C in its discussion of "children" and in the difficulty that R. Yoḥanan has with "children" in both of the steps. Still, I admit that important connections can also be found with the lengthy section that follows, so these sections should be read together as well as apart from one another.

   The first portion of this section is, as mentioned earlier, a quotation of a tradition found also in the lengthy discussion of suffering in the Mekhilta and Sifrei. What is notable about its present quotation is the seemingly minor but (I shall argue) actually rather significant omission of the introduction to R. Shimeon's comment as recorded in those midrashim. Here the Talmud merely commences by saying, "three good gifts did the Holy One . . . ," whereas in the midrashim R. Shimeon's opinion is introduced with the words "*suffering is precious,* for three good gifts. . . ." Because the tradition appears, in the midrashim, in the context of a series of statements commencing with this introductory formula, it might be thought that this introduction was added under the influence of that formulaic context. It might be imagined, therefore, that the Bavli's version is more "original." Whether or not that is so, we could easily suppose that the Bavli merely preserved a slightly different version of this tradition, and we might therefore conclude that this difference—this omission in the Bavli's version—is insignificant. However, as we shall see, the question of whether "suffering is precious" plays a crucial role in the present deliberation. Below, several sages are addressed with the question "Is suffering precious to you?" (the Hebrew adds only one word to change the affirmative declaration into a question). Each time the question is asked, the answer is direct and unambiguous: "neither they [= the sufferings] nor their reward!" With this utter rejection of the preciousness of suffering, it is difficult to avoid the conclusion that the omission of this comment in the baraita of R. Shimeon b. Yoḥai is, in fact, significant. If nothing else (that is, if the phrase was not actually excised by the author of the Bavli's deliberation), then, at the very least, this omission shows that the Bavli is not predisposed to agree that "suffering is precious." For this reason (either intentionally or unwittingly) it chooses a version of this tradition that does not include this expression.

   The second segment of the present text (B) begins by arguing again on behalf of the benefits of suffering. If these forms of suffering lead to the forgiving of sins, then they must surely be suffering of love. But R. Yoḥanan's response reveals, now more explicitly, that the apologetic for suffering is not as simple as it might appear. The problem is that, while R. Yoḥanan can indeed find scriptural support for the claims concerning Torah and deeds of lovingkindness, he allegedly cannot find such support for the claim that the loss of one's children leads to the forgiving of sins. But the text gives us every reason to question this failure. First, his proofs for Torah and lovingkindness require the combination of three verses; the proof for burying one's children requires only two. Second, his proof is original, while the proof he fails to offer has already been expressed in the tradition (by R. Shimeon b. Yoḥai). Third, the proof that he fails to supply is given by some anonymous elder; is it possible that the great R. Yoḥanan is unable to find a simple proof where an unnamed elder can?! Finally we learn (at C.2.a) that there is good reason for R. Yoḥanan to have difficulty with "burying one's children"—he himself was forced to do so and thus he knew this pain intimately. Is it this pain, we are forced to ask ourselves, that doesn't allow him to find scriptural proof for the benefits of losing one's child?

Turning to C, we again learn that R. Yoḥanan has misgivings about suffering that involves "children"; he is unwilling to admit that either it or skin afflictions is suffering of love. It must be noted: the text signals us here that something is awry. Unlike all of the traditions that have come before this, R. Yoḥanan's statement is built of two points, not three. With respect to his dissent on skin afflictions, some equilibrium is quickly recovered—three solutions to the problem of the apparent contradiction of his statement with another authoritative teaching are offered. But the number three appears nowhere in the discussion of "children," not in the problem and not in the solution.

Oddest of all is the way that R. Yoḥanan's dissent on "children" is challenged: he can't mean what he appears to say because he was also accustomed to say "this is the bone of my tenth son." Apparently the gemara is suggesting that, for some reason, this statement should be taken as evidence that the loss of one's child, obviously experienced by R. Yoḥanan himself, is in fact suffering of love.[15] But we ourselves would be tempted to say that for precisely this reason R. Yoḥanan is unwilling to accept such an experience as suffering of love! Would we be impious for arriving at such a conclusion? Are we to conclude, despite alternative and possibly better interpretations, that R. Yoḥanan does, in fact, believe that the loss of one's children is suffering of love, as the gemara here demands? Since R. Yoḥanan's statement ("this is the bone") is presented here as deriving from another context, we can really judge only if we consider the context from which it was taken. Fortunately, the Talmud supplies us later with a context that is clearly more original and thus we will be invited to judge for ourselves. I will argue that, in light of the "original" context, the meaning given to this statement here becomes highly implausible. In my opinion, the author of this deliberation intentionally asks us to reconsider and ultimately to reject his conclusions here.[16] At this point it is sufficient to note that there are already several signals, both formal and substantive, that cause us to respond to the gemara's present arguments with misgivings.

Now, in the penultimate section of this deliberation, we are introduced to "the real R. Yoḥanan" and we learn, in the course of this introduction, a great deal about R. Yoḥanan's attitudes concerning suffering.

Part III

A. R. Ḥiyya b. Abba became ill. R. Yoḥanan went in to him.
  1. He said to him: Is suffering dear to you?
  2. He said to him: Neither it nor its reward.
  3. He said to him: Give me your hand.
  He gave him his hand and raised him.
B. R Yoḥanan became ill. R. Ḥanina went in to him.
  1. He said to him . . .
  2. He said to him . . . [all same as in A]
  3. He said to him . . .
  He gave him his hand and raised him.
  (And why? Let R. Yoḥanan raise himself [for we have seen that he has the power to do so in the prior story]! They say, "One who is imprisoned does not release himself from prison.")[17]
C. R. Eleazar became ill.[18] R. Yoḥanan went in to him. He saw that he was lying in a dark room. [R. Yoḥanan] uncovered his arm and a light fell [over the room] and he saw that R. Eleazar was crying.
  1. He said to him: why are you crying?
    a. If it is because of Torah that you have not [studied] sufficiently, we have taught [in m. Men. 13:11], "it makes no difference whether one does much or little, provided that he directs his heart to heaven."
    b. And if it is because of food, not every man may merit two tables [= wealth].[19]
    c. And if it is because of children, *this is the bone of my tenth son* [emphasis added].
  2. He said to him: I am crying on account of this beauty that will rot in the earth.[20]
  3. He said to him: For this you should surely cry
  And the two of them cried together.[21]
  4. He said to him . . .
  5. He said to him . . . [all same as in A and B]
  6. He said to him . . .

In this segment of the deliberation, the present consideration of suffering comes to a climax. The essential point is made in the first two virtually identical sections (A and B). When questioned regarding their attitudes toward their suffering, both sages respond by declaring that neither it nor its reward is desired by them. To put it in other words, if this is what is necessary to attain reward, keep it! Both parties would rather be spared the suffering.

The response to suffering modeled here is quite startling. To begin with, it should be recognized that the suffering experienced here is some kind of illness; each sage is confined to his bed, and it is necessary that each be raised (= healed). At the same time, there is no explicit evidence that we are speaking of suffering so severe that it would render the sufferers unable to pray or study—though, to be sure, if we (mistakenly) sought to reconcile this with what came earlier we could insist upon such a reading. Nor, obviously, is the present suffering related to the loss of one's children or to skin afflictions. According to all parties, therefore, this is suffering that might qualify as suffering of love.

But this cannot be suffering of love because, as we learned above (at I.B.2), to be suffering of love, adversity must be accepted with love, and that clearly is not the case here. Neither, however, can it be deemed suffering of punishment, for these sages actively intercede to eliminate the suffering of the other. If this suffering were understood as God's punishment, there could be no justification for their initiatives.[22] In fact, these masters evidently do not accept—as the Yerushalmi would have liked—that their suffering is the direct will of God at all. But if not the direct will of God, then what is it? What in the attitudes or beliefs of these rabbis leads them to respond as they do?

Unfortunately, answers to these questions are not readily forthcoming in this text. But certain possibilities are negated, at least, in the more complex final section (C). Upon discovering R. Eleazar weeping, R. Yohanan asks him why he is doing so. Yohanan does not wait for an answer, but instead rejects what he believes to be certain obvious possibilities. If it is because of lack of sufficient study, he says, no problem! It is not quantity that counts but proper intention. Again, R. Yohanan works against more conventional opinions expressed much earlier: lack of sufficient Torah study ("neglect of [study of] Torah" at I.A.2) was offered, it will be recalled, as good reason for suffering. Not so, says R. Yohanan. Alternatively, if it is because of the lack of wealth, coventionally understood as reward from God (its inverse must therefore be punishment), this, too, is not to be interpreted in this way. Again, no reason to cry. And, says R. Yohanan, if it is because of "children," neither is this reason to cry, for, Yohanan points out to Eleazar, "this is the bone of my tenth son."

How are we to understand this last step in R. Yohanan's comforting of R. Eleazar? The comment regarding "children" is found in a series of statements regarding what R. Eleazar lacks. He believes that he lacks sufficient Torah and he sees that he lacks wealth. The possible problem is not the loss of something but its absence to begin with. Conversely, when Yohanan responds that there is good reason to cry, it is for something that he most assuredly has—his own beauty. The contrast is between something now enjoyed and something never possessed. Therefore, it seems likely that the same is being said about children: lack of children is not something to cry about. Why? Because "this is the bone of my tenth son." In other words—

it now seems clear—R. Yoḥanan comforts his friend by indicating that things could have been much worse. If he thinks that childlessness is painful, look at the alternative. Far more painful is the loss of a beloved child.

I am arguing for this understanding based upon purely literary considerations, signals to the reader given in this text alone. It may be objected that R. Eleazar is known in the Talmud to have had at least one son (R. Pedat; see Ber. 11b and M.Q. 20a). However, it seems to me that there is no reason to admit that knowledge here. Signals given in the present context should be considered far more powerful than details that might be available from elsewhere (unless we could show that that other information is assumed to be common knowledge, which is not the case here). Lest there be doubt concerning the sense of the present text, I refer the reader's attention to the comment of Tosafot at Nid. 8a (s.v. *"v'amar"*):

> [Commenting on the fact that R. Pedat is identified in this text as being the son of R. Eleazar:] And should you say that in the first chapter of Berakhot [5b, our text here] R. Yoḥanan said to R. Eleazar, "If because of children, this is the bone of my tenth son," *suggesting that R. Eleazar did not have children,* it could be said [in response to this problem] that he was born to him after [this story in Berakhot] or that he had many children and some of them died. . . . [emphasis added]

So Tosafot, too, believe that the clear sense of the present text is that R. Eleazar has no children. The meaning of R. Yoḥanan's statement, therefore, is just as I have said: the lack of children is insignificant next to their loss.

I inquire into the precise meaning of this exchange because of its implications for our understanding of the earlier segment of this deliberation, at II.C.2. If there is no reason to understand R. Yoḥanan's statement as evidence that he believes that the loss of children is suffering of love, as now seems clear, then we should finally reject the forced conclusion of that step above. As we have now learned, Yoḥanan grieves the loss of children deeply. It is for this reason that he rejects such suffering as "suffering of love"— precisely as we had preferred earlier. Are we to be troubled by the contradiction between this conclusion and the conclusion expressed explicitly at II.C.2? I think not. First, it will be recalled that the formulation of the text itself invited us to question the sincerity of its explicit avowal. Moreover, now the gemara has given us precisely the evidence we need to challenge its claim above. Of course, it did not need to do so. By supplying this information, the gemara is inviting us to reread and to reevaluate. By doing just this, we discover that the gemara, too, was not fully comfortable with its first tentative interpretation of R. Yoḥanan's bitter statement.

Thus we see R. Yoḥanan is extremely bitter about his suffering. He has suffered the loss of a child and he is in no mind to accept this suffering. He would be willing to forgo the reward if he could avoid the suffering. But where, in the opinion of R. Yoḥanan, is value to be found? What truly is worth crying about? The answer, we see in the final crucial step of this last exchange (2–3; the final exchange [4–6], if it belongs at all,[23] is a mere formulaic repetition of what has come before), is this beauty—the beauty of R. Yoḥanan—that will, with his death, rot in the ground. In the end, it is all reduced to the simple and undeniable beauty of the mundane. Grander conceptions, those which transcend the mundane, are dismissed as being (at the very least) inscrutable or, possibly, without redeeming value. Apologies for God's ultimate justice and the meaning of God's world find no hearing with these masters. As Qohelet (Ecclesiastes) himself might remark, only that which can be definitively grasped has enduring value.[24]

But, almost perversely, this is not the end of this deliberation on suffering. Someone has added a very different conclusion, one that returns us to pieties apparently long put aside (in this context).

Part IV

a. R. Huna, four hundred barrels of wine turned sour on him.

b. R. Judah the son of R. Sala the Pious and the sages (and there are those who say it [was] R. Ada b. Ahava and the sages) went in to him and said: The master should examine his ways [to see if there was any sin that caused this punishment].

c. He said to them: And am I suspect in your eyes?

d. They said to him: Is the Holy One, blessed be He, suspected of doing judgment without justice?

e. He said to them: If there is someone who heard something about me, let him speak.

f. They said to him: This is what we have heard, that the master has not given vines [due in payment] to his hired man.

g. He said to them: Is anything left to me from him? He has stolen everything!

h. They said to him: This is what people say, "The one who steals from a thief tastes the taste [of his theft]."

i. He said to them: I accept upon myself that I will give it [his due] to him.

j. There are those who say that [as reward for his "repentance"] the vinegar once again became wine,

k. And there are those who say that [as reward] vinegar went up in price and sold for the same amount as wine.

The point of this narrative is the same as so many: suffering, even of the economic sort, must be punishment for sin. Therefore, the first thing to do when one experiences such suffering is to examine one's ways (b = I.A.1 above); we have come full circle.

But how are we to respond to this in light of what has come before? When we hear the question, "Is the Holy One, blessed be He, suspected of doing judgment without justice?" we are tempted to say, "What about R. Yoḥanan and his loss of his child? Was that justice? Certainly, R. Yoḥanan was not willing to admit to this."[25] Against the tense struggle with the meaning of suffering that has preceded this, this final piety fails to convince.

Moreover, this final narrative is also formally distinct from the prior deliberation. Unlike almost everything above, the stamp of tripartite formulation is completely absent from this segment of text. Even in the most artificial way, it is difficult to see a triplet in this exchange.[26] So not only the substance of what is said here but also the way in which it is said sets this last section off from the rest.

What does the Bavli seek to communicate by adding this story at the end of the lengthy prior deliberation? It may wish to indicate some discomfort with the implications of the earlier discussion and allow the reader to recover more conventional views.[27] But if this is the intent, the efforts are ironically thwarted. The challenge of what comes above cannot easily be put behind. If it means to take issue with what came before, the contrast that the placement of this story has highlighted only calls into question the assumptions upon which the story is built. Which is more powerful, after all, the lengthy, detailed struggle represented in the earlier deliberation or the conventional conclusions offered here? If this represents a retreat from the more radical statements that have come earlier, it has (in this immediate context) ultimately failed. If, instead, the intent is to invite us to compare and contrast the opinion with which we began—repeated here again—with those opinions we have encountered in the course of deliberation, then this has been accomplished brilliantly. Returning to this position at the end, we *are* forced to ask whether it can be upheld against the bitter rejections we heard earlier. At the very least, after following R. Yohanan through his struggle with suffering, no reader can be sure that this final, very ancient opinion is one that he or she can fully accept.

Finally, it is the sense of struggle which emerges most resoundingly from this lengthy deliberation. The problem of suffering and the question of its meaning is difficult—perhaps too difficult—precisely as the very difficulty of this text illustrates. Having worked through the various approaches to the problem, we are left with no obvious solutions. That may indeed be the point which the final authorship of this sugya wanted to make.

Ḥagiga 4b–5a

The final text to be examined in this chapter, at Hag. 4b–5a, is a lengthy and sometimes internally contradictory deliberation on suffering, God's justice, and the condition of Israel in this world. It is included here because of the radical view concerning premature death expressed in one segment of the lengthier sugya.

Before commencing analysis, let me clarify my claim at the opening of this chapter that this text is without precedent. The common structural element that ties the deliberation as a whole together is the statement, "R. so-and-so, when he arrived at this scripture, he would cry (quote scripture) (explanation)." The Yerushalmi, at Hag. 2:1 (77a), records a tradition that there are six scriptures that Rabbi would read and cry. The scriptures enumerated there are, with one exception, all quoted in the Bavli's present deliberation as well. But there the parallel ends. The attributions are all different. The explanations that so emphatically clarify the point in the Bavli are, with one exception, completely absent in the Yerushalmi (so much so that one commentator on the Yerushalmi, the *Qorban ha-'eda*, is forced to quote the Bavli's explanations in order to render the Yerushalmi fully comprehensible). More important, there are thirteen cases of such scriptures outlined in the Bavli, not a mere six, as in the Yerushalmi. Furthermore, the scriptures are simply referred to in the Yerushalmi (with one exception); no compositional relationship is created between them. In contrast, the Bavli formulates a context to create a message that transcends the individual scriptures. Finally, and most crucially for our discussion here, the scripture that yields the most radical view in the Bavli has no parallel in the Yerushalmi. Thus, when speaking of the opinions expressed at the Bavli's compositional level, it is correct to say that there is no precedent elsewhere in rabbinic literature.

Before the segment of text that will most concern us, the gemara in Ḥagiga makes reference to seven other scriptures that provoked one sage or another to cry upon reading them. The first two traditions, attributed to R. Huna, speak of the sorrow caused when being reminded, in two specific scriptures, that God has distanced Israel from God, despite earlier expressions of desire for closeness. The second two speak of the fear that must overcome a person when anticipating God's judgment. These enunciate more explicitly the theme which will dominate the deliberation that follows.

The fifth through seventh steps, attributed to R. Ammi and R. Asi, quote scriptures that list various extremely righteous or pious acts that a person can undertake and yet, according to each scripture, such undertakings only possibly guarantee divine reward or protection; as each sage remarks, "all of this and [only] 'perhaps'?!" The quotation of these scriptures out of context and with this added emphasis has an important effect. In their original prophetic contexts (Lam. 3:29, Zeph. 2:3, Amos 5:15) it seems likely that this conditional "perhaps" should be understood as saying, "If you improve your deeds now, *perhaps* these deeds will bring you enough merit either to avert the evil that should follow from your sins or to give you hope after the punishment has already come"—the "perhaps" because the meritorious deeds done now still have to be weighed against the iniquities that preceded them. However, as quoted here, the impression is clearly given that no matter how good one's deeds are, and in complete disregard of what they might be balanced against, still, all that can be guaranteed is a "maybe." To some extent, the system of balances, of appropriate reward and punishment, cannot be assured—there is something arbitrary in the whole system that does not permit confidence. This lack of confidence, this fear of arbitrary nonjudgment, causes these sages to cry.

This insistence that the system of correct justice cannot be guaranteed—supported, it will be recalled, with full scriptural "proof"—sets the stage for the most radical possibility. The text is this:[28]

a. R. Joseph, when he would arrive at this scripture, he would cry: "there are those who find their end without judgment." (Prov 13:23, translated for context)

b. He said:[29] But is there [one] who passes [away] not in his [proper] time?

c. Yes!

d. As [in] this [case] of R. Bibi b. Abbaye, who was found in the presence of the Angel of Death.

e. He [= the Angel of Death] said to his messenger: Go bring to me Miriam the Hairdresser.[30]

f. He went [and] brought to him Miriam the raiser of children.

g. He [= the Angel of Death] said to him: I said to you Miriam the Hairdresser!

h. He said to him: If so, I will return her.

i. He [= the Angel of Death] said to him: Since you have brought her, let her be in [my] number [= let her remain among the dead]. But, [tell me] how were you able [to take] her [being that it was not her appointed time]?

j. [He answered:] She took a shovel in her hand and she was raking [the coals in] the oven. She took it and placed it on her knee [and] she burned [herself] and her luck went bad and [an opening was thus provided and so] I brought her.

k. [Having witnessed this exchange,] R. Bibi b. Abbaye said to him [or, to them]: Have you permission to do this?

l. He [= the Angel of Death] said to him: And is it not written, "there are those who find their end without judgment [or, justice]?!"

m. He said to him: But is it not written, "One generation goes, another comes?" (Eccl 1:4) [thus implying, as understood by R. Bibi b. Abbaye, that each generation has an appointed time which must be fulfilled]

n. He [= the Angel of Death] said: [This verse merely requires] that I accompany them until the generation is completed and then I give them to Duma [see Ps. 115:17].

o. He [R. Bibi] said to him: In any case, what did you do with her years [those that were rightly due to Miriam or to anyone who similarly died prematurely]?

p. He said: If there is a student of sages who forgives [others] I will add them [= the years] to him and he will be the other's replacement.

The simple story line is straightforward enough. Rabbi Bibi b. Abbaye witnesses an exchange between the Angel of Death and his messenger. Having been sent to bring a certain Miriam—it being her appointed time to die—the messenger brings the wrong Miriam. Asked by the Angel of Death himself how he was able to do so, the messenger replies that this wrong Miriam had an accident that provided the opportunity for her life to be taken. Rabbi Bibi b. Abbaye then intervenes, challenging the idea that the Angel of Death and his messenger have permission to take someone before his or her appointed time. The Angel of Death says he can and justifies his actions with the very same scripture that had caused R. Joseph to cry. Bibi quotes another scripture, which he takes to suggest that such premature death is not permitted, and the Angel of Death explains how both scriptures can be accommodated. Crucially, the Angel does not yield his right to take life prematurely (that is, before the time appointed by God's justice). An artificial accounting, whereby the unused years will be taken advantage of by someone (to fill out the "generation"), is all that is necessary.

Before even taking our analysis any further, the opinion of this story, in all of its radicalness, is perfectly clear. There can be premature death. God's justice is not necessarily done. The Angel of Death or his messenger can entirely disregard what God's will requires. In an extreme and explicit way, this narrative eliminates all of the many rationalizations of suffering (in this case, premature death) that came before it and returns, almost perversely, to the opinion that a collective—now some ill-defined entity called a "generation"—is all that counts in the justice of this world. But distinguishing this treatment from earlier collective treatments is the fact that here the concern is undoubtedly the individual; reference to the collective is a mere lame rationalization—not the real point at all.

The composition of this story supports the lesson just outlined in a variety of remarkable ways. The first and most obvious element of this composition is the complete absence of any explicit mention of God. Thus the author signals in his composition the point that he otherwise makes in the narrative: God is not involved here. God is not an active participant in this death or related matters of justice. God does appear, though only by implication, in the scriptures quoted, which are of course understood by the rabbi or rabbis who composed this text and by their readers to be in some way words of the Divine. It turns out, then—ironically and remarkably—that the very justification for the Angel of Death and his messenger acting in disregard of God's specific will (1) is the words of God, which the Angel uses to serve his purpose. In an extreme application of the principal, "It is not in Heaven" (b. B.M. 59b), the Angel of Death uses God's word against God, a perversion over which God has no power (or, if you prefer, chooses to have no power). Again, God's disembodied word appears here but, as in the premature death of one poor Miriam, God Godself is nowhere to be found.

Related to these points is the fact that, as this story has it, it is the Angel of Death who here sends an agent. It will be recalled that it is the Angel of Death who is meant to serve as God's agent (Greek: "*angelos*" = messenger). In all of the Babylonian Talmud there is not another angel who sends a messenger. Yet here, the Angel of Death does. It is the Angel of Death, in other words, who stands, in this story, in the place otherwise occupied by God. God is removed from the scene; the Angel of Death takes God's place. Moreover, by positing that the death itself is effectuated by an agent of the agent of God, the narrative serves further to symbolically remove this death from God. God is removed in every sense from the death described here. The opinion is thus stated quite eloquently: this death, at least, has nothing to do with God.

But it is essential to recognize that the lesson articulated here is not meant to be narrowed to this single death. The point of R. Joseph's crying in response to the verse from Proverbs is that its teaching has a far more general application. The same is evident in the final exchange between R. Bibi and the Angel of Death; "have you permission?" (k) is a broad question, and the angel's response makes it clear that he feels he has the overall right to take lives prematurely. If there is any limitation on this power, it is not spelled out. Only an accident is needed before the angel's right is activated, and there can be little question of the prevalence of such accidents.

It is virtually impossible to miss the meaning of this story. On the foundation of what precedes it—a foundation that remarks that reward and justice are only possible, not assured—this sequence illustrates just how unassured justice is. How startling a claim this is! The lessons of this story were so troubling to some later readers that R. Ḥananel (tenth century, North Africa), for example, remarks here:

> There is one who says that [R. Bibi b. Abbaye] saw a kind of dream here, and, not only so, but R. Bibi b. Abbaye was involved in seeking demons. For this reason, one may say, he saw something like this [the story reported here], and we do not depend on this [story to draw authoritative conclusions]. Indeed, there is an explanation [of the verse] "there are those who find their end . . ."—such as where a person killed his fellow.

For this commentator, to accept what this story clearly says would be unthinkable. It must be the result of some dangerous and improper speculation! Besides, the verse can be explained without problem: murder can end a life even before its appointed time. This explanation is acceptable because people have free will (even to murder). Otherwise, however, God's justice and God's will prevail.

Of course, the Talmud records not the opinion that R. Ḥananel would prefer but the one we described above. Had it been thought to be unacceptable or merely the result of hallucination, there would have been no reason for the Talmud to record it. Therefore, this must be deemed a legitimate opinion at the level of the Talmud's redaction. And, it must be recalled, it is deemed legitimate in rabbinic circles, in all of its harsh reality, only in the Bavli.[31]

Just how provisional the foregoing opinion is, even in this context, is evident in a step that follows shortly after the one just analyzed. Again, attentions turn to the problem of premature death:

> *a*. R. Yoḥanan, when he arrived at this scripture, would cry, "He puts no trust in His Holy ones" (Job 15:15)—If He will not put trust in His Holy ones, in whom will He put trust?
> *b*. One day he [= R. Yoḥanan] was walking on the road. He saw a certain man picking figs. He left those that were ripe and took those that were not ripe.
> *c*. He said to him: Are not these [others] better?

d. He said to him: I need these for the road. These will keep [while] these will not keep.

e. [R. Yoḥanan] said: This is what is written, "He puts no trust in his Holy ones." [Rashi: "(Just as, with respect to) the good (figs) he is afraid that they will rot, so too are righteous youth brought to death (prematurely) lest they sin."]

f. Is this so? But [there is the case of] that student who was in the neighborhood of R. Alexandri and he died prematurely, and he [= R. Alexandri] said: "If this student had wanted he could have lived [by living righteously]." And if this principle [spelled out in the prior story] pertains, perhaps he [= this student] was of "the Holy ones" [whose lives are taken early so that they not sin].

g. That one [= the student] was rebellious against his teachers.

How different is the tone of this story from the one above! The story admits that there are some who die prematurely, but only because God wants to "protect them from the road," to assure that they not "rot." This is the meaning of the verse: "He puts no trust in His Holy ones"; instead, God takes them to assure that they will remain holy. But this pertains only to those who are genuinely holy. Those who have sinned are punished accordingly, and this is the explanation of the premature death of the certain student.

Here there is no admission of the lack of God's justice. On the contrary, justice prevails in all realms. Even premature death is just because it may be understood either as punishment or as protection of those who have not yet sinned. They, of course, will be rewarded in the world-to-come (not stated here explicitly, but clearly assumed).

This text as a whole gives no indication of which of the expressed views, this or the one examined earlier, is to prevail. Perhaps it would be best to read their combination here canonically, that is, as a case where contradictory opinions, juxtaposed, are simultaneously to be considered legitimate options. However, in light of the careful composition of this text as it progresses, it is likely that there is a better explanation of the present contradiction.

The text that follows the first story above is, with some variation and room for expansion, structured around this common formula: "R. Yoḥanan, when he came to this scripture, he cried. . . . [He said:] a servant whose master does thus-and-so to him, has he any [hope of] remedy?" (The only exception to this formula in the primary structure is this last story regarding premature death.) The master in each case is, of course, God, and the general point is that a variety of scriptures may be understood to say that God is particularly harsh in judgment against Israel. In the thematic progression of this long sugya, the present sequence may be understood as saying, "Not only are chances of being rewarded for righteous acts dubious, but also God is so exacting with Israel that what are seemingly the most minor transgressions will lead to punishment." Included among the sins that are mentioned to illustrate this point are giving charity to the needy in public, which leads, presumably, to their embarrassment. Another example, well below this, is speaking to one's wife with undue levity while making love.

This sequence of traditions built around the statements of R. Yoḥanan assumes divine justice of a sort—as stated, a particularly harsh sort. In this respect, this segment of text is even more ominous than what came before. In the earlier part of the deliberation at least there was a chance, no matter how uncertain in might have been. Now, that chance is defined as being ever more remote because of the strict application of justice. Ironically, the radical possibility enunciated earlier is now left behind, but with far harsher consequences. As has been noticed in many earlier deliberations on God's justice, if such justice is too consistently applied, mankind will have difficulty surviving its application. Without mercy or, here, at least some degree of arbitrariness, "Has he any [hope of] remedy?"

The pessimistic tenor of this text is reinforced in its final steps, where the theme becomes the hiding of God's face. As is stated, "anyone who is not in [a state of] 'the hiding of [God's] face' . . . [and] in [a state of] 'they shall be ready prey' (both, Dt 31:17) is not of them [= of Israel]." The condition of being Israel today demands that one be prey to the nations and demands that one feel the distance of God's presence. Both these conditions are an outcome of divine justice, a justice which, however, does not (at the present time, at least) offer much hope. Hope is found only in the next stage of this text, in a transition away from this immediate discussion, from which we learn that God does, at least, cry for our catastrophe.

A quick review of the themes that provoke crying makes clear the direction that this text wants to point us. It begins with distancing from God, then goes on to the fear of judgment. Next comes the play of the arbitrary— the complete absence of justice. But then comes the even more difficult condition to confront: the complete and unyielding application of justice. We conclude with God's intentional absence, which, the gemara says, is too harsh—at least God must weep. It is evident, from this review, that a logically consistent analysis of God's justice has never been the point, thus logical contradictions are not a problem. The author has been interested in leading us along the progressively bitter path of individual and collective Jewish experience. Notably, when it appears that Rava is living too comfortably, though in secret he too may be prey to the government's lust for wealth, this appearance must change (for this, see 5b, top). The author of this text is a resolute and almost unyielding pessimist. It is this attitude and emotion that he has shared with us.

Of the several more radical expressions regarding suffering and its relation to divine justice, none is entirely without precedent in biblical literature. The protest of R. Yoḥanan and his colleagues in Berakhot is really no more extreme (and far less eloquent) than that of Job. And the skepticism articulated in the story of the wrong Miriam is no more doubting than that of Ecclesiastes. However, unlike Job (the book), the rabbis saw no possibility of a thundering *deus ex machina* in their time, and the piety that probably saved Ecclesiastes for the canon (its final two verses)—providing hope against the wise man's lack thereof—are in Ḥagiga the end of hope: if God will bring all of a person's actions to judgment, even that which is hidden from him, then what hope is there? These small differences are very important. They make the protest more biting, the skepticism more stinging. They give a new voice to views that were not fully articulated in the first go around.

In fact, it may be that it is this giving of new voice that represents the Bavli's most radical departure from earlier rabbinic forays. It is one thing to quote scripture—if an opinion is scriptural, it is legitimate. But it is another thing entirely to express these opinions in the rabbis' own idiom, using rabbinic authorities and employing contemporary reality for illustration. In doing this, the Bavli admits above all that the reality perceived by Job or by Ecclesiastes is also part of its own reality, a courageous and possibly even dangerous admission. Moreover, expressing these views in its own voice, the Bavli takes full responsibility for them. What an astounding responsibility it is.

Understanding the Bavli

The Bavli's teachings on suffering are extremely varied, ranging from the most antique of biblical views to the far more radical possibilities just examined. In terms of their numbers, most of the Bavli's treatments probably recreate the most traditional possibilities, though these expressions tend to be brief and peripheral to the discussions at hand. Many are ambivalent or express their challenge *sotto voce*, showing the Bavli's broad willingness to give an ear to protest or complaint. The relatively common presence of such texts shows that their uneasiness with simplistic theodicies is at least approvingly understood by the Bavli's authorship, if not widely shared. The Bavli makes it clear that even outright protest is to be tolerated.

Notably, in extended theoretical discussions of justice as such (as opposed to deliberations on personal suffering), the Bavli says little to distinguish itself from earlier rabbinic texts. It is fully able to speak on behalf of the reality of God's justice, and the schemes it employs to justify that support are themselves ancient and often repeated. If these were the only expressions in the Bavli that related to the present concerns, we might have concluded that the Bavli, like the Yerushalmi, for example, insisted upon complete adherence to the age-old pieties.

However, it is impossible to separate discussions of justice from those relating to suffering. The texts that address the problem of suffering are also discussions of God's justice. And, as we have seen, the Bavli does express alternative, even angry views. Numerous texts are not at all confident of the justice so unhesitatingly supported in others. How, then, are we to understand the difference in approach between these two sorts of texts?

In the introductory chapter, I suggested that my decision to focus primarily on texts that relate to suffering as such was motivated by the apprehension that theoretical discussions of "justice"—a concept, not a reality—

were more susceptible to intellectualized speculation than discussions of suffering. Justice can be worked out in theory; when one rationalization is confronted by too many anomalies, adjustments can be made to account for the troublesome reality. As long as we remain in the realm of theory, a perfect system of justice can be maintained. When speaking of suffering, on the other hand, it is far more difficult to escape the genuine problem presented by the individual experience. As long as the discussion has no name, we may rationalize all we wish. As soon as we must speak of R. Yoḥanan's loss or of R. Eleazar's illness, it is impossible not to hesitate and to allow questions to resound, plaguing us once and then again.

If I am correct in what I have here suggested—and here the argument becomes circular—then it may be that the difference between Bavli texts that speak of suffering and those that restrict themselves to divine justice lies precisely in the distinction between theory and insistent reality. Theory stands undisturbed in many of these texts. Application of the theory to individuals is what provokes misgivings and protest.

How may we understand the Bavli's variety in the context of its composition? The Bavli, we said, is the voice of the rabbinic community in sixth-century Babylonia. This community remained but a small proportion of Babylonian Jewry as a whole and, though by this time the rabbis exerted considerable influence in the Jewish population at large, they were still an intellectual-religious elite. As such, they were undoubtedly distinguished by a variety of in-group rituals and regulations: they were particularly meticulous in the observance of eating and sexual taboos, they avoided coarse speech and improper dress, and they were required to show extraordinary deference to the most learned of their number.[32] Yet it would be a mistake to imagine that the rabbis were a sect of religious pietists. On the contrary, the rabbis' avowed ideology required them to be in constant contact with common Jews, whom they hoped to persuade of the correctness of rabbinic customs and interpretations. The rabbis struggled not to separate from other Jews, but to remake all Jews in the image of their Torah. Thus they not only judged and regulated other Jews—to the extent that they were granted authority over local Jewish courts and marketplaces—but they also could, and undoubtedly did, eat and pray with those other Jews. In all of this, they had only limited official power to enforce their own views; the bulk of their influence was dependent upon their ability to gain the voluntary support of the ancient Babylonian community.[33]

Even within the rabbinic party itself, rabbinic power was ironically limited. Groups of rabbis were scattered throughout Babylonia, with no recognized center or superior authority. Different masters and their disciples had different opinions concerning matters of practice and doctrine, and local rabbinic groups had no choice but to respect the decisions of rabbinic groups in other locales.[34] Inner-rabbinic hierarchies were strong, and more junior scholars understood that they were expected to show deference to superior scholars.[35] But such hierarchies were also fluid, with more than one rabbinic story telling of the deposition of one academy head in favor of another.

Moreover, the position one held within the rabbinic hierarchy was not ascribed. Birth was officially worth nothing in the rabbinic movement, and there is little evidence of, say, family dynasties within Babylonian rabbinism.[36] The rabbinic mythology itself represents its greatest paragons as individuals who, though beginning life modestly, attained high station in the rabbinic hierarchy by force of their own brilliance.

To state matters as succinctly as possible, the Babylonian rabbinic community was relatively more fluid and relatively less able to coerce obedience than other Rabbinic communities before it. Notions of inside and outside (the rabbinic community) were less distinct, and questions of status were subject to competition, not assignation. Mary Douglas has observed that social structures defined by these characteristics are more likely to support certain kinds of cosmological and metaphysical belief systems. To be precise,

> [A]s [assigned status] weakens, there will be increasing scope for scepticism about metaphysical principles and their fit to experience. There will be pressure to doubt any mutual support between theories about God, nature and reality. . . . The same atmosphere of intellectual openness will foster tolerance, for the grounds for intolerance are eroded and the power to suppress contrary views is weakened. . . . Individual variation will be tolerated, no longer a symbol of threatened classification.[37]

Douglas speaks of the most extreme manifestation of these trends, where what might be called free-market individualism reigns supreme. The Babylonian Jewish community certainly did not approach this condition. However, when compared with the religion of Priestly Israel or even the rabbinic movement in Palestine, the Babylonians were certainly closer to what Douglas calls "low group and grid"[38] than Jews had been before. The greater plurality observed in the Bavli's record, along with the greater willingness of its authors to express skepticism concerning traditional systems of reward and punishment—even the willingness to entertain the possibility of chaotic and unjust forces—all may be explained in light of the correspondences which Douglas suggests. If we are open to the general thesis which underlies her proposal that "it takes a certain kind of social experience to start to worry about the problem of evil,"[39] then we will not fail to see the correlation between the social structures of rabbinic Judaism in Babylonia and the opinions and ideologies it came to express.

Another factor which may help explain the Bavli's variety and openness is the relative security these Jews enjoyed. Crucially, the rabbis of this time confronted no urgent historical-theological crises. If we understand the defensive insistence of fifth-century Palestinian documents to be, at least in part, a reaction to the challenge of the Christian triumph and related developments, then the absence of such forces in the Babylonian context may explain the absence of a similar reaction in the pages of the Bavli. The Babylonian sages had the luxury of being less defensive, more questioning and skeptical. By virtue of both their social and historical situation, they could tolerate possibilities which their brethren to the west could not. Of course, nothing in this context required that such alternatives be preferred, and, in the absence of fragmentation or breakdown, it also remained possible for these same rabbinic masters to appropriate earlier traditions and explanations without apology or regret. Such traditions had worked in the past. There was nothing in recent experience which necessarily challenged their ongoing validity. Where the rabbis so chose, they could thus repeat earlier teachings without significant alteration.

No final decision was insisted upon in the Bavli's pages. Some declared that suffering must be punishment for sin, others insisted not. The canonical Bavli, in its characteristic fashion, supported both. As they record in the pages of this Talmud, its final authors evidently felt, "These and these are the words of the living God."

11

Summary and Conclusions

Canonical rabbinic teachings relating to the problem of suffering are first found in the Mishnah. The Mishnah, as already observed by Neusner,[1] overwhelmingly neglects the imperfections of history, preferring to picture a world controlled and stabilized by Torah—a world more perfect. Thus the Mishnah has little direct to say on matters of suffering, and what it does say supports the dominant biblical explanation according to which suffering is punishment for sin. Suffering, in this view, is not evidence of imperfection but, on the contrary, evidence of the perfection of God's justice in this world. Accordingly, teachings which relate to divine justice also speak unapologetically about reward and punishment and even imagine—in archaic biblical fashion—that such reward or punishment may be imparted in this world. The world-to-come is available, in the Mishnah's system, to supply a corrective when present reality offers troublesome testimony, but this by now traditional view is not deemed essential in all Mishnaic discussions. Even more literal applications of ancient biblical promises are supported.

The next stage of rabbinic composition, beginning with the Tosefta, makes only modest steps beyond the Mishnaic precedent. The Tosefta's comments on relevant Mishnahs tend merely to offer additional examples or to supplement the base-Mishnah in expected ways. With relation to personal suffering and divine justice, the Tosefta repeats the archaic vision of the Mishnah. Only in its comments on the destruction of the Temple does the Tosefta mark new ground. While, on the one hand, the Tosefta contains tractates which speak of the Temple and sacrificial law as though

211

the subject of its discussions were still in operation, the Tosefta also introduces comments on the destruction and expressions of hope for restoration in numerous places where the Mishnah records no such statement. True,
the Tosefta's explicit explanation of the destruction returns us to reward-
and-punishment ideology at its purest. But the fact that the Tosefta is willing to discuss the destruction at all shows its openness to the imperfections
of history. Its hopes for restoration similarly reveal its sense that the world
is tragically flawed, that restoration is indeed necessary. If we view the destruction as emblematic of the suffering of the people as a whole, as seems
reasonable, then we will appreciate the Tosefta's comments here as the first
step toward confronting the problem of suffering more directly.

The halakhic midrashim, in all probability only slightly later in their composition than the Tosefta, include the first significant examples of rabbinic
deliberations on suffering, now undeniably recognized as at least a potential problem. The greater frequency of such deliberations is the first notable
development at this stage. This development may perhaps be explained, at
least in part, by the fact that the midrashic compositions attend not only to
the Torah's law but to its narrative portions as well. But this explanation
does not fully account for the noted increase, for the precise nature of the
comments to find record in these documents was the choice of the rabbinic redactors. Should they have wanted to avoid discussion of suffering,
this was their choice to make. Therefore, even if we account for the difference in genre, the marked contrast with the Mishnah and the Tosefta suggests that rabbinic sensibilities have begun to shift.

The second important development is the powerfully apologetic nature
of these discussions. Despite the reality which Jews (like others) every day
confront, particularly during the period in which these midrashim took
place, there is still, in their pages, no admission that the problem is a genuine one. Whatever one views in reality can be explained in light of available
explanations—so these midrashim insist. Significantly, to support these
apologia, the midrashim recover resolutions to the problem of suffering that
were offered by different Jewish groups long before but which the rabbis,
in the Mishnah and the Tosefta, had mostly neglected. These include a far
more powerful dependence on reward and punishment in the world-to-
come, the notion that suffering can bring expiation, the suggestion that
suffering is somehow covenantal, and others. With these explanations, the
present authors believe they have resolved any apparent problems observers of the mundane world might have, so they insist that suffering be
accepted graciously and with perfect faith. Those who question God's justice are not believed to offer proper models of piety.

The next stage of the record of rabbinic beliefs in Palestine, completed
more than a century later in the aftermath of world-transforming events, is
somewhat more varied but, on the explicit level at least, not significantly
different from earlier rabbinic expressions. The most outstanding element
in the Yerushalmi's response to suffering is its unbending condemnation of
those who would reject God's justice. The questioner, in its view, is likely

to become the apostate. No room is made for the possibility that traditional explanations might not work. In fact, it is the most common of traditional explanations which the Yerushalmi insists do work, with reward and punishment playing virtually the same role here as in the Mishnah. Suffering is judgment; sin leads to suffering. Reward or punishment will come, if not now then in a future world. Less frequent alternatives, such as the suggestion that suffering leads to expiation, merely repeat rabbinic opinions first expressed a century or more before.

Midrashim of this period are somewhat more complex. Like the Yerushalmi, their explicit message condemns questioning, and they repeat many of the traditional explanations of suffering. The abundance of their comments on God's preference for mercy over strict justice is notable, suggesting a shift in concerns and sensibilities. But more important is the evident ambivalence in the rhetoric of many midrashic compositions which relate to suffering and divine justice. To borrow a phrase from popular discourse, "their mouths say no! no! [to questioning and protest] but their eyes say yes! yes!" Whatever their explicit message regarding the expression of doubt, the subtle articulation of such doubt is more than occasional in these texts. For the most part, these doubts are conveyed through imperfect parables or internal literary contradictions. But on one or two important occasions the doubts become far more explicit, showing that, whatever agreement there might be in the rabbinic community at the level of full articulation, the difficulties of individual authors with the realities they perceive will not be completely suppressed.

But it is the Bavli which, characteristically, gives voice to the fullest range of explanations and responses, and allows for even the most radical expression of questioning or doubt. Once again, all of the views that found earlier record in rabbinic texts have their place here. Deliberations which limit their focus to the theoretical question of divine justice are particularly conservative in their approach. But, at the same time, the subtle criticism of earlier views finds considerably more latitude in this work, and several major deliberations are quite explicit in their radical critique of traditional alternatives. So, at Shab. 55a–b, the authorship insists that there may be suffering or death without prior sin. At Hag. 4b–5a, the authorship admits that death may be premature, arbitrary, accidental, and even contrary to God's presumed will. And at Ber. 5a–b, the authorship critiques the range of earlier explanations of human suffering, concluding simply with rejection: "I want neither sufferings nor their reward!" each of the suffering rabbis is made to say.

It is not only these radical possibilities which distinguish the Bavli, but the range of options that is canonically juxtaposed. Indeed, the Bavli's range may be likened to the range of the biblical canon itself, where Deuteronomy, Ezekiel, Job, and Ecclesiastes are all offered as authoritative (= divine) alternatives. The Bavli legitimates the same and more. To begin with, the fact that the Bavli even recovers this range, when the latter expressions had been neglected or suppressed earlier in the rabbinic record, is significant.

If all the Bavli did was to recover the equivalent of the voices of Job and Ecclesiastes, this would be a considerable inner-rabbinic development. But the Bavli is willing to articulate Job's complaint even without holding forth the possibility of a divine revelation in response. It sees fit to appropriate the dismissive skepticism of Ecclesiastics even without adding (in the immediate context) the equivalent of that book's final, more traditional coda. In the Bible, where the voices are assumed to be, on some level, divine, the impression conveyed by such doubts is somehow mediated. In the Bavli, where the voice is more obviously a human one, the questions are more biting, the critiques more severe.

This, in brief, is the range and development of classical rabbinic responses to suffering and related issues. It needs to be emphasized that these are *rabbinic* responses. Because our evidence has been rabbinic documents alone, we must limit the conclusions we draw from that evidence. To put the matter simply, these materials tell us little about the beliefs of Jews in general, that is, Jews who have not yet, at any given stage, been rabbinized; moreover, they don't necessarily reveal much about the belief of rabbinized Jews who are not themselves rabbis. To appreciate these limitations fully, it is necessary to expand upon these observations in some greater detail.

Nonrabbinic Jews

It is by now a commonplace in histories of Judaism during these centuries that the rabbis and their followers were through most of this period but a minority, with increasing influence but not, until the end, with recognized dominance. Jacob Neusner's history is punctuated with numerous observations regarding the limits of the rabbinic movement in the context of third- to sixth-century Babylonian Jewry. There is considerable evidence of nonrabbinic forms of Judaism, both in Palestine and Babylonia, for the entire period.[2] The evidence at hand causes Shaye J. D. Cohen to judge that rabbinic Judaism did not "triumph" over alternative and more ancient forms until the seventh century at the earliest.[3]

What this means is that the material reviewed in earlier chapters is inarguably relevant to only a small proportion of ancient Jewry as a whole. We have no way of being certain whether the precise developments we have noted characterized other Jews as well, or whether the range of responses legitimated in the rabbinic canon would have been accepted by other contemporary Jews. Still, we may make a reasoned judgment in this matter, and the testimony of the rabbis is not useless for reconstructing the ideologies of nonrabbinic Jews.

I would propose that several factors allow us to extend certain conclusions suggested above to nonrabbinic Jews. First, there can be no doubt that the predominant biblical view was that suffering is punishment for sin. If nonrabbinic Jews were in a significant sense *prerabbinic* Jews (that is, their beliefs were profoundly influenced by the Bible, if not yet by the rabbis), then we would expect the legacy of biblical ideology to have loomed large in the nonrabbinic population. Since, in any case, this biblical opinion, revised to admit the completion of judgment in the world-to-come, was the dominant view expressed in rabbinic texts until the very latest stages of antiquity as well, it would seem reasonable to surmise that this was the most popular explanation of suffering for all Jews, rabbinic and nonrabbinic alike. Moreover, I will argue shortly that the rhetoric which the rabbis directed toward Jews whom they intended to rabbinize, as opposed to their expressions to their own disciples, was also dominated by the opinion that suffering should be understood as part of the equation of divine reward and punishment. Recognizing that rhetoric, to be effective, needs to address an audience in terms with which they already identify (the more alien the ideas expressed, the more difficult will any persuasion be), then this too would suggest that suffering as punishment for sin was the most common view among Jews at large.

But this obviously does not mean that this was the only belief concerning suffering held by nonrabbinic Jews. Apocryphal works, along with the writings of Philo and Josephus, already provided evidence that Jews in the late prerabbinic and early rabbinic periods entertained a variety of explanations of suffering, including the belief that it was fate or that it was a test which improved the sufferer. Many of these opinions were held by the contemporary Hellenistic population of the Near East, and the broad influence of the contact between Jew and non-Jew during this period has been well-documented. Thus there is good reason to expect that these alternative explanations of suffering would also have been shared by Jews at large. And though the rabbis neglected or suppressed such beliefs in their early compositions, there is no basis on which to conclude that other Jews ceased to hold these beliefs. Moreover, as we have seen, the rabbis themselves reappropriated many of these earlier opinions as their movement developed. It is likely that they did not create them *ex nihilo*. Rather, it is more reasonable to suppose that these opinions continued to be expressed among Jews in general and that the rabbis readmitted them to their canon as their deliberations on suffering came to respond more and more to the conditions of their day.

Non-Rabbis

I suggested that the range of responses to suffering recorded in rabbinic documents—particularly those expressions of ambivalence, doubt, or outright protest which we saw in later documents—most likely speaks for rabbis alone and not for rabbinized Jews who were not rabbis. This conclusion is necessary if we consider the audience to which the written rabbinic record was addressed. I spelled out earlier, in our discussions on the Bavli, the reasons why it is reasonable to believe that that document was directed to the rabbinic elite alone.[4] The level of literacy required to study the document, the difficulty of its deliberations, and similar factors, support this evaluation. The levels of literacy and intellectual sophistication required to master the Yerushalmi are certainly not significantly lower, so the same judgment seems reasonable in its case as well. Richard Sarason has suggested the same conclusion, convincingly in my opinion, with respect to the classical aggadic midrashim.[5] And even the Mishnah, apparently the "easiest" of all of the rabbinic works, makes considerable demands: high literacy, assumed familiarity with scripture, command of many obscure or specialized terms, institutions, and methods, and significant intellectual capabilities (to understand categories, preserve order in the midst of abundant and potentially chaotic details, and so on).[6] Therefore, whatever the rabbis may have communicated to rabbinized Jews who were not rabbis, we do not find actual record of it in the written documents which they have left us. Well, if not here, where?

The answer, I believe, lies in the complex of prayers and blessings the rabbis sought to promulgate in the Jewish population at large. Unlike "Torah study," which (understood in the rabbinic sense) was restricted to rabbis and their disciples, these observances were intended for performance by all Jews at regular intervals. Though the rabbis may have held forth an ideal that all male Jews should study Torah, it is not realistic to suppose that most Jews would have had the time, financial means, and inclination to fulfill that ideal. Thus if the rabbis wished to communicate at least some of their ideas to non-rabbis—as they most assuredly did—they could not effectively have done so in those documents which became the focus of rabbinic study. Instead, it was through popular liturgies that the rabbis could influence those Jews who accepted rabbinic practices. If Jews made it their custom to pray and recite blessings, as instructed by the rabbis and according to their formulations, then they would regularly be subject to the subtle influences of the formulas they recited. To discover the rabbis' public message, therefore, we must examine the ideologies of the popular formulas which they composed.

We begin with the prayer liturgy proper. The first of the major components of rabbinic prayer, perhaps appropriated from prerabbinic liturgy, is the Shema.[7] The Shema is comprised of three scriptural passages surrounded by blessings. The scriptural passages are already clearly identified in the Mishnah (Ber. 2:2), and the middle passage—Deut. 11:13–21—is crucial to our discussion. This Torah text articulates as clearly as any the classical vision of reward and punishment. It proposes that, if the people do not observe God's will, God "will shut up the skies so that there will be no rain and the ground will not yield its produce; and you will soon perish from the good land. . . ." Punishment is collective, it occurs in this world, and it is what we would call suffering. This is the classical biblical paradigm at its most literal, and nothing in context serves to modify the paradigm. It is offered here as the centerpiece (literally) of what is arguably the most important part of the regular rabbinic liturgy. Thus the Jew who fulfills his obligation will recite this passage twice a day, every day of his life (beginning from young childhood). This will serve powerfully to reinforce the ancient biblical approach, without so much as a hint that alternatives are available.

The next major element of the regular daily liturgy is the Amidah, the silent prayer. The Mishnah already speaks of this prayer as being composed of eighteen blessings (Ber. 4:3), but it does not specify what these blessings might be. Still, it is clear that a regular formulation is assumed in the Mishnah, and several of the blessings are referred to by name in both the Mishnah (5:2) and the Tosefta (see Tosefta Berakhot, chapter 3). Whether the full array of blessings is yet formulated at that early stage (and, in light of the specific number, it seems quite likely that it is), all of the blessings are already designated, by name and in order, in both the Yerushalmi (Ber. 2:4, 4d–5a) and the Bavli (Meg. 17b).

What is of concern to us is the sequence of blessings which begins by thanking God for giving us discernment, then asks God to help us repent, proceeds to ask God for forgiveness of sins, and concludes by asking God to redeem us. The order has a clear purpose: discernment enables us to distinguish between right and wrong; then, with God's help, we will be able to repent; repentance, properly done, will lead to redemption. The assumption is that the absence of redemption is a function of sin (= that which must be repented for) and full repentance, eliminating the stain of the sin, will thus lead to redemption. The ideology, and even the vocabulary, are strongly prophetic, and the classical system of divine reward and punishment is behind it all. Again, if a Jew recites these words several times each day[8] (with the exception of Sabbath and festivals), then the cause-and-effect system propounded here will be powerfully reinforced. Furthermore, as he considers the redeemed world defined in the subsequent blessings—in which the sick are healed, the fields are full with produce, the exiles are returned, judges are restored, the wicked are judged according to their wickedness, the righteous are rewarded, Jerusalem is restored, and sovereignty is returned to the House of David—he will also note that the absence of these things in the present is a result of the sins of Israel. He will not miss the fact that this absence—of health, of abundant food, and the like—is what we call suffering, and he will thus have a ready explanation for why such suffering exists.[9]

The same message is communicated in the blessing a Jew is required to say upon hearing a bad report. The Mishnah defines the obligation in this way: "Upon hearing bad tidings, one says 'blessed is the true judge'" (Ber. 9:2). The Mishnah does not specify further the sort of occasion that would be appropriate for the recitation of this blessing, but both the Yerushalmi (9:2, 13a) and the Bavli (59b) suggest this formula as a proper response to hearing of the death of one's parent. Indeed, this is accepted Jewish custom. But the blessing is not limited to this circumstance alone, and Lieberman observes that the Tosefta (Ber. 6:1) deems it appropriate to include such a phrase in the blessing after meals in the house of a mourner.[10] Whatever its context, the message of this blessing could not be any clearer. If something bad happens, if a loved one dies, it is an act of divine justice. Once again, in the rabbis' popular liturgy, no alternative is entertained.

The context for the recitation of this latter blessing shows the importance of this message in the eyes of the rabbis. When one hears bad news, and particularly of the death of a parent, one may well be tempted to respond in anger or protest. This is the moment when one's emotions are likely to be least in control, when a cry of anger might emerge spontaneously. Yet this is precisely the time when the rabbis view the need to ritualize the response, and the response they propose insists on order and divine design where common people may see chaos and arbitrary cruelty. God is the never-failing judge—this is the message the rabbis want us not to forget.

We see, then, that the rituals which the rabbis promulgated for the common Jew—the Shema, prayer, blessings—all support the same view, the same explanation of suffering and misfortune. It is, we have seen, that explanation so often offered in the Bible, and it is found in these liturgies in virtually unmodified form. Notably, this is the same ideology supported by the Mishnah, and because these prayers and blessings are first defined in that document, it is not surprising that its stamp is felt here so powerfully. In their subsequent, more elite expressions, the rabbis explored and supported a variety of other approaches to the problem of suffering, yet there is no evident influence of such alternative speculations in the popular liturgies as they unfold in these later documents. The Bavli, though it is willing to entertain possibilities which are distinctly contrary to the classical biblical view, nevertheless continues to insist upon this view in the public formulas that it demands. There are thus two levels of rabbinic wisdom pertaining to these matters: a popular level, which supports more conventional pieties, and an elite level, which allows for less traditional speculation as well.[11]

The History of Religious Ideas and Rabbinic Judaism

The present history chooses one of two competing models for the conduct of such a study and carries it through to its conclusions. For reasons spelled out in the first chapter, I eschew the earlier paradigm, represented in the work of E. E. Urbach[12] and adopt instead the model proposed by Jacob Neusner. Having completed this study, we are now in a position to compare the two methods and to ask which compels greater support.

Urbach's treatment of these same subjects attends almost exclusively to the opinions of individuals. These opinions may be gathered from any classical rabbinic document, whatever the time or place of its composition— the attributions given in these works are accepted virtually without question. The presumed views of these teachers are then organized according to the logical associations of Urbach's categories.

Aside from the basic methodological objections already spelled out in Chapter 1, Urbach's approach involves several other problems. First, Urbach neglects entirely the context in which opinions are recorded. The purpose for which they are quoted, the function they serve in context, the ways they may have been transformed for context—for him these are all minor questions at best. As a consequence, the opinion which is conveyed in the final documentary formulation and, in the case of the Talmuds, the anonymous voice of the final authorship, are also entirely ignored. Whatever the historical value of individual attributed opinions, then, the one opinion that can be dated with the greatest certainty (even when questions remain) gets no hearing in the pages of his study. For Urbach, there is no text; there are only isolated teachings. It is he who provides the primary context for understanding them, as though the original rabbinic documents did not do so first.

Second, Urbach's approach tends to smooth over differences between earlier and later expressions. Because later documents, like earlier documents, also quote opinions attributed to earlier sages, when we pay attention to names instead of documents, the differences between early and late mostly disappear. What we viewed in earlier chapters as developments in rabbinic expression turn out to be, in the view of this method, merely different categories of response. To be sure, Urbach perceives important developments when comparing pre- to postdestruction traditions (where postdestruction can include even reportedly tannaitic views which are recorded for the first time only in later documents). And he also isolates expressions attributed to rabbis who experienced the Hadrianic persecutions, which make good sense against the background of those events—again ignoring the fact that these expressions may have been thus attributed only centuries later. But Urbach may otherwise draw upon teachings from any period, and the only distinction which emerges forcefully is the categories he has himself defined. For the most part, then, not only literary context but also historical context are rendered irrelevant.

The differences in the approach we have taken will be immediately evident. To begin with, this study has primarily been concerned with final documentary expressions. Text comes first and then individual opinions only in consideration of their contexts. To be sure, if the views of individuals were preserved in a form that approaches the original, we have not captured their voices, but we can never be certain whether or not this was the case. On account of such uncertainty, we have judged such losses necessary. Instead, we have preferred to recover views which find expression in the final documentary context, opinions which represent the canonical opinions of a community of authors and editors and not merely those of individuals. Furthermore, we are able to interpret and appreciate these opinions in light of the contexts in which they took shape. It is this possibility that enables us to construct a history of religious ideas, a possibility which, as we saw, was largely unavailable by means of the alternative method.

Our specific conclusions support Neusner's broader project in important ways, though certain revisions and more significant corrections are also suggested.[13] The Mishnah's denial of a more complex reality and projection of a world in perfect order—in which suffering is punishment for sin and reward or punishment might be realized even in this world—corresponds precisely with Neusner's more general characterization of the Mishnah's system.[14] The postures of the Yerushalmi and, in the same context, the classical aggadic midrashim (Genesis Rabbah, Leviticus Rabbah, and so on) also reflect, in significant ways, Neusner's broader observations concerning those documents. The Yerushalmi's refusal to admit question or protest is indicative of its general quest for certainty, as is its assertion that the classical system continues to operate without a hitch. The insistence of the midrashim that God judges with mercy, along with their wider recognition of the redemptive qualities of suffering, are appropriate specifics in the more general program of redemption suggested in these documents. In these ways, Neusner's intuitions are powerfully confirmed. At the same time, the fact that the aggadic midrashim are rhetorically not as certain (or as unified) in their redemptive visions as Neusner suggests lends support to the correctives offered by David Stern and others;[15] they are certainly correct that Neusner's insistence on discovering integrated documentary programs goes too far. Nevertheless, the value of Neusner's reading remains, as does the merit of his viewing these literary developments in their historical contexts.

In the case of the Bavli, my own earlier work is at serious variance with Neusner's, and I believe the evidence of this study supports my conclusions against his. Neusner's claim is that the Bavli speaks with a single, uniform, consistent, monotonous voice. This alleged singleness of voice suggests, in his view, a singleness of purpose: to demonstrate the perfection of the rabbinic Torah as embodied in the Mishnah. If the Bavli's demonstration is convincing, then Israel, who abides by the Mishnah, will occupy a social utopia, a perfect realization of God's will.[16]

In contrast, I have argued that the Bavli is characterized primarily by argumentation, a discourse composed of multiple voices in which the multiplicity of those voices is not lost. Instead, one voice finds a place next to its contrary, and the Bavli prefers to support these opposing views, side by side, rather than deciding definitively in favor of one or another. Different opinions of law can be equally well defended in its pages, as can differing interpretations. The reasons for this support of multiplicity, for this extended attention to diverse opinions, are themselves multiple, but ultimately, I think, the Bavli's posture is due to the recognition on the part of its authorship that the divine will, preserved in Torah, is accessible only through the acutely human act of interpretation. If interpretation is human, then it is by definition imperfect, and thus any single interpretation or opinion (itself based upon an interpretation) can at best be only a partial realization of the dictates of the divine will. In light of this condition, the authorship of the Bavli recognized the need to learn from multiple, equally imperfect opinions.[17]

The Bavli's opinions concerning suffering are multiple and often at odds with one another. Some support the most ancient of biblical explanations of suffering, others reject such explanations outright. Some see suffering and death as punishment for sin, others reject this view as a matter of principle. Some deliberations offer defenses of divine justice against apparently contradictory evidence, others angrily reject the promised value of suffering. If we had to characterize the Bavli's position on these matters in "a single voice," we would be restricted to saying "the Bavli deems it legitimate to respond in diverse ways to one's suffering." The Bavli does not insist upon unity. Instead, it recognizes that Torah and reality are both complex, and different experiences of that complexity justify different interpretations of its meaning.

I suggested in the previous chapter that the Bavli's tolerance of diversity may reasonably be explained on the basis of several factors. First, the distance of the Bavli's community from the sorts of crises which afflicted Palestinian Jewry in earlier centuries meant that the defensive postures assumed in Palestinian rabbinic documents were unnecessary in the Bavli. The Bavli's context was one of relative stability and perhaps (if we are correct in dating its composition to the mid-sixth century) even peace. In such a setting, challenging views are less threatening, particularly (as proposed earlier) when expressed in the company of the rabbinic elite.

Second, the rabbis in Babylonia were distributed over a greater geographical area than their Palestinian counterparts, constituting small groups in a larger, often nonrabbinized Jewish population. They had little official authority, little power to enforce their views. Whatever influence they gained they had to work for; they had no choice but to compete with other, more ancient Judaisms. No position came to them by "natural" right. Only by persuading the Jewish population of the wisdom of their ways could the rabbis gain the ascendancy they sought.

By contrast, the rabbis in Palestine were concentrated in the north, particularly in Tiberius and its environs. By virtue of this concentration, the movement could demand greater uniformity of its adherents. Unlike their Babylonian counterparts, the rabbis of Palestine were less compelled to tolerate diversity of opinion or practice. Moreover, because of the smaller geographical extent of Palestine, the smaller Jewish population (at least in the latter centuries of this era), and the fact that the rabbis had once controlled the office of the patriarch,[18] it is likely that they exerted greater power here than did their counterparts in Babylonia. It is also likely that the population as a whole was rabbinized at an earlier stage than in the east.[19] Consequently, the rabbis in Palestine were in a better position to insist upon limited, perhaps more traditional views—especially among their own number—and they had greater authority to insist upon these views than did their distant colleagues.

The preceding comments are built on the recognition that social constellations relate to religious ideologies in significant ways. It is not enough to examine religious expression in its gross historical context and suggest a cause-and-effect relationship. For this reason, Neusner's accounts of the Mishnah, the Yerushalmi, and the aggadic midrashim, valuable as they are, remain incomplete. It is not sufficient to note the juxtaposition of the

Mishnah's utopia with the catastrophes of the previous century and a half. One must also account for the social structure of the rabbinic movement in Palestine in the late second century: its small size, its strict internal hierarchies, its official power side by side with its limited religious control, and so on. These factors too affect the nature of the rabbis religious program at this stage. The same may be said regarding the later documents. This is not to suggest that the Yerushalmi's "quest for certainty" (using Neusner's phrase) is not, in part, a reaction to the upheaval of the prior century—that, too, is surely a factor. It is simply to suggest that different social orders in the same historical context will support different ideological structures, and a more complete account of the development of religious ideas must make room for this sort of observation as well.

The Growth and Flexibility of a Religious Canon

In reviewing the history of the canonization of Hebrew scripture, James A. Sanders writes:

> [W]hile rabbinic Judaism was closing its ranks, shedding all denominations save one and considerably restricting its canon, Christianity, on the other hand, was spreading out into the Roman-Hellenistic world, becoming pluralistic in itself and significantly keeping its canon open-ended.[20]

In Sanders's view, the restricted canon of the Bible (= the Tanakh) as accepted by the rabbis is evidence of their intolerance of alternatives. Whatever the merit of this precise characterization,[21] there is no doubt that he is in some measure correct; the early rabbis were a small group with a very precise and relatively limited vision. Not only is this quality evident in the rabbis' biblical canon but, significantly supporting Sanders, in the Mishnah and its (lack of) range of ideologies as well.

But it would be a mistake to look to the canon of Hebrew scripture alone for its testimony concerning the rabbis' alleged intolerance of alternatives. Not only is the rabbinic biblical canon itself an immensely diverse one (as we have often discussed) but, at the same time as the biblical canon was closing for the rabbis, another one was opening: their own.[22] Admittedly, at its inception this canon tolerated far fewer alternatives than even the Tanakh, but as it grew it became considerably more varied, and views which had long before lost currency in rabbinic circles found new expression. In the history which we have traced this development is particularly powerful.

We have had frequent occasion to note the renewed presence in rabbinic literature of explanations of suffering which had earlier been excluded from the recognized biblical canon or from the first rabbinic works or, sometimes, from both. These included suffering as a refining test, suffering as a means for achieving atonement, early death as sparing or redemptive, and the protective power of the suffering of the righteous. There is even one midrash relating to Daniel which borrows some of that book's apocalyptic qualities. In fact, the range of explanations and responses in rabbinic literature quite parallels the range represented by earlier Jewish compositions, whether included, ultimately, in the biblical canon or not.

There are, in my reading, only two significant differences between the rabbinic record, considered as a whole, and the earlier Jewish corpus. The first is the prominence of apocalypses in Jewish works composed between the second century BCE and the first century CE, compared with the almost complete absence of this genre in rabbinic compositions. The rabbis do not imagine an impending end-time; they condemn those who insist upon a precise accounting of history and its expected conclusion (though, to be sure, there is some small record of rabbis who engaged in such speculation). For the rabbis, this world and this history are what we must continue to work with. Therefore, explanations which suggest that current suffering should be understood as the birth pangs of the messianic age find no hearing in rabbinic texts.

This emphasis on the present makes one important escape valve available to earlier Jews unavailable to rabbinic Jews: the apocalyptic explanation of suffering, just discussed, could not be called upon. Perhaps for this reason, at the latest stage of the development of classical rabbinic Judaism, at least, expressions of rejection, protest, or anger had to be allowed. The apocalypses salvaged a system of reward and punishment; without the same option, the rabbis were forced, on rare occasion, to reject this same system. Such outright and explicit rejection is not found in earlier Jewish materials, save for Ecclesiastes, and the position of Ecclesiastes finds no voice in Jewish materials between the Bible and the Bavli. Thus, even despite the precedent of one unconventional biblical book, this final rabbinic possibility genuinely represents a new direction for the tradition.

In their deliberations on suffering, the rabbis show themselves at their most adaptive and creative. New social and historical circumstances lead to new explanations and reactions. If one lived to witness the publication of the Mishnah, one could not possibly have predicted the quality of reflections on human suffering which would find a place in later rabbinic "commentaries." But if one lived in sixth-century Babylonia, one could be sure that, without the alternatives now recorded in the last classical rabbinic work, Judaism could not possibly have survived the storms of antiquity. Whether we attribute the relative openness of the Bavli to religious genius or to the forces affecting a society in history makes little difference. What is important is that so significant a range of human emotional expression and religious insight found a home in the rabbinic context. On the foundation of this enlarged and varied canon, Judaism (now mostly rabbinic Judaism) was well-equipped to survive the many sufferings subsequent centuries would bring.

Notes

Chapter 1

1. For a broad discussion of religious responses to suffering, see John Bowker, *Problems of Suffering in Religions of the World* (Cambridge: Cambridge University Press, 1970).

2. See Peter Berger's discussion, *The Sacred Canopy: Elements of a Sociological Theory of Religion* (New York: Anchor Books, 1969), p. 53ff.

3. The phrase is Berger's. Ibid., p. 73.

4. See Jon D. Mikalson, *Honor Thy Gods: Popular Religion in Greek Tragedy* (Chapel Hill: University of North Carolina Press, 1991), p. 18, and, in considerable detail, Robert Parker, *Miasma: Pollution and Purification in Early Greek Religion* (Oxford: Clarendon Press, 1983), pp. 198–256 (a summary of the whole is found on pp. 255–56). The same belief carried forward into Roman paganism; see Ramsay MacMullen, *Paganism in the Roman Empire* (New Haven: Yale University Press, 1981), pp. 74, 76, and 82.

5. Mikalson, *Honor Thy Gods*, p. 5 and elsewhere.

6. Ibid., p. 5.

7. Euripides, *Medea*, 1. 755, quoted in Mikalson, ibid., p. 83.

8. Ibid., pp. 18, 25. For the same belief in Roman paganism, see MacMullen, p. 82.

9. Translations of the texts referred to herein may be found in *Textual Sources for the Study of Zoroastrianism*, ed. and trans. Mary Boyce (Chicago: University of Chicago Press, 1990; 1st pr. Manchester University Press, 1984). The present texts are found on pp. 28, 35, and 37.

10. Ibid., p. 39. See also Yasna 30, p. 35.

11. Later Zoroastrian tradition also spoke explicitly of resurrection. One wonderful account of the judgment to take place at the time of resurrection de-

scribes the following scene: "All mankind will arise, whether just or wicked . . . everyone will behold his own good or bad deeds, and the just will stand out among the wicked like white sheep among black. Fire . . . will melt the metal in the hills and mountains, and it will be upon the earth like a river. Then all men will be caused to pass through that molten metal. . . . And for those who are just it will seem as if they are walking through warm milk; and for the wicked it will seem as if they are walking in flesh through molten metal." See Boyce, *Textual Sources,* p. 52.

12. Ibid., p. 30.

13. Ibid., p. 35. See also Yasnas 45 and 32, p. 36.

14. Ibid., p. 50.

15. See Jon D. Levenson, *Creation and the Persistence of Evil* (San Francisco: Harper and Row, 1988).

16. A more detailed examination of biblical responses to and explanations of suffering is found in Chapter 2.

17. Dio Cassius, Roman History 69.14, trans. E. Cary (Loeb Classical Library, 1925), p. 451.

18. It is likely that this term for suffering originates with the use of the same root in Deut. 8:5: "As a man chastens his son, so does the Lord, your God, chasten you." The same association of suffering and divine chastening is, notably, also found among Israel's neighbors. See, for example, Plutarch, *De Sera numinis vindicta* 550a: "[T]he cure of the soul, which goes by the name of chastisement and justice, is the greatest of all arts." In *Plutarch's Moralia 7,* trans. Phillip H. DeLacy and Benedict Einarson (Loeb Classical Library, 1959), p. 191.

19. Solomon Schechter, in *Studies in Judaism: First Series* (Philadelphia: Jewish Publication Society, 1911), pp. 213–32; reprinted in *Studies in Judaism: Essays on Persons, Concepts, and Movements of Thought in Jewish Tradition* (New York: Atheneum, 1970), pp. 105–22.

20. E. E. Urbach, *The Sages: Their Concepts and Beliefs,* trans. Israel Abrahams (Jerusalem: Magnes, 1975), vol. 1, pp. 420–48.

21. See Yaakov Elman, "The Suffering of the Righteous in Palestinian and Babylonian Sources," Jewish Quarterly Review 80, no. 3–4 (January–April 1990): 315–39.

22. Yaakov Elman, "Righteousness as Its Own Reward: An Inquiry into the Theologies of the Stam," *Proceedings of the American Academy of Jewish Research* 52 (1990/1991): 35–67.

23. Elman, "The Suffering of the Righteous," p. 315.

24. A concise expression of Neusner's oft-repeated critique is found in his overly polemical *Reading and Believing: Ancient Judaism and Contemporary Gullibility* (Atlanta: Scholars Press, 1986), pp. 119–26.

25. See William Scott Green, "What's in a Name? The Problematic of Talmudic 'Biography,'" in *Approaches to Ancient Judaism: Theory and Practice,* ed. W. S. Green (Missoula, Mont.: Scholars Press, 1978).

26. See M. I. Finley, *Ancient History: Evidence and Models* (New York: Elisabeth Sifton Books and Penguin Books, 1986), p. 18.

27. Martin S. Jaffee discusses this imprecision in detail in his "How Much 'Orality' in Oral Torah? New Perspectives on the Composition and Transmission of Early Rabbinic Tradition," *Shofar* 10, no. 2 (Winter 1992): 62–67.

28. See my "On the Reliability of Attributions in the Babylonian Talmud," *Hebrew Union College Annual* 60 (1989): 175–90.

29. See Elman, "Righteousness as Its Own Reward," pp. 40–45.

30. Ibid., p. 59.

31. Ibid., and notes 58 and 59 there.

32. This is true even of Elman in his "Righteousness as Its Own Reward," despite promises to the contrary. His "The Suffering of the Righteous," on the other hand, goes much further in respecting and giving attention to the final documentary hand.

33. See my "Composition and Meaning in the Bavli," *Prooftexts* 8, no. 3 (1988): 271–91.

34. See Neusner, *The Bavli and Its Sources: The Question of Tradition in the Case of Tractate Sukkah* (Atlanta: Scholars Press, 1987).

35. See Boyarin, *Intertextuality and the Reading of Midrash* (Bloomington: Indiana University Press, 1990), pp. 13–14.

36. I have in mind, of course, Neusner's many studies of the documents of classical rabbinic Judaism. The reader will find, in most of the chapters where I consider rabbinic responses, that I offer Neusner's claims for the religious history of rabbinism as the essential foundation for comparison and critique. To his credit, Neusner is the only one to have written extensive religious histories of the development of rabbinic documents and so, even where I disagree with particular analyses, I record his view for consideration. The only exception is the chapters on the Bavli, in connection to which I think Neusner's work is extremely misguided. In those chapters, I offer for comparative consideration my own *The Mind of the Talmud: An Intellectual History of the Bavli* (New York: Oxford University Press, 1990).

Chapter 2

1. I include in this assertion even rabbinic Judaism as represented in the Mishnah. Neusner, in his ground-breaking work on the Mishnah, properly notes the important discontinuities between that document and the various documents of the Bible, emphasizing in particular the fact that the Mishnah rarely quotes or justifies its rulings based upon explicit biblical sources. However, the Mishnah frequently *intimates* a biblical foundation and, as Neusner also highlights, the agenda of the Mishnah, both as a whole and in many of its specifics, is predominantly the agenda set out by the priestly author in the Torah. For these reasons, I am confident of the accuracy of my present assertion. For Neusner's discussion, see *Judaism: The Evidence of the Mishnah* (Chicago: University of Chicago Press, 1981), especially pp. 167–229.

2. Relatively conservative views of the canonization of Hebrew scripture—views, that is, that argue for an earlier rather than a later conclusion to the canonization process—are found in Sid Z. Leiman, *The Canonization of Hebrew Scripture: The Talmudic and Midrashic Evidence* (Hamden: Connecticut Academy of Arts and Sciences, 1976), and Roger T. Beckwith, *The Old Testament Canon of the New Testament Church* (Grand Rapids, Mich.: Eerdmans, 1985). The opposing view is taken by James A. Sanders, *Canon and Community* (Philadelphia: Fortress Press, 1984). An important critique of virtually all scholarship on the canonization of Hebrew scripture is Jack N. Lightstone's "The Formation of the Biblical Canon in Judaism of Late Antiquity: Prolegomenon to a General Reassessment," *Studies in Religion* 8, no. 2 (1979): 135–42.

3. See the discussion of this matter in Sanders, *Canon and Community*, p. 11.

4. For more on common assumptions that characterize the reading of canonical works, see John B. Henderson, *Scripture, Canon, and Commentary: A Comparison of Confucian and Western Exegesis* (Princeton: Princeton University Press, 1991), pp. 89–138.

5. A schematic history of this topic, particularly in postexilic biblical documents and in nonbiblical second-Temple literature, may be found in Shaye J. D. Cohen, *From the Maccabees to the Mishnah* (Philadelphia: Westminster Press, 1987), pp. 87–101.

6. Not surprisingly, a good number of books have been devoted to the subject of responses to suffering in the Bible. A concise critical bibliography of major works before 1955 may be found in Jim Alvin Sanders, "Suffering as Divine Discipline in the Old Testament and Post-Biblical Judaism," *Colgate Rochester Divinity School Bulletin* 28 (1955): 124–25, to which should be added, of course, Sanders's work itself. Of late, this subject has been less the focus of attention in book-length scholarship.

7. Biblical translations are taken from the New JPS Version (Philadelphia: The Jewish Publication Society, 1988). Here, the translator notes that the "precise nature of these ills is uncertain."

8. The longest threat of punishment for transgression, again manifest through a wide variety of plagues and diseases (in a word, suffering), is Deut. 28:15–68. The details there are more dramatic, but nothing of the overall lesson is changed.

9. The history of the chronicler shares the overall Deuteronomic ideology in its explanation of suffering. The editorial evaluations also appear in Chronicles; see, for example, 2 Chron. 25:2, 14–15, and 26:4. Individual afflictions are similarly explained as punishment; see 2 Chron. 32:24ff. Menasseh's transgressions, too, are offered as explanation for his capture and temporary captivity in Babylon; see 2 Chron. 33.

10. See also Pss. 1, 5, 7:9ff., 9:3–5 and 9, and 18:21–25.

11. See also Prov. 10:6–10, 10:27, 10:30, 12:7, 13:21, and so forth.

12. See Prov. 3:11, 6:23, 10:17, 12:1, and 15:10. Sanders, in "Suffering as Divine Discipline," concludes that only 3:11 and 15:10 bear this precise sense in Proverbs; see pp. 33, 40, and 44. However, he shows that discipline imposed by a parent also often involves hardship or suffering (see p. 40) and the verb YSR (= instruction) is taken by Sanders to involve hardship in fully one-third of its biblical uses (p. 42). It seems to me, therefore, that the sense suggested clearly in these verses, in Proverbs and elsewhere, is by association implied in others as well; Sanders also often describes a use of this term as speaking of "general" instruction.

13. Of course, the ancient Israelites were by no means unique in making this connection, as discussed in Chapter 1. See also Parker, *Miasma*, pp. 235ff.

14. Literally: "known."

15. This is the translation of Charles A. Briggs in the *International Critical Commentary, Psalms*, vol. 1 (New York: Charles Scribner's Sons, 1906), p. 91. RSV has "The Lord tests the righteous and the wicked."

16. For a review of the range of possibilities and the scholarship in support of each proposal, see the *Anchor Bible*, vol. 20 (Garden City, N.Y.: Doubleday, 1968), pp. xliii–lx, and, absent the more recent work but in greater detail, H. H. Rowley, *The Servant of the Lord and Other Essays on the Old Testament* (London: Lutterworth Press, 1952). Whatever the intended identity of the servant from a source-critical perspective (that is, when this chapter is considered as originally an

independent source), the present context strongly suggests that the servant is Israel. See 41:8, 44:2, 44:21, and 49:3.

17. I make no judgment here concerning whether the original audience of this communication were readers or listeners (I assume they were the latter). I speak of readers because our concern is the rabbinic audience of this prophecy, and they were certainly readers.

18. See note 16.

19. Clear, that is, outside of an apologetic reading of this much-polemicized text. I find Harry Orlinsky's denial of this sense of Isaiah's message to be completely unconvincing; see his "The So-Called 'Suffering Servant' in Isaiah 53," *The Goldenson Lecture of 1964* (Cincinnati: Hebrew Union College Press, 1964).

20. Y. Kaufmann, *The Religion of Israel*, trans. Moshe Greenberg (New York: Schocken, 1972), p. 399.

21. Kummel notes Isa. 24–27, Zech. 9–14, and the book of Joel as earlier "predictions of the apocalyptic type." But, he goes on to say, these are not "apocalypses proper . . . the first and most important of . . . which . . . is the book of Daniel." See his *Introduction to the New Testament*, 17th ed., trans. Howard Clark Kee (Nashville: Abingdon Press, 1975), p. 453.

22. Ibid., pp. 453–54.

23. By the time of the composition of 2 Maccabees, no more than sixty years later, this confidence would be present; see Chapter 3.

24. Kaufmann, *The Religion of Israel*, p. 399.

25. See Gerhard von Rad, *The Message of the Prophets*, trans. D. M. G. Stalker (New York: Harper and Row, 1965), p. 159.

26. See Pss. 35:17, 22–24, 42:10, 43:2, 44 (all), and 74 (all).

27. A partial bibliography may be found in the works selected for inclusion in Nahum N. Glatzer's *The Dimensions of Job: A Study and Selected Readings* (New York: Schocken, 1969), along with his bibliography there, pp. 299–303. See also Brevard Childs's selected bibliography, *Introduction to the Old Testament as Scripture* (Philadelphia: Fortress Press, 1979), pp. 526–28. On the relationship between Job and cognate literatures, see Gerhard von Rad, *Old Testament Theology*, vol. 1, trans. D. M. G Stalker (New York: Harper and Row, 1962), p. 408, n. 55, and idem, *Wisdom in Israel* (Nashville: Abingdon Press, 1972), p. 9. This latter piece speaks of the relationship of ancient Near Eastern wisdom and biblical wisdom in general.

28. On the apparent confusion in Eliphaz's first speech, see von Rad, *Old Testament Theology*, p. 410.

29. There is widespread critical agreement that this section of Job, the speeches of Elihu (chapters 32–37), are a later addition to the text; see Childs, *Introduction to the Old Testament as Scripture*, p. 529. I include these references in light of their established position in the final canonical context, the context which was, after all, known and accepted uncritically by the rabbis.

30. See Stephen A. Geller, "'Where Is Wisdom?': A Literary Study of Job 28 in Its Settings," in *Judaic Perspectives on Ancient Israel*, ed. Jacob Neusner, Baruch Levine and Ernest Frerichs (Philadelphia: Fortress Press, 1987), p. 173, for the same point.

31. Glatzer, *The Dimensions of Job*, Chapters 5 and 6.

32. Ibid., pp. 63, 70.

33. Geller, "'Where Is Wisdom?'" p. 170.

34. Ibid., p. 173.

35. See Ibid., pp. 169–75. See also von Rad, *Old Testament Theology*, p. 413.

36. See Sanders, "Suffering as Divine Discipline," p. 1. Cf. H. W. Robinson's enumeration in *Suffering Human and Divine* (New York: Macmillan, 1939), pp. 34–48.

Chapter 3

1. For an excellent review of this literature, see George W. E. Nickelsburg, *Jewish Literature between the Bible and the Mishnah* (Philadelphia: Fortress Press, 1981).

2. See the comments of George W. E. Nickelsburg in *Jewish Writings of the Second Temple Period*, ed. Michael E. Stone (Assen: Van Gorcum; Philadelphia: Fortress Press, 1984), pp. 33 and 89–90.

3. Translations of works of the Apocrypha are those of Edgar J. Goodspeed, *The Apocrypha: An American Translation* (New York: Vintage Books, 1959).

4. Cf. Isa. 57:2.

5. Many of the following texts are discussed in far greater detail in George W. E. Nickelsburg, *Resurrection, Immortality, and Eternal Life in Intertestamental Judaism* (Cambridge, Mass.: Harvard University Press, 1972).

6. This new anticipation of reward and punishment following death in postbiblical Jewish works has often been explained as a consequence of Hellenistic influence. Mikalson comments, however, that "Expectations of rewards [in the afterlife] are rare, tentative, and do not involve the common dead." In general, he describes evidence of reward and punishment in the afterlife as "meager" in Greek tragedies. Perhaps, then, this connection has been overdrawn. For Mikalson's discussion, see *Honor Thy Gods*, pp. 119–20.

7. Dated by Nickelsburg (*Jewish Literature*, p. 48) to before 175 BCE (that is, earlier than the latter chapters of Daniel).

8. The translator (M. A. Knibb) notes that this should perhaps be corrected to four. See *The Apocryphal Old Testament*, ed. H. F. D. Sparks (Oxford: Clarendon Press, 1984), p. 211, n. 26.

9. See Nickelsburg, *Jewish Literature*, pp. 149–50.

10. Though the process is less clear than here, a similar recording is presumably imagined in the book spoken of in Dan. 12:1. See the thorough discussion of this matter in *The Book of Daniel*, The Anchor Bible, vol. 23, trans. with introduction and commentary by Louis F. Hartman and Alexander A. Di Lella (Garden City, N.Y.: Doubleday, 1978), p. 306.

11. The translation is that of R. H. Charles in *The Apocryphal Old Testament*.

12. "Rise up" is Nickelsburg's translation in *Resurrection*, p. 32. The reader should see Nickelsburg's full discussion of the present passage from Jubilees, pp. 31–33.

13. This story and its various later retellings, and particularly that of 4 Maccabees, are discussed by Moses Hadas in his introduction to 4 Maccabees, in *The Third and Fourth Books of Maccabees*, ed. and trans. M. Hadas (New York: Harper and Brothers, 1953), pp. 91–135. The multiple versions are also discussed by Y. Gutmann in "The Mother and Her Seven Sons in the Aggadah and in II and IV Maccabees" (Hebrew), in *Sefer Yohanan Levi* (Jerusalem: Magnes, 1949), pp. 25–37. See also Nickelsburg's important discussion of this text, *Resurrection*, pp. 93–109.

14. M. Fishbane, for example, takes it this way. See *Biblical Interpretation in Early Israel* (Oxford: Oxford University Press, 1985), p. 493.

15. Resurrection is also assumed elsewhere in this literature; see, for example, Ps. of Sol. 3:12.

16. Norman Golb has challenged the common view that the Dead Sea Scrolls are the exclusive library of a particular sect; see "The Dead Sea Scrolls: A New Perspective," *American Scholar* 58, no. 2 (Spring 1989):177–207. Whatever the merit of his claims for the Qumran site and the actual history of the library, I find his characterization of the nature of the scrolls corpus completely convincing. The present hymn offers no sign of sectarian origin (if apocalyptic is necessarily sectarian, then what do we do with Daniel?) and thus may be taken as evidence of broader Jewish currents in the late second-Temple period.

17. Translations of Qumran documents are those of Theodor H. Gaster, *The Dead Sea Scriptures* (Garden City, N.Y.: Anchor Books, 1976). The present text is found on p. 399.

18. Golb's thesis, discussed in note 16, obviates the need to reconcile the many contradictions between this document and the Code of Discipline. The late-second-Temple period was characterized by extreme sectarianism and thus it may well be that the different sectarian writings found in this corpus do not derive from the same sects.

19. There are also possibly other minor additions to the main body of the text, as well as emendations that were necessitated by the course of history immediately following its composition. See Goodspeed's introduction in *The Apocrypha*, pp. 39–40. Translations that follow are taken from that volume. Important discussions of the theodicy of this work may be found in Alden Lloyd Thompson, *Responsibility for Evil in the Theodicy of IV Ezra*, SBL Dissertation Series, 29 (Missoula, Mont.: Scholars Press, 1977) and Tom W. Willet, *Eschatology in the Theodicies of 2 Baruch and 4 Ezra* (Sheffield: Sheffield Academic Press, 1989).

20. Jacob M. Myers, in *The Anchor Bible*, vol. 42 (Garden City, N.Y.: Doubleday, 1974), p. 166, translates "exceeds [what is yet to come]" without "far." In his commentary (pp. 183–84) Myers clarifies that the intent is to describe the imminence of the anticipated end.

21. Translations to follow are by R. H. Charles, revised by L. H. Brockington, in *The Apocryphal Old Testament*. On the ideologies of Baruch, see Gwendolyn B. Sayler, *Have the Promises Failed? A Literary Analysis of 2 Baruch*, SBL Dissertation Series, 72 (Chico, Calif.: Scholars Press, 1984).

22. The parallels between 4 Ezra and 2 Baruch are detailed in G. H. Box, *The Ezra-Apocalypse* (London: Society for Promoting Christian Knowledge, 1912), pp. lxix–lxx. A more recent detailed discussion of similarities and differences may be found in Thompson, *Responsibility for Evil*, pp. 121–48.

23. See also the Apocalypse of Abraham for a similar approach.

24. A more detailed description of the narrative may be found in Nickelsburg, *Jewish Literature*, pp. 49–54.

25. Supporting this interpretation, see Paul D. Hanson, "Rebellion in Heaven, Azazel, and Euhemeristic Heroes in I Enoch 6–11," *Journal of Biblical Literature* 96, no. 2 (1977): 195–233, esp. pp. 201–2.

26. See Nickelsburg, "Apocalyptic and Myth in I Enoch 6–11," *Journal of Biblical Literature* 96, no. 3 (1977): 395, 388.

27. See John J. Collins, "Methodological Issues in the Study of I Enoch: Reflections on the Articles of P. D. Hanson and G. W. Nickelsburg," SBL Seminar Papers, vol. 1 (Missoula, Mont.: Scholars Press, 1978), pp. 317–19.

28. All of the following statements are found at 1QS iii, 13–iv, 26.

29. Josephus, *Jewish War*, trans. H. St. J. Thackeray (Loeb Classical Library, 1926).

30. For similar beliefs, see the Testament of Job 1–27 (a detailed description may be found in Nickelsburg, *Jewish Literature*, pp. 241–48).

31. The translation is that of Moses Hadas in *The Third and Fourth Books of Maccabees*.

32. This was the common belief of Greek and Roman religion; see my discussion in Chapter 1 and references there.

Chapter 4

1. Neusner, *Judaism: The Evidence of the Mishnah*, p. 27, emphasis added.

2. See Neusner's discussions in *Messiah in Context: Israel's History and Destiny in Formative Judaism* (Philadelphia: Fortress Press, 1984), pp. 31–42, and in *Judaisms and Their Messiahs at the Turn of the Christian Era*, ed. J. Neusner, W. S. Green and E. Frerichs (Cambridge: Cambridge University Press, 1987), p. 276.

3. Neusner, *Judaism: The Evidence of the Mishnah*, p. 235.

4. Ibid., p. 41.

5. See Joseph B. Soloveitchik, *Halakhic Man*, trans. Lawrence Kaplan (Philadelphia: Jewish Publication Society of America, 1983), pp. 23–24.

6. Neusner, *Judaism: The Evidence of the Mishnah*, pp. 167–229.

7. Neusner illustrates this graphically in *Judaism: The Evidence of the Mishnah*, p. 240.

8. MS Paris 328–29 has "Eleazar b. R. Shimeon." MSS Kaufmann and Parma consider this the continuation of the previous tradition, attributed to R. Judah.

9. The tradition of the Kaufmann and Parma manuscripts makes this even clearer; there the speaker adds: "And what caused me to be sustained with pain? Say: *My sins!*" (emphasis added). Unmistakably, it is present, personal sin that is considered crucial here.

10. The text printed at the end of tractate Pe'a (not part of the original Mishnah; see below), while not repeating the present principle explicitly, quite clearly assumes it in its affirmation of active divine justice. Thus "anyone who is not [truly] lame, nor blind, nor crippled [in two limbs], and makes himself as one of them [in order to pervert justice] will not die from old age until he will be [in fact] like one of them. . . ." In each case described in this text, the punishment reflects precisely the nature of the perversion of justice. Though this text is not actually a Mishnah—see J. N. Epstein, *Mevo lenusaḥ ha-Mishnah*, vol. 2 (Jerusalem: Merkaz, 1948), p. 975—it loyally recreates the ideology first spelled out (in the rabbinic context, that is) in Mishnah Sotah.

11. Urbach makes this same point in *The Sages: Their Concepts and Beliefs*, vol. 1, p. 439, and vol. 2, p. 881, n. 68.

12. Cicero, *De legibus*, trans. Clinton Walker Keyes (Loeb Classical Library, 1928).

13. A discussion of this principle of justice in these and other sources may be found in I. Heinemann, *Philons griechische und judische Bildung* (Breslau: M. & H. Marcus, 1932), pp. 369–83.

14. See Epstein, *Mevo lenusah*, vol. 2, p. 1306, on the latter part of the final Mishnah and the probability that it is not original to the Mishnaic text.

15. Ibid., p. 722.

16. Lieberman, in *Tosefta kifeshuta*, vol. 5 (New York: Jewish Theological Seminary of America, 1955), p. 1023, supports this reading of the Mishnah. He explains the commentary of the Yerushalmi by suggesting that "the Yerushalmi had difficulty, [asking] is it so that troops pass one by one? For this reason they interpreted . . . so as to say [that what is meant in the Mishnah is that they are judged] as a troop [passing] on this path on the crest [of a mountain]." In other words, the Mishnah did not, in fact, say that they are judged individually. The Yerushalmi, which wanted this to be so, therefore had to interpret the Mishnaic metaphor as referring to very specific and unusual conditions.

17. See David Halivni, *Meqorot umesorot, seder nashim* (Tel Aviv: Dvir, 1968), pp. 660–62.

18. For an excellent review of references to the world-to-come and other eschatological images in the Mishnah, see Anthony J. Saldarini, "The Uses of the Apocalyptic [*sic*] in the Mishnah and Tosepta," *Catholic Biblical Quarterly* 39 (1977): 396–409.

19. Epstein, *Mevo lenusah*, vol. 2, p. 1133.

20. Immediately before the reference to the Temple's destruction, there is a mention of the death of the "first [= early] prophets." Following the description of the consequences of the destruction, the text goes on to speak of the "War of Vespasian." If there is a chronological order to the Mishnah's list, then it would appear that the first destruction is intended. This is supported by the first described consequences of the destruction (for example, the elimination of the legendary worm, who would carve the stones for the Temple's construction). Nevertheless, the proximity of this discussion to the discussion of the Vespasian war (= the war during which the second Temple was destroyed) makes it likely that there is an intentional blurring here.

21. Mention of the destruction is also found in a section of this text marked as Mishnah 15 of the same chapter. This is not, however, original to the Mishnah; see Epstein, *Mevo lenusah*, vol. 2, pp. 949 and 976–77, and *The Babylonian Talmud with Variant Readings, Tractate Sotah* (II), ed. Rabbi Abraham Liss (Jerusalem: Institute for the Complete Israeli Talmud, 1979), p. 352, n. 157.

22. Neusner considers this text in some detail in his discussion of the Mishnah's theory of history; see *Messiah in Context*, pp. 25–38. Remarkably, Neusner devotes the largest part of his discussion to the latter portion of Mishnah 15—which he sees as the most significant piece of this text—despite the fact that it is not actually a part of the Mishnah (see previous note)! His comments are thus irrelevant to the Mishnah's theory of history and the Messiah.

23. Mishah Maaser Sheni refers to the possibility of rebuilding in a matter-of-fact manner, as a mere detail that affects the status of certain ritual practices. The hope expressed at the end of tractate Taanit is not part of the original Mishnah; see Epstein, *Mevo lenusah*, vol. 2, p. 686.

24. See his comments quoted earlier in this chapter.

25. Briefly, what I am arguing in this paragraph is that, relative to what they would become in later centuries, the rabbis, at this early stage, were what Mary Douglas would call "high group and high grid." See Douglas, *Natural Symbols* (New York: Random House, 1973), pp. 134–36; and *In the Active Voice* (London: Routledge and Kegan Paul, 1982), pp. 210–11.

26. See, for example, Ḥanokh Albeck, *Mishnah*, 6 vols. (Jerusalem: Bialik Institute; Tel-Aviv: Dvir, 1953), vol. 4, p. 367.

27. See also "Mishnah Avot" 6:5—actually a later addition to Avot—which repeats this same belief. In this respect, the appendix is one in spirit with the text to which it is appended.

28. Offered first in his commentary, this interpretation is apparently preferred by R. Obadiah of Bertinoro. This is also the sense that is assumed by Neusner in his translation of Avot, as well as by Yaakov Elman in "When Permission Is Given: Aspects of Divine Providence," *Tradition* 24, no. 4 (Summer 1989): 24.

Chapter 5

1. The precise relationship of the Tosefta and the Mishnah is conveniently laid out by Neusner in *The Tosefta: Its Structure and Its Sources* (Atlanta: Scholars Press, 1986).

2. Regrettably, Saul Lieberman, the outstanding modern scholar of the Tosefta, did not offer his opinion concerning the dating of this work. Ḥanoch Albeck argued forcefully that the Tosefta as we know it (as opposed to some of the traditions which came to be included in it) was a post-Talmudic creation; see *Mavo la-talmudim* (Tel-Aviv: Dvir, 1969), pp. 54–72. In my opinion, the assumptions upon which his argument is built may readily be challenged and his conclusions, therefore, are not compelling.

3. Neusner, *Midrash in Context: Exegesis in Formative Judaism* (Philadelphia: Fortress Press, 1983), pp. 2–12.

4. The outlines of the history of this period are presented concisely in Elias Bickerman and Morton Smith, *The Ancient History of Western Civilization* (New York: Harper and Row, 1976), pp. 185–88.

5. See J. Boardman, J. Griffin, and O. Murray, eds., *The Oxford History of the Classical World* (Oxford: Oxford University Press, 1986), p. 808.

6. For a detailed history of this period in Palestine see M. Avi-Yonah, *The Jews of Palestine: A Political History from the Bar Kokhba War to the Arab Conquest* (New York: Schocken, 1976), pp. 89–136.

7. See Lee I. Levine, "The Jewish Patriarch (Nasi) in Third Century Palestine," in *Aufstieg und Niedergang der römischen Welt II*, vol. 19, no. 2, ed. H. Temporini and W. Haase (Berlin and New York: De Gruyter, 1979), pp. 649–88. The strength of Levine's conclusions requires moderation because of his almost exclusive dependence upon rabbinic sources, whose self-interest is obviously served by claiming greater authority for the rabbinic patriarch.

8. Page numbers refer to Lieberman's edition of the Tosefta (New York: Jewish Theological Seminary of America, 1955–1988).

9. See my discussion of this Mishnah in "Composition and Meaning in the Bavli," pp. 281–82.

10. See Lieberman's comment to p. 79, l. 83, *Tosefta kifeshuta*, vol. 9, p. 184.

11. Note again that the original Mishnah ended before the tradition of "R. Judah in his name." What follows is a later addition.

12. The fact that the Tosefta omits tractates Tamid and Middot may be significant in this connection. These are the two tractates that are most closely wedded to the Temple as an everyday institution—Tamid describing the order of the daily service in the Temple and Middot describing the dimensions of the Temple itself. Is their absence mere accident, or may we attribute more meaning to it?

13. See *Tosefta kifeshuta*, vol. 5, pp. 1115–16.

14. I follow the version of the Erfurt manuscript. Other versions sometimes differ significantly, so much so that Lieberman, in a rare judgment, prints all of Erfurt side by side with his base text.

15. See also Taan. 2:3 and 4:6.

16. For another case where the reality of the destruction is brought in where the corresponding Mishnah fails to recognize the same reality, see Yoma 1:9.

17. Neusner, *Messiah in Context*, p. 60.

18. Ibid., p. 72.

19. See J. Neusner, W. S. Green, and E. Frerichs, eds., *Judaisms and Their Messiahs at the Turn of the Christian Era* (Cambridge: Cambridge University Press, 1987). See especially Green's introductory chapter.

Chapter 6

1. Albeck, *Mavo la-talmudim*, p. 106.

2. He merely makes reference to M. D. Herr's article in *The Encyclopedia Judaica*; see Neusner, *The Midrash: An Introduction* (Northvale, N.J.: Jason Aronson, 1990), pp. 31–32. Astoundingly, Neusner accepts Herr's date though he disagrees in all details with the bases of Herr's argument. Herr accepts Albeck's argument that the midrashim are unknown by the Talmuds (including the Bavli) and accepts the traditional dating of the Bavli at c. 427 (the death of R. Ashi, its purported redactor). But Neusner assumes as a commonplace that the Talmuds know the halakhic midrashim and, besides, dates the Bavli c. 600 or later. Thus Herr's dating is unsupportable if one accepts Neusner's conclusions elsewhere. For my dating, see below.

Note that Neusner's present book, *Midrash: An Introduction*, provides a concise sample of his more extended works on the midrashim, listed in the complete bibliography included in the volume, pp. 221–29. The entries relevant in this context are found on pp. 222–24.

3. See again Neusner's comments in *Midrash in Context*, pp. 2–12.

4. See the basic conclusions of these studies as offered in Neusner, *The Midrash: An Introduction*, pp. 31–137.

5. See David W. Nelson, "Responses to the Destruction of the Second Temple in the Tannaitic Midrashim," Ph.D. dissertation, New York University, 1991, pp. 365–68.

6. Page numbers refer to standard editions, listed in the bibliography.

7. The translation of the latter verses is modified from the JPS translation for the present context.

8. Translation modified for context.

9. Translation adjusted for context.

10. Translation adjusted for context.

11. I confess that I do not understand the relationship between the final claim and the verse that is quoted here. The argument as a whole is, in any case, easily understood.

12. A similar point is made at Mekhilta *deshira* par. 3, p. 128, ll. 6–8.

13. See David Nelson's discussion of this text and others in which God is described as regretting his punishment of Israel; "Responses to the Destruction," pp. 224–28.

14. See, for example, G. Alon, *The Jews in Their Land in the Talmudic Age*, ed. and trans. Gershon Levi (Jerusalem: Magnes, 1984), vol. 2, p. 635.

15. See the Mekhilta texts at pp. 78–79 and 81, and also Sifrei Num. 106, p. 105.

16. The same assumption is also shared by Sifrei Num. 115, p. 129.

17. "With favor" is the translator's (New JPS) interpolation. It does, however, capture the correct sense of the Hebrew original.

18. Important discussions of the rabbinic *mashal*, commonly translated (as I have here) as "parable," may be found in David Stern, *Parables in Midrash: Narrative and Exegesis in Rabbinic Literature* (Cambridge, Mass.: Harvard University Press, 1991), and Daniel Boyarin, *Intertextuality and the Reading of Midrash*, pp. 80–92.

19. Translation adjusted for context.

20. I follow Finkelstein's emendation in translating here. See his note on p. 346, l. 10.

21. Plutarch, *Consolation to His Wife*, trans. Phillip H. de Lacy and Benedict Einarson (Loeb Classical Library, 1959), 610–f, p. 597.

22. See also Sifra, *milu'im*, 23.

23. This characteristic of the halakhic midrashim is so powerful that it causes Finkelstein to conclude—against the canons of contemporary scholarship in rabbinic literature—that "the core of the Sifra [is] a Temple textbook for priests"; see his "The Core of the Sifra: A Temple Textbook for Priests," *Jewish Quarterly Review* 80, no. 1–2 (July–October 1989): 15–34.

24. The same narrative is quoted at Tosefta Yoma 1:12 and Tosefta Shev. 1:4. In neither case, however, is the event connected with the destruction of the Temple—that is the innovation of the present text.

25. The discussion of the ninth of Ab and the commemoration of the Temple's destruction, at 31 (p. 51), is not original to the Sifrei text; see Finkelstein's note to p. 50, l.

26. There are many variants of this attribution; see the apparatus there.

27. The same claim is evident, though without explicit reference to the Temple's destruction as such, in *ba-ḥodesh* 1 (pp. 203–4); see David Nelson's discussion in "Responses to the Destruction," pp. 41–45.

28. Nelson notes a significant development in texts in this category, that is, their common claim that God accompanies Israel into exile and suffers with them in their exilic condition. These traditions respond, obviously, to the question, "What is God's relationship to Israel after punishment?" and answer that God's love remains strong—so strong that God experiences the same pain. No doubt such a view would be a significant source of comfort for those who lived after the destruction. Still, it must be emphasized that these traditions offer no revision of the transgression–punishment theology, nor is the love they speak of inconsistent with the anger that must be attributed to God before the punishment. Witness the parent who, after punishing a child for misbehavior, nevertheless suffers at the child's pain.

29. See Levine, "The Jewish Patriarch (Nasi) in Third Century Palestine," pp. 681–84.

30. See Ket. 110b–11a.

Chapter 7

1. Neusner's review of these events, heavily dependent upon Avi-Yonah's history, may be found in *Judaism in Society: The Evidence of the Yerushalmi* (Chicago: University of Chicago Press, 1983), pp. 3–26.

2. A detailed history of this development may be found in Ramsay MacMullen, *Christianizing the Roman Empire, A.D. 100–400* (New Haven: Yale University Press, 1984).

3. See *The Jews in Roman Imperial Legislation*, ed. with commentary by Amnon Linder (Detroit: Wayne State University Press; Jerusalem: Israel Academy of Sciences and Humanities, 1987), pp. 320–21.

4. Avi-Yonah devotes but a few pages to the fifth century following the demise of the patriarch. See *The Jews of Palestine*, pp. 236–41 (this includes his record of the sixth century, though some of what he says is also relevant for the fifth).

5. See Shaye J. D. Cohen, "Epigraphical Rabbis," *Jewish Quarterly Review* 72 (1981–1982): 1–17.

6. Neusner, *Judaism in Society*, p. 26.

7. This sentence is missing in the body of the MS Leiden but is recorded in the margin.

8. Translated for the present context.

9. This tradition is missing in MS Vatican 133 but is found in MS Leiden.

10. The same tradition is found at Gen. R. 33, 3 and 96, 9, and the protective power of the suffering of the righteous (Rabbi) is similarly assumed in each. The Palestinian sources are of a single fabric in their approach to this legend; important elaboration is found only later in the Bavli.

11. The first printing (Venice) has at this point in the narrative "*keshera,*" a word without any sense in this context. The Vilna printing therefore "corrects" it to "*keshehaya*" ("when he was departing to his house"). The Leiden manuscript has "*kesheR'*" = "when Rabbi (= R.) departed. . . ." See Saul Lieberman, *HaYerushalmi kifeshuto* (Jerusalem: Darom, 1934), p. 193.

12. Lieberman notes that "the Hebrew *din* often means torture." See "Roman Legal Institutions in Early Rabbinics and in the Acta Martyrum," *Jewish Quarterly Review* 35, no. 1 (1944): 15, n. 99.

13. This translation is based upon the clearly preferred reading of the version at Sotah and the Leiden and Vatican manuscripts in Berakhot (for the printed RHTT, Leiden has V'TT and Vatican has V'T'). The Leiden script is somewhat unclear and could easily have been confused for RHTT.

14. Neusner's translation. Boyarin, in *Intertextuality and the Reading of Midrash*, p. 126, translates "deaf." Neusner's translation seems better to me, though both are possible in context ("deaf" would be understood in the sense of "fool," a common connotation of this word in rabbinic usage). Whichever the case, our concern here is the next phrase in this statement.

15. The same contrast between the two Talmuds may be evident in their respective comments on Job (y. Sot. 5:6, 20c and b. B.B. 15a). The Yerushalmi objects to a tradition, attributed to R. Shimeon b. Laqish, that "Job never existed and never will exist." It concludes that "He existed but his suffering never happened." So why, the Yerushalmi wants to know, did the biblical text report that it had happened? "To say that if they [= the sufferings] had come upon him he could have withstood them." With this resolution, the Yerushalmi accomplishes two purposes: (1) it removes the obvious injustice assumed by the book (Job was righteous, therefore it would have been improper for God to permit him to suffer in order to accept Satan's challenge); (2) it demonstrates that a righteous individual (Job) could, if necessary, withstand suffering—apparently without protest or complaint. This latter understanding is in accord with the Yerushalmi's opinion, discussed above. In contrast, the Bavli records the opinion that Job never existed

(among many different opinions) without such a revision and without reference to the problem of nonsubmissive responses to suffering.

Chapter 8

1. I omit discussion of the opinions of Ecclesiastes Rabbah. Herr puts its redaction in the eighth century ("Ecclesiastes Rabbah," *Encyclopedia Judaica*, vol. 6, p. 355) and, though Marc Hirshman (*Midrash Qohelet Rabbah*, Ph.D. dissertation, Jewish Theological Seminary of America, 1982, vol. 1, pp. 58–107) argues against the necessity of such a late dating, the matter is sufficiently in doubt to exclude consideration of this midrash here. Regarding Song of Songs Rabbah, Herr ("Song of Songs Rabbah," *Encyclopedia Judaica*, vol. 15, p. 153) suggests a probable date of the mid-sixth century, but Samuel Lachs ("Prolegomena to Canticles Rabba," *Jewish Quarterly Review* 55 [1965]: 249) argues for a *terminus a quo* of 625. He finds support for this conclusion in what he views to be the probable dependence of several passages in this midrash on the Bavli (p. 250 and n. 82 there). I restrict discussion of opinions in this midrash to a few highly pertinent texts.

2. Neusner, *The Midrash: An Introduction*, p. 148.

3. Neusner, *Judaism and Scripture: The Evidence of Leviticus Rabbah* (Chicago: University of Chicago Press, 1986), p. 93. The earlier quote is taken from p. 110. Neusner's entire exposition here, pp. 59–136, merits detailed attention.

4. See Stern, *Parables in Midrash*, p. 152.

5. Margulies's text does not include this tradition. However, as his apparatus indicates, most manuscripts and versions do. We may, on that account, consider this tradition integral to Leviticus Rabbah.

6. See also Gen. R. 55, 1 (p. 585); 57, 4 (p. 618); 93, 10 [11] (p. 1170); Lam. R. proem 11; and Lam. R. III, 31.

7. Pages given in parentheses refer to *Bereshit (Genesis) Rabbah*, ed. J. Theodor and Ch. Albeck (Jerusalem: Wahrmann Books, 1965).

8. *Midrash Rabbah: Genesis*, trans. Rabbi Dr. H. Freedman (London: Soncino, 1983), p. 215.

9. See Albeck's comment, vol. 1, p. 251, bottom.

10. For suffering as "reproofs of instruction," see also Lev. R. 30, 2; 29, 4 (in the printed edition) with parallel in Pesiqta de Rab Kahana, p. 338 (Mandelbaum edition); also Pesiqta, p. 405.

11. The same text is paralleled, with mostly minor differences, in Lev. R. 27, 1 (pp. 613–14).

12. This theme is reiterated with slightly different nuances several times in this immediate context; see Gen. R. 8, 4 and 8, 5 (pp. 59ff.). See also Burton Vizotsky's discussion of these texts, *Reading the Book* (New York: Doubleday, 1991), pp. 192–96.

13. This tradition is repeated at Pesiqta 23, 3 (pp. 336–37). With slight differences, the theme is reiterated at 23, 8 (p. 341) and 23, 11 (p. 344).

14. Again, the tradition is repeated in Pesiqta 23, 9 (p. 342).

15. This same midrash appears at Gen. R. 39, 6 (pp. 368–69) and 49, 20, and also at Lev. R. 10, 1 (pp. 196–97).

16. Despite methodological flaws discussed in the first chapter, Urbach's discussion of divine mercy (in *The Sages*) is extremely valuable.

17. Translation adjusted for context.

18. Printed editions and some manuscripts have "the good."

19. The tradition attributed to R. Simlai appears also in the Yerushalmi (Sot. 1:5, 17a). There, however, the latter part of the statement—"and slays both the beautiful (good) and the bad"—is not included, and the Greek term here translated as "general undiscriminating punishment" (a simpler translation, independent of this context, might be "plague"; see Margulies's note, p. 539, and Henry G. Liddell and Robert Scott, *Greek-English Lexicon* (Oxford: Clarendon Press, 1968), p. 1060) stands without elaboration. Without such elaboration the emphasis on the indiscriminate nature of the punishment is, at best, implied. Certainly, the explicit articulation that is central to this midrash's expression is missing in the Yerushalmi.

20. Stern, *Parables in Midrash*.

21. Ibid., p. 60.

22. Ibid. See also Stern's discussion of complaint meshalim, pp. 130–45, and his analysis of the literary function of gaps, especially pp. 80–81.

23. There are various minor differences between the three versions, none of which affects the sense of the text. This translation follows the latter version.

24. Translation adjusted for context.

25. Manuscripts record multiple variants of this text. The present version captures the intent of this tradition. See Albeck's comment, p. 1137.

26. MS Vatican has here *yehi* = "so may it be."

27. See Albeck's comment, p. 1138.

28. See also Song of Songs Rabbah I, 60 and 61, where the righteous are valued as being able to declare "enough!" to strict divine justice.

29. I follow Kummel's general definition of apocalypse; see *Introduction to the New Testament*, pp. 453–54. Essential to the apocalyptic genre, by this definition, are eschatological thought, an otherworldly perspective, the penetration of extra-Jewish concepts, and the expression of ideas through parables and symbols. Essential, too, is that the apocalypse be presented as a "revelation" from God, as, of course, the term suggests. Finally, not emphasized by Kummel but no less vital to the genre is the urgency with which it anticipates the end-time. See the following note.

30. Anthony J. Saldarini, in "The Uses of Apocalyptic in the Mishna and Tosepta," reviews what he terms apocalyptic themes in earlier rabbinic literature. Unfortunately, because of the suppression of genuine apocalyptic traditions in rabbinic literature, Saldarini is forced to define apocalyptic in the broadest possible terms, including any messianic or eschatological reference whatsoever. Nevertheless, it should be noted, he is able to identify relatively little. If one insists upon a more limited definition of the genre, as suggested in the previous note, then he, in fact, identifies no evidence at all of the apocalyptic genre in earlier rabbinic literature. The present case, with its claim for a fixed end-time, its self-representation as a dialogue with the Divine (= revealed dialogue, at least on the one side), its greater urgency, and its use of Daniel, is the closest we will come to genuine apocalyptic expression in rabbinic literature even in its later classical stages.

31. See Jacob Neusner, *The Midrash Compilations of the Sixth and Seventh Centuries*, vol. 1, *Lamentations Rabbah* (Atlanta: Scholars Press, 1989), pp. 176–87, and Shaye J. D. Cohen, "The Destruction: From Scripture to Midrash," *Prooftexts* 2 (1982): 18–39. Cohen writes, "Fourteen of the thirty-six proems to the book close with the phrase 'since they sinned, they were exiled,' and at least three others close with equivalent admissions of guilt. The midrash affirms that good befalls the doer of good, and bad befalls the doer of wickedness" (p. 26).

An important reading of the rhetoric of Lamentations Rabbah may also be found in Alan Mintz, *Hurban: Responses to Catastrophe in Hebrew Literature* (New York: Columbia University Press, 1984), pp. 49–83.

32. See Cohen, "The Destruction," pp. 26–28.

33. I follow the text of S. Buber (repr. Hildesheim: Georg Olms Verlagsbuch-handlung, 1967). There are frequent differences, sometimes important, between his text and that of printed editions. In the present context, none of the differences is severe enough to challenge the integrity of the basic point of each quoted narrative.

34. Cohen, "The Destruction," pp. 26–28.

35. See Stern's discussion, *Parables in Midrash*, pp. 130–45.

36. On these elements in the narrative, see Jonah Fraenkel, "Bible Verses Quoted in Tales of the Sages," in *Studies in Aggadah and Folk-Literature*, ed. Joseph Heinemann and Dov Noy, Scripta Hieroslymitana, vol. 22 (Jerusalem: Magnes, 1971), pp. 80–87.

37. Neusner remarks, in connection with this story, "I do not see any real proposition in the long story about the destruction of the Second Temple and Johanan ben Zakkai"; *The Midrash Compilations*, p. 184. In light of the proposition that I have here identified—that the destruction might also be interpreted in human terms—perhaps his judgment should be revised.

38. For other cases in which Lamemtations Rabbah "was capable of seeing the catastrophe in purely human terms," see Cohen, "The Destruction," pp. 25–26.

39. See David Stern, "Imitatio Hominis: Anthropomorphism and the Character(s) of God in Rabbinic Literature," *Prooftexts* 12 (1992): 173, n. 25. Stern's entire analysis of this text is superb, especially pp. 158–64.

40. See Buber's edition, p. 25, n. 15, p. 26, n. 18, and p. 28, n. 23.

41. See Buber, p. 28, n. 23.

42. Stern, "The Character(s) of God in Rabbinic Literature," p. 164.

Chapter 9

1. For an extended description of the Bavli, its approach, and its foundational ideologies, see my *The Mind of the Talmud*, especially Chapters 5 and 6. Jacob Neusner's first synthetic work on the Bavli, *Judaism: The Classical Statement* (Chicago: University of Chicago Press, 1986) is, despite serious flaws in some details, worth consideration (on one such flaw, see my "Scripture Commentary in the Babylonian Talmud: Primary or Secondary Phenomenon?" *AJS Review* 14, no. 1 [March 1989]: 1–15). Neusner's subsequent work on the Bavli is largely superficial and misguided, though recent monographs offer more challenging readings. See my review of his *Talmudic Thinking: Language, Logic, Law*, in the *AJS Review*, forthcoming.

2. For more on this approach to reading the Bavli, see my "Composition and Meaning in the Bavli," and the various references there, especially J. Muilenburg, "Form Criticism and Beyond," *Journal of Biblical Literature* 88 (1969): 1–18. On reader-response concerns, see my "The Intended Reader as a Key to Interpreting the Bavli," *Prooftexts* 13, no. 2 (May 1993): 125–40.

3. The other sort of reading that has been called "canonical" is one that asks how an authoritative text was received into a community of believers or adherents. That is not what I intend here.

4. See M. Kadushin, *The Rabbinic Mind* (New York: Bloch, 1952; 3rd ed., 1972), pp. 131–42.

5. An excellent illustration of this approach may be found in Donn F. Morgan's analysis of the canon of biblical "Writings," in *Between Text and Community: The "Writings" in Canonical Interpretation* (Minneapolis: Fortress Press, 1990).

6. For a fuller description of canonical criticism, see Sanders, *Canon and Community*.

7. See B. M Lewin's edition of the *Epistle of R. Sherira Gaon* (repr. Jerusalem: Makor, 1972), p. 99.

8. See *The Cambridge History of Iran*, vol. 3(1), ed. Eshan Yarshater (Cambridge: Cambridge University Press, 1983), pp. 153–62; Jacob Neusner, *A History of the Jews in Babylonia*, vol. 5 (Leiden: Brill, 1970), pp. 79–85.

9. *The Cambridge History*, p. 161.

10. A more detailed discussion of the social and political situation of the rabbis at this time is found in my concluding analysis of the Bavli in the next chapter. The reader will find accompanying documentation there, as well.

11. Though there are, of course, two Talmuds, I use the terms "Talmud" and "Talmudic" in this chapter and the next to refer to the Babylonian Talmud, unless otherwise specified.

12. See also A.Z. 18b for a similar formulation.

13. The same explanation of suffering, and the claim that what pertains to our biblical ancestors pertains to us as well, is found in one of the Bavli's two extended discussions of the destruction of the Temple or Temples, at Yoma 9b. See my discussion of this text in the appendix to this chapter.

14. "Joy" or "happiness," as used in such contexts, may better be understood as "willingness." See Yohanan Muffs, *Love and Joy: Law, Language and Religion in Ancient Israel* (New York: Jewish Theological Seminary of America, 1992), pp. 121–38.

15. Manuscript variants have: "Anyone who is happy with suffering in this world brings himself salvation in the world to come." See R. Rabbinovicz, *Diqduqei soferim*, 2 vols. (New York: M.P. Press, 1976).

16. On the face of it, these two observations—that Rabbi accepted suffering and that they came upon him as punishment for wrongdoing—contradict one another. Nevertheless, the rhetorical point—that suffering willingly accepted is superior—is effectively made. For a source-critical analysis of this problem, see Shamma Friedman, "*La'aggadah hahistorit batalmud habavli*," in Sefer hazikharon lerabbi Shaul Lieberman (Jerusalem: Jewish Theological Seminary of America, 1989), p. 17. For Friedman's overall analysis of the present text, along with the Yerushalmi parallel, see there, pp. 1–27.

17. Other aspects of this same text are analyzed in detail, from a very different perspective, in Daniel Boyarin, "The Great Fat Massacre: Sex, Death and the Grotesque Body in the Talmud," in *People of the Body: Jews and Judaism from an Embodied Perspective*, ed. Howard Eilberg-Schwartz (Albany: SUNY Press, 1992), pp. 69–100.

18. Translation adjusted for context.

19. Yaakov Elman discusses this and related texts in "When Permission Is Given."

20. This is the version of manuscripts; see *Diqduqei soferim*. The printed text follows Rashi's emendation.

21. "Again" is missing in several manuscripts and versions.

22. "Horrible illnesses" is missing in several manuscriupts and versions. Of course, this in no significant way changes the point regarding suffering.

23. The context in which this brief deliberation appears offers no key to interpretation. The broad discussion relates to the obligation to reprove one's neighbor. Clearly, suffering is understood as reproof from God and, on that basis, this exchange finds a home here. Formally, the question with which this discussion begins ("What is the limit of suffering?") echoes questions posed previously ("What is the extent of reproof?"), thus also providing an impetus for its inclusion here. But substantively the present discussion stands independent of its context, so we are left with very few clues for deciphering its intent.

24. See *Diqduqei soferim*, ad loc.

25. Essentially the same explanation, similarly rejecting the notion held by earlier Greeks that "the sins of the parents on the children the gods do visit," is found in Plutarch, *De sera numinis vindicta*, 562f–563a. The parallels in the development of Greco-Roman and Jewish ideas in these matters is notable, though it is impossible to establish direct influence.

26. See Marcus Jastrow, *A Dictionary of the Targumim, The Talmud Babli and Yerushalmi, and the Midrashic Literature* (New York, 1886–1903; rept. New York: Judaica Press, 1971), pp. 1309–10, s.v. "*qibl'a*, III."

27. One version has not "suffering" but "prison," a reading supported by its closer parallel to the first part of the tradition, which reads "a charm against [damage in] the out-house is modesty and silence." We could easily understand why advice regarding two "houses" of danger (the "house of the chair" and the "house of prisoners") would be put together; it is more difficult to understand why "suffering" enters this tradition, if not by scribal error. If this alternative is correct, of course, then nothing is being said here directly about suffering at all.

28. The confusion between "Rava," "Rabbah," and "Rav" in different manuscripts and versions of this text renders determination of a "correct" reading impossible. I follow the Vilna printing in my translation. In any case, I treat all of what is recorded here as the opinion of the Bavli.

29. This introductory phrase is missing in manuscripts; see *Diqduqei soferim*.

30. Here, as elsewhere throughout this text, there is a wide variation in the amount of each verse that is quoted in different manuscripts. For present purposes, the variations make little difference.

31. This step is missing in several manuscripts and versions; see *Diqduqei soferim*.

32. I follow Neusner's translation for context.

33. For more on the differences between the Bavli and the Yerushalmi in their responses to suffering, see Elman, "The Suffering of the Righteous in Palestinian and Babylonian Sources."

Chapter 9: Appendix

1. "The welcoming of guests"— omitted in my translation though present in the printed edition—is found neither in the Mishnah, its manuscripts, and records, nor, obviously, in the version of the Mishnah that is interpreted below, at 40a—where the biblical sources of the other phrases are provided but not a source for this. Whatever its source, therefore, it is clearly not original.

2. On this final phrase, see my discussion in *The Mind of the Talmud*, p. 161.

3. The meaning of this comment and its relation to the following comment of Rava is a matter of some confusion; see the commentaries of Rashi and Tosafot.

4. See Elman, "Righteousness as Its Own Reward," especially pp. 49–52 and following.

5. It should be recalled that the Mishnah was originally copied in whole chapters at the beginning of each chapter of Talmudic deliberation. Its distribution to various points in the Talmudic text is a later printing convention. Nevertheless, manuscripts of this section, as far as I have been able to check, do include a *pisqa* (a brief quotation calling reference to the relevant Mishnah) at this same stage in the text, and so caution is warranted here. Still, I think that matters of substance and formulation are persuasive and the contrary evidence of the *pisqa* should, therefore, be put aside.

6. See the footnote in *Diqduqei soferim* for a list of versions that follow this reading.

7. See Haim Z. Dimitrovsky, *S'ridei Bavli*, vol. 1 (New York: Jewish Theological Seminary of America, 1979), p. 144.

8. See the note in *Diqduqei soferim.*

9. My present analysis differs in significant ways from that of Robert Goldenberg in "Early Rabbinic Explanations of the Destruction of Jerusalem," *Journal of Jewish Studies* 33 (1982): 523. The difference is a consequence of the fact that he reads the tradition of R. Yoḥanan b. Torta in isolation from the larger context, whereas I read only the context as a whole. Furthermore, I cannot agree that the various explanations offered for the destruction of Jerusalem at Shab. 119b (profanation of the Sabbath, failure to recite the Shema, failure to educate children, and so on) are "trivial" (see Goldenberg, pp. 519–20). On the contrary, I read these statements as rabbinic claims that the offenses listed are tantamount, in rabbinic terms, to repudiation of the Covenant. Thus I see the Bavli's deliberations on the destruction as far more traditional than does Goldenberg.

Chapter 10

1. There are numerous variants in the details of this text in manuscripts and versions. None affects the substance of the text and I have thus not called attention to them.

2. See Tosafot, s.v. *"v'shema mina."*

3. See Kraemer, *The Mind of the Talmud*, Chapters 5–6.

4. I discuss, at length and in detail, the phenomenon of definitive refutations in the Bavli in "The Rhetoric of Failed Refutation in the Bavli," *Shofar* 10, no. 2 (Winter 1992): 73–85. Documentation for the claims made here can be found there.

5. See L. Jacobs, "Are There Fictitious Baraitot in the Babylonian Talmud?" *Hebrew Union College Annual* 42 (1971): 185–96.

6. An important analysis of this same text is offered by Yaakov Elman in "Righteousness as Its Own Reward," pp. 40–45. Though emphasizing different points in his analysis, Elman's conclusions are very similar to mine.

7. See my "The Intended Reader as a Key to Interpreting the Bavli."

8. I emphasize this point because Louis Jacobs, in his very different outline of this sugya, lists these comments as the first steps of the sugya on suffering. For the reasons just articulated, I do not view them as part of the sugya proper. Jacobs

admits that the step that intervenes between those just quoted and what follows "has no connection at all with the theme of sufferings" (p. 33) and he omits it from his outline of the sugya (p. 40) but does not justify on literary grounds his doing so. For Jacobs's analysis of this text, see "The *Sugya* on Sufferings in B. *Berakhot* 5a, b," in *Studies in Aggadah, Targum and Jewish Liturgy in Memory of Joseph Heinemann*, ed. Jakob J. Petuchowski and Ezra Fleisher, eds. (Jerusalem: Magnes and Hebrew Union College Press, 1981), pp. 32–44. His outline of the text is found at pp. 40–41.

9. Better: "Rava said R. Seḥora said R. Huna said." See *Diqduqei soferim*, ad loc.

10. Translated for context.

11. Here I follow Neusner's translation.

12. Or, "causes the sacrifice to cleanse"; see the various alternatives recorded in *Diqduqei soferim*.

13. Louis Jacob's analysis of this text (above, note. 8) ignores important substantive and literary characteristics of the text as a whole. For example, while he lists the replies to one objection to an opinion of R. Yoḥanan (below, II.C.1.a–c) as one of his steps (no. 13), he omits the reply to another objection (below, II.C.2.b). What is the difference? Why count one but not the other? I invite the reader to compare my analysis with his. Nevertheless, I support Jacobs's overall argument that this text requires careful literary analysis and I agree wholeheartedly with his claim that "we do not have here a simple anthology of teachings on sufferings, but a carefully thought-out pattern" ("The *Sugya* on Sufferings," p. 41).

14. The version in MS Munich is this: And are "children" not suffering of love? But did not R. Yoḥanan say. . . .

15. Rashi suggests this logic: "A great man like R. Yoḥanan would not be visited by suffering that is not [suffering] of love." Tosafot suggest, in contrast, that "since R. Yoḥanan was accustomed to comfort others with this [that is, by producing the bone of his son], we should learn from this that [he thought that] they were sufferings of love." I strongly prefer the second explanation, first, because Rashi forces us to ignore the fact that, as Tosafot point out, "many righteous individuals have had no children," despite the gemara's conclusion here that infertility is not suffering of love, and second, the gemara below supplies an "original" context for R. Yoḥanan's comment in which his clear intent is to comfort another with his act.

16. The sort of reading demanded by this text (by any text, I would argue, but particularly here) is well articulated by Steven D. Fraade, in *From Tradition to Commentary* (Albany: SUNY Press, 1991), p. 125.

17. MS Munich begins with the story of R. Yoḥanan (B) and then, to make the point that R. Yoḥanan should raise himself, refers back to an as yet untold story of R. Yoḥanan's healing of R. Ḥiyya b. Abba. Other versions also differ in various details. These differences eliminate the complete structural balance of the present text but do not affect the substance of the discussion in any essential way.

18. The printed text has Eliezer, a common error.

19. Tosafot offers this reading in place of "no man merits two tables," for obvious reasons. The original version, rejected by Tosafot, is supported by MS Munich and several other records of this text. See *Diqduqei soferim*.

20. Manuscripts make it clear that the intent is to "your beauty," that is, the beauty of R. Yoḥanan.

21. This narrative statement and the exchange that follows, identical with

preceding exchanges, are missing in MS Munich and certain versions. See *Diqduqei soferim*.

22. As evidence that the Bavli recognizes this connection, see Ber. 60a, bottom.

23. See above, note 21.

24. I cannot for a moment agree with Jacobs's suggestion that these steps are intended to be humorous ("The *Sugya* on Suffering," p. 44). There is nothing humorous about suffering or in the deliberation on it in this text. Its striking him as humorous can only be on account of the immense irony of the skepticism which it expresses.

25. It should be noted that even the author of the Tosafot on this page (s.v. "*dina*") is brought to voice such a protest. In his words, "There are many righteous people who are afflicted both in their bodies and their property!" So much for justice.

26. Jacobs manages to find a triplet, but only, as I have said, in the most artificial way; see his outline at p. 41 of "The *Sugya* on Suffering." He leaves out numerous steps from the narrative (the initial suggestion that Huna examine his ways—so important for echoing the statement at the beginning of the sugya, the statement by his interlocutors of the sin of which he is suspect, and so on) without any rhyme or reason. He is merely forcing the text into his preconceived schema.

27. Jacobs calls this a "happy ending" (ibid., p. 42).

28. There are many minor differences in this text found in manuscripts and versions. None substantially affects the present analysis.

29. Rashi, Tosafot, and others, seek to eliminate this attribution. It makes no difference, for our discussion, whether what follows is to be attributed to R. Joseph or should be understood merely as the voice of the Talmud.

30. Manuscripts and early versions do not have the term "hair" (see *Diqduqei soferim*, ad loc.), in which case the translation would be something like "Miriam the raiser of women," whose meaning is entirely unclear. This has no consequence, however, for the present analysis.

31. Urbach downplays the implications of this story, claiming that the Angel of Death has difficulty responding to R. Bibi b. Abbaye's challenge (L) and thus implying that the force of what comes before is attenuated. Urbach, in truth, is unwilling to grant the force of this story and he disregards completely the literary-compositional features that support the opinion of the author, as I have spelled them out. See Urbach, *The Sages*, vol. 2, pp. 810–11, n. 74.

32. The post-Talmudic tractate *Derekh Eretz Zuta* preserves many Talmudic traditions which speak to the special conducts expected of a sage or a disciple of sages.

33. See Jacob. Neusner, *There We Sat Down* (Nashville: Abingdon Press, 1972), pp. 90–136.

34. The multiplicity and variety of opinions recorded in the Talmud, from different times and places, attest to the reality here described. The Bavli's discussion at Yeb. 14a is particularly relevant to the question of the rabbinic movement's ability to enforce uniformity upon its adherents.

35. See Richard Kalmin, "Collegial Interaction in the Babylonian Talmud," *Jewish Quarterly Review* 82, no. 3–4 (January–April 1992): 383–415.

36. See Avraham Grossman, "From Father to Son: The Inheritance of Spiritual Leadership in Jewish Communities of the Middle Ages," in *The Jewish Fam-*

ily: Metaphor and Memory, ed. David Kraemer (New York: Oxford University Press, 1989), 116–18.

37. M. Douglas, "Cultural Bias," Royal Anthropological Institute, Occasional Paper 35 (1978), reprinted in *In the Active Voice* (London: Routledge and Kegan Paul, 1982), pp. 194–95.

38. An excellent brief presentation of Douglas's analytical system may be found in Ross Shepard Kraemer, *Her Share of the Blessings* (New York: Oxford University Press, 1992), pp. 14–17.

39. See Douglas, *Natural Symbols,* p. 145.

Chapter 11

1. See also B. Z. Wacholder, "Messianism and Mishnah: Time and Place in Early Halakhah," *The Louis Caplan Lecture on Jewish Law, March 28, 1978* (Cincinnati: Hebrew Union College Press, 1979).

2. See, for example, the discussions of Erwin R. Goodenough, *Jewish Symbols in the Greco-Roman Period,* abr. ed., ed. J. Neusner (Princeton: Princeton University Press, 1988), and Neusner, *A History of the Jews in Babylonia,* vol. 5 (Leiden: Brill, 1970), pp. 217–43 (the chapter is entitled "Other Jews, Other Magicians"). Much evidence will also be found in Lee I. Levine, *The Rabbinic Class of Roman Palestine in Late Antiquity* (Jerusalem: Yad Izhak Ben-Zvi; New York: Jewish Theological Seminary, 1989). Though Levine downplays the significance of this evidence (see p. 127), his counterargument is almost entirely dependent upon the testimony of rabbinic literature itself, testimony which is obviously self-serving and which should therefore be treated far more skeptically than it is by Levine. Note that Levine proposes a number of only one thousand rabbis in all for the entire third and fourth centuries in Palestine. There is no doubt that he is correct when he characterizes the rabbis as "a small, closely knit coterie of savants." See p. 66, n. 117 and p. 67.

3. See Cohen, *From the Maccabees to the Mishnah,* p. 221.

4. Again, for the more detailed argument, see my "The Intended Reader as a Key to Interpreting the Bavli."

5. See Richard S. Sarason, "Toward a New Agendum for the Study of Rabbinic Midrashic Literature," in *Studies in Aggadah, Targum and Jewish Liturgy in Memory of Joseph Heinemann,* ed. Jakob J. Petuchowski and Ezra Fleischer (Jerusalem: Magnes, 1981), pp. 65–66.

6. Neusner suggests a similar conclusion regarding the Mishnah's audience. See *Judaism: The Evidence of the Mishnah,* pp. 246–47.

7. The Shema has commonly been spoken of by scholars as a practice which was already in force during the second-Temple period. Most have simply accepted the testimony of Mishnah Tam. 5:1, which has the Shema as part of the Temple ritual, without recognizing that this report comes from the rabbis at least 130 years after the fact. Of course, it is evident that the rabbis would have served their own interests by claiming that a practice which they invented was more ancient and part of the Temple ritual. Therefore, the rabbinic testimony here is suspect and unreliable. Reference has also commonly been made to Josephus, *Antiquities* 4.8.13 (212), but Josephus speaks only of the custom of giving thanks to God, morning and evening, for having delivered the Jews from Egypt. Mention of the Exodus is found in the third paragraph of the Shema, but it is hardly the way someone would characterize the Shema as a whole. Moreover, though it is true that

Josephus' report is found in the midst of his exposition of that section of Deuteronomy which begins the Shema, he does not propose that mention of the laws of phylacteries and door amulets (tefillin and mezuzah) is part of the recitation or praise. For this reason, his report raises more doubt than support concerning the practice of reciting the Shema. The fact that two of the paragraphs which come to constitute the Shema are found in ancient (predestruction) tefillin and amulets proves nothing. They are included in these objects because these are the passages which are understood to require these practices.

8. The Mishnah is explicit in indicating that recitation of prayer is required of women as well as of men (see m. Ber. 3:3). In the absence of an explicit qualification in context, there is no good reason to conclude that this refers to anything but *the* rabbinic prayer, which we are now discussing.

9. An excellent analysis of the rhetoric of these blessings, and of this prayer as a whole, is Reuven Kimelman's "The Daily ʿAmidah and the Rhetoric of Redemption," *Jewish Quarterly Review* 79, no. 2–3 (October 1988–January 1989): 165–97.

10. See Saul Lieberman, *Tosefta kifeshuta*, 2nd ed., vol. 1 (New York: Jewish Theological Seminary, 1992), p. 102.

11. This distinction is crucial, for messages which might threaten the religious beliefs of common folk would not similarly threaten the commitments of the rabbinic elite. In recognition of this distinction, the apparently subversive consequences of certain deliberations in the Bavli should be far less troubling. Though the rabbis behind the Bavli thought it appropriate to share these possibilities among themselves, they did not consider them proper for public discourse. For a more detailed discussion of the distinction suggested here, see Kraemer, "The Intended Reader as a Key to Interpreting the Bavli," pp. 127, 133, and 138.

12. Urbach, *The Sages*, Chapter 15.

13. Neusner's relevant works are referred to in my introductions to earlier chapters.

14. See our discussion in Chapter 4.

15. See Sterm. *Parables in Midrash*, p. 152 and references in note 1 there.

16. See Jacob Neusner, *Talmudic Thinking: Language, Logic, Law* (Columbia: University of South Carolina Press, 1992), pp. 175–87.

17. The argument encapsulated here may be found, at length, in Kraemer, *The Mind of the Talmud*, pp. 99–170.

18. See Levine, "The Jewish Patriarch (Nasi) in Third Century Palestine," pp. 649–88. As Levine notes, non-Rabbinic (= non-Jewish) sources speak almost exclusively of the patriarch during the fourth and early fifth centuries, during which time the office was clearly very powerful but nonrabbinic (thus, in all probability, explaining the increasing hostility of later rabbinic sources toward the patriarch). Concerning the second and third centuries, non-Jewish sources say almost nothing and rabbinic sources say a great deal, including the assertion that the patriarch was a rabbi. There is thus reason to be suspicious of rabbinic reports; Levine's conclusions for the third century, built entirely upon traditions preserved in rabbinic texts, are less than secure. Nevertheless, R. Judah I (= the Patriarch) seems to have enjoyed Roman support and therefore, even if the powers of the rabbinic patriarchate were less than rabbinic sources claim, it is still reasonable to believe that rabbis did achieve significant political power in Palestine during this period.

19. The epigraphic evidence analyzed by Shaye J. D. Cohen supports the conclusion that the rabbinic presence, and therefore likely influence, was signifi-

cantly greater in Palestine than in any of the diasporas throughout these centuries. See his "Epigraphical Rabbis," pp. 15–17.

20. Sanders *Canon and Community*, p. 11.

21. Cf. Shaye J. D. Cohen, "The Significance of Yavneh: Pharisees, Rabbis, and the End of Jewish Sectarianism," *Hebrew Union College Annual* 55 (1984): 27–53.

22. See my fuller discussion of this matter in "The Formation of Rabbinic Canon: Authority and Boundaries," *Journal of Biblical Literature* 110, no. 4 (1991): 613–30.

Bibliography

Rabbinic Texts, Standard Editions

(numbers given in parentheses in Chapters
5, 6, and 8 refer to these editions)

Bereshit (Genesis) Rabbah. 3 vols. Ed. J. Theodor and Ch. Albeck. Berlin, 1903–
1936. Reprinted with corrections, Jerusalem: Wahrmann, 1965.

Mekhilta de-Rabbi Ishmael. Ed. H.S. Horovitz and I. A. Rabin. 2nd ed., Jerusalem: Wahrmann, 1970.

Pesiqta de Rab Kahana. 2 vols. Ed. B. Mandelbaum. New York: Jewish Theological Seminary of America, 1962.

Sifre Devarim. Ed. L. Finkelstein. Berlin, 1939. Reprint, New York: Jewish Theological Seminary of America, 1969.

The Tosefta: According to Codex Vienna. 5 vols. Ed. S. Lieberman. New York:
Jewish Theological Seminary of America, 1955–1988.

Vayyiqra (Leviticus) Rabbah. 5 vols. Ed. M. Margulies. Jerusalem, 1953–1960.
Reprint, Jerusalem: Wahrmann, 1972.

General Bibliography

Albeck, Ḥanoch. *Mavo la-talmudim.* Tel-Aviv: Dvir, 1969.

Alon, G. *The Jews in Their Land in the Talmudic Age.* 2 vols. Ed. and trans. Gershon
Levi. Jerusalem: Magnes, 1984.

The Apocrypha: An American Translation. Trans. Edgar J. Goodspeed. New York:
Vintage Books, 1959.

The Apocryphal Old Testament. Ed. H. F. D. Sparks. Oxford: Clarendon Press,
1984.

Avi-Yonah, M. *The Jews of Palestine: A Political History from the Bar Kokhba War to the Arab Conquest.* New York: Schocken, 1976.

Beckwith, Roger T. *The Old Testament Canon of the New Testament Church.* Grand Rapids, Mich.: Eerdmans, 1985.

Berger, Peter. *The Sacred Canopy: Elements of a Sociological Theory of Religion.* New York: Anchor Books, 1969.

Bickerman, Elias, and Smith, Morton. *The Ancient History of Western Civilization.* New York: Harper and Row, 1976.

Bokser, Baruch. "*Maᶜal* and Blessings over Food: Rabbinic Transformation of Cultic Terminology and Alternative Modes of Piety." *Journal of Biblical Literature* 100, no. 4 (1981): 557–74.

——. "The Palestinian Talmud." In *Aufsteig und Niedergang der römischen Welt II.* Vol. 19, no. 2, pp. 139–256. Reprinted in *The Study of Ancient Judaism,* vol. 2. Ed. Jacob Neusner. Hoboken, N.J.: Ktav, 1981.

The Book of Daniel. The Anchor Bible, vol. 23. Trans. with introduction and commentary by Louis F. Hartman and Alexander A. Di Lella. Garden City, N.Y.: Doubleday, 1978.

Bowker, John. *Problems of Suffering in Religions of the World.* Cambridge: Cambridge University Press, 1970.

Boyarin, Daniel. "The Great Fat Massacre: Sex, Death and the Grotesque Body in the Talmud." In *People of the Body: Jews and Judaism from an Embodied Perspective.* Ed. Howard Eilberg-Schwartz. Albany: SUNY Press, 1992.

——. *Intertextuality and the Reading of Midrash.* Bloomington: Indiana University Press, 1990.

The Cambridge History of Iran. Vol. 3(1). Ed. Eshan Yarshater. Cambridge: Cambridge University Press, 1983.

Childs, Brevard. *Introduction to the Old Testament as Scripture.* Philadelphia: Fortress Press, 1979.

Cohen, Shaye J. D. "The Destruction: From Scripture to Midrash." *Prooftexts* 2 (1982): 18–39.

——. "Epigraphical Rabbis." *Jewish Quarterly Review* 72 (1981–1982): 1–17.

——. *From the Maccabees to the Mishnah.* Philadelphia: Westminster Press, 1987.

——. "The Significance of Yavneh: Pharisees, Rabbis, and the End of Jewish Sectarianism." *Hebrew Union College Annual* 55 (1984): 27–53.

Douglas, Mary. "Cultural Bias." Royal Anthropological Institute, Occasional Paper 35 (1978). Reprinted in *In the Active Voice.* London: Routledge and Kegan Paul, 1982.

——. *Natural Symbols.* New York: Random House, 1973.

Elman, Yaakov. "Righteousness as Its Own Reward: An Inquiry into the Theologies of the Stam." *Proceedings of the American Academy of Jewish Research* 57 (1990/1991): 35–67.

——. "The Suffering of the Righteous in Palestinian and Babylonian Sources." *Jewish Quarterly Review* 80, no. 3–4 (January–April 1990): 315–39.

——. "When Permission Is Given: Aspects of Divine Providence." *Tradition* 24, no. 4 (Summer 1989): 24–45.

Epistle of R. Sherira Gaon. Ed. B. M. Lewin. Reprint, Jerusalem: Makor, 1972.

Epstein, J. N. *Mevo lenusaḥ ha-Mishnah.* 2 vols. Jerusalem: Merkaz, 1948.

——. *M'vo'ot l'sifrut ha-amoraim.* Jerusalem: Magnes, 1962.

Finkelstein, L. "The Core of the Sifra: A Temple Textbook for Priests." *Jewish Quarterly Review* 80, no. 1–2 (July–October 1989): 15–34.

Finley, M. I. *Ancient History: Evidence and Models.* New York: Elisabeth Sifton Books and Penguin Books, 1986.

Fishbane, M. *Biblical Interpretation in Early Israel.* Oxford: Oxford University Press, 1985.

Fraade, Steven D. *From Tradition to Commentary.* Albany: SUNY Press, 1991.

Fraenkel, Jonah. "Bible Verses Quoted in Tales of the Sages." In *Studies in Aggadah and Folk-Literature.* Ed. Joseph Heinemann and Dov Noy. Scripta Hieroslymitana, vol. 22. Jerusalem: Magnes, 1971.

Friedman, Shamma. *"La'aggadah hahistorit batalmud habavli."* In Sefer hazikharon lerabbi Shaul Lieberman. Jerusalem: Jewish Theological Seminary of America, 1989.

Geller, Stephen A. "'Where Is Wisdom?' A Literary Study of Job 28 in Its Settings." In *Judaic Perspectives on Ancient Israel.* Ed. Jacob Neusner, Baruch Levine, and Ernest Frerichs. Philadelphia: Fortress Press, 1987.

Glatzer, Nahum N. *The Dimensions of Job: A Study and Selected Readings.* New York: Schocken, 1969.

Golb, Norman. "The Dead Sea Scrolls: A New Perspective." *American Scholar* 58, no. 2 (Spring 1989): 177–207.

Goldenberg, Robert. "Early Rabbinic Explanations of the Destruction of Jerusalem." *Journal of Jewish Studies* 33 (1982): 517–25.

Goodblatt, David. "The Babylonian Talmud." In *Aufstieg und Niedergang der römischen Welt II.* Vol. 19, no. 2. Reprinted in *The Study of Ancient Judaism,* vol. 2. Ed. Jacob Neusner. Hoboken, N.J.: Ktav, 1981.

Goodenough, Erwin R. *Jewish Symbols in the Greco-Roman Period,* abridged ed. Ed. J. Neusner. Princeton: Princeton University Press, 1988.

Green, William Scott. "What's in a Name? The Problematic of Talmudic 'Biography.'" In *Approaches to Ancient Judaism: Theory and Practice.* Ed. W. S. Green. Missoula, Mont.: Scholars Press, 1978.

Gutmann, Y. "The Mother and Her Seven Sons in the Aggadah and in II and IV Maccabees" (Hebrew). In *Sefer Yohanan Levi.* Jerusalem: Magnes, 1949.

Halivni, David. *Meqorot umesorot.* Jerusalem: Jewish Theological Seminary of America, 1982.

———. *Meqorot umesorot: seder nashim.* Tel Aviv: Dvir, 1968.

———. *Meqorot umesorot: yoma-hagiga.* Jerusalem: Jewish Theological Seminary of America, 1975.

———. *Midrash, Mishnah and Gemara: The Jewish Predilection for Justified Law.* Cambridge, Mass.: Harvard University Press, 1986.

Heinemann, I. *Philons griechische und jüdische Bildung.* Breslau: M. & H. Marcus, 1932.

Henderson, John B. *Scripture, Canon, and Commentary: A Comparison of Confucian and Western Exegesis.* Princeton: Princeton University Press, 1991.

Hirshman, Marc. *Midrash Qohelet Rabbah.* Ph.D. dissertation, Jewish Theological Seminary of America, 1982.

Jacobs, L. "Are There Fictitious Baraitot in the Babylonian Talmud?" *Hebrew Union College Annual* 42 (1971): 185–96.

———. "The *Sugya* on Sufferings in B. *Berakhot* 5a, b." In *Studies in Aggadah, Targum and Jewish Liturgy in Memory of Joseph Heinemann.* Ed. Jakob J. Petuchowski and Ezra Fleischer. Jerusalem: Magnes and Hebrew Union College Press, 1981.

Jaffee, Martin S. "How Much 'Orality' in Oral Torah? New Perspectives on the

Composition and Transmission of Early Rabbinic Tradition." *Shofar* 10, no. 2 (Winter 1992): 53–72.

Jastrow, Marcus. *A Dictionary of the Targumim, the Talmud Babli and Yerushalmi, and the Midrashic Literature.* New York, 1886-1903. Reprint, New York: Judaica Press, 1971.

The Jews in Roman Imperial Legislation. Ed. with commentary by Amnon Linder. Detroit: Wayne State University Press; Jerusalem: Israel Academy of Sciences and Humanities, 1987.

Kadushin, M. *The Rabbinic Mind.* New York: Bloch, 1952; 3rd ed., 1972.

Kalmin, Richard. "Review of 'Midrash, Mishnah and Gemara: The Jewish Predilection for Justified Law,' by David Halivni." *Conservative Judaism* 39, no. 4 (Summer 1987): 78–84.

Kasovsky, C. Y. *Otzar leshon ha-Mishnah.* 4 vols. Tel-Aviv: Massadah Publishing Co., 1957, 1967.

———. *Otzar leshon ha-Talmud.* 41 vols. Jerusalem: Ministry of Education and Culture of the Government of Israel and Jewish Theological Seminary, 1958–1982.

———. *Otzar leshon ha-Yerushalmi.* Vols. 1– . Jerusalem: Jewish Theological Seminary, 1979–

Kaufmann, Y. *The Religion of Israel.* Trans. Moshe Greenberg. New York: Schocken, 1972.

Kraemer, David. "Composition and Meaning in the Bavli." *Prooftexts* 8, no. 3 (1988): 271–91.

———. "The Formation of Rabbinic Canon: Authority and Boundaries." *Journal of Biblical Literature* 110, no. 4 (1991): 613–30.

———. "The Intended Reader as a Key to Interpreting the Bavli." *Prooftexts* 13, no. 2 (May 1993): 125–40.

———. *The Mind of the Talmud: An Intellectual History of the Bavli.* New York: Oxford University Press, 1990.

———. "On the Reliability of Attributions in the Babylonian Talmud." *Hebrew Union College Annual* 60 (1989): 175–90.

———. "The Rhetoric of Failed Refutation in the Bavli." *Shofar* 10, no. 2 (Winter 1992): 73–85.

———. "Scripture Commentary in the Babylonian Talmud: Primary or Secondary Phenomenon?" *AJS Review* 14, no. 1 (March 1989): 1–15.

Kraemer, Ross Shepard. *Her Share of the Blessings.* New York: Oxford University Press, 1992.

Kummel, W. G. *Introduction to the New Testament,* 17th ed. Trans. Howard Clark Kee. Nashville: Abingdon Press, 1975.

Leiman, Sid Z. *The Canonization of Hebrew Scripture: The Talmudic and Midrashic Evidence.* Hamden: Connecticut Academy of Arts and Sciences, 1976.

Levenson, Jon D. *Creation and the Persistence of Evil.* San Francisco: Harper and Row, 1988.

Levine, Lee I. "The Jewish Patriarch (Nasi) in Third Century Palestine." In *Aufstieg und Niedergang der römischen Welt II.* Vol. 19, no. 2. Ed. H. Temporini and W. Haase. Berlin and New York: De Gruyter, 1979.

———. *The Rabbinic Class of Roman Palestine in Late Antiquity.* Jerusalem: Yad Izhak Ben-Zvi; New York: Jewish Theological Seminary, 1989.

Lieberman, Saul. *Ha Yerushalmi kifeshuto.* Jerusalem: Darom, 1934.

———. *Hellenism in Jewish Palestine.* New York: Jewish Theological Seminary of America, 1950. Reprint, 1962.

———. *Tosefta kifeshuta.* 9 vols. New York: Jewish Theological Seminary of America, 1955–1988.

Lightstone, Jack N. "The Formation of the Biblical Canon in Judaism of Late Antiquity: Prolegomenon to a General Reassessment." *Studies in Religion* 8, no. 2 (1979): 135–42.

MacMullen, Ramsay. *Christianizing the Roman Empire, A.D. 100–400.* New Haven: Yale University Press, 1984.

———. *Paganism in the Roman Empire.* New Haven: Yale University Press, 1981.

Mikalson, Jon D. *Honor Thy Gods: Popular Religion in Greek Tragedy.* Chapel Hill: University of North Carolina Press, 1991.

Mintz, Alan. *Hurban: Responses to Catastrophe in Hebrew Literature.* New York: Columbia University Press, 1984.

The Mishnah. 6 vols. Ed. Hanokh Albeck. Jerusalem: Bialik Institute; Tel Aviv: Dvir, 1953.

Morgan, Donn F. *Between Text and Community: The "Writings" in Canonical Interpretation.* Minneapolis: Fortress Press, 1990.

Muffs, Yohanan. *Love and Joy: Law, Language and Religion in Ancient Israel.* New York: Jewish Theological Seminary of America, 1992.

Muilenberg, J. "Form Criticism and Beyond." *Journal of Biblical Literature* 88 (1969): 1–18.

Nelson, David W. "Responses to the Destruction of the Second Temple in the Tannaitic Midrashim." Ph.D. dissertation, New York University, 1991.

Neusner, Jacob. *The Bavli and Its Sources: The Question of Tradition in the Case of Tractate Sukkah.* Atlanta: Scholars Press, 1987.

———. *A History of the Jews in Babylonia.* 5 vols. Leiden: Brill, 1965–1970.

———. *Judaism: The Classical Statement.* Chicago: University of Chicago Press, 1986.

———. *Judaism: The Evidence of the Mishnah.* Chicago: University of Chicago Press, 1981.

———. *Judaism and Scripture: The Evidence of Leviticus Rabbah.* Chicago: University of Chicago Press, 1986.

———. *Judaism in Society: The Evidence of the Yerushalmi.* Chicago: University of Chicago Press, 1983.

———. *Messiah in Context: Israel's History and Destiny in Formative Judaism.* Philadelphia: Fortress Press, 1984.

———. *The Midrash: An Introduction.* Northvale, N.J.: Jason Aronson, 1990.

———. *The Midrash Compilations of the Sixth and Seventh Centuries.* Vol. 1. *Lamentations Rabbah.* Atlanta: Scholars Press, 1989.

———. *Midrash in Context: Exegesis in Formative Judaism.* Philadelphia: Fortress Press, 1983.

———. *Reading and Believing: Ancient Judaism and Contemporary Gullibility.* Atlanta: Scholars Press, 1986.

———. *Talmudic Thinking: Language, Logic, Law.* Columbia: University of South Carolina Press, 1992.

———. *There We Sat Down.* Nashville: Abingdon Press, 1972.

———. *The Tosefta: Its Structure and Its Sources.* Atlanta: Scholars Press, 1986.

Neusner, J., Green, W. S., and Frerichs, E., eds. *Judaisms and Their Messiahs at the Turn of the Christian Era.* Cambridge: Cambridge University Press, 1987.

Nickelsburg, George W. E. *Jewish Literature between the Bible and the Mishnah.* Philadelphia: Fortress Press, 1981.

———. *Resurrection, Immortality, and Eternal Life in Intertestamental Judaism.* Cambridge, Mass.: Harvard University Press, 1972.

The Oxford History of the Classical World. Ed. J. Boardman, J. Griffin, and O. Murray. Oxford: Oxford University Press, 1986.

Parker, Robert. *Miasma: Pollution and Purification in Early Greek Religion.* Oxford: Clarendon Press, 1983.

Rabbinovicz, R. *Diqduqei soferim.* 2 vols. New York: M.P. Press, 1976.

Rowley, H. H. *The Servant of the Lord and Other Essays on the Old Testament.* London: Lutterworth Press, 1952.

Saldarini, Anthony J. "The Uses of the Apocalyptic [*sic*] in the Mishnah and Tosepta." *Catholic Biblical Quarterly* 39 (1977): 396–409.

Sanders, James A. *Canon and Community.* Philadelphia: Fortress Press, 1984.

Sanders, Jim Alvin. "Suffering as Divine Discipline in the Old Testament and Post-Biblical Judaism." *Colgate Rochester Divinity School Bulletin* 28 (1955).

Sarason, Richard. "Toward a New Agendum for the Study of Rabbinic Midrashic Literature." In *Studies in Aggadah, Targum and Jewish Liturgy in Memory of Joseph Heinemann.* Ed. Jakob J. Petuchowski and Ezra Fleischer. Jerusalem: Magnes, 1981.

Sayler, Gwendolyn B. *Have the Promises Failed? A Literary Analysis of 2 Baruch.* SBL Dissertation Series, 72. Chico, Calif.: Scholars Press, 1984.

Schechter, Solomon. "The Doctrine of Divine Retribution in Rabbinical Literature." In *Studies in Judaism: First Series.* Philadelphia: Jewish Publication Society, 1911. Reprinted in *Studies in Judaism: Essays on Persons, Concepts, and Movements of Thought in Jewish Tradition.* New York: Atheneum, 1970.

Soloveitchik, J. B. *Halakhic Man.* Trans. Lawrence Kaplan. Philadelphia: Jewish Publication Society, 1983.

Stern, David. "Imitatio Hominis: Anthropomorphism and the Character(s) of God in Rabbinic Literature." *Prooftexts* 12 (1992): 158–74.

———. *Parables in Midrash: Narrative and Exegesis in Rabbinic Literature.* Cambridge, Mass.: Harvard University Press, 1991.

Textual Sources For the Study of Zoroastrianism. Ed. and trans. Mary Boyce. Manchester: Manchester University Press, 1984. Reprint, Chicago: University of Chicago Press, 1990.

The Third and Fourth Books of Maccabees. Ed. and trans. M. Hadas. New York: Harper and Brothers, 1953.

Thompson, Alden Lloyd. *Responsiblity for Evil in the Theodicy of IV Ezra.* SBL Dissertation Series, 29. Missoula, Mont.: Scholars Press, 1977.

Urbach, E. E. *The Sages: Their Concepts and Beliefs.* 2 vols. Trans. Israel Abrahams. Jerusalem: Magnes, 1975.

Vizotsky, B. *Reading the Book.* New York: Doubleday, 1991.

von Rad, Gerhard. *The Message of the Prophets.* Trans. D. M. G. Stalker. New York: Harper and Row, 1965.

———. *Old Testament Theology.* Vol. 1. Trans. D. M. G. Stalker. New York: Harper and Row, 1962.

———. *Wisdom in Israel.* Nashville: Abingdon Press, 1972.

Willet, Tom W. *Eschatology in the Theodicies of 2 Baruch and 4 Ezra.* Sheffield: Sheffield Academic Press, 1989.

General Index

Abraham, 122, 128, 130, 144
Adam, 18, 55, 89, 123
Afterlife, 39–40, 230n.6
Aggadic midrashim, 115–49, 213
Ahura Mazda, 5
Albeck, H., 79, 234n.2
Amos, 22
Angel of Death, 86, 124–25, 137, 162, 202–4
Angels, rebellious, 45
Antiochan persecution, 6, 26, 41
Apocalypse, 7, 25, 26–27, 40–44, 46, 52, 84, 140, 223, 239n.30
Apocrypha, 63, 215
Aqiba, Rabbi, 87, 111–13, 169–70

Bar Kokhba, 7, 52, 74, 107, 140–41, 181
Bavli, 150–210, 213–14
  characteristics of, 151–52, 220–21
  dating of, 152–53
Belial. See Satan
Berger, Peter, 3, 225nn.2–3
Bible and suffering, 6, 17–35
Birth pangs, 43, 51, 223
Book (of life), 39, 230n.10
Bowker, John, 225n.1
Boyarin, Daniel, 14
Boyce, Mary, 225n.9, 226nn.11–14
Buber, Martin, 32
Buber, S., 144

Camus, Albert, 3
Cain, 18
Canonical criticism, 152
Canonization of the Hebrew Bible, 17, 222, 227n.2

Christianity, 79, 100, 102–3, 109, 147
Christians, 15
Cicero, 58
Code of Discipline, 46–47
Cohen, Shaye J.D., 103, 141–42, 214, 239n.31
Collins, John J., 45
Complaint, 27–33, 142, 148, 159. See also Suffering: critique of; Suffering: protest of
Constantine, 102

Damascus Covenant, 41
Daniel, 6
David, 20
Dead Sea Scrolls, 15, 37, 41
Death, 86, 89, 136–39, 184–88. See also Suffering
  premature, 200–207
Demons, 4, 5, 6
Deuteronomy, 6
Dio Cassius, 7
Divine justice, 9, 18–22, 31, 59, 63, 70–73, 105, 116–20, 146, 160, 162, 172–76, 207, 211
  denial of, 164–65, 184–207
Divine mercy, 57, 72, 113–14, 120–24, 147
Douglas, Mary, 209, 233n.25
Dualism, 5, 7, 45–47, 118, 136

Ecclesiastes, 6, 33–34, 84, 206–7, 213–14, 223
Elisha b. Abuya, 170, 175
Elman, Yaakov, 10–12, 175, 227n.32

Index of Primary Sources

Hebrew Bible

Genesis
3 18
4 18
6 18
18 18
Leviticus
26 19
Numbers
12 18
13–14 18
16 18
20 18
Deuteronomy
4 19
7:15 19
8:5 22–23, 226n.18
11:13–21 19, 216
28:15–68 6
Judges
2:10–19 20
2 Samuel
11–12 20
1 Kings
16 20
2 Kings
17 21
Isaiah
2:2–4 25
2:12 25
52:13–53:12 23–24, 37
Jeremiah
12:1–4 28
31:30 21
Ezekiel
18:21–24 21, 71

Amos
2:2–4 22
3:2 23
Habakkuk
1 25, 27–28
2:3–5 25
Malachi
3 25–26
Psalms
10–13 29
11:5 23
34:16–20 21–22
73 28
77 29
82:2–3 29
88 29
Proverbs
3:12 23
3:33 22
Job
30–33
29–31 32
32–37 229n.29
38–end 32–33
42:7–8 33
Ecclesiastes
33–34
1:18 126
Daniel
8 26–27
12:2–3 27

Apocryphal Works

2 Baruch
43–44, 51
1 Enoch
6–11, 45

22:9–11 39
96–105 39
4 Ezra
41–43, 51
Jubilees
4:32 57
7–15 45–46
23 40
2 Maccabees
6:13–16 38
6 89
7 40
4 Maccabees
48–49
Testament of Gad
5:11 57
Wisdom of Solomon
87
2:23–3:3 39–40
4:7–9 38
4:11 38

Philo

De providentia
49–50

Josephus

Jewish War
6.310–11 48

New Testament

Matthew
7:2 57–58
Mark
4:24 57–58

259